EMPLOYEE ASSISTANCE PROGRAMS

Second Edition

EMPLOYEE ASSISTANCE PROGRAMS

A Basic Text

Edited by

WILLIAM S. HUTCHISON, JR.

WILLIAM G. EMENER

Tampa, Florida

C H A R L E S C T H O M A S • P U B L I S H E R, L T D.
Springfield • Illinois • U.S.A.

Published and Distributed Throughout the World by

CHARLES C THOMAS • PUBLISHER, LTD.
2600 South First Street
Springfield, Illinois 62794-9265

© *1997 by* CHARLES C THOMAS • PUBLISHER, LTD.

ISBN 0-398-06781-3 (cloth)
ISBN 0-398-06782-1 (paper)

Library of Congress Catalog Card Number: 97-13474

With THOMAS BOOKS *careful attention is given to all details of manufacturing
and design. It is the Publisher's desire to present books that are satisfactory as to their
physical qualities and artistic possibilities and appropriate for their particular use.*
THOMAS BOOKS *will be true to those laws of quality that assure a good name
and good will.*

Printed in the United States of America
SC-R-3

Library of Congress Cataloging-in-Publication Data

Employee assistance programs : a basic text. — 2nd ed. / edited by
William S. Hutchison, Jr., William G. Emener.
    p.   cm.
Includes bibliographical references and index.
ISBN 0-398-06781-3 (cloth). — ISBN 0-398-06782-1 (paper)
    1. Employee assistance programs—United States.   I. Hutchison,
William S.   II. Emener, William G. (William George)
HF5549.5.E42E47   1997
658.3′82—dc21   97-13474
                                                                  CIP

To
Dr. Carolyn B. Dickman
and
her children and family,

Be it known that
this book is dedicated to

a loving Husband
a wonderful Dad
a #1 Grandpa

and
a Pioneer,
a Great Friend and Colleague

Dr. J. Fred Dickman
(1926–1995)

AUTHORS' BRIEF BIOGRAPHICAL SKETCHES
J. "FRED" DICKMAN
(1926-1995)

The counselors of the world lost an exceptional friend and advocate with the passing of Fred Dickman. Fred was the consummate teacher, having attained both his masters and doctorate degrees from the University of Florida, and for more than 25 years training substance abuse counselors at the University of South Florida.

Fred Dickman had been a counselor since his days as an Episcopal priest at Saint Andrew's Church in Tampa, and at the time of his death was continuing as counselor and director of Seminole Heights Counseling Center.

In addition to being an addictions professional, Fred was certified as a rehabilitation counselor, an employee assistance professional, psychologist, and licensed as a mental health counselor and school psychologist.

As a professor at USF, Fred was responsible for the development of special studies and practicums in alcoholism and other addictions, and had developed a proposal for master's degree track in substance abuse.

Fred Dickman was a dynamic force in the establishment and operation of Florida Alcoholism Counselor Certification Board (FACCB) and the eventual transformation to the Certification Board for Addiction Professionals of Florida (CBAPF).

Throughout the nation, but primarily within his home state, Dr. Dickman was called upon for guidance and support in the areas of substance abuse prevention intervention and treatment. He was truly an innovator and leader in our field.

Fred Dickman was first and foremost a counselor, although he was also an educator, a consultant, an author, a lecturer, a spiritual adviser, an advocate, an innovator, an active participator in every aspect of our profession, and to most who knew him—a valued friend.

Fred Dickman, your knowledge and your spirit live on through those of us you have touched.

(From: *Florida/NAADSAC News,* 1996, *1*(2), p. s)

EDITORS

William S. Hutchison, Jr. is an Associate Professor of Social Work of the School of Social Work at the University of South Florida. He earned his Ph.D. in Adult Education with a cognate in Staff Development and Training in 1992 from the University of South Florida. In addition, he received his M.S.W. degree from the University of Georgia and his B.A. in psychology from David Lipscomb College. He has worked as a clinical social worker in health, mental health, alcohol and drugs, and child welfare treatment settings. His clinical practice in these settings has included individual, couple, family, group, and psychodrama treatment methods. He has taught social work practice in four universities and two colleges. Dr. Hutchison has authored and coauthored ten treatment training manuals, coauthored *Counseling the Troubled Person in Industry,* and has presented numerous invited papers on social work practice at professional meetings. He is a member of the National Association of Social Workers and the Academy of Certified Social Workers. In addition, he is a Board Certified Diplomate in Clinical Social Work and a licensed clinical social worker.

William G. Emener, Ph.D., CRC is a Distinguished Research Professor in the Department of Rehabilitation Counseling and a former Associate Dean at the University of South Florida, Tampa, Florida. He has worked as a rehabilitation counselor and supervisor as well as a rehabilitation counselor educator and program director at three other universities (Murray State University, Florida State University, and the University of Kentucky). Dr. Emener's publications and writings include six research monographs, seven books, numerous book chapters in ten different texts, over 25 nonpublished professional papers, 95 authored/coauthored articles in 17 different professional refereed journals, and over 100 professional papers presented at professional meetings. He has been an editor/coeditor of over 20 special publications, and was Coeditor of the *Journal of Applied Rehabilitation Counseling* from 1978–1982. Dr. Emener's recognitions include being a recipient of the *1980 American Rehabilitation*

Counseling Association Research Award, a recipient of the National Rehabilitation Administration Association's *The Advancement of Research in Rehabilitation Administration Award,* and is a *Fellow* of the American Psychological Association. He was the 1983–1984 President of the National Rehabilitation Administration Association and was the 1989–1990 President of the National Council on Rehabilitation Education. Dr. Emener has had a private practice as a licensed psychologist for the past 25 years (in Florida and Kentucky), and has developed and coordinated numerous employee assistance programs.

CONTRIBUTORS

CHERYL ANDREWS, CEAP
Summit EAP
Tampa, Florida

MAX BROMLEY, ED.D.
University of South Florida
Department of Criminology
Tampa, Florida

WILLIAM BLOUNT, Ph.D.
University of South Florida
Department of Criminology
Tampa, Florida

ALISSE C. CAMAZINE
Love, Lacks & Paule
St. Louis, Missouri

B. ROBERT CHALLENGER
Tampa, Florida

HELEN DAHLHAUSER
Clearwater, Florida

FRED DICKMAN, Ed.D. (Deceased)
University of South Florida
Department of Rehabilitation Counseling
Tampa, Florida

WILLIAM G. EMENER, Ph.D.
University of South Florida
Department of Rehabilitation Counseling
Tampa, Florida

MARK EVANS
EVA-Tone, Inc.
Clearwater, Florida

RICHARD E. GENTRY, ESQ.
South St. Augustine, Florida

BEN HAYES, B.A.
St. Petersburg, Florida

WILLIAM S. HUTCHISON, JR., M.S.W., Ph.D.
University of South Florida
School of Social Work
Tampa, Florida

JAN LIGON, M.S.W.
The University of Georgia
School of Social Work
Athens, Georgia

DONALD W. MAGRUDER
Director
Employee Assistance Program
Anheuser-Busch Companies
St. Louis, Missouri

CARNOT E. NELSON, Ph.D.
University of South Florida
Department of Psychology
Tampa, Florida

DIANA NORRIS, M.A.
Tampa, Florida

CALVIN M. PINKARD, Ph.D.
University of South Florida
Department of Rehabilitation Counseling
Tampa, Florida

MICHAEL RANK, Ph.D.
University of South Florida
School of Social Work
Tampa, Florida

MONA SCHONBRUNN
Longboat Key, Florida

G. DOUGLAS TALBOTT, M.D.
Smyrna, Georgia

HARRISON M. TRICE, Ph.D.
Cornell University
Ithaca, New York

ELOISE WILLIAMS, MSW, CEAP
Tampa, Florida

TENNYSON J. WRIGHT, Ph.D.
University of South Florida
Department of Rehabilitation Counseling
Tampa, Florida

BONNIE L. YEGIDIS, Ph.D.
The University of Georgia
School of Social Work
Athens, Georgia

FOREWORD TO THE SECOND EDITION

The nature of business is changing, from a manufacturing-based economy to a service- and information-based economy, and as these changes take place, the workforce is undergoing a dramatic shift. It is becoming older and more female. It is becoming better educated. Its values are changing and its emphasis is shifting more toward family life and the home.

Business must accommodate these changes if it is to survive and remain viable. No longer are family issues, for example, something that corporate executives can ignore and expect employees to deal with on their own or on their own time. Restructuring the business to deal with these and other employee concerns and personal problems is *not* an exercise in altruism; *it is a way of improving the bottom line, a means to increased competitiveness.* Competition of the future will not focus solely on attracting and keeping customers for a company's products, it will include attracting and keeping the best of a dwindling pool of potential employees who create those products. Employee assistance programs (EAP), from an employer's viewpoint, are becoming essential to the success of today's businesses.

For these reasons, the employee assistance professional is becoming more and more an integral part of the corporate policymaking team. The chief executive officers and union leaders are looking to these professionals for guidance and in maintaining that most important resource of all: the people who make a company work.

This second edition has been carefully updated and constructed to help employee assistance and human resource professionals do their jobs better. It is a distillation of many years experience and aims to give the building blocks for a successful EAP. Its approach to this complex subject is practical, not academic, and while no two EAPs are exactly alike, the fundamentals in this book will apply to all worksites.

The profession of employee assistance has developed extensively over 25 years, and today's employers can build on the experiences of major firms that have developed effective EAPs by trial and error. This book has been written with the help of many people, including human resources, research, EAPs, labor, law enforcement, clinical and managed care professionals. In the end, this book is about how to help people live happier, more productive lives by providing them with the resources to deal with personal problems—to the advantage of all concerned.

George T. Watkins, M.A., CEAP
Publisher
EAP Digest Magazine

FOREWORD TO THE FIRST EDITION

Over the past several years, there has been tremendous growth in all phases of the Employee Assistance Programming field. The rapid growth in programs initiated, designed, and implemented by, with and for both labor and management, has placed a great demand upon the qualified resources now available. If we are to meet this growing demand, indeed, the quality, quantity, and opportunity to attract qualified professionals working in the field needs to be enhanced and increased.

We are on the threshhold of professional certification and credentialing, EAP curricula for colleges and universities, and a growing host of workshops, seminars, and conferences—all on EAPs. All of this necessitates a significantly larger library of available resources and knowledge bases, relative to all phases of the Employee Assistance Program enterprise.

This book represents the effort of numerous experienced and noted EAP practitioners in the fields of Occupational Alcoholism and Employee Assistance Programming. It is through these types of undertakings and the willingness of professionals to share knowledge, skills, and expertise that will enhance the growth of the EAP field and enable it to flourish and reach its professional potential. Thus, the authors are to be commended for their initiatives and leadership to "pass it along" and maximize our abilities to assist a special group of our citizenry—our troubled employees.

John J. Hennessey
President of ALMACA 1984–86

PREFACE TO THE SECOND EDITION

The dawn of the second edition of this book was born during a conversation between its two editors, Bill Emener and Bill Hutchison, specifically when their dialogue turned to their departed friend and colleague, Dr. J. Fred Dickman. Grieving can be painful at times, yet the energy it can engender can likewise be productive. Such was the case during this aforementioned conversation. "What better way to honor Fred than to carry on his dream of providing important cutting edge information to students, colleagues, and fellow professionals."

The editing processes that ensued were guided by three definitive goals for this second edition: (1) to honorously savor the historical and developmental considerations of the *past;* (2) to surface and discuss the avant-garde issues and developmental accomplishment of the *present;* and (3) to update and hone our predictions, concerns, and recommendations regarding the *future.* Needless to say, these three expectations indeed were challenging.

This second edition has the same titled eight Parts as did the first edition. A careful study of the 40 chapters in the first edition, however, rendered a decision to reprint 26 of the chapters from the first edition, unedited and unabridged. (Four of these 26 chapters actually had been reprinted in the first edition from our first edited book in 1985, *Counseling the Troubled Person in Industry.*) Two chapters from the first edition were edited and updated by their author(s) specifically for this second edition. Thus, 12 chapters from the first edition were eliminated from this second edition. Four of the 26 unedited and unabridged chapters from the first edition are accompanied in this edition by a "Comment/Update" authored by carefully chosen professionals from the field having specialized expertise and experience in the respective areas of the chapters. Six of the 33 chapters in this second edition were authored by experts especially for this edition. In sum, it is the belief of the editors that the three goals for this second edition are accomplished in the blending and special tailoring of attention to the past, the present, and the future.

As addressed throughout this volume, and specifically in the "future directions" writings in the last chapter, employee assistance programs have made and are continuing to make meaningful, helpful impacts on the lives of employees *and* on the efficiency and effectiveness of American business and industry. We are confident, moreover, that you, the reader, the student, the professional of today, will successfully confront the unique challenges facing the future of employee assistance programs. And when it is necessary and appropriate for a third edition of this book to be prepared, we trust that we will again rise to the occasion and successfully confront that challenge. Together, we can move closer to seeing Fred's dream come true.

William S. Hutchison
William G. Emener

PREFACE TO THE FIRST EDITION

The genesis for this text, commensurate with the intentions of most human service professionals, emanated from our compassionate and genuine commitment to ameliorate self-destruction, pain, and sorrow. Collectively, we have provided 110 years of human services to individuals and families in need of special professional assistance. Our actual work on this volume, however, was initiated by perceived and real needs for it within the Employee Assistance Program movement. The personal and intrinsic satisfaction we derive from helping others provided the impetus and energy for this endeavor; our individual and collective research, scholarship, and clinical experience provided the wisdom and guidance.

In 1978, faculty in the College of Social and Behavioral Sciences at the University of South Florida began offering masters level courses on alcoholism and alcoholism counseling. These courses have been in such demand that the first editor of this book, Fred Dickman, was released half time for teaching them and continuing curriculum developments. Concomitantly, the third editor, Bill Hutchison, was developing and teaching specialized courses in substance abuse and family intervention. In the past two years, their respective departments, Rehabilitation Counseling and Social Work, have focused concentration tracks in these areas with special considerations in the industrial work world. Fred, who also coordinates industrial EAP programs, and Bill, who also consults with EAP programs, realized a student demand for coursework specific to EAPs. Thus, during the summer of 1983 they offered a special EAP course. While being overwhelmed by large enrollments, they also observed a scattered dearth of professional literature specific to EAPs. During a professional conference with their colleague, Bill Emener, a counseling psychologist who also worked with industry and EAP clientele, the idea for the first book, *Counseling the Troubled Person in Industry,* eventually emerged into a reality.

Since the publication of *Counseling the Troubled Person in Industry,* Bob

Challenger emerged on the scene. As First Vice President of the Institute for Human Resources Bob has become an invaluable asset to the EAP community in Florida in general and the Tampa Bay Area in particular. He became a coteacher in the EAP course cosponsored by the Departments of Social Work and Rehabilitation Counseling at the University of South Florida. Bob brings 40 years of experience in the EAP field which is evident in his efforts as an author and coeditor of this new book. Among the numerous purposes of this book, one has loomed in the forefront: **to provide a meaningful updated collection of readings basic to the understanding, development, implementation, evaluation, and future continuation of Employee Assistance Programs in the United States.** In short, this book is designed to serve as a basic text covering the important aspects and critical issues concerning EAP professionals.

In many ways this is an original text. An analysis of the specific contents of this book (i.e., its 40 chapters), indeed delineates its existence as an original work on our behalf as its authors. Ten chapters are carefully selected reprints of previously published works by experts in the field. The four of us contributed to three of the 14 authored and coauthored chapters which were written specifically for this book by leading, nationally recognized experts. Moreover, the four of us authored and coauthored (exclusively) three chapters which were previously published works, and authored and/or co-authored 19 chapters which were originally written for this book (three of them with professionals other than ourselves). **Overall,** the four of us individually and collectively authored and/or co-authored 25 of the 40 chapters in this volume. We are very appreciative of our professional colleagues and associates throughout the United States who assisted us with this endeavor. We enjoy full responsibility for our final selection of all previously published chapters and our choices of the authors of all original chapters in this book. Nonetheless, it must be noted that the specific content of each chapter remains the sole responsibility of the author(s) of each chapter.

Part I provides a background, historical appreciation, and philosophical orientation for EAPs in the United States. Part II articulates and refines the basic ingredients, components, administrative aspects, and critical attributes of a successful EAP. Part III surveys the predominant characteristics of EAP clientele and the clinical approaches designed to ameliorate the problems and difficulties that EAP clients tend to be experiencing when they come for assistance. Part IV discusses basic aspects of program evaluation relevant to an EAP. Part V discusses on the EAP professional and professional education, training and development with emphasis upon the growing demand for professionalism in the EAP movement. Part VI looks at special issues currently in debate including legal aspects of EAPs and drug testing in industry as an EAP dilemma. Part VII highlights a few selected examples of EAP populations requiring special attention and procedures, while the last part looks at future directions of the EAP movement.

Admittedly, our intentions were ambitious and could very well have been beyond what reality would allow in one single volume. Fittingly, we ask you, the reader, to study the contents of this book and join us in our initiatives and endeavors to continue to develop the best EAP programs we can, conduct them in the most efficient and effective manner possible, appropriately evaluate them, and thus ensure their continuing developments into the future. Millions of America's workers and their families, as well as American industry itself, have, are, and will continue to benefit from EAPs. With reasons such as these, our labors of love shall prove to be eminently worthy of our efforts.

B. Robert Challenger
Fred Dickman
William G. Emener
William S. Hutchison

ACKNOWLEDGMENTS

Attempting to acknowledge genuine and sincere appreciation to a large number of individuals for their exceptional work and valuable assistance always is a difficult task. And in the case of a second edition of a book such as this one, it is extremely difficult. Thus, should we have accidentally failed to mention anyone who indeed did make a contribution to this initiative, we extend our sincerest apologies.

First and foremost, we want to thank Dr. Carolyn B. Dickman, who not only did extensive library research work for the first edition, but also openly gave her permission, encouragement, and enthusiasm to this second edition.

For their organizational and administrative assistance, and also for their timely typing, indexing, and proofreading skills, we graciously acknowledge Ms. Keely Hutchison, Ms. Valerie Keeth, Ms. Ruby Walker, and Ms. Marianne Bell. For their unending support and love, Bill thanks his wife Glenda Hutchison and their daughters Angie and Keely.

Without hesitation, Dr. William G. Emener and Dr. Carnot Nelson updated their chapter from the first edition for assuring its cutting edge quality on this second edition. For purposes of retaining historical perspectives, numerous chapters also were identified as "in need of cutting edge updating," and to the authors of the special, originally written "Comment/Updates" affixed to these chapters, we extend our sincerest appreciation: Cheryl Andrews; William G. Emener; Mark Evans; Sylvia Straub; William S. Hutchison, Jr.; and Eloise Williams.

As mentioned in the Preface, this second edition contains six "new" chapters, especially written for this book. To the top-notch professionals who made valuable time in their very busy schedules, we extend a hearty "Thank-You!": Max Bromley, William Blount, William G. Emener, William S. Hutchison, Jr., Jan Ligon, Michael Rank, and Bonnie Yegedis.

Having the Foreword to the Second Edition especially prepared for the book by George Watkins, was received as a true compliment to the book. We indeed appreciate George's valuable contribution!

A second edition to a book always has its unique challenges and what we call "literary speed bumps." For his patience and genuine understanding, we deeply express a "Thank-you again!" to Michael Thomas of Charles C Thomas, Publisher.

As is known by many, Dr. William S. Hutchison, Jr. is a Professor in the Department of Social Work and Dr. William G. Emener is a Distinguished Research Professor in the Department of Rehabilitation Counseling, both in the College of Arts and Sciences at the University of South Florida. To our Department Chairs, Jean Amuso and John Rasch, our colleagues and staff, and specifically to our students, we say, "Thanks so much for your patience and understanding—especially when we seemed preoccupied, extremely busy, and very tired in the mornings." Dr. Hutchison especially thanks his student Sylvia Grimsley for her library research.

The wisdom and courage we self-perceived in moving on to produce this second edition primarily came from the thousands of clients and EAP professionals with whom we have worked over the years. To you, we owe our deepest and sincerest gratitude.

William S. Hutchison
William G. Emener

CONTENTS

PART III. CLIENT CHARACTERISTICS AND SERVICES

PART IV. PROGRAM PLANNING AND EVALUATION

PART V. PROFESSIONAL AND PARAPROFESSIONAL TRAINING AND DEVELOPMENT

EMPLOYEE ASSISTANCE PROGRAMS

PART I
HISTORY AND PHILOSOPHY

The opening part of this book traces the development of industrial-based Alcoholism Recovery Programs, the early philosophy involved, and some later developments as the original Alcoholism Recovery Programs and Occupational Alcoholism Programs began to expand their horizons and encompass other disabling, human problems and conditions.

Chapter 1, by Trice and Schonbrunn, documents the roots of today's programs as lying in the bedrock foundation of Alcoholics Anonymous, founded on June 10, 1935. The Twelve Steps of Recovery and the publication of the "Big Book" in 1939 played a most important role in the early formation of recovery programs. The backbone of these early semiformal rehabilitative efforts was the utilization of a recovering person whose personal and experiential encounters with alcoholism provided the understanding, empathy, commitment, and patience to work in the industrial setting as an in-house intervener/counselor.

In Chapter 2, Challenger discusses the early years of employee assistance programs (EAPs) and highlights rationale underlying the need for EAPs throughout the United States. In the accompanying Update/Comment, Hutchison and Emener identify and discuss additional, compelling rationale which underscore the need for EAPs circa the 1990s.

Rounding out Part I's focus on historical and philosophical considerations of EAPs, Dickman and Challenger, in Chapter 3, identify and discuss pertinent, historical and philosophical developments of EAPs in the United States.

It is assumed that with careful reading and a thorough, overall digestion of the writings in this Part, the reader will further appreciate the "roots" of EAPs and enjoy a richer understanding of them.

Chapter 1

A HISTORY OF JOB-BASED ALCOHOLISM PROGRAMS 1900–1955

HARRISON M. TRICE AND MONA SCHONBRUNN

The early history of job-based alcoholism programs can be traced to efforts to eliminate alcohol from the workplace that were prevalent into the early years of the 20th Century, and to subsequent socioeconomic factors which mandated a change in long-accepted behaviors and employer policies. Numerous forces, including World War II and its impact on the labor market, led to the need for rehabilitating alcoholics in the workforce, a need recognized by a number of sensitive and innovative industrial physicians. Evidence supports the conclusion, however, that without the existence of Alcoholics Anonymous, and the dedication and almost superhuman efforts of some of its members in developing and supporting the early programs, few of these programs would have survived.

In an attempt to describe partially the events, forces, and individuals involved in the formative period of occupational alcoholism programs during the 1940s and 1950s, the authors have collected material from a variety of sources, including many firsthand accounts from persons directly concerned in early program development. It is hoped that this material will promote increasing interest in the history of job-based alcoholism programs and generate further input from sources that can contribute to knowledge about this movement which has had such a strong impact on the progress of alcoholism intervention practices.

INTRODUCTION

Although there has been a trend in recent years to eulogize the "new" and to discredit the early focus of job-based programs on alcoholism, there is a growing interest in the history of this movement. Many practitioners express a curiosity about the earlier efforts, often believing them to be rich in anecdote and interesting personalities, and perhaps

Reprinted with permission from the authors and the *Journal of Drug Issues, Inc.,* Spring 1981, pp. 171–198. This chapter is reprinted from *Employee Assistance Programs; A Basic Text* (1988) with permission of the author, the book's editors (Dickman, Emener, & Hutchison, Jr.) and the publisher (Charles C Thomas, Publisher).

5

searching for the increased sense . . . derived from knowledge about one's predecessors.

In an effort to partially describe some of the forces, events, and persons who were involved in the early formative period of the 1940s and 1950s, we have been collecting data from a variety of sources. First and foremost, we attempted to locate and secure the recollections of those persons involved in early programs who are still alive. Where we found such people, we tried to secure a taped, face-to-face interview, or alternatively, asked them to tape for us, following uniform guidelines. In other cases the persons wrote their recollections in letter form.

Our next source was the literature of the period and, to a degree, of the first decades of this century prior to World War II. In addition, we visited the General Service Office of Alcoholics Anonymous and were provided with copies of relevant correspondence (anonymous). The Christopher D. Smithers Foundation allowed us to make use of their historical materials. Yvelin Gardner, long-time Associate Director of the National Council on Alcoholism (NCA), used his files and those of NCA to help us. We also gained access to the collection of papers of Mrs. Marty Mann, founder and for years Executive Director of NCA, in the archives of Syracuse University Library. We were fortunate in securing the cooperation of Lewis F. Presnall, former Director of Industrial Services at NCA; Presnall provided us with five background tapes. Also, J. George S., one-time Director of the Milwaukee Information and Referral Center, shared historical recollections with us.

Despite all this help, we felt rather uneasy about many of our descriptions and ask readers to realize that this article is our first effort to pull together the materials we have collected over the past five years. For those who believe we are in error, and we are sure we have made errors relative to specific points and conclusions, we make a special request. Since this article represents a first "take," so-to-speak, we extend to you an invitation: Please share with us whatever historical materials you have; we will treat them in a professional manner and use them to correct or supplement what we have begun here. We should all profit from a more abundant knowledge of early program formation and the dedicated pioneers who led the way in this important and innovative movement toward the rehabilitation of alcoholic employees.

EARLY ROOTS OF JOB-BASED PROGRAMS

Ironically, the common use of alcohol as a mainstay of the workplace was the ground in which the first roots of job-based programs took hold. Throughout much of the first half of the nineteenth century, workers in practically all occupations drank on the job, frequently at the employer's expense, and often during specific times set aside for imbibing (Krout, 1925; Furnas, 1965). In the southern United States, for example, men often took off from work for "elevenders," a whiskey and brandy version of the coffee break (Janson, 1935). In England, dock workers during this period, and on into the twentieth century, typically had at least four or five drinking breaks with "practically no restrictions on the worker's access to liquor during the hours of labor" (Sullivan, 1906:508). These practices were even more evident in 18th century England. In London during this century, it was commonplace for workers in many trades to be directly dependent upon tavern keepers, since taverns were the employment agencies of that period. In one extreme instance, men who worked on coal-carrying ships were almost required to drink specific amounts each day; the cost of the assigned amount was taken from wages—whether it was drunk or not (George, 1925). Other employers sold drinks in the workplace and frequently charged these costs against wages.

Apparently, such drinking was deeply embedded in both the leisure and job behavior of working class people . . . permeated much, if not all, of frontier life, where there was "liberal and frequently excessive consumption of alcohol" (Winkler, 1968:415). The repeated waves of immigrants had somewhat different, but generally supportive drinking norms. These served to reinforce the widespread use of alcohol in some form, both on and off the job (Sinclair, 1962). Despite numerous efforts to remove this practice from worker behavior (Gutman, 1977), it persisted well into the latter part of that century and on into the twentieth (Stivers, 1976).

Probably the first expression of concern for on-the-job drinking, and dealing with the problem in a nonpunitive sense, came from the Washingtonians (Fehlandt, 1904). This society—in some ways a forerunner of Alcoholics Anonymous (AA) in that it advocated total abstinence, group meetings, and the "carrying of the message"—flourished for a brief time in the mid-1800s, until political and religious entanglements led to its demise. It did, however, very early on set something of a precedent for the heavy involvement of AA in job-based programs during the 1940s and 50s. It was a policy among Washingtonians that "each one bring one," and working men were a primary target. Members frequently would seek out excessive drinkers from their work settings, often asking employers and coworkers for suggestions about whom to approach with their message. For example, during the Civil War, and immediately thereafter, Washingtonians became active among the employees of a prominent Chicago publishing and printing house.

Because there is a strong concentration in the literature on "problem drinking," and a neglect of functional or "payoff drinking" (Bacon, 1976; Trice and Beyer, 1977), little is known about the positive functions of alcohol use in working class life. Apparently, however, there were perceived to be many. As a result, the first intensive effort to excise alcohol from the workplace, which came from farmers and employers from the 1880s to the 1920s who were attempting to discipline and organize a dependable, predictable workforce (Gutman, 1977), was a lengthy and difficult task, fraught with intense value judgements. It is within this context that the first roots of job-based programs can be found. Despite strong and deep-seated opposition, the early decades of this century saw the disappearance of condoned drinking on the job.

All segments of American society had become caught up in the Temperance Movement. Employers, in particular, were committed to the removal of alcohol in order to eliminate one of the main problems in socializing a reliable workforce. Among the most prominent examples were the employers in the steel industry (Hendrick, 1916), where all sorts of persuasions—including discharge—were used to stop drinking in the workplace. By the turn of the century numerous American railroads required total abstinence, both on and off the job (Timberlake, 1963).

Directly reinforcing the Temperance Movement efforts was the "gospel of efficiency" (Haber, 1964, IX) that came to be the predominant ideology of the second and third decades of the twentieth century. One form of this "gospel" was commercial efficiency. Apart from the moralistically desirable personal characteristics of discipline, self-reliance, and hard work, there was the ideal of the profit-making, efficient, commercial enterprise that utilized the efficient worker and operated within an efficient community. That ideal then spread to housewives, clergymen, and teachers. Taylorism was the epitome of this ideology within the workplace. This set of carefully calculated studies of how jobs could be most efficiently done, with the least amount of time spent, created an atmosphere in which there was precious little acceptance for time off for a beer! There was even less tolerance for unproductive workers, regardless of why they were that way. Alcohol became anathema to efficiency.

Equally potent was the emergence of workmen's compensation in the various states. Under these laws, employers were held financially responsible for many of the injuries incurred by employees on the job—regardless of who was actually at fault. Thus, there was a heightened concern and fear that drinking workers would injure either themselves, fellow workers, or both. In sum, the Temperance Movement, Taylorism, and Workmen's Compensation combined to drive alcohol from the workplace.

These efforts rapidly became fraught with punitive measures which soon carried over in many quarters to judgmental attitudes of anger and disgust for individuals who drank to intoxication, even though off the job. It may not be an exaggeration to conclude that much of the stigma which came to be attached to alcoholism arose from these repressive efforts to drive alcohol from the job environment.

Whatever the motives, a genuine concern for the effects of alcohol intoxication, of problem drinking, and of alcoholism on performance marked this period and was in sharp contrast to the long-standing encouragement or acceptance by employers of drinking on the job. A concerted drive to bring awareness of these problems to industry was evident during the first two decades of the century. Sullivan (1906) stated that "industrial alcoholism" was a particularly debilitating form, derived from workers' use of alcohol as an aid to heavy labor. Citing the high rates of alcohol-related pathologies among English dock workers, where industrial drinking was high, and the low rates of similar disorders among coal miners, where such drinking was low, he urged that on-the-job use of alcohol be eliminated rather than encouraged. According to him, such a program would strike at the main source of alcoholism. The American Museum of Safety published, and sold to employers on a large scale, a compilation of European methods for discouraging drinking while working. It stressed, providing some evidence, that the major reason for such company actions should be the loss of efficiency and increased chances for accidents if drinking occurred in a mechanized workplace (Tolman, 1911).

Following this, in 1915, *The Outlook* published a succinct account of how 63 large firms in the Midwest had discovered that alcohol in almost any quantities damaged efficiency, and how they used all manner of ways, including discharge, to discourage its use. This effort was attributed to the "new campaign for scientific efficiency in industry." A review of the evidence that had accumulated during this period was one of the first publications of the Yale Center of Alcohol Studies in the early forties (*Quarterly Journal of Studies on Alcohol,* 1942). In many ways it was an enlargement and refinement of an earlier approach, attributed to an unidentified vice president of a large iron works during the early teens. He explained the positive effects of the evangelist Bill Sunday on work productivity by saying that religion had little to do with it. "The thing that made those men efficient was cutting out the drink" (Theiss, 1914:856). Thus, impaired job performance became a major focus on the concern about drinking on the job during these decades prior to World War II, although a great deal of awareness had already emerged just prior to World War I. Those who came to emphasize the point were first and foremost workworld people; moreover, they were not staff people such as medical or personnel; nor were they persons from the outside who sought to influence employers. Rather, they were largely line managers, whose chief concern was "getting the job done." More basic, however, is the fact that these very early efforts were exclusively directed toward alcohol and alcohol problems only. Even though other personal problems were to attract much attention later in Employee Assistance Programs the origin of job-based programs was undeniably in alcohol problems within the workplace.

The Early and Mid-Forties: Actual Programs Emerge

Three potent forces combined during this period to capitalize on the already present and widespread concern about the effects of alcohol on job efficiency. First was the birth and sudden growth of Alcoholics Anonymous (AA). Second, influential and dedicated medical directors came to support and actively initiate programs during this period, providing a high status leadership to the emerging programs. Third, this development converged with the unique labor market conditions during World War II.

In 1938, there were three AA groups and approximately 100 members. By 1944, the movement had 10,000 members in just over 300 groups in America and Canada. Widespread favorable publicity about the "Big Book," *Alcoholics Anonymous,* created a wave of interest about AA during 1939 and 1940. An article in the *Saturday Evening Post* in 1941 accelerated the sale of the book and a flood of interest in AA activity (Trice, 1958). In 1945, a film, "Problem Drinkers," in the *March of Time* documentary series, focused on AA, the newly formed National Committee for Education on Alcoholism (NCEA), and the Yale Center of Alcohol Studies.

Probably of equal significance was the fact that AA had come to the attention of a few influential medical directors and industrial physicians who became very prominent in developing many of the early programs. From the recollections of our various sources come numerous names of company medical directors during this period. One source believes that Dr. Daniel Lynch, Medical Director of the New England Telephone Company in the thirties, "could be the very first in point of time who conducted a program for alcoholics in industry; he was conducting his one-man Medical Director program as early as the mid-thirties." Other sources mention Dr. George Gehrmann of DuPont, Dr. John L. Norris of Eastman Kodak, Dr. John Witmer and Dr. S. Charles Franco of Consolidated Edison, Dr. W. Harvey Cruickshank of Bell Canada, Dr. James Roberts of New England Electric, Dr. Clyde Greene of Pacific Telephone and Telegraph, Dr. Robert Page of Standard Oil of New Jersey, Dr. Harold Meyer of Illinois Bell Telephone, and Dr. James Lloyd of North American Aviation. We will discuss some of these individuals and programs in more detail in a later section.

To a very large degree, underlying motivation for rehabilitative action came from the unusual labor market conditions during World War II. The enormous production requirements of the war resulted in a careful measurement of productivity at a time when many companies were "scraping the bottom of the barrel" for employees. Under the pressure for the "fullest possible production" (Stevenson, 1942:661), significant losses of efficiency by only a few workers created a noticeable problem. Fox (1944:257) described the personnel demands as a "drastic change from a period of recession to one of maximum production (which) brought many new problems to industry, including those arising from the employment of workers who would hardly be hired under normal conditions." As a result, many cases of problem drinking and alcoholism which would otherwise have remained largely outside the typical workplace, came to the attention of managers and medical directors. For example, Dr. James Roberts of the New England Electric Company said that during the war years the company was desperately in need of employees, especially at the wage earning level, and began recruiting from employment agencies in the Bowery area of New York. Many of these employees were near skid row types, and efforts to devise rehabilitation for them was unsatisfactory. Dr. Roberts underscored that the company program evolved from necessity rather than benevolence.

Aside from the need to hire "marginal" workers, other factors also contributed to management's awareness of alcohol-related problems in the workplace during the war years. As the association between alcohol abuse and absenteeism became more and more obvious (Industrial Medicine, 1943), this became the most significant part of the awareness (Jukes, 1943). Shift work also produced on-the-job drinking with its safety and disciplinary problems. Rapid, sudden expansion of productivity necessitated long working hours, making for a use of alcohol and for management's toleration of it that was reminiscent of a century earlier.

There were also indications that conditions just after the war exacerbated employee drinking problems. One factor was the problem of readjustment for millions of returning soldiers. Another was the large scale readjustment of industry and business itself to peacetime conditions. Henry A. Mielcarek, Director of Personnel Services at Allis Chalmers during the postwar period, observed that these problems continued on into the fifties (Mielcarek, 1951).

Although labor conditions had a great deal of influence on the development of the early "near programs," union involvement was practically nonexistent. It should be noted that true management involvement was also minimal during this time. The truly early programs were often so "informal" and "unwritten," that only those directly involved knew what was going on. For example, great pains were taken at DuPont for three or four years after program inception to "keep quiet what was being done." [Quotation marks, without a designation, indicate a direct quote from one of our sources.] If management was kept uninformed, labor unions were consulted even less. Although union organization and strength were well advanced during this period, it was not until the late forties and early fifties that unions became involved. Even then it was largely on their own initiative. There is evidence that for quite some time programs were seen as management-based. When Eastman Kodak and DuPont made their programs public, no union was involved, and as other companies explored programs following the war, this same attitude prevailed. Although this was slowly to change, it set a pattern for future programming, and one that was to be a source of much confusion and conflict.

Pioneer Companies: The Unheralded and the Famous

There is substantial evidence in our accumulated materials that there were numerous employers who were taking some form of action approaching a program during the war years. Some branches of the military also appeared to be taking steps to combat alcoholism. Rather early on the Merchant Marine found that combat pressures were so strong for some men that they resorted to heavy alcohol use. As a result, this service developed its own rehabilitation centers and encouraged an open recognition of the problem (JIF, 1947). There is also some evidence in our materials that the U.S. Navy had a similar concern.

Among companies who may have been developing some form of program—often dubbed "informal" or "quasi-private"—during or just after World War II, some appear at least twice in our materials, but are difficult to corroborate. Among these are the Hudson Department Store of Detroit and Thompson Aircraft Products of Cleveland. Similarly, Schlitz Brewery received some mention, but the lead is difficult to substantiate.

Most tangible evidence exists concerning a cluster of companies who appear to have had some of the basic ingredients of alcoholism programs in the early forties. The Pacific Telephone and Telegraph Company in 1940 made one of its many modifications and additions to its employee benefit plan; it decided that disability directly or indirectly due to intoxication or use of alcohol would be covered by the plan; prior to this such coverage had been discretionary. The New England Electric Company, responding to many of the pressures of World War II, began an organized effort to control and rehabilitate problem drinkers in the mid-forties. There are also indications that the Illinois Bell Telephone Company began working with alcoholics toward the end of the war. The work "was done quietly with no formal management support." In other words, the approach was a rehabilitative one, but it was "unwritten." Just why there was so much emphasis on "keeping it quiet" during this period is a question never answered by our sources; however, one may guess that the stigma attached to alcoholism played an important part.

In the Western Electric Company a series of memos in the early forties set forth a rehabilitative approach, although the company made no formal public statement. One source indicated that such guidelines existed in the late 1930s when he began working for Western Electric. According to this source, unions were cooperative from the beginning—an exception to the general rule of not involving unions.

Although there is some evidence that an "unwritten policy" had existed earlier, the Caterpillar Tractor Company's "formal" efforts to deal with alcoholism began in 1945. In that year, the company's medical department and personnel from the Medical College of Cornell University developed a comprehensive, company-wide mental health program that included alcoholism (Vonachen et al., 1946). In many ways, this was an early Employee Assistance Program (EAP) rather than a plan which focused solely on the alcoholic employee. It seems to be the only example of an explicitly EAP approach in this entire period, though one survey observed that "there is also a marked trend to integrate industrial alcoholism activities with broader health and personal programs" (Henderson and Straus, 1952). This reference may have been to the kind of personnel counseling programs that also were active in Western Electric's Hawthorne plant, and in the Chino Mines Division of Kennecott Copper Company. Our evidence, however, suggests a sharp separation between these programs and job-based alcoholism ones. Alcoholism programs focused on alcoholism and alcoholism only—other drugs were rarely, if ever, mentioned in the literature or other source material.

Other early approaches also seemed to be moving toward the status of a program, yet are largely unheralded as such today. The first semi-formalized effort on the West Coast was started by North American Aviation in 1944. Webb Hale, Manager of Personnel Administration, instituted the program with Earl S. (where private or AA sources were used, an effort has been made to respect AA members' anonymity in the spirit of AA's traditions by using the first name and the first initial of the last name. We especially tried to follow this policy with living AA members who helped us), a recovering alcoholic, was employed as a counselor and soon began to work with various other company locations. Although there is a question in our materials about how much top management recognized this "program," there still was some formalization.

Just after the war, Dr. W. Harvey Cruickshank of Bell Telephone of Canada became interested in the problem of alcoholism in the workplace. However, a program was not formalized for some years to come, due in large part to management resistance.

Against this background of unheralded employers who were taking bits and pieces of programmatic action in the war years, and immediately thereafter, it is revealing to look at the widely publicized "pioneers." Probably the most celebrated are those at E.I. DuPont de Nemours and Company and at the Eastman Kodak Corporation. They are linked together for a good reason. Apparently, Dr. John L. Norris of Eastman Kodak and Dr. George H. Gehrmann of DuPont played very similar roles at about the same time in the very early forties, although they never met until a conference in 1949. Both were much impressed with the effectiveness of AA in arresting problem drinking among employees and encouraged the use of AA by utilizing the services of recovering alcoholics who worked in the plant. However, while both of these often publicized "pioneers" started from much the same point, they nevertheless diverged considerably in their approaches in program development with one moving toward a more formalized internal program with a policy statement and coordinator, while the other initiated an informal network of information and action directed toward outside community agencies.

Dr. Gehrmann developed the DuPont program with the help of a member of AA, David M., who was hired specifically for that purpose. Dr. Gehrmann's interest was in part due to several severe drinking problems among highly valuable DuPont employees. Also, important was the interest of high status managers in the company. Apparently the activity at DuPont became more formalized as the war ended.

In contrast, the situation at Kodak remained informal during this period, with the medical department and a network of AA members inside the company operating with the "quiet acceptance" of management. Nor is there evidence that an awareness of alcoholism among higher status employees operated at Kodak, although it might have done so. In any case, Dr. Norris developed the tie with AA in a way which emphasized it as a community resource, and followed through with this approach by helping to form one of the first Councils of Alcoholism, in Rochester, New York, under whose aegis an outpatient clinic was established.

Given this examination of the history of both the publicized and unpublicized early programs, it is difficult to speak of a "first." Clearly, North American Aviation on the West Coast developed the basic elements of a program at about the same time as did DuPont and Kodak on the East Coast, and in somewhat the same way. Other companies were also active, with many having dedicated, energetic AA persons working with them, but many always remained "informal." DuPont and Eastman Kodak operated a very low-key program indeed during the late war years and immediately thereafter, but both had medical directors who used their status and expertise to initiate, innovate, and break precedent. Perhaps this sponsorship by relatively influential staff officers constituted the major differences, insuring some continuity and recognition. This may be particularly true of Dr. Gehrmann, who decided to concentrate internally. He thereby slowly built a program inside DuPont, rather than relating primarily to community resources and agencies.

This notion of an "in-house" program received support from the next pioneer company to emerge, the Consolidated Edison Company of New York. In many ways it represents a transition from the informal, unwritten practices that characterized the start of the earlier programs. Early in 1947, Consolidated Edison officially recognized alcoholism as a medical disorder and set up a three-fold procedure for dealing with it. Behind this decision were factors quite different from those operating at Kodak and DuPont. Dr. John J. Witmer, Vice President of Industrial Relations in 1947, seemed to be a moving force, although there is some evidence that the Chairman of the Board, Ralph Tapscott, initiated the idea following complaints about the discharge of a long-term problem drinking employee from a local clergyman. Dr. Witmer had consulted on several occasions with Dr. Gehrmann of DuPont, as well as with Professor Selden Bacon of Yale. Unlike the case with DuPont and Kodak, there is a conspicuous absence of reference to counselors, AA groups, or AA members within the company. Instead, an influential medical director and department, encouraged by top management, apparently devised the plan largely on their own, a play relying heavily on the authority of the company to legitimately intervene. In many ways what is now called "occupational programming" had come into being. For example, there is good reason to believe that the union was quite active, and that the company incorporated it into the planning. The company also took the position that they would openly describe their policy, despite some unfavorable publicity. In terms of modern day programs, it may well be that Consolidated Edison was really "number one."

AA Pioneers

There are two persons who can truly be called pioneers in job-based programs. The earliest, and truly the first, was the previously mentioned David M., who started a one-man, persistent campaign within the Remington Arms Company of Bridgeport, Connecticut, a subsidiary of the DuPont Company. He was to continue this work inside that same company until his retirement in 1967. Although he came to have some influence outside DuPont (he was invited to participate in the industrial seminar at Yale, the first University of Wisconsin Summer School, and later on at Rutgers University industrial workshops) he nevertheless was largely a pioneer within the company. He can be called an "inside" change agent. The second pioneer, Ralph "Lefty" Henderson, was a sharp contrast. From his position as industrial consultant with the Yale Center of Alcohol Studies, he began in 1948 to range far and wide, contacting and encouraging organizations by the dozens, traveling practically all over the country to start programs. If David M. was "Mr. Inside," Lefty Henderson was "Mr. Outside."

Both came from the same background of severe, chronic alcoholism and recovery through Alcoholics Anonymous. Both were products of the very early period of AA's growth—both joining AA in 1940—and both manifested an almost super-human tenacity and persistence, restrained by a worldly-wise finesse. Both had high status and influential collaborators who should share in their pioneer standing. Certainly this is true of David M.'s association with Dr. George H. Gehrmann, long-time Medical Director at DuPont. Henderson's affiliation was with Professor Seldon D. Bacon, Director of the Yale Center of Alcohol Studies. Although Bacon's direct involvement was much shorter than that of Gehrmann, it was for a time intense. Perhaps the Fates also deserve recognition for bringing the individuals of these two pairs together. There is little doubt that, despite many differences in background and status, there was a compatability, a "chemistry," in each pair that sparked action.

David M.: A Dedicated Inside Change Agent

Dave M. was the first industrial counselor hired to work with alcoholic employees. His early experience in the industrial environment and determined efforts at the Remington Arms Company are best described in his own words:

> One of the officers of the tennis club (where I worked) was Vice President of the Remington Arms Company and I told him about this very vivid and wonderful experience of AA. I told him that I wanted to get out of tennis and that I felt industry could use something of this kind. He seemed quite understanding and he said certainly the members of the Club had noticed quite a difference. I advertised in the paper that an AA group was starting in the Bridgeport-Fairfield area. Then came along a case of a shift supervisor in Remington Arms. This man responded very well, so I went to the Vice

President and asked him if I could approach the people at Remington Arms to see if they would rehire this supervisor. I saw the head of personnel and the welfare man. They were both very understanding, but then they took it up with the Medical Director; Dr. _____ was adamant that the man would not be allowed to return to work at Remington Arms. Dr. _____ had fired him and he was going to stay fired.

That summer I finished my work at tennis hoping to get started in industry with Remington Arms, but I found out that I only had my first citizenship papers. I had to wait until March. I went from September (I'd given up my job at Aiken) to March without any work of any kind because there was nothing to do without my second citizenship papers. Finally I did start with Remington Arms in March 1942. I particularly wanted to get into the shop to get a better idea of industry in general. I was put on a job as an inspector, inspecting bullet jackets as they were made. I started at 75¢ an hour after I'd been making $5.00 to $6.00 an hour at tennis. [For five months] my job was working from 11:00 at night until 7:00 in the morning. It was quite a rich experience. I picked up a couple of alcoholics and got them interested in coming to our AA meeting in Bridgeport.

Then with quite an effort, I got transferred to the personnel department as a terminator-exit interviewer. I met with people who were leaving the company after being fired, or going into the service, or becoming pregnant. In this particular job the alcoholic had to come through me and this was where we were able to get them interested in coming into AA. Before I left Remington Arms, I was able to keep 22 employees working steady and sober with AA.

When I was in personnel, I contacted about 3 or 4 of the manufacturing supervisors—top men—and told them about my experience and asked if they had any employees with a drinking problem and said I'd be only too pleased to help. In my particular office I was soon able to get supervisors to give these people who were being let go another chance and the success rate was extremely high. They were very pleased, but when I approached top management in Remington Arms about what more could be done officially, I was told that there was not enough of a problem to justify a program. I asked permission to approach the DuPont Company, in Wilmington, Delaware. I had to go through Dr. _____ to be allowed to approach DuPont, the parent company. Again, I got a very emphatic no from Dr. _____.

In September 1942, I got a letter of introduction to two of the bigshots in Wilmington: Mr. Maurice DuPont Lee and Emile DuPont. I got the letter of introduction from a Vice President of the Guarantee Trust Co. who at this time was active in AA himself. I made arrangements and went down to see Mr. Lee and Mr. DuPont. I explained the work that had been done at Remington. They were very gracious, and thanked me for the time and effort, but they didn't feel that drinking was a major problem. They said they had picked up a few cases over the years that could have been helped, but they could see no need for anything in the way of a program.

On the way down to make the visit, I had stopped at the AA clubhouse in

Philadelphia. I got friendly with one of the members there and I told him about the work I'd done at Remington Arms and my intention of going to DuPont. He said the Medical Director of DuPont, Dr. Gehrmann, had been to two or three meetings and that he was red hot as far as AA was concerned. The AA said I should be sure to see Dr. Gehrmann while I was in Wilmington.

After I had been to see Mr. Lee and Mr. DuPont, I went over to Medical, but Dr. Gehrmann happened to be out of town, so I didn't see him. Two weeks later, I got a letter from Mr. Lee thanking me again but saying that they could see nothing in the way of a program in the future. Naturally, I was quite disappointed.

About 3 weeks after that I got a layoff notice. Remington Arms was cutting back from 15,000 to 7,000 practically overnight. So by December 1, 1943, I had a month's notice to leave. With that, I got on the phone to call Dr. Gehrmann and explain that I was in AA, that I had been in AA 3 years, and what I'd done at Remington Arms. Gehrmann's answer was 'By God, you're just the guy I'm looking for . . .' He said he'd been to some AA meetings in Philadelphia, was deeply impressed, and would like to get a group started in the company or in Wilmington. He said, 'I'll arrange for you to come down and talk it over and see what we can do about a transfer.'

So that's what happened. I went down and saw Dr. Gehrmann and we seemed quite pleased with each other. In the meantime, I talked it over with Bill Wilson and I said 'If I take a job like this would I be a professional AA?' He said 'No, not unless you actually took money for direct therapy. If a company wants to hire someone to give information and to teach them about the problem and give some direction there is no one more qualified than the recovered alcoholic.' So in that case I felt free, and he said he thought it would be a wonderful thing if I could work something out.

Dr. Gehrmann wanted to set me up in Medical, but I suggested I stay anonymous and find a job that would keep me busy. In the meantime, I'd start a group in Wilmington that could absorb any DuPont employee. I transferred there in January 1944.

Once "on board," Dave M. quietly, but with determination and Dr. Gehrmann's backing, began to approach employees. Apparently supervisors would confront employees with poor performance, decide whether or not the problem was alcohol-related, and refer at once to the medical department. Henrietta Gehrmann, the widow of the medical director, stated that "Dr. G. gave him (Dave M.) names of men he was to approach." He would tell these employees about the AA group he and a few others had started in Wilmington, Delaware. At the same time he made it clear that it was the employee's choice to decide whether to join or not. In the meantime the employee would have the general help of the medical department, but unless he took steps to overcome his problem he would be discharged. These points, and others such as probation for three months, came to be formalized by Gehrmann over the next four years into company policy and procedure (Gehrmann, 1955). This tough "constructive coercion" position is one that has been substantially muted into what is today called "constructive confrontation" (Beyer and Trice, 1980).

Dave M. was a naturalized citizen of the U.S. He was born in the north of Ireland and lived in England until he was 21 where he was educated and developed his love for tennis. He came to this country in 1923 during the Prohibition era. By 1928–29 he had become an active alcoholic, growing worse and worse over a twelve-year period. During this time, he made his living as a coach and professional tennis player. He learned about AA when he read an article about the group in *Liberty Magazine.* He sent away for the AA book and in early 1940 and, greatly impressed by it, contacted the organization.

Dave M. was in his early forties when, after joining AA, he worked for Remington Arms, and then transferred to DuPont. For a quarter of a century, he pursued the growth and development of the alcoholism program within DuPont and its many locations and subsidiaries, making this his major life's work until he retired in 1967. Bill W., the cofounder of AA, in a letter to Dave M. in 1968 refers to "the marvelous job that you turned in as the first pioneer of alcoholic rehabilitation in industry." There seems little doubt that he was a true innovator, joined by another innovator—a dedicated, powerful medical director—to launch a new and practical approach to alcoholism.

We know much less about what Dr. Gehrmann's experiences and attitudes were during the late 1930s and early 1940s, but there are some clues. At the time Dave M. called him in 1943, he had, like Dr. Norris, experienced numerous failures with alcoholic employees. He later declared that "for twenty-eight years I struggled without AA and my results were zero; with AA over the past five years, I got 65 percent (recovery)" (National Industrial Conference Board, 1958:36). Also like Dr. Norris, he was much impressed by AA and the results it had achieved. He had referred professional employees to it and had himself attended some meetings. He was at the time a well-established professional and an administrative officer in the company, and had been with DuPont since 1915, about 25 years, allowing for service during World War I. He had been medical director since 1926 and was not to retire until 1955. Of the numerous industrial physicians who played a role in the emergence of job-based programs, he was probably one of the best positioned to initiate the innovation and keep it alive.

There is also good reason to believe that some of the top management at DuPont was sympathetic, although not necessarily convinced. Dr. Thomas Hogshead, a psychiatrist in private practice in Wilmington, and who knew the principals involved, has identified Maurice DuPont Lee as a person "who was also quite instrumental in the inauguration and development of this program." Maurice DuPont Lee's interest may have come about because of a chance meeting, while on vacation with Bill W. Other sources mention Henry DuPont and Emile DuPont as also having been sympathetic. In any case, there apparently was no opposition to what Dr. Gehrmann and Dave M. were doing; although there may not have been active encouragement. The best conclusion is that, as far as the company policy was concerned, Dr. Gehrmann "carried the ball" alone.

Ralph "Lefty" Henderson:
A Peripatetic and Influential "Outside Change Agent"

Many of the early forces operating to produce job-based programs culminated in the person and work of Ralph McComb Henderson. For the last ten years of his life (1948–1958) he was the industrial consultant for the Yale Center for Alcohol Studies, traveling constantly in an effort to influence both small and large companies, and unions as well, to take positive rehabilitative action toward their problem drinking employees. Probably no other single person invested as much time, effort, and energy to this general task. R. Brinkley Smithers stated that Henderson aided greatly in installing programs in numerous small companies in New Haven and vicinity where the Yale Center was located. Professor Milton Maxwell, who succeeded Henderson at Yale, observed in 1958 that Henderson "had a small or large hand in just about every occupational program in existence." Mark Keller, long-time editor of the *Journal of Studies on Alcohol*, describes him as "our man for industry and he was often on the road promoting the Yale Plan for Business and Industry." He goes on to say that he believes Henderson to be the main initiator, with Professor Selden Bacon of Yale, of the Allis Chalmers program in Milwaukee. Bacon himself spent much time in the early fifties on the road with Henderson, explaining the Yale Plan and soliciting funds for an industrial unit at the Yale Center. Bacon describes him as an "itchy-foot AA who was eager to get to the big boys and tell them the facts of life about boozers," and as "a frequent traveler who, when on the road, talked and talked and talked and was enormously welcome as a talker."

Henderson could be termed the first occupational program consultant (OPC) with a territory that covered the Northeast, the Midwest, and probably even beyond. Lewis Presnall, in fact, tells of him visiting the Chino Mines Division of Kennecott Copper in Hurley, New Mexico, in the early fifties. Henderson's second wife, Esther, relates how he was often invited to the Minneapolis-St. Paul area where he consulted with numerous industrial representatives. She says that he "traveled all over creation—I wouldn't be surprised if he used American Legion contacts, law contacts, contacts made when he was in industry, but above all AA contacts, and of course the NCA staff; he was getting in touch with various people in industry all over America."

George S. describes several visits that Henderson made to the Milwaukee area. Accompanying him on these visits were such prominent persons as Marty Mann, Leo Greenberg, and Selden Bacon. According to George S., Henderson played an "integral part in setting up the Milwaukee effort." Under the auspices of the Milwaukee Information and Referral Center, the first meetings in the area to discuss job-based programs were set up to include fourteen employers, among whom were International Harvester, Huebsch Manufacturing, Trackson Co., Wisconsin Electric, A.O. Smith, American Laundry, Schlitz Brewery, Cudahy Packing Co., Allis Chalmers, and Marathon Paper. Apparently strongly influenced by Henderson, George S. stimulated a cooperative network of companies who agreed to participate in a demonstration program of the Yale Plan. This may well have been the first consortium. Henderson first came to Milwaukee in 1950, and upon his third trip there (two years later) was badly injured in a car accident. Because of this, and George S.'s departure from Milwaukee in 1953, the program for all practical purposes lapsed at this point.

Henderson's work in the Northeast is described by Charles Rietdyke, who as Coordinator of Supervisory Training at the Scovill Manufacturing Company in Waterbury, Connecticut, worked with Henderson to develop Scovill's alcoholism policy. Rietdyke describes Henderson's influence in starting programs at Scovill, Armco Steel, and Waterbury Brass Works in the early fifties. Elizabeth Whitney (now Elizabeth Whitney Post), detailed Henderson's dedication and enthusiasm in making numerous trips to Boston to talk with industrial groups and fraternal organizations. Like George S. in Milwaukee, she was greatly influenced and aided by Henderson in her work among New England companies. Henderson also had a substantial effect on the developing policy at Standard Oil of New Jersey. The AA General Services Office used his name, with that of Dave M. as a reference person, in answering mail inquiries about job-based programs in the early fifties. Seldon Bacon estimates he corresponded with over fifty companies and unions during that time.

Even before taking the Yale position, however, Henderson's travels had been extensive to say the least. The year before joining the Yale Center (1947), he had worked as a field representative of the then National Committee for Education on Alcoholism. During that year, according to his annual report, he visited 43 different cities in 14 different states and one in Canada, often two and three times. In the early 1940s, when Henderson worked for the Wedge Pipe Company in New Orleans, "he made speeches to business and industrial groups all over the South," as well as literally hundreds of AA talks. Beyond doubt Ralph "Lefty" Henderson sowed the seeds of job-based programs wider and further than anyone before him, and probably anyone since.

Henderson's personality apparently fitted his mobility in that he was outgoing, gregarious, and extroverted. Those who saw him in action usually had similar impressions and their descriptions were always very affectionate in tone. To one observer, he was "a bear-like man, a friendly, husky St. Bernard with a twinkle in his eye." Yet another vividly described him as a very persuasive "unmade bed." To another, he was a "gruff, eager beaver AA who told it like it was." One informant described how Henderson, on one occasion, had to be corrected on "scientific matters" while lecturing at the summer school, and that he boasted in an AA talk in 1954 that he was "proud that I'm no scholar." He was, however, a well-educated, colorful, and dynamic speaker who could command both humor and respect. One of the students in his industrial seminar in 1954 likened him to Will Rogers or Wallace Beery, describing how he used commanding gestures with "ham-like hands." Bacon said Henderson "was the most magnificent platform artist I ever saw." Apparently his earlier skills as a trial lawyer had found new and different expressions.

He was born in Armour, South Dakota in 1895; in 1919, he graduated from Law School at the State University. After private practice in his own law firm as a trial lawyer, he became active in the American Legion—he had served in World War I. In 1933–34, he was made state Commander of the Legion and soon thereafter was Assistant Attorney General of South

Dakota for a brief time. In 1939, he was a State Chairman for the Republican National Convention and participated in the nomination of Alf Landon.

He developed a severe drinking problem during this period of his life. In one of his taped AA talks in 1954, he estimated that there were "seven or eight years when I was just lost from my associates, lost from my family, and actually lost to myself." He and his first wife were separated and ultimately divorced. In the late thirties he experienced skid row in many states. His turning point came in 1939 when a municipal judge in Chicago precipitated a crisis by threatening to "put him away" if he didn't join AA. Also his wife-to-be, Esther, provided moral support and encouraged him to learn about and locate AA. At that time AA was, in his words, "rather hard to find." When he did finally make contact, according to his AA story, he discovered the judge was already a member himself!

Upon affiliating with AA in 1940, he took a job with the Wedge Pipe Company of Chicago. He worked out of the firm's New Orleans office and was, according to his obituary (*Quarterly Journal of Studies on Alcohol* 1958:374) an "industrial personnel specialist." Having spent the war years in this capacity he probably saw firsthand some of the ways in which a specific workplace dealt with problem-drinking employees. In 1946 the company transferred him back to Chicago where a new phase of his life began. He married for the second time, and in 1947 both he and his wife attended the Yale Summer School Alcohol Studies. While there, Esther Henderson accepted a position as Secretary/Treasurer with Professor Selden Bacon at the Center of Alcohol Studies. Ralph Henderson took a position as Assistant to the Executive Director of NCEA, Mrs. Marty Mann. During 1947 he traveled extensively for NCEA throughout the Southeast, Northeast, and Midwest, establishing a mobile pattern which soon accelerated and became his trademark. The following year, 1948, he accepted an offer from the Yale Center to serve as their industrial consultant.

From 1948 until 1958, Henderson developed the work world approach to problem drinking at the Yale Center. He lectured at the summer school, conducting an industrial seminar there, and engaged in what could be termed "outreach" to a wide variety of employers and unions. During his first years at Yale, he sketched out, with Selden Bacon, the "Yale Plan for Business and Industry" (Henderson and Bacon, 1953). In this article he developed a concept that was to become widely used, the "half man" description of alcoholic employees. The Plan contained a series of specific suggested policy guidelines a company could follow to openly deal with the problem-drinking employee, containing sections on the pivotal role of line supervisors, location of coordinators in the company, and counseling-referral. It put frequent emphasis upon alcoholism as a health problem and upon the alcoholic as a sick person. As mentioned previously, the Plan was a focal point for a series of conferences in Milwaukee, Wisconsin under the auspices of the Milwaukee Information and Referral Center. Henderson acted as a "spark plug" in the entire effort although it later collapsed. Apparently only one company carried through and that was Allis Chalmers, which was to produce a classic example that would be cited and studied worldwide. The death of Henderson in 1958 meant the loss of an energetic pioneer who had both a keen personal knowledge of alcoholism and a working knowledge of, and experiences with, the dynamics of the workplace—a combination of attributes that was often to be in short supply as job-based programs grew in numbers and size in the coming years.

There are certainly other AA "pioneers" of job-based alcoholism programs about whom we unfortunately have less background information. One such person is Warren T., the first counselor with the Great Northern Railroad (presently Burlington Northern Railroad) in the early fifties. We have some tantalizing glimpses of his earlier pioneering efforts through Dave M., and the AA General Services Headquarters in New York, but few solid facts. In the AA files, we find a letter written in March 1943, signed Warren T., which reads, "I am now in the loan department, under a personnel manager who is a most tolerant person, and I am to take care of the alcoholic problems. This I believe is the first firm to take on an AA for that sole purpose. I have been here on the new job four days and have conferred with 17 cases (which I write up) of men who admit their alcohol problem and are looking for help." He then refers to the "shipyard" where he works. Dave M. says that Warren T. worked for the Kaiser Shipyards near Oakland, California in a job not unlike the one Dave M. had with Remington Arms in 1941. That is, he was in the personnel department where he could readily encounter employees with drinking problems. Although his letter fails to mention these assumed details, they nevertheless seem plausible. In spite of the optimistic tone of the letter to AA Headquarters, Dave M. has said that Warren T. had trouble getting management support—the same problem which he himself had with Remington Arms. Whether or not Warren T.

was able to continue in this type of work after the shipyards closed down in 1946 is unclear. On the other hand, in a speech at the Twentieth Anniversary Convention of Alcoholics Anonymous in St. Louis in 1955, he remarked that "I've worked on this problem in industry for more than 12 years . . . " but in a July 1951 letter to AA headquarters, telling them of his appointment at Great Northern he observes that "I am most grateful for the opportunity to again get back into active work of this type that I like so well."

One thing seems clear. Warren T. was an experienced man with employed alcoholics when he came to work for Great Northern, and that he gained this experience on the West Coast during the forties. Much like Dave M. he was motivated by his AA affiliation. He worked in a somewhat more receptive company, but started approximately two years later, and probably had to cease his efforts because the war ended and management was unwilling to go formal. In contrast, Dave M.'s job accelerated following the war. In any event, it seems likely that Dave M. (1941) was followed by Warren T. (1943), with Henderson capping off the AA pioneers of this period (1949).

Two other AA members, Elizabeth W. in Boston and George S. in Milwaukee, also played an important role in the field of alcoholism programming in the mid-1940s, but with a somewhat different focus. Both approached the question of job-based programs from the stand-point of broad-based community action organization. Their approach contrasted with both Dave M.'s and Warren T.'s and to some degree with Henderson, who were all more oriented to single, specific work organizations. George S. left Milwaukee in 1953 and continued his community-based approach in Canada. Elizabeth W., however, continued to generate considerable activity over a long period of time among local work organizations in the Boston area. For a quarter of a century, she served as the Executive Director of the Greater Boston Council on Alcoholism, an organization she founded in 1945. The Council, the first volunteer community health organization in the U.S. to deal with alcoholism, became the first affiliate of NCA. She recognized early on the importance of working together with industry in order to effectively rehabilitate alcoholics. Through the Greater Boston Council on Alcoholism she established the Consultation and Guidance Service on Alcoholism for Business and Industry, a service designed to educate companies in the greater Boston area on the problem of alcoholism and provide them with information about community treatment facilities. For five years the

Greater Boston Council cosponsored a two-credit course for personnel workers entitled "Problem Drinkers in Business and Industry" together with Boston University and the Personnel Managers Club of the Chamber of Commerce. One day institutes were presented at the Harvard Business School, Tufts, and MIT during a seven-year period.

Among the many companies in the Boston area with which she worked are Dow Chemical, Bell Telephone, General Electric, Hood Milk, Raytheon, Woolworth, Allis Chalmers, First National Bank of Boston, Eastern Gas and Fuel, New England Electric, Foxboro Company, New England Telephone, and Liberty Mutual. The widespread support that Boston industry committed to the efforts of the Boston Council is a reflection of the capabilities of Elizabeth W.

Elizabeth W. is the most prominent woman in the early period of job-based programs, although by no means the only one. Although Marty Mann's concentration was not specifically directed to such programs, she constantly supported and "did everything possible to promote them," throughout her long career as founder of NCA. Other women worked in more specialized ways. Warren T.'s wife, Alice, worked directly with her husband, while Esther Henderson worked as an administrator and sympathetic supporter of Ralph Henderson. Also, during the surge of interest in the Milwaukee area, two industrial nurses were particularly active: Phoebe Brown of the Schlitz Brewery and Kathleen Russell of International Harvester. At approximately the same time, Metropolitan Life Insurance Company in New York appointed Dr. Lydia Giberson as a member of the President's staff to counsel on medical-behavioral problems.

THE UPSURGE OF PROGRAMS—
LATE FORTIES AND EARLY FIFTIES

In a broader view, a more discernible coherence in efforts to develop job-based alcoholism programs emerged as the 1950s approached, with a resultant burgeoning of activity. There was a sharp increase in the number of formal, written policies and a diminution of the "quietly started" ones. A number of factors were involved.

Major Contributing Factors

AA continued to provide a widespread impetus; its General Services Office continued to respond to inquiries about job-based programs from both members and nonmembers. Between 1949 and 1954, there was an increase of almost 50 percent in the number of inquiries about work world programs, although inquiries leveled off. AA itself continued to grow during these years. By 1950, there were approximately 90,000 members in 3,000 groups spread throughout the world (Trice, 1958).

The efforts of the Yale Center were sharply increasing. Not only did the major part of Ralph Henderson's work take place during this time, but he was often joined by Selden Bacon. The latter recalls the entire effort as a "tremendous campaign," saying, "I personally visited 40 or 50 directors (or presidents or executive vice presidents) of the 65 largest corporations in America and discussed this alleged problem with all of them at considerable length; this traipsing around may have had some impact; we may never know." The Yale group devised a card file about large employers, used by both Bacon and Henderson, but there were many turndowns and "deaf ears." Efforts during 1948–50 produced a tentative plan for one giant corporation. The entire thing collapsed because "the top man was a teetotaler." Yet inquiries grew. Among those who became interested were the Department of Labor and the Federal Security Agency.

In the early fifties the Christopher D. Smithers Foundation was established; in October 1952 it was formally incorporated. It soon became—and remains today—the only private foundation actively promoting education and action program on alcoholism. Although its focus was much broader than industrial alcoholism, it soon came to regard industry as a major arena for programs and prevention efforts. Moreover, its early emphasis was on the need for labor and management participation in joint planning and action. It actively encouraged labor-management committees in the National Council on Alcoholism and developed foundation bulletins directed toward job-based programs (Smithers Foundation, 1977). The Foundation collected information on individual company programs, which resulted in the first publication that surveyed the developments of the forties and fifties (Smithers Foundation, 1958). Since this early beginning, the Foundation, and its President, R. Brinkley Smithers, have actively supported and helped to develop job-based programs.

Publicity also began to play a part in the upsurge of activities. At least two companies, Allis Chalmers and Consolidated Edison, openly publicized their programs. Henderson received good press coverage on the subject indicating that his subject matter was newsworthy. Charles P. Frazier, a New York City journalist and later Director of Education for the Christopher D. Smithers Foundation, wrote a series of articles that attracted much attention and came to be dubbed "The Billion Dollar Hangover." Copyrighted by the United Features Syndicate, the three-piece series appeared in over 250 newspapers and magazines. In his introduction, Frazier wrote: "Alcoholism has grown to be a billion-dollar a year headache in industry and a few enterprising companies have taken steps to combat it therapeutically" (Frazier, 1957).

In addition, there was radio coverage starting in 1950. Elizabeth W., Executive Director of the Greater Boston Council on Alcoholism, produced and moderated a weekly radio program entitled "Alcoholism is Everybody's Business." She interviewed various community leaders, many of whom were leaders in business and industry, on the program. She also invited speakers from various industrial companies from all over the country to be interviewed. Among her guests were industrial physicians, psychologists and nurses who discussed the problem of and programs for the alcoholic employee. This long-running radio program had a listening audience of 150,000.

During this period, the American Association of Industrial Physicians and Surgeons (currently known as the American Occupational Medical Association) formed a Committee on Alcoholism. In 1950 its name was changed to the Committee on Problem Drinking and Dr. R. Gordon Bell of Toronto became its chairman. The committee's efforts were directed toward changing the disinterested and negative attitude held by numerous members of the industrial medical community toward the alcoholic employee. Membership on the committee included such well-known physicians as Dr. James Roberts of New England Electric, Dr. Harvey Cruickshank of Bell Telephone of Canada and Dr. Edward Byneski of General Electric in Cincinnati. During the Association's 1949 annual meeting, a symposium addressing the topic "Alcoholism as a Medical Problem in Industry," was presented by Drs. Gehrmann and Norris.

More concrete action came from Consolidated Edison Company in New York City during the same period of time. Dr. Franco was instrumental in establishing the Consultation Clinic for Alcoholism at University Hospital, New York University Bellevue Medical Center. Many other industrial physicians in the New York City metropolitan area soon joined with Dr. Franco in referring problem drinking employees to the Clinic.

Consistent with these developments was the inclusion of materials on alcoholism in textbooks on occupational medicine. Dr. Gehrmann authored a chapter for a widely circulated book that described the DuPont Company program (Gehrmann, 1954). Ten years earlier, the watchword had been "keep it quiet," even for Gehrmann. Now programs for alcoholic employees were part of a textbook. Other forms of institutionalization of programs also occurred among industrial physicians during this period. Dr. John Witmer passed on the developing program at Consolidated Edison to Dr. S. Charles Franco in 1951 who in the early seventies passed it on to a younger associate of his, Dr. Thomas Doyle. At DuPont, when Dr. George Gehrmann retired, Dr. Gerald Gordon followed him and continued to work with Dave M. At Illinois Bell, Dr. Harold Meyer turned the program over to Dr. Robert Hilker who directed it during the seventies. At Eastman Kodak, upon the retirement of Dr. John Norris, Dr. William Hoskin carried the program forward.

These developments were accompanied by an outcropping of special conferences that focused on the topic of alcoholism in the workplace. In addition, more broadly-oriented Summer Schools of Alcohol Studies followed the lead of the Yale School by including in their programs lectures and seminars on the subject. The University of Wisconsin's Adult Extension Division, for example, began to sponsor a week-long conference on alcoholism in 1949; Henderson held a session there on industrial alcoholism throughout the early fifties. The University of Utah presented a similar conference. In the same year the Chicago Committee on Alcoholism sponsored the first national conference on the subject of problem drinking and the workplace. Entitled "The Problem of Alcoholism in Industry" it featured both Drs. Gehrmann and Norris.

Between 1949 and 1951, the Milwaukee Information and Referral Center sponsored a series of conferences that involved at least eighteen companies in the Milwaukee area. In 1951, an Institute on Alcoholism was established at Marquette University's Labor College. That year Henry Mielcarek presented a session at the Institute which described the origins and procedures of the Allis Chalmers program. By 1952, the previously mentioned course for personnel managers established by Elizabeth W. at Boston University entitled "The Problem Drinker in Business and Industry" was instituted.

A natural concomitant of these conferences was the emergence of relevant research. In 1946 Dr. Elvin M. Jellinek made his now famous *What Shall We Do About Alcoholism* speech to the Economics Club of Detroit. Published in 1947 (Jellinek, 1947), it contained a series of carefully calculated estimates of the impact of problem drinking on employee absenteeism, job-related accidents, and its costs to business and government. (It is interesting to note that the same issue of the journal carrying Dr. Jellinek's speech also carried a speech about how Alcoholics Anonymous came into being and was organized.) An enlargement of these facts and estimates soon followed. Bacon published articles directed toward both industrial physicians and business people that expanded on the factual points in Jellinek's speech and pointed out the dollar and cents costs of alcoholism to employers (Bacon, 1948; 1951).

In 1950, the Yale Center set up an Industrial Research Council on Alcoholism with representatives from prominent companies. From this group came a pioneering piece of research in 1951 that was to break with the global, overall estimates that characterized the earlier reports and effectively dispelled the skid row stereotype of the alcoholic. The research, carried out by Robert Straus and Selden Bacon of the Yale Center of Alcohol Studies on 2,000 male patients from nine outpatient clinics, produced evidence that there was a "hitherto unrecognized segment of alcoholics who display a relatively high degree of social and occupational integration" (Straus and Bacon, 1951:238). This was a landmark piece of research, often cited even today, setting the stage for the legitimacy of job-based programs. It played a pivotal role, together with earlier research, in the formation of the Yale Plan for Business and Industry, and was the backdrop against which Henderson developed his widely used "half man" description of problem drinking employees.

Less profound, but nevertheless useful research, also appeared as part of the general upswing of activities. Allis Chalmers (1950) published a follow-up report of the first eight months of its program. Seventy-one cases were studied; of these, 51 employees were still working and had so curtailed their drinking that it did not interfere with their jobs. The remaining employees were in various undetermined categories. Only five employees had to be discharged. This was perhaps the first evaluation of a company program. It set the pattern of unusual success that was to be frequently reported in future years. The Allis Chalmers program also provided data for an empirical study of absenteeism: the 174 disciplinary cases involving use of alcohol at the time the program began were absent an average of 26 days annually (O'Brien, 1949). A few years earlier, Benson Y. Landis (1945:212), commenting on data about the absenteeism of factory workers relative to drinking, reported they had lost, "on the average 3 days per month, or 36 (days) per year." Other published research attempted to make estimates of the actual number of alcoholic employees in a given workplace (Page, et al., 1952).

Surveys were not neglected in the upswing of research activity. The Greater Boston Council on Alcoholism conducted a survey of 400 Boston area companies in 1952 in an effort to determine industrial interest in job-based programming. Eighty-five of the companies surveyed indicated their interest in job-based programming. Eighty-five of the companies surveyed indicated their interest in an alcoholism program that could be incorporated into their company health policy. The Opinion Research Corporation, Princeton, N.J. (1952) conducted a survey for the Licensed Beverage Industry. The results of this study which sampled medical and personnel directors from 433 manufacturing companies reported that in their opinion "chronic alcoholism" was not considered an important problem. And a 1954 Kansas survey of 364 companies reported a policy of immediate dismissal for detected alcoholics (Community Studies, 1954).

Although job-based programs tended to be seen initially as purely management-oriented, union involvement and interest became manifest during the late forties and early fifties. This trend emerged despite the fact that the Yale Plan made no mention of unions. Typical of the early management-based orientation was the statement of Dr. Robert Page, Medical Director of Standard Oil of New Jersey, that a program "must be oriented, sold all down the line, and carried out by management." As R. Brinkley Smithers observed, this had often been an obstacle in implementing programs during the early period. Since that time, not only has union interest increased, but more programs have direct union involvement.

Leo Perlis, longtime Director of the Department of Community Services, AFL–CIO, recounts how alcoholism became a part of the CIO Community Services "agenda" beginning in late 1948 along with heart disease, cancer, and "all sorts of problems." Unions were actively involved in a number of seminars during the late 1940s and early 1950s. During 1948 and 1949 the CIO Community Services Committee sponsored a series of seminars and workshops where they had large locals. The Steel Workers of America held two conferences in Youngstown, Ohio in 1950. In 1953, the Utility Workers of America, CIO, and the International Brotherhood of Electrical Workers, AFL, jointly sponsored several meetings on the topic "Problem Drinking and Industry" at the New York Academy of Medicine. Perlis met and conferred a number of times with Mrs. Marty

Mann, Executive Director of NCA. An outcome of these meetings was the publication of a pamphlet entitled "What Every Worker Should Know about Alcoholism." This was the first labor printed publication on the subject of alcoholism.

Also important was the effort to place labor representatives on the Board of Directors of NCA. Berkeley Watterson, staff member from CIO Community Services, was an NCA Board member in the early fifties, and Walter Reuther, President of the United Automobile Workers, was an early member also. Interestingly enough, there was some resistance from the Brewery Workers Union who feared that the entire operation might be prohibitionist. Apparently this fear faded when members learned of the disease concept of alcoholism. Perlis summarized the early period as follows: "Our own records show that we first initiated a nationwide program on alcoholism in 1950. That was under the auspices of the National CIO Community Services Committee. While there was no great enthusiasm among union leaders, there was even less enthusiasm among corporate executives. This was so even though we proposed joint union-management sponsorship and a policy to keep alcoholism outside the controversial area of collective bargaining."

The CIO sent a number of its community services representatives to the Yale Summer School of Alcohol Studies in the early fifties. Henderson, using the CIO pamphlet, encouraged union representatives to be active in his industrial seminars and generally recognized the value of the union in job-based programs. In a 1953 letter he expressed this point succinctly. "The mere fact that the union recognizes the problem and has gone on record will be a great help in the development of programs in plants where the CIO is involved." Bacon recalls a lengthy discussion he had with officers of the Steel Workers Union; members were initially undecided on the issue of problem drinking behavior; finally they agreed it was indeed a union problem. Meanwhile local counselors of Community Services in New York City and Chicago had begun openly to work with alcoholism cases. In Buffalo, N.Y., the Steelworkers Local availed themselves of the knowledge and advice of Dr. Marvin Block, a widely recognized authority on the medical aspects of alcoholism, who was instrumental in initiating many alcoholism programs.

But these union achievements came at the expense of some internal conflict. Because unions were first and foremost political organizations there were real risks involved for union officers who might appear to be embracing a policy that was often seen as management inspired or controlled. For example, unions at Allis Chalmers were not involved in the initial planning of the program in the late forties. They heard about it only when the publicity occurred, and angrily threatened a strike. Matters became so bad in 1949 and 1950 that Walter Reuther, President of the United Automobile Worker, was asked to mediate. He convinced management that they should go over the entire plan with the union. When an agreement to consult with union officials was reached, and union representatives were included in training sessions, the conflict over the program ceased and there was general union support. Surprisingly, the two unions involved said that if management did not set up a program, they would.

The Programs

The late 1940s and early 1950s saw the emergence of a large number of company programs and policies on alcoholism. Selden Bacon, referring to the emergence of open, more explicit efforts, says: "I think this sort of thing was going on all over in the fifties." Programs that developed during this period were often more formalized than earlier efforts. The alcoholism programs that were started at Allis Chalmers in Wisconsin, at Bell Telephone in Canada, at the Great Northern Railroad in Minnesota are among the best known programs of the time period.

Of these three companies, the most publicized program was at the Allis Chalmers Manufacturing Company. As with many of the earlier efforts, an AA member, George S., was a key figure in starting the program. In 1948 he organized the Milwaukee Information and Referral Center and directed his attention toward business and industry. Presumably he got a favorable reception from top management in Allis Chalmers, or perhaps he stimulated it. In any event, Walter Geist, company president during the late forties seemed to be quite motivated. An informational flyer on the Allis Chalmers program states that "Since October 1947 our company has had a plan for the rehabilitation of alcoholic employees... " Henry Mielcarek, then Personnel Services Manager, described how "in March 1948 a committee was appointed to study alcoholism at Allis Chalmers" (Mielcarek, 1951:152–153). However, as often happens, there came a lull in activity for almost two years. George S., however, continued to urge Geist to launch a program. Early in 1949 Geist directed Mielcarek to get a plan together and the latter reports that "In May, 1950, an experienced counselor, a former secretary of the local AA group, was employed to handle the situation" (Mielcarek,

1951:152–153). The program was set up in the Personnel Services Division, which also administered a wide variety of employee benefits: home benefits, physical illness benefits, retirement, recreation, and "general counseling." Initially the Medical Department was not involved, although "two or three years later" they did begin to participate, but how and to what degree is unclear.

The public relations department, on the other hand, took an active interest from the start. One observer noted that "the P.R. aspect of the program was a big factor in moving it from the drawing board to actual operation." According to several of our sources the program was publicly announced before it was actually in operation. One informant recounts how the public relations and advertising people—particularly one person— "saw all kinds of potential in it . . . He spared no effort and no dollars and it became known worldwide; and almost overnight they had visitors from all over coming to learn how they dealt with alcoholics."

Henry Mielcarek himself traveled to Wilmington to visit with Dr. Gehrmann and also attended the Yale Summer School. He seemed to have accepted the strategy, to a degree, of DuPont and Consolidated Edison: "In our alcoholic approach, we have used the philosophy that it is our job to straighten the man out and not to punish him" (Mielcarek, 1951:159). One anecdote that seems to be fairly accurate is about his effect on a sales convention of heavy machine manufacturers in Kansas City (or St. Louis) in 1949. He included in his talk a description of the Allis Chalmers plan and this immediately generated some new accounts, especially from the deep South where some dealers thought Allis Chalmers already had an active program. One version of that incident has Mielcarek "making a great sales pitch and dominating the total sales convention." It is clear that public relations had come to play a prominent part in job-based alcoholism programs. More and more it would become a regular part, making for a sharp reversal of the "keep it quiet" atmosphere that had characterized practically all of the efforts of the early forties. As a matter of fact, it had become so much a part that when the first AA counselor hired for the Allis Chalmers program had a bad "slip" it created "some real live problems." Another important feature was the role of the labor unions in the Allis Chalmers program. As mentioned previously, the initial lack of union involvement almost precipitated a strike. For this reason, unions were involved in early program development at Allis Chalmers, probably for the first time.

In contrast to the Allis Chalmers program, the program that emerged at Bell Telephone in Toronto, Canada, was almost purely a medical department matter, without any AA or personnel department involvement. It grew largely from the experiences and knowledge of one man: Dr. W. Harvey Cruickshank. Dr. Cruickshank's correspondence has provided us with much insight into the behavior and attitude of Canadian industry during the forties. Just prior to the war, when he was taking his degree in psychiatry, "attempts at rehabilitation were seldom considered and most never successful," and the AA movement was not yet active. During the war, Dr. Cruickshank worked with both the Ontario Department of Health and the Canadian Army Medical Corps in Canada and overseas. In neither case did anyone "give alcoholism or alcohol a second thought." But later, during the postwar changes in Canada, with the impetus toward industrial medicine engendered by the war and the improvement in economic conditions, with rising pensions and sickness benefits, he observed a growing awareness of the "great cost of employee marginal ill health and absences." As a result, top management became more and more oriented to the "human resources of the business."

Against this background, Dr. Cruickshank took a position as Medical Director of Bell Canada immediately following the war. However, it was not alcoholism that at first concerned him. Rather he was originally interested in the "main causes of illness and absences and their effects upon the business." His studies quickly identified the absent-prone and sickness-prone employee who accounted for a large percentage of the disruptive problems. Dr. Cruickshank recalls that as he and his staff "began to study in detail the absent-prone employee we ran head-on into the problem of alcoholism and, after seeing the extent of it began to spend more and more time on it." Such a position implied that rehabilitation should receive greater attention than it had previously. Slowly, from 1947 to 1950, he and his staff began to train and inform managers, but "it was slow going." There was resistance at all levels, though the medical department found that a "fair number (of problem drinkers) could be rehabilitated."

Because there were over 8,000 managers, there arose in the late forties a real need for an official company policy to guide managers in detecting and referring problem drinking employees. Gradually, Dr. Cruickshank and his staff thrashed out a policy statement that alcoholism was a health problem, that it was treatable, that the condition be considered eligible for sickness benefits, and that disciplinary actions be delayed until health factors had been adequately reviewed. "By 1950, we had quite a large number of success stories among some very highly skilled and talented people and the skeptics became less vocal," he wrote. But it was not until there had been a "lot of selling on the part of a great number of people at all levels" that a formal policy became possible. This was in 1951. Although AA had become very active during this time and "spread far and wide," its services were apparently not used. Dr. Cruickshank also writes that he knew "of no significant initiatives by personnel staff people," and that, although there was union support, even the "trade union movement had not really taken any initiative in this area." It is obvious that the program began and remained based in the medical department in this company.

Another prominent example of the emergence of stable programs during this period was that developed at the Great Northern Railroad. John M. Budd, the company president, had become aware of a definite problem among his employees as early as 1951 and hired Warren T. as the company's first alcoholism counselor. Budd had come up through the ranks and had seen firsthand, and at all levels, the problems that alcohol could create in running a railroad. Thus, he was intensely interested and Warren T. reported directly to him. Not only did the Great Northern program enjoy this unusually strong management support, but it appears to have had a broader scope than others in some ways. As mentioned earlier, Warren T.'s wife, Alice, played a part in this, working in "debt adjustment" at Great Northern, where she helped with the debt-ridden nature of problem drinkers as well as with their creditors. In 1956, Les V. succeeded Warren T. His wife, Kay, also worked with him, but added a new development: she was a charter member of Al-Anon and so introduced the family dimension to their approach. They covered an enormous system of 25,000 miles on a regular basis, slowly winning support from the railroad unions.

The period saw the appearance of numerous, relatively formal, open policy approaches which are less well-known than those at Allis Chalmers, Bell Canada and Great Northern. The number of these companies further demonstrated the rapid upswing of activity in the latter part of the forties and early fifties.[2]

There was even some activity in the military at this time, though it can hardly be termed either open or explicit. In 1949 and 1950, T/Sgt. William Swegan attended the Yale Center of Alcohol Studies. A chaplain on the Mitchell Air Force Base, N.Y. (Major Thomas Adams) helped him secure a leave of absence for six weeks and $150.00 for expenses. For the refresher in 1950 he received a five-day leave, but not monetary support. After much delay, Sgt. Swegan managed to secure a transfer to Lackland Air Force Base in San Antonio, Texas in 1953, where he was fortunate in working with an interested psychiatrist, Dr. Louis West. A "small experimental program was initiated in 1953 at the 700th USAF Hospital with the approval of the Hospital and Base Commanders and the Office of the Surgeon General (West and Swegan, 1956:1004).

SOME CONCLUSIONS

The roots of job-based alcoholism programs can be traced back to the late 19th/early 20th century efforts by employers to eliminate the long-accepted use of alcohol in the workplace. Even though these efforts were largely successful, the process took roughly 50 years, and the repressive measures used created stereotypes that may well have contributed substantially to the stigma surrounding the disorder of alcoholism. Actual programs came into being in an effort to reduce this stigma and treat the problem drinking employee in a constructive, rehabilitative fashion rather than a punitive one. Programs sprang from the workplace itself and from employers' concern about job efficiency, workmen's compensation, and mechanization. Moreover, they grew solely from a concern for alcohol use, and rarely, if ever, dealt with other kinds of drugs or personal problems.

Three forces combined in the late thirties and during the war years to escalate these concerns into embryonic programs. These were the rapid rise of Alcoholics Anonymous, the sudden and enlarged need for workers during the war, and the concern of industrial physicians. Persons who were active and highly committed innovators capitalized upon these ingredients during the war, molding them into specific, but "quiet" programs. These formative forces spun off additional ones immediately after the war. Some top managements became interested; various unions and their community services programs became openly active. The "keep it quiet" theme of the early forties rapidly gave way to more open publicity in the latter part of the decade. The Yale Center of Alcohol Studies became very active, efforts of AA members grew rapidly, and industrial physicians organized their interests more formally than before. Serious research efforts appeared and found their way into program planning. By the mid-fifties there were full-blown efforts underway in at least 50 or 60 companies and unions. Ten years earlier there had been only the quasi-secret activities of a handful of dedicated AAs and influential industrial physicians.

The dim shape of an intervention strategy for combating alcoholism in the workplace had surfaced during this short, but active period. The Yale Plan had made no mention of poor work performance and relied largely upon supervisors as liaisons with counselors and referral agents, but it did urge the developments of AA groups, even within the plant itself. There was, however, no connection seen between the AA notion of "hitting bottom" and using the authority of the workplace to precipitate this in the Plan.

Others, however, were making the connection. Dr. Witmer at Consolidated Edison tended to reject the prevailing notion that pressure from the workplace hindered rather than helped. Rather, he advocated that company pressure on the problem drinking employee to do something about his drinking and his poor performance be used to promote acceptance of help and treatment. At DuPont, Dave M. was telling alcoholic employees that the company's concern involved job performance deterioration and a desire to protect its investment in the employee. Dr. Gehrmann went further and openly advocated that supervisors directly confront problem drinking employees, telling them the company could no longer tolerate poor performance because of drinking, that discharge could ensue, but that AA and medical help would be available while the employee made up his or her mind. The outlines of what was later to be called constructive confrontation had been sketched out and an intervention strategy was born (Beyer and Trice, 1980).

Finally, it is obvious that many of these early efforts disappeared; we know little about them or why they died. Two speculations are, however, supported by historical evidence. First, where there was a combination of top management encouragement, a motivated high status staff person, and a dedicated AA counselor, there seems to have been more continuity. Secondly, and more basic, when a program had these ingredients, and also planned for its own continuance by institutionalizing and formalizing its efforts, it tended to survive. In contrast, when it relied heavily upon the zeal and dedication of one person, regardless of who he/she was, it was likely to disappear.

NOTES

[1]The following individuals and organizations contributed to this study. There were many others, however, too numerous to list here, whose contributions were invaluable. Tapes were provided by those with an asterisk.

AA General Services Office, Selden Bacon*, Charles J. Barron, R. Gordon Bell*, Marvin Block, John M. Budd, John Carney, The Christopher D. Smithers Foundation, William Cowan, W. Harvey Cruickshank, Ralph Daniels*, S. Charles Franco*, Charles Frazier*, Yevlin Gardner*, Henrietta Gehrmann, Claude Green, Esther Henderson, R. J. Robert Hilker, Thomas Hogshead, John Kaczmarowski, Mark Keller, William Knaut, Earl H. Loomis, Marty Mann Collection of Private Papers, University of Syracuse Library, Syracuse, NY, Milton Maxwell*, David Meharg*, Harold Meyer, Virgil J. Meyers*, John L. Norris*, Leo Perlis*, R. H. Porter*, Lewis Presnall*, Charles Rietdyke*, James Roberts, R. Brinkley Smithers*, George Strachan*, William Swegan, C. L. (Les) Vaughan, Elizabeth (Post) Whitney*.

[2]Armco Steel Corporation of Ohio, Bell Telephone of Detroit, Bethlehem Steel Co., Chino Mines Division of Kennecott Copper, Chicago Rawhide Company, Cone Mills Corporation, Greensboro, NC, Corning Glass Works, Corning, NY, Detroit Edison, Dow Chemical, Midland, Michigan, Equitable Life, New York City, General Electric, Lynn, Massachusetts, Inland Steel Company, International Harvester, Peoria, Illinois, Kemper Insurance Company, Liberty Mutual of Boston, Lockheed Aircraft, Burbank, California, Metropolitan Life, New York City, New England Electric Company, Westboro, Massachusetts, New England Telephone, Boston, New York Telephone, New York City, New York City Transit Authority, Norton Company, Worchester, Massachusetts, Peoples Gas Light and Coke Company, Chicago, Raytheon Corp., Boston, Scovill Manufacturing Company, Waterbury, Connecticut, Southern New England Telephone Company, New Haven, Connecticut, Standard Oil Company of New Jersey, Waterbury Brass Company in Connecticut.

REFERENCES

Allis-Chalmers Manufacturing Company (1950). Results to Date—March 15, 1950. Milwaukee, Wis.: Privately Printed. (March 15).

Bacon, Selden (1948). Alcoholism in Industry. *Industrial Medicine*, 17:161–167.

Bacon, Selden (1951). Alcoholism and Industry. *The Civitan Magazine*, March, 3–57.

Bacon, Selden (1976). Concepts. Pp. 57–134 in Filstead, W. J., J. J. Rossi, and M. Keller (eds.) *Alcohol and Alcohol Problems.* Cambridge, MA: Ballinger Publishing Co.

Beyer, Janice & Harrison Trice (1980). The Design and Implementation of Job-Based Alcoholism Programs: Constructive Confrontation Strategies and How They Work. Papers Presented for N.I.A.A.A. Research Workshop on Alcoholism in the Workplace, Reston, Virginia, May 24, 1980, Government Printing Office, Forthcoming.

Community Studies, Inc. (1954). Alcoholism Survey: State of Kansas. Kansas City, pp. 76–80.

Fehlandt, August (1904). *A Century of Drink Reform in the United States.* Cincinnati: Jennings and Graham Publishers.

Fox, John (1944). Some Implications of Expansion in War Industries. *Quarterly Journal of Studies on Alcohol,* 3:646–649.

Frazier, Charles P. (1957). Firms Fight Alcohol Waste. *New York World Telegram and Sun,* April 8, 9, 10.

Furnas, C. (1965). *The Life and Times of the Late Demon Rum.* New York: Capricorn Books.

Gehrmann, George & John Norris (1949). Alcoholism in Industry—Symposium: Thirty-Fourth Annual Meeting, American Association of Industrial Physicians and Surgeons, Detroit, Michigan, April 16.

Gehrmann, George (1954). The Rehabilitation of the Alcoholic in Industry. In Arthur Fleming & C. A. D'Alonzo, *Modern Occupational Medicine.* Philadelphia: Lea & Febiger, Chapter 16.

Gehrmann, George (1955). How DuPont Combats Alcoholism. *Petroleum Refiner,* July, pp. 23–28.

George, M. Dorothy (1925). *London Life in the 18th Century.* New York: Knopf.

Gutman, Herbert (1977). *Work, Culture, and Society in Industrializing America.* New York: Vintage Books.

Haber, Samuel (1964). *Efficiency and Uplift.* Chicago: University of Chicago Press.

Henderson, Ralph & Robert Straus (1952). Alcoholism: 1941–1951. A Survey of Activities in Research, Education and Therapy. *Quarterly Journal of Studies on Alcohol,* 13:472–495.

Henderson, Ralph & Selden Bacon (1953). Problem Drinking: The Yale Plan for Business and Industry. *Quarterly Journal of Studies on Alcohol,* 14:247–262.

Hendrick, Burton (1916). How Business Fights Alcohol. *Harper's Monthly Magazine,* August: 425–431.

Industrial Medicine (1943). Absenteeism—Unauthorized Time Away from the Job. 12:338–341.

Janson, Charles (1935). *The Stranger in America, 1793-1806.* New York: Press of the Pioneers.

Jellinek, Elvin J. (1947). What Shall we do about Alcoholism? *Vital Speeches,* 13:252–254.

J.I.F. (1947). Alcoholism: An Occupational Disease of Seamen. *Quarterly Journal of Studies on Alcohol,* 8:498–505.

Jukes, Robert (1943). Industrial Absenteeism; Its Medical Phase. *Industrial Medicine,* 12:553–556.

Krout, John (1925). *The Origins of Prohibition.* New York: Alfred A. Knopf.

Landis, Benson (1945). Some Economic Aspects of Inebriety. In *Alcohol Science and Society.* New Haven: Yale University Press, pp. 212–268.

Mielcarek, Henry (1951). Alcoholism in Industry. In *Proceedings of the Institute on Alcoholism,* October 10–December 12, Marquette University Labor College, pp. 150–161. Milwaukee, Wisconsin.

National Industrial Conference Board (1958). *The Alcoholic Worker.* Studies in Personnel Policy, number 166. New York: National Industrial Conference Board.

Norris, John L. (1968). *Alcoholism in Industry: Lecture in Honor of Dr. George Gehrmann.* Annual Meeting of the American Academy of Occupational Medicine. Boston, February 8th.

O'Brien, Charles (1949). Alcoholism Among Disciplinary Cases. *Quarterly Journal of Studies on Alcohol,* 10:268–278.

Opinion Research Corporation (1952). *Chronic Alcoholism in Industry as viewed by Medical and Personnel Directors.* Princeton, NJ, privately printed.

The Outlook (1915). Alcohol and Efficiency. Vol. III, Oct. 13, p. 350.

Page, Robert, J. J. Thorpe, & D. W. Caldwell (1952). The Problem Drinker in Industry. *Quarterly Journal of Studies on Alcohol,* 13:370–396.

Quarterly Journal of Studies on Alcohol (1942). Alcohol and Industrial Efficiency. Lay Supplement #3, New Haven, Conn.

Sinclair, Andrew (1963). *Prohibition: The Era of Excess.* Boston: Little, Brown and Co.

Smithers Foundation, The Christopher D. (1958). *A Basic Outline for a Company Program.* New York.

Smithers Foundation, The Christopher D. (1977). *25th Anniversary Report: Pioneering in the Disease of Alcoholism.* Mill Neck, New York.

Smithers Foundation, The Christopher D. (1979). *Pioneers We Have Known in the Field of Alcoholism.* Mill Neck, NY: The Christopher D. Smithers Foundation.

Stevenson, Rachel (1942). Absenteeism in an Industrial Plant due to Alcoholism. *Quarterly Journal of Studies on Alcohol,* 2:661–668.

Stivers, Richard (1976). *A Hair of the Dog.* University Park, PA: Penn State University Press.

Straus, Robert & Selden Bacon (1951). Alcoholism and Social Stability. *Quarterly Journal of Studies on Alcohol,* 12:231–260.

Sullivan, W. C. (1906). Industry and Alcoholism. *Journal of Mental Science,* 52:505–514.

Theiss, Lewis (1914). Industry vs. Alcohol. *The Outlook,* 107:856–861.

Timberlake, James (1963). *Prohibition and the Progressive Movement, 1900–1920.* Cambridge: Harvard University Press.

Tolman, William (1911). *Alcoholism in Industry.* New York: American Museum of Safety.

Trice, Harrison (1958). Alcoholics Anonymous. *Annals of American Academy of Political and Social Science,* 315:108–116.

Trice, Harrison (1959). The Problem Drinker on the Job. Bulletin #40. New York State School of Industrial and Labor Relations, Cornell University, Ithaca, NY.

Trice, Harrison & Janice Beyer (1977). A Sociological Property of Drugs. *Journal of Studies on Alcohol,* 38:58–74.

Vonachen, Harold, Bela Mittelmann, & Milton Kronenberg (1946). A Comprehensive Mental Hygiene Program at Caterpillar Tractor Co. *Industrial Medicine,* 15:179–184.

West, Louis & William Swegan (1956). An Approach to Alcoholism in the Military Service. *American Journal of Psychiatry,* 112:1004–1009.

Winkler, Allan (1968). Drinking on the American Frontier. *Quarterly Journal of Studies on Alcohol,* 129:413–445.

Chapter 2

THE NEED FOR
EMPLOYEE ASSISTANCE PROGRAMS

B. Rorbert Challenger

Over the years there has been a continual escalating of the cost nationally of the work-related problems, most of which are resolvable through Employee Assistance Programs. The expansion of services now being provided through the EAP models has been tremendous over the past few years. It sometimes appears that EAPs are trying to be all things to all people.

The Early Years

In the formation days of Alcoholism Recovery Programs, a team, comprised usually of a "caring" physician and a recovering alcoholic, provided the system within the organization that enabled many sufferers to begin the long journey to becoming once again a productive and healthier human being. Much of this early activity was carried on at some risk to the providers and usually operating in a semi-covert manner. As long as large waves were not made, boats were not rocked and success stories were available to be pointed out, these informal programs were permitted "to do their thing." Results were visible, but not statistically recorded and evaluated. The by-product accomplishments of a single recovery were not considered. The team of two was usually hard pressed to handle just the obvious problem cases and had little time, and in some cases, lacked the expertise to measure results in a truly acceptable academic manner.

Any policies and procedures that dealt with these efforts were:

This chapter is reprinted from *Employee Assistance Programs; A Basic Text* (1988) with permission of the author, the book's editors (Dickman, Emener, & Hutchison, Jr.) and the publisher (Charles C Thomas, Publisher).

43

a. Limited in content and scope
b. Not disseminated throughout the organization
c. Reactive in nature
d. Absent of any educational or preventative measures
e. Lacking inclusion of family members
f. Solely directed at alcoholism

Terms such as women's issues, adult children of alcoholics, family treatment, teenage alcoholism, genetic components, and all the "syndromes" were unheard of. Withdrawal treatment was referred to as "the drying out farm." Inpatient treatment was usually a few beds in a governmentally operated psychiatric center, where alcoholic patients were treated as stepchildren and second class citizens.

Despite the lack of knowledge about the illness, adequate funds to operate programs effectively, trained personnel, and a willingness to openly face and discuss issues (the stigma was ever so present), using "Twelve Stepping" as a method and "Don't Drink and Go to Meetings" as a hope, these programs worked. Many of the pioneers in this field can attest to this.

Typical Cases

The use of alcohol, almost to the point of condonement, has been and still is a way of life in most business settings. Practically all conferences, seminars, sales meetings, outings, and annual get togethers are anointed and capped off by cocktail parties, open bars, and extended drinking sessions. In some cases it appears to be a contest. Picture if you will,

> a young engineer from an alcoholic family, veteran of a war where drinking was prevalent and accepted, a graduate of a prominent university where the veterans continued their drinking habits, is now placed in this type of industrial setting: the proverbial sitting duck with an outcome that is predictable.
>
> Or a female advertising employee, who when recently promoted to an executive position, found herself involved in martini lunches and extended after work cocktail gatherings, during which much business was transacted. The choices soon became apparent: retain her newly acquired position in the organization by maintaining this "way of life" (as expected) or remove herself from the scene.

These are typical cases and too often the scenario.

The Problem

Recent federal reports proclaim the following:

- There are **18 million** adults (18 years of age or older) who have alcohol-related problems.
- Of these, **10 million plus** suffer from the disease of alcoholism.
- There are over **4 million** teenage problem drinkers.
- This results in an economic loss nationwide of $144.2 **billion** annually.
- Adding mental health problems, the losses in the workplace total a "whopping" $102.3 **billion each year.**

When you couple these staggering figures with the destruction of families, marital devastation, the catastrophic effect upon the younger generation, it can only point out the desperate need for Employee Assistance Programs that:

1. Incorporate early identification and intervention.
2. Provide proactive education and prevention arms.
3. Utilize quality yet economically priced treatment modalities.
4. Are equipped to provide a full array of follow-up and evaluative data.

Rationale for EAPs

There are five major reasons for the implementation of these comprehensive programs. These are:

1. **Reduction of Costs:** The opportunity to reduce drastically the enormous dollar burden that the workplace now bears.
   a. The containment of health care costs through early identification and treatment prior to a crisis situation.
   b. The possible prevention of potential problems through training and education of **all.**
   c. Potential for an increase in productivity for a minimum investment.
2. **Rehabilitation Rate:** The capability of retaining 70 to 80 percent of the troubled employee population.
   a. Through family coverage and involvement, the opportunity to reach into the homes for domestic problems.
   b. Through utilization of improved and sound economical treatment modalities, maintain a high level recovery value.
   c. Provision of support for the use of self-help groups.
3. **Enhancement of Labor/Management Relations:** The opportunity for labor and management to jointly tackle a problem that will benefit all concerned.

      a. To jointly remove the "games played" by troubled employees.

4. **No-lose Situation:** The opportunity to provide a benefit to employees and families that returns more than its costs.

5. **Humane Aspects:** The capability of projecting a "caring" image internally and externally.

      a. Fulfilling a corporate responsibility within the community.

      b. The possibility of saving valued employees and their jobs.

      c. The possibility of restoring families.

      d. The capability of saving lives.

What Needs to be Done

For a long time, we in the field have mouthed the disease concept when discussing alcoholism. As Neil Scott, Editor, reported in his Alcoholism and Addictions Magazine (May/June 1987), "The fact is that alcoholism is a disease, plain and simple." Likewise, the EAP movement needs to recognize that the EAP "concept" is no longer a concept. It is a fact, plain and simple. Organizations like DuPont do not support, operate, and maintain a program for 45 years based on a concept. In fact, to the best of my knowledge, DuPont has undertaken only one evaluation study of their program (in 1966), some 24 years after its inception, and found the results so overwhelmingly positive that it has never seen the need to conduct another one.

The basic need is **commitment;** commitment at the top of every organization that EAPs will be implemented. Commitment by every aspect of the world of work that "this will be a way of life in the workplace." A commitment to the realization the Employee Assistance Programs are factual, beneficial and the best way to resolve personal/behavioral problems in the workplace.

From the *Scottish Himalayan Expedition* by W. H. Murray:

> *Until one is committed*
> *There is hesitancy, the chance to draw back,*
> *Always ineffectiveness.*
> *Concerning all acts of initiative (and creation),*
> *There is one elementary truth,*
> *The ignorance of which kills countless ideas*
> *And splendid plans:*
> *That the moment one definitely commits oneself,*
> *Then providence moves too.*
> *All sorts of things occur to help one*
> *That would never otherwise have occurred.*

A whole stream of events issues from the decision,
Raising in one's favour all manner
Of unforseen incidents and meetings
And material assistance,
Which no man could have drempt
Would have come his way.

COMMENT/UPDATE

WILLIAM S. HUTCHISON, JR. AND WILLIAM G. EMENER

In The Need for Employee Assistance Programs, Bob Challenger states that EAPs are trying to become all things to all people. When this chapter was written there was a developing awareness that Employee Assistance Programs had gone from occupational alcoholism programs to broad brush programs that addresses problems in living of employees and family members as well as promoting health and wellness.

Problems of living included substance use disorders, psychological problems, marriage and family problems and legal/financial problems.

These categories continue to be relevant for Employee Assistance Programs. Indeed, changes in our society and at the workplace have produced additional specific problems that readily fit in the Employee Assistance program structure and philosophy to provide organizations and employees professional assistance with personal and workplace problems as well as opportunity to develop healthy lifestyles and a wellness philosophy.

Newly emerged personal problems include HIV/AIDS, domestic violence, single parenthood, unwed teenage parenthood and newer substances of abuse including crack, crank, ice, designer drugs such as ecstasy and the rape drug Rufunol.

Likewise, the workplace has changed. The concept of downsizing to increase corporate profits has left many managers and workers without jobs with options to move and change jobs or to accept early retirement or to change careers entirely. This has created an additional and underlying stress. In addition, technology has expanded rapidly: voice mail, computers, e-mail, internet, user networks and video conferencing are realities requiring the development of new skills for those who don't bring them to the workplace from their education or previous on the job training experience.

Workplace violence has increased as it has increased in society.

Nationally, some ten percent of teachers are assaulted by students and student-student assaults occur at a similar rate. Some 5,000 murders occurred at work in 1996. Assault rates were 15% at worksites nationally.

Employee assistance programs have expanded and developed additional services to address these new demands. Traumatic stress debriefing has become a standard EAP service along with anger management and conflict resolution training. HIV/AIDS and domestic violence awareness have also been added to the training and education function of EAPs. Formal connections have been established between drug free workplaces and EAP clinical services. EAPs professionals work actively with organizations to plan, coordinate and deliver new workplace programs such as day care for employees' children, financial and retirement employee benefits programs such as Family Leave and Health Insurance.

The changing demands and opportunities of the American workplace continues to produce the need for broad brush EAP services. The unique structure and philosophy of EAPs, that it is an employee benefit that if provided free of charge and with employee confidentiality assured, continue to provide a unique opportunity to organizations to address the changing workplace and the needs of employees and families in a responsible, safer, and potentially growth productive manner.

Chapter 3

EMPLOYEE ASSISTANCE PROGRAMS:
A HISTORICAL SKETCH

FRED DICKMAN AND B. ROBERT CHALLENGER

It is well documented that the employee assistance program (EAP) movement has gained astounding momentum in recent years, with EAPs in over half of the largest industries found in Fortune's "500" (Busch, 1981; Dickman & Emener, 1982; Land, 1981; Roman, 1981; Sonnenstuhl & O'Donnell, 1980). Increasing numbers of smaller (250 employees) companies are interested in EAPs (Phillips, 1983), and community observation reveals that mental health centers, alcoholism treatment centers, social service agencies, etc. are literally rushing to get "into the act" and secure EAP contracts with industry. A strong and viable association, Association of Labor and Management Administrators and Consultants on Alcoholism (ALMACA), exists for EAP professional personnel. Undoubtedly, the movement will grow and as it does, at least some broad knowledge of its history and early philosophy is important.

History and Philosophy

EAP history is intertwined closely with that of Alcoholics Anonymous (AA). AA, it is well known, began in Akron, Ohio on June 10, 1935 when Bill Wilson talked for hours with Dr. Bob Smith in an attempt to help himself stay sober. Bill, a stockbroker from New York, had five months "release" from the "compulsion." Following a business failure on a trip to Akron, he was craving a drink (Kissin & Begleiter, 1970). This meeting was essentially the founding of AA, as each man learned he could stay

The original version of this chapter was prepared specially for *Counseling the Troubled Employee in Industry* (1985) as chapter 1, pp. 7–12. For purposes of being accurately advantgarde, it was updated by its authors and reproduced in this book with their permission as well as the permission of the publisher (Charles C Thomas, Publisher). This chapter is reprinted from *Employee Assistance Programs; A Basic Text* (1988) with permission of the author, the book's editors (Dickman, Emener, & Hutchison, Jr.) and the publisher (Charles C Thomas, Publisher).

sober by talking about his alcoholism to another. When it is recalled that in 1935 alcoholic people were given up by medical and psychological practitioners as "incurable" and, as a rule, were institutionalized under life commitment, this chance encounter seems nothing short of miraculous (Leach & Norris, 1977).

By 1939, the AA movement had spread throughout the midwestern and northeastern United States, and more people were getting into "recovery." Many of these recovering people were members of the work force, and it is reasonable to assume their transformation was not lost on factory supervisors and higher level management.

One alcoholic worker was eager to communicate his experience, strength and hope to his fellow suffering worker (Trice & Schonbrunn, 1981). Hence, the EAP movement began—amateurishly if you will—with one recovering alcoholic worker sharing his recovery with another.

These occupational alcoholism programs (OAPs) were so successful in terms of saving money, of increased production, and of ultimately "rehabilitated" skilled workers that it was reasonable to assume that such an approach to alcoholism problems would be effective for other human problems as well.

In 1962, the Kemper Group launched its program of rehabilitation of its alcoholic personnel and expanded the program's thrust to reach families of alcoholic workers and to persons with "other living problems." This enlarged scope of OAPs led to the modern employee assistance program (EAP) known as the "broad brush" approach to human problems in industry. This approach basically increases the services of the assistance program to include marriage and family problems, emotional problems, financial and legal problems, and other problems with drugs in addition to alcohol. This became the typical industrial counseling approach by the end of the 1970s, and during the 1970s the broad brush approach exploded.

The tremendous growth in the 1970s of EAPs was accompanied by (and perhaps contributed to) the following:

1. The Hughes Act

In 1969 Senator Harold Hughes of Idaho deplored the lack of federal and state involvement in the treatment of alcoholism. The next year Congress passed the Federal Comprehensive Alcohol Abuse and Alcoholism Prevention Treatment and Rehabilitation Act and created the National Institute of Alcoholism and Alcohol Abuse (NIAAA) to administer monies and provide leadership in the alcoholism field. The next year (1971) most states followed federal lead and enacted legislation to decriminalize public intoxication and treat alcoholism as a medical disease rather than a legal issue.

2. NIAAA

In 1971, the National Institute of Alcoholism and Alcohol Abuse (NIAAA), commissioned to treat and research alcoholism, saw the workplace as a potentially effective early intervener. Consequently, establishment of EAPs in each of the various states had a high priority. Grants were made to the various state alcoholism authorities to train and hire EAP specialists. Through these grants, many mental health districts and community alcoholism services hired specialists and instituted efforts to reach smaller, local industries as individuals randomly reached national industry in the 1940s, 1950s, and 1960s (Trice & Schonbrunn, 1981).

3. National Council on Alcoholism

In the 1970s, the NCA established the Occupational Alcoholism Bureau and under the leadership of Ross Von Wiegand began to publish helpful materials, sponsor seminars and conferences and spread the EAP concept.

4. ALMACA

Another major thrust of the 1970s was the organization of the Association of Labor and Management Administrators and Consultants on Alcoholism (ALMACA) in 1971. ALMACA provided a forum for dissemination and enhancement of knowledge among professionals, published a directory of specialists, and generally increased community and industrial awareness of the EAP concept today.

5. Treatment Centers

The proliferation of alcoholism treatment centers since the Hughes Act of 1970 is nothing short of phenomenal. In 1969, there were three treatment centers in Florida, one publicly funded by the state, and two privately funded. Today, the author knows of twenty-plus private centers in four counties—just in the Tampa Bay area. Each of these centers has an EAP specialist whose major endeavor is to reach industry. These private centers are in addition to several public agencies in this same location. Perusing national magazines and professional journals, it is not difficult to see this same phenomenon throughout the nation. There is no way to accurately estimate just how many EAP endeavors exist at the present time.

6. Change Human Services Funding

Another force fueling the EAP fire at the present time may be the most significant EAP event of the 1980s. This involves public centers and private practitioners. The economic situation of the early 1980s and, to a real extent, governmental philosophy have forced significant cutbacks in every phase of human services. Both public mental health agencies, alcohol/drug treatment centers, and private counseling firms tend to see future survival in a partnership with industry and are eager to enter the EAP field. This event is labeled potentially most significant, as it may well change the major philosophy and thrust of the EAP movement.

As noted, the early movement provided an innovative and effective approach to alcoholism identification and treatment by means of early intervention and confrontation. Its philosophy was that alcoholism was treatable, and since the average alcoholic industrial employee was a ten-year skilled worker, the bottom line was that to remediate this employee ultimately saved the company money (Brisolara, 1979; Land, 1981). This philosophy developed (World War II and two decades beyond) when a premium was placed on high productivity and during a period in which there was a shortage of trained persons. This, coupled with the fact that OAP/EAP personnel had a high commitment to alcoholism rehabilitation, made for strong motivation to identify and treat the alcoholic workers.

The situation may now be changing. Skilled workers are waiting in line for jobs, and EAP personnel often do not have the training or the commitment of their predecessors to identify and rehabilitate alcoholic people. In addition, many managers in local industry do not want to believe they have alcohol/drug problems among their work force. A change, or at least confusion, may be witnessed in the philosophy and thrust of the EAP of the 1980s. What will take its place?

7. Reduction of Stigma

Significant in the 1970s and 1980s is a reduction of the stigma pertaining to alcoholism. In 1976 at a National Council on Alcoholism annual meeting, 50 prominent Americans publicly proclaimed their recovery from the addiction to alcoholism. Since that time countless other nationally known persons have done the same. This has led to a gradual reduction in the stigma attached to alcoholism and directly influenced the growth of the EAP concept.

A new concept is gaining momentum and may threaten or even supplant the EAP movement. This is increasingly known as the employee enhancement program (EEP). It claims preventive capabilities by concentrating on stress management, holistic health concepts, and other "addiction" problems such as smoking, overeating, overworking, etc. It purports that if stress is controlled and employees are taught healthy life-styles, such problems dealt with by OAPs and EAPs may be prevented. However controversial this new thrust may be, no one doubts that it may be the "industrial counseling" concept of the 1980s (see Fig. 1). Hopefully, this new "preventive" approach will add to the old and that remedial work with alcoholics and other troubled employees will continue to be refined and enhanced.

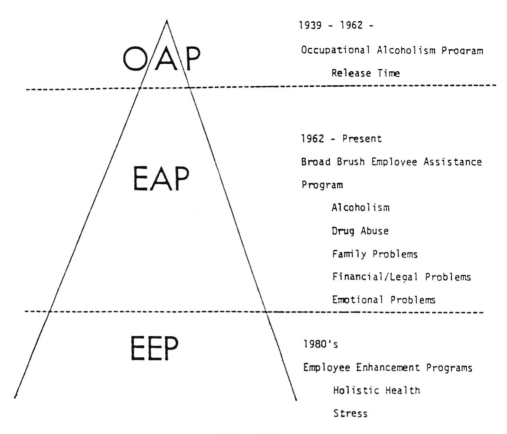

Figure 3-1.

REFERENCES

Brisolara, A. (1979). *The alcoholic employee: A handbook of useful guidelines.* New York: Human Sciences Press.

Busch, E.J. (1981). Developing an employee assistance program. *Personnel Journal, 60*(9), 708–711.

Dickman, F., & Emener, W.G. (1982). Employee assistance programs—basic concepts, attributes and an evaluation. *Personnel Administrator, 27*(8), 55, 56, 58–61.

Kissin, B., & Begleiter, H. (Eds.) (1977). *Treatment and rehabilitation of the chronic alcoholic.* New York: Plenum Press.

Land, T. (1981). Global strategy: Confronting alcoholism at the workplace. *Alcoholism, 1*(6), 41–42.

Leach, B., & Norris, J.L. (1977). Factors in the development of Alcoholics Anonymous (AA). In B. Kissin & H. Begleiter (Eds.): *Treatment and rehabilitation of the chronic alcoholic.* New York: Plenum Press.

Phillips, E.A. (1983). Employee assistance programs: A survey of selected firms in Pinellas County, unpublished survey.

Roman, P.M. (1981). From employee alcoholism to employee assistance. *Journal of Studies on Alcohol, 42*(3), 244–272.

Sonnenstuhl, W.J., & O'Donnell, J.E. (1980). EAP's: The why's and how's of planning them. *Personnel Administrator, 25*(11), 35–36.

Trice, H.M., & Schonbrunn, M. (1981). A history of job-based alcoholism programs: 1900–1955. *Journal of Drug Issues.*

PART II
STRUCTURE AND ORGANIZATION

The initiation, design, planning, implementation, evaluation and continuation of efficient and effective employee assistance programs, require in-depth understanding and appreciation of the structure and organization of business and industry. Moreover, it is incumbent upon employee assistance program professionals involved in such activities to be knowledgeable of the organizational and structural aspects of employee assistance programs and the dynamic interface between those of an industry or business and those of an employee assistance program serving it. The five chapters in this part of this book are designed to individually and collectively address these important phenomena as well as to discuss selected critical issues and considerations surrounding them.

With an overall purpose of providing a basic framework for the other chapters in this part, Nelson and Emener (in Chapter 4) examine the structure of business and industry and labor unions, and describe and discuss key organizational dynamics in industrial organizations. In Chapter 5, Dickman discusses 11 key ingredients of an employee assistance program: (a) management endorsement; (b) labor endorsement; (c) the industry's policies regarding its EAP; (d) confidentiality; (e) supervisor and steward training; (f) financial aspects and insurance coverage; (g) professional personnel; (h) broad service components; (i) accessibility; (j) EAP awareness; and (k) program evaluation. In her Comment/Update to this chapter, Eloise Williams elaborates on how these critical elements have evolved to date. Specific details on alternatives for funding EAPs, methods of promoting employee awareness of the EAP and the continued centrality of client confidentiality highlight this article.

It has been suggested that an employee assistance program is the "third arm of industry"—management and labor being the other two. Fittingly, in Chapter 6, Dickman and Emener emphasize the importance of mutual involvement and trust on behalf of management and labor, and discuss the benefits of these attributes to labor (the union), to management (the business or industry), to an employee assistance program, and to employees.

The editors of this book adhere to the tenet that every employee assistance program is different and unique, and the designers and planners of each should develop a model specific to their own. Toward that end and for purposes of appreciating the specifics of a historically successful employee assistance program, Chapter 8, by Magruder, discusses the key elements of the Anheuser-Busch Company's Employee Assistance Program (which in the late 1980s encompassed approximately 40,000 employees and their dependent family members). In effect, Chapter 8 explicitly and implicitly illustrates many of the qualities and characteristics of successful employee assistance programs.

Chapter 4

WORK ORGANIZATIONS; STRUCTURE AND ORGANIZATIONAL DYNAMICS CRITICAL TO EMPLOYEE ASSISTANCE PROGRAMS

CARNOT E. NELSON AND WILLIAM G. EMENER

Central to the initiatives, missions, goals, and objectives of employee assistance programs is a uniquely defined and targeted constituency group—troubled employees in work organizations. Fittingly, employee assistance program professionals, in order to be effective and efficient in their efforts of assisting troubled employees, must understand work organizations. Importantly, an understanding of a work organization demands a thorough comprehension and appreciation of **both** its structure and organizational dynamics. Nonetheless, work organizations do not exist in isolation; rather, they are influenced by many "outside" organizations and individuals. For example, a primary outside organization which highly influences a work organization and its respective employee assistance program is a labor union (Beyer, Trice & Hunt, 1980; Dickman & Emener, 1982; Emener & Dickman, 1983; McWilliams, 1985). The overall, guiding purposes of this chapter are twofold: (a) to examine the structure of business and industry and labor unions; and, (b) to describe and discuss key organizational dynamics of industrial organizations. It should be noted that throughout this chapter the terms work organization, business, and industry are used interchangeably.

Structure

A typical definition of an organization includes the planned coordination of the activities of two or more people in order to achieve some common and explicit goal through a division of labor and a hierarchy of

This chapter was written specifically for the 1988 version of this book and revised by the authors for this second edition.

authority (Robbins, 1983). Thus, even though they may differ in many ways (e.g., size, goals, activities, and ownership), General Motors, a university, and a local doctor's office can be viewed as organizations. Importantly, each of these three work organizations have a common characteristic—they have structure.

The concept of structure denotes the way in which an organization combines its human resources for its goal-directed activities. Structure can be viewed as consisting of three primary dimensions: (1) complexity; (2) formalization; and (3) centralization. **Complexity** refers to the differentiation within an organization—the greater the differentiation, the greater the complexity. There are three types of differentiation: (a) horizontal; (b) vertical; and, (c) spatial. Horizontal differentiation is concerned with the differences between work units in terms of tasks performed and the requisite education and training of the individuals working within them. Vertical differentiation refers to the number of steps in the chain of command within an organization (more complex organizations tend to have more steps). When an organization has plants and offices in a number of different geographical locations, this is considered spatial differentiation. **Formalization** refers to the degree to which jobs in an organization are standardized or the degree to which individuals working in the organization have individual discretion over what they should do, and how and when they should do it. **Centralization** is concerned with the degree to which formal decision-making powers are concentrated in a single position within an organization. Thus, it is eminently important for employee assistance professionals to be very cognizant of an organization's complexity (e.g., how is it differentiated?), its formalization (e.g., what levels of autonomous functioning do various groups of employees have?), and its degree of centralization (e.g., where and within whom is decision-making power vested?) in the processes of initiating, developing, implementing, and evaluating an employee assistance program.

There are four basic determinants of organizational structure: (a) its size; (b) technology; (c) environment; and (d) power-control. Large organizations (e.g., Westinghouse), by their very size, tend to be complex in that there is a vast amount of all three types of differentiation. Moreover, large organizations tend to be decentralized and formalized. The former primarily due to the fact that no one individual could keep track of all decisions that have to be made (not to mention the vast amount of information that would have to be maintained in order to make so many decisions). "Control" in large organizations tends to be developed through formalization with the utilization of specialized implementation techniques such as detailed job descriptions, formal rules and regulations, and standardized operating procedures.

The technology of an organization refers to what it does—how it transforms "inputs" into "outputs"—how it produces products from raw materials. Within an organization, there can be many levels of technology which can be understood in terms of their amounts of routinization. For example, some job tasks such as those found on assembly lines can be viewed as highly routinized; the job tasks of research chemist, on the other hand, tend to be very nonroutinized. Fittingly, highly routinized jobs tend to be very formal while nonroutinized jobs typically are not. Thus, while not implying an over-generalization, it hereby can be appreciated that an employee assistance program for predominately assembly line industry understandably would have different perspectives on its EAP clients than an employee assistance program for a chemical research company.

The environment of an organization also influences its structure. In order for an organization to survive, it must adapt to (or at least accommodate to) its environment. In placid environments with little change, for example, a centralized, complex and formal organization would tend to function most efficiently. In rapidly changing environments, on the other hand, highly decentralized structures would tend to be preferred in order to provide the needed flexibility to confront and accommodate the rapidly changing environmental conditions and constituencies. It recently has been critical for employee assistance programs in the airline and banking industries, for example, to be cognizant of the turbulent environments in which these two large industries strive for survival and viability.

Although the phenomenon of "power" will be discussed in detail later in this chapter, at this point it is important to note that the power-control explanation of organizational design focuses on the politics within the organization. Quite frequently within an organization there are individuals and/or units seeking to enhance and further their own interests. Central to this observation is that those in power in an organization tend to prefer an organizational structure that maximizes their control within (or over) the organization. Thus, a manager may make a decision that minimally satisfies or enhances the organization while maximizing his or her interests (e.g., level and span of control). From an overall perspective, it is important to remember that **business is structured top-down.** Operationally, authority is vested in the ownership of a company and then delegated to boards of directors, chief executive officers, managers, supervisors, etc. While remaining open-minded in their perceptions of leaders in business and industry, it is also important for employee assistance program professionals to be cognizant of not only **who** people are, but **where they are in the company as well.**

Culture

According to Schein (1990), organizational culture is a pattern of basic assumptions that are invented, discovered, or developed by a group as it learns to cope with its problems of external adaptation and internal integration. This pattern of assumptions, if it works well, is adopted and taught to new members as they enter the organization. An organization's culture can be thought of as "the way we do things around here." Each organization has its own unique culture. Organizational culture is a socially-constructed concept that provides organization members with a way of understanding events. The use of symbols, sagas, and stories is a major component of organizational culture.

Symbols are essential elements of managing people in organizations. Symbols are important for control and motivation in any social system. For example, in some organizations, wearing a special pin is a symbol of achievement. Even in child-focused groups such as the Girl Scouts or Boy Scouts, symbols are important. Symbols provide a way to control and guide behavior in the direction that the organization chooses.

Sagas and stories usually involve a retelling of how the organization was started or of some great accomplishments by someone in the organization. In many cases, the stories involve relating how someone's hard work and sacrifice resulted in a major benefit for the company or society. The stories and sagas are passed along and as with most stories are distorted and exaggerated. The stories and sagas serve much the same purpose as the symbols—they can be used to control and motivate people.

Schein (1990) recommended that organizations and managers learn to use organizational culture to control and motivate employees. However, he cautioned that organizational culture, once established, is only changed with great effort.

Labor Unions

As mentioned at the beginning of this chapter, labor unions play vital and pivotal roles in the employee assistance programs where they exist. Dickman and Emener (1982), for example, boldly stated: "An EAP cannot be meaningful if it is not backed by the employees' labor unit" (p. 56). With regard to structural considerations of work organizations, however, it is important to remember that whereas in industry authority flows "top-down," in unions power flows "bottom-up." In a union, the workers it represents are its members—thus, the goals and accomplishments of the union must reflect the members' interests. In unions, the leadership is elected by the members and contracts typically are ratified by the members.

The labor movement in the United States exists at three levels: (a) local unions; (b) national unions; and, (c) labor federations. Prior to discussing these three components of labor, however, an important distinction that cross-cuts all of labor must be noted. In general, there are two types of unions: (1) craft unions; and (2) industry unions. An example of the former would be the carpenters' union; an example of the latter would be the auto workers' union.

The local union is the formal organization through which the member deals with his or her employer on a day-to-day basis. Typically, "locals" represent workers in a single industry or job classification in a single locality, and frequently bargain with a single employer. Smaller locals which deal with a single employer typically elect part-time officers to run the union. Locals which deal with multiple employers, as is frequently found with construction unions, employ a business agent who is charged with the responsibility to see that the members' contractual rights are not being violated and for referring members to available employment. In industrial organizations, the key union officer is the "steward." He or she is responsible for ensuring that management (especially first-line supervisors) complies with the union contract. Also, the steward represents the employee when grievances are aired, and in most instances is the union representative with whom employee assistance program professionals work with the closest.

The national or international union is the body that holds the basic authority within the labor movement. Interestingly, most local unions are chartered by a parent national union, and many local activities are constrained, governed and/or must be approved by the respective national (parent) union. For example, local unions usually are required to obtain permission from their national unions before striking or ratifying a contract. The employees of national (parent) unions tend to be full-time employees and work hard to assist their local unions in a wide variety of activities. Thus, while it is critical for employee assistance program professionals to develop close working relationships with local union officials (e.g., the stewards and elected officers), it is also very important for them to develop good relationships with representatives of respective national (parent) unions.

The structure of national unions, depending upon the nature of the industry involved, varies widely. For example, the United Auto Workers has national departments, each representing one of the major auto manufacturers. Because the auto industry is centralized, so is the national union representing auto workers. The Carpenter's Union, on the other hand, tends to bargain at the local or regional level because the industry is decentralized.

The American Federation of Labor and the Congress of Industrial Organizations (AFL–CIO) is a federation of 99 national unions. Although it has many missions, goals, and objectives, it basically is designed to facilitate some overall direction to the labor movement and provide technical assistance to its national unions. There are also state and local labor organizations which are affiliated with local unions; however, these organizations tend to be primarily involved in political and lobbying activities.

McWilliams (1985), in articulating the benefits of a joint union-management employee assistance program, poignantly stated, "Programs [EAPs] achieve maximum effectiveness only when unions and managements are joint partners—when the program is neither a 'union' program nor a 'management' program but a joint 'people' program" (p. 56).

Employee assistance program professionals not only recognize the meaningfulness of this cooperative relationship between management and labor, but are committed to enhancing it. The more knowledgeable, understanding and appreciative employee assistance professionals are the structure of work organizations and labor unions, and **how they interface and work together and with each other,** the more effective and efficient they will be in providing meaningful employee assistance programs for troubled employees.

Organizational Dynamics

Power

A key element in understanding how an organization functions is power. In terms of organizational functioning, the concept of power (as used by the authors of this chapter) refers to an interpersonal or intergroup relationship in which one individual or group has the ability to cause another individual or group to take an action that would not be taken otherwise (Steers, 1984). Obviously, power is closely related to the concepts of authority and leadership. Authority includes the right or legitimacy of seeking compliance to one's requests that is absent in the concept of power. Leadership, on the other hand, refers to the ability to influence another person above that required by the situation. It, indeed, is critical for employee assistance program professionals to know who is in authority or who is in the position of leadership. Nonetheless, it is also important to know who or which group has what power.

According to French and Raven (1968) there are five bases of social power; these will provide the grounding for the following discussions of power in organizations. **Reward power** exists when person A perceives that person B controls his or her rewards. In **coercive power,** person B perceives that person A will punish him or her if B does not comply to A's request.

A most important source of power within organizations is **legitimate power.** Here, person B perceives that person A has the right to exert power and B has an obligation to comply. This, of course, is what is meant by authority. When person B complies with person A's request because B admires or likes A, this is referred to as **referent power.** The fifth source of power is called **expert power** and exists when person B perceives that person A has knowledge or expertise relevant to him or her. The ability to recognize and understand the variety of types and sources of power is very important to the employee assistance program professional. For example, if one employee or a group of employees are having difficulties relating to another employee(s) in their work area and the situation becomes troublesome, it would seem appropriate to suggest that the employee(s) discuss the matter with the individual central to the situation. Should the response to such a suggestion be akin to, "I/we can't because that person has too much power," it would be very beneficial to explore the type and magnitude of the power that the individual is perceived to have. Given the basic differences among French and Raven's

(1968) five sources of power in organizations, differential intervention/remediation strategies would be needed in each individual situation. What works in one power situation may be totally ineffective in another power situation.

Politics

Closely associated with the concept of power is politics. In terms of the relevance of power and politics in the work organizations germane to employee assistance programs, the concept of "politics" basically will refer to the resolution of differing preferences in conflicts over the allocation of scarce and valued resources (Steers, 1984, p. 314). Many organizations, businesses, and industries circa 1987 are highly political entities for two understandable reasons (among others). First, resources are scarce. Today, a common business slogan is "lean and mean." Companies like AT&T, for example, are "downsizing" (i.e., reducing staff). Second, rapid changes in the environment call for increasing numbers of nonprogrammed decisions—decisions that are novel or unstructured (vis-à-vis decisions that are more routine and structured). Moreover, politics become more prevalent when: (a) the goals of a department, unit or organization are ambiguous; (b) the external environment is more complex and (c) during periods of organizational change. It is important for employee assistance program professionals to be acutely aware of the politics in the work organizations which their employee assistance programs serve. Among the many reasons why such awareness is important are: (a) the professionals would be better postured for accurately predicting changes in the organizations that may affect the employee groups they serve; (b) they would be more insightful in assisting their clients (employees) in understanding resulting changes and impacts; and, (c) they would be in a more advantageous position of assisting organizations in understanding ways and means by which the organizations could be more caring about the employees being affected by resulting changes in the organizations.

Decision-making

A key element in any organization is decision-making. In the context of the phenomena being addressed in this chapter, "decision making" is being referred to as a process of selecting among alternatives. For example, it is very appropriate for an employee assistance professional to be curious about "Who makes what decisions within the organization?", and

"How and by what processes are such decisions made?" Interestingly, Heller (1973) pointed out that: (a) if a decision is important for the organization, a nonparticipative style of decision-making is likely to be used; (b) if a decision is important to the subordinates in the organization in terms of their work, a more participative decision-making approach would likely be used and (c) if the organization's decision-makers believe that the subordinates in the organization have something to contribute to the decision-making and/or its implementation, then participative decision-making is even more likely to be used. Another way of viewing this is to consider topics of importance to the organization as "managerial decisions" and decisions concerning the employees' (subordinates') work as "technical decisions."

Two basic models of decision-making are the "economic man model" and the "bounded rationality model." The economic man model assumes that people are economically rational (i.e., they desire to maximize gains and minimize losses), and that they do this in an orderly and systematic manner. Fundamentally, this model posits that people discern the symptoms of a problem, define the problem to be solved, develop criteria to evaluate alternatives, systematically explore all alternatives, evaluate each alternative, select the "best" alternative, and finally implement the decision. Although on the surface this model appears reasonable and appealing, it is woefully inadequate in describing actual and/or typical decision-making behavior. First, it assumes that individuals or groups can gather all the relevant information necessary to make a given decision. Second, it assumes that all relevant information can be stored and processed. Obviously, these assumptions are false and actually can be misleading to employee assistance program professionals in their attempts to comprehend decision-making in business, industries, and work organizations.

Simon (1957) presented a much more relevant and appropriate model for the employee assistance program professional, the "bounded rationality model," which assumes that people consider alternative solutions sequentially. Operationally, this model postulates that if a solution meets a minimum set of criteria, then it is accepted; if not, then another solution is examined. (It is important to note here that it is not the "best" solution that is sought; rather, it is a "satisfactory" solution that is sought.) Decision-makers are assumed to use "heuristics"—rules that guide the search for alternatives into areas with high probabilities of yielding satisfactory solutions. For example, a company will tend to

promote employees who have attained certain scores on selected performance measures because in the past employees with such scores have
succeeded.

Employee assistance program professionals have found that their knowledgeable awareness of decision-making phenomena is very useful in
their understanding of the organizations which their programs serve.
Moreover, such expertise can facilitate helpful self-insights into how
employee assistance program professionals, themselves, make their own
day-to-day decisions.

Communications

Communication can be considered the "life blood of an organization."
In fact, five decades ago Barnard (1938) postulated that communication
is the basis of organizations and that without communication organizations cannot function. The following section of this chapter will examine
the relationship between organizational structure and communication,
the direction(s) of communication within organizations, and selected
problems in organizational communication.

Communication networks portray the impact of organizational structure
on communications. Additionally, communications networks reveal the
paths of communication between and/or among individuals in a group.
Consider, for example, the difference between the "chain" versus the
"wheel" types of communication networks. In the chain, each member of
the group can only communicate to two other members (except at the
ends). The typical "chain of command" communication in work organizations is a good illustration of this communication mode. In this type of
network, however, the centralization of power is high and the satisfaction
of group members tends to be low. The wheel type of communication
network can be conceptualized as a wheel—with a hub and spokes. In
this mode, members of the group all communicate with the same (one)
person. A common work organization illustration of this type can be
found in formal work groups where all members communicate (individually) with their leader, e.g., their foreman or unit supervisor. As
mentioned earlier, in this mode there is a highly centralized form of
authority and satisfaction among the members tends to be low. "Common,"
or complete communication, on the other hand, allow everyone on the
group to communicate freely with everyone else. This communication
network type can be observed, for example, in a human development/
training seminar for first-line supervisors. There is no centralization of

authority and power, and satisfaction of the members tends to be high. Employee assistance program professionals conducting seminars such as these, need to be cognizant of the fact that the communication network mode that the supervisors may experience in the seminar (i.e., the common type) is most likely quite different from the type of communication network they experience when they have their monthly meetings with their division manager (i.e., the wheel type). These structures also differ in terms of their relationship to the accuracy of communication. In the chain, for example, written communication tends to be high on accuracy and verbal communication tends to be low on accuracy.

Communication in organizations can flow three ways: horizontally, upward and downward. **Horizontal communication** involves communication between or among individuals at the same level within the organization. There are two types of horizontal communication: (a) within subunit; and, (b) between subunit. Within subunit communication typically is informal and focuses on the coordination of work activities. For example, rehabilitation counselors and social workers within a district office may work together very closely on a special project calling for high levels of within subunit cooperation and coordination. Between subunit communication, both face-to-face and written (e.g., between district offices), although not sanctioned in bureaucratic organizations, tends to be common. Between subunit communication such as this has been referred to as "Fayol's Bridge"—without it the communication system would become completely clogged. For example, in a bureaucratic hierarchy such as a governmental agency, direct communication between or among different subunits (e.g., district offices) typically is difficult to develop because in a bureaucratic hierarchy communications predominately are directed upward in the chain of command until the point where the hierarchies of the two subunits come together (e.g., the regional office). The between subunit type of communication thus saves time, enhances good cooperation, and allow for the development of reasonable solutions to complex problems and situations. However, it should be noted that this type of communication can lead to conflict; for example, different subunits may view the world differently and have different vocabularies.

Upward communication flow is not very common in most traditional work organizations; it tends to be circumscribed. For example, subordinates are very careful of what they say to their superiors. Employees tend to tell their superiors what their superiors want to hear. Moreover, they tend to emphasize the positive and eliminate or downplay the negative in upward communication. Essentially, the element of trust plays a major role in the accuracy and honesty of upward communication; usually, the higher the level of trust, the higher level of accurate and honest upward communication.

Downward communication involves five important elements (Katz & Kahn, 1978). First is "job instruction" which basically refers to the employee being taught and/or told what he or she is expected to do. Second is the "rationale for the task" and an understanding of where it fits into the total organization. Third is "information" regarding rules and regulations, policies, procedures, and practices within the organization. The fourth element is the giving of feedback to the individual employee regarding his or her performance. The fifth element involves an attempt on behalf of the organization to indoctrinate subordinates into the organization's goals and values.

As most experienced employee assistance program professionals know, there are numerous problems and difficulties in organizational communications. The following four, however, appear to be especially relevant to their work. **Omission** occurs when aspects of a message are either not (a) sent by the sender, (b) understood by the receiver, (c) accurately transmitted by a middle or interim person, or (d) understood completely by the recipient. **Distortion** is the alteration of the meaning of messages as they pass through the organization. **Overload** occurs when an individual receives too many messages to adequately understand and respond appropriately (it must be remembered that a person's capacity to comprehend and remember information is finite). The substance, style, and tone of communications can have interfering emotional influences on a receiver to the extent that such an experience renders the communication cycle as ineffective. In such cases, the receiver typically has **unrealistic expectations** regarding the communication, disappointment as well as a whole cadre of other kinds of emotional reactions emerge, and the receiver understandably focuses his or her attention on the essence of the communication rather than its substance. For example, an employee assistance program counselor may meet with an upset employee who says, "My manager has been a good friend of mine for years, yet he sends me these stuffy, pushy, cold-sounding and demanding memos!" Here is where a helpful EAP counselor can facilitate an understanding of the communication style appropriate and necessary for this employee's manager (in view of his position in, and the nature of, the organization—vis-à-vis his friendship with his subordinate).

Labor Relations and Collective Bargaining

How an organization treats its employees is an important aspect of organization dynamics. Fittingly, this is also an important consideration for employee assistance programs! In organizations where unions are involved, relationships between management and unions are referred to as **labor unions.** The key element to such relationships is the development and implementation of collective bargaining agreements. **Collective bargaining** is a human institution in which the representatives of management and employees establish the terms and conditions of employment (Mills & McCormick, 1985). The process of collective bargaining is the primary means through which labor and management come to terms and settle disputes. Whenever possible, representatives from an organization's employee assistance program should have a consultative role in the development of the organization's collective bargaining agreement(s) in order to assure a synergistic relationship among three missions and goals of the three arms of the enterprise: management, labor and the employee assistance program (Dickman & Emener, 1982; Emener & Dickman, 1983).

The collective bargaining agreement typically covers a wide variety of topics. First and foremost are wage and benefit issues. Included here are not just pay per hour but a variety of fringe benefits as well (e.g., health and dental insurance, vacations, holidays, pensions, etc.). Interestingly, because of burgeoning medical and other health care costs, documented advancements, benefits, and appreciations of employee assistance and wellness programs, and assorted cultural phenomena such as a rise in the leisure ethic, employers are becoming much more concerned with benefits than previously. Fittingly, nonwage issues increasingly are becoming integral parts of collective bargaining agreements. Issues such as these include hours of work, length of contracts, management and union rights, procedures for disciplining and discharging employees, grievance and arbitration procedures, seniority and job security, and working conditions and safety. Obviously, the development of a collective bargaining agreement is a complex process in which both sides are adversaries who must cooperate if the company is to prosper and an acceptable contract is to be reached. Assuring that the contract is in keeping with the missions and objectives of the organization's employee assistance program (e.g., especially in terms of how it relates to troubled employees), constitutes a very important consultative role on behalf of the employee assistance program professional.

Resource Allocation

Much valuable information can be learned about an organization from an understanding of how it allocates its resources. The ultimate goals and priorities of an organization become clear and concrete in the process(es) of resource allocation. In almost every case, an organization's resources are finite, and how and in what ways an organization allocates its resources constitute key managerial functions.

Among the variety of resources of an organization, the following five are not only precious to most organizations but also highly relevant to the initiatives and activities of employee assistance program professionals. The first is time.—how should an employee spend his or her time on the job? Most jobs involve a variety of job tasks—what are the priorities by which an employee's tasks should be initiated and/or completed? An organization has a finite amount of **financial resources** —how should they be allocated? For example, should a company increase employees' salaries, dividends to stockholders, purchase new equipment, take over another company, "save it for a rainy day," etc.? **Personnel** is another resource that must be allocated. For example, should a terminated employee be replaced or should that line be transferred to another unit within the company?

When "times are bad" and there has to be a reduction in the work force, who gets fired? **Materials** also are considered a valuable resource to an organization. For example, should a new computer system be purchased for the front office or should new typewriters be purchased for the front office or should new typewriters be purchased for all the unit offices? What will be the differential effects and impacts of these two alternative purchases? Finally, there are **physical resources.** What types of new buildings need to be constructed or what existing building should be renovated? Again, what would be the rationale for such alternatives— e.g., the predicted effects on work output, the status needs of management, the job satisfaction level of on-line employee, etc.? Importantly, it can be extremely beneficial to everyone concerned when an organization's employee assistance program's professionals are formally or informally consulted when resource allocation decisions need to be made. There is no substitute for accurate predictions of the outcome effects of such decisions, and the adage "an ounce of prevention is worth a pound of cure" assuredly verifies this assertion.

Concluding Comment

This chapter has examined key structural components of business and industry, and described and discussed dominant considerations of the organizational dynamics of industrial organizations—all of which are relevant, critical, and pivotal to the work of employee assistance program professionals. Obviously, the space available in one chapter can only scratch the surface in terms of all of the phenomena known, understood and appreciated by the successful employee assistance program professional. Fittingly, employee assistance program professionals are urged to develop a professional life-style in which they will always be a "student" of organizational structure and organizational dynamics. The world is ever changing—rapidly changing—and remaining on top of "what's going on" in the work organizations that their employee assistance programs serve, is tantamount to being an efficient and effective employee assistance program professional.

Acknowledgement. Sincerest appreciation is extended to Margaret A. Darrow, a Masters Candidate in the Department of Rehabilitation Counseling at the University of South Florida, for her technical assistance and critical reading of earlier drafts of this chapter.

REFERENCES

Barnard, C. (1938). *The functions of the executive.* Cambridge, MA: Harvard University Press.

Beyer, J.M., Trice, H.M., & Hunt, R. (1980). Impact of federal sector unions on supervisor's use of personnel policies. *Industrial and Labor Relations Review, 33,* 212–231.

Corneil, W. (1982). Initiating a joint labor management EAP. *EAP Digest, 2*(5), 22–27.

Dickman, F., & Emener, W.G. (1982). Employee assistance programs: Basic concepts, attributes and an evaluation. *Personnel Administrator, 27*(8), 55–62.

Emener, W.G., & Dickman, F. (1983). Corporate caring: EAPs solve personnel problems for business benefits. *Management World, 12*(1), 36–38.

French, J.R.P., & Raven, B. (1968). The basis of social power. In D. Cartwright & A. Zanden (Eds.), *Group dynamics.* New York: Harper and Row.

Heller, F.A. (1973). Leadership decision making and contingency theory, *Industrial Relations, 12,* 183–199.

Katz, D., & Kahn, R.L. (1978). *The social psychology of organizations,* rev. ed. New York: John Wiley and Sons.

McWilliams, E.D. (1985). The values of a joint union-management program. In J.F. Dickman, W.G. Emener, & W.S. Hutchison, Jr. (Eds.), *Counseling the troubled person in industry.* Springfield, IL: Charles C Thomas, Publisher.

Mills, D.A., & McCormick, J. (1985). *Industrial relations in transition: Cases and context.* New York: John Wiley and Sons.

Robbins, S.P. (1983). *Organizational behavior: Concepts, controversies and applications (2nd ed.).* Englewood Cliffs, NJ: Prentice-Hall.

Schein, E.N. (1990). Organizational Culture, *American Psychologist,* 45, 109–119.

Simon, H.A. (1957). *Administrative behavior (2nd ed.).* New York: The Free Press.

Steers, R.M. (1984). *Introduction to organizational behavior.* Glenview, IL: Scott, Foresman and Company.

Chapter 5

INGREDIENTS OF AN EFFECTIVE EAP

FRED DICKMAN

Employee Assistance Programs (EAP) are extensive and widespread (U.S. National Institute on Alcohol Abuse and Alcoholism). In addition, their goals, structures, and types of personnel vary extensively in order to meet the specific program needs for which they were developed (Beyer & Trice, 1978). Yet to reach a high degree of effectiveness, every EAP requires identifiable minimum ingredients (Dickman & Emener, 1981; Dunkin, 1982). These necessary ingredients and their specific uniqueness comprise the primary thrust of this chapter.

I. Management Endorsements. It is absolutely necessary that management, at its highest level, endorse and actively support their Employee Assistance Program (EAP). To begin with, backing simply from middle management and/or the Industrial Relations Department is not enough. Management endorsement and active involvement from the very top of the corporate structure is required if an EAP is even to get off the ground. This is true whether the industry is a large corporation such as General Motors or whether it is to serve a small distributorship such as one with 50 employees.

Top management backing can insure that the following will happen:

- Doors will open to EAP personnel at all other levels of management.
- Adequate financial support to begin the EAP will be made available for mail-outs, lower supervisory training, and initial diagnostic sessions.
- Enthusiastic support of middle and lower management more likely will model and reflect top management initiative.
- A beginning to enlist the support of local top management will be maximized.

This chapter is reprinted from *Counseling the Troubled Person in Industry* (1985) with permission of the author, the book's editors (Dickman, Emener, and Hutchison, Jr.) and the publisher (Charles C Thomas, Publisher).

In this author's experience, no elaboration is strong enough to stress the above principle. He coordinates, on a local level, four EAPs, all of which abide by this first principle by beginning the EAP with support at the highest corporate level. This has meant he has had access and friendly receptivity to top level local management. From the beginning and throughout the past five years this enthusiastic support is largely responsible for each of the local branches achieving a penetration rate of 8 percent and very high employee, management and labor satisfaction with the program (Dickman & Emener, 1982).

II. Labor Endorsements. Organized labor on a national level has wholeheartedly endorsed the EAP concept, and other experts in the field have expounded the value of labor-management cooperation in implementing an effective program (Beyer, Trice, & Hunt, 1980; McWilliams, 1978). Such cooperation, in this author's experience, is crucial when the industry involved is union organized and will increase EAP participation by a meaningful degree. The following anecdotes illustrate this point.

Two of the several EAPs with which the author is under contract to coordinate in the Tampa Bay area are union shops. Both unionized companies had national union EAP endorsement but local business managers were cautious and hesitant. Such reticence could have hindered the progress of this "new idea" at the area. Fortunately, opportunities to demonstrate EAP value came early.

Two illustrative incidents in one shop involved alcoholism and both occurred late in 1979. In the first incident, the author was "beeped" by his answering service in the middle of a Saturday morning. It appeared that a worker (with seven years of seniority) had had an emotional breakdown during the midnight shift. During a disagreement with a foreman he had "lost it" and thrown a bottle at the foreman (which fortunately missed but crashed through a plate glass window of the foreman's office). The caller (to the EAP office) was a labor steward who quickly asked, "Could the worker be seen?" He was seen an hour later, initially diagnosed as "withdrawal—acute," and was referred that day to a treatment center. It was clear he was blacked-out during most of his shift. He was treated, suspended for several months (the EAP is often an alternative to discipline but not a substitute), continued in a recovery program, returned to work, and today is a fully functioning sober, effective employee. No doubt his job, seniority and expertise would have been lost had not the labor steward acted quickly and had the EAP not been there.

The other incident concerned an older, skilled employee who was brought to the EAP office by another labor steward. The employee was intoxicated and was attempting to start his car to drive home at the end of his shift. The steward persuaded the worker to let him drive and went directly to the EAP office. He was persuaded to go that day to a treatment center and today is a recovering employee of 20 years seniority who is rated to be even more competent than he had been. In both cases, families and coworkers were aware of these two person's problems, but did not know what to do nor how to do it before the company (and union) provided the EAP.

As of this writing, four years later, these cases have been replicated with the EAP identifying and securing proper treatment for alcoholism, drug abuse, and many other productivity-reducing problems. And incidentally, local union management, at all levels, is solidly behind the program and provides 20–25 percent of the referrals. Where labor is involved it is imperative to secure its support.

III. Policy Statement. Every industry instituting an EAP must have a clear policy statement as to the philosophy and intent of the program. The policy statement makes it clear that human problems are inevitable, that these problems often interfere with work performance, and that, rather than terminate the impaired, troubled employee, the company would prefer to restore the employee to full capacity by providing the appropriate assistance in a confidential and professional manner. An effective policy statement makes clear the following:

- To have problems is human, and the workplace is not immune.
- The company prefers the interfering problem to be dealt with professionally as early as possible.
- Problems brought to the EAP will be treated confidentially and will not become a part of an employee's personnel file.
- Alcoholism and other drug abuse is a disease to be treated and not a behavior to be punished.
- The EAP exists to assist employees and their families, not as a substitute for usual disciplinary principles and policies.
- In no case will the employee be coerced to use the EAP.

These basic principles are necessary as minimum components of the company's statement that its employees are its most valuable asset. In addition, these principles, properly stated, serve to protect employees who choose to use the EAP.

IV. Confidentiality. Confidentiality is the cornerstone of an effective EAP. All employees have the right to seek help for their problems and know that their problems will be kept in the strictest confidence. In addition, when a worker is referred to the EAP by a supervisor (rather than self-referred), he or she needs to know that under no circumstances will this information be noted in any official files. Further, any employee needs to know that nothing of the nature of his or her problem will get back to supervisors or anyone else. Unless absolute confidentiality is kept at all levels, the EAP will not be successful. It is that simple. Only the employee himself or herself may (and often does) reveal his or her treatment (often the best EAP referral source) but no one else may, including the referring supervisor or labor steward, a manager, or, of course, the EAP personnel who are bound by professional ethics. Holding to this important ethic and principle overtly is not enough. There are many ways to break confidentiality in an Employee Assistance Program inadvertently. Following, in a tongue-in-cheek fashion, are some of the ways this can be done:

1. How to Break Client Confidentiality Without Even Trying

Schedule clients from the same industry too close together. Usually the EAP counseling office is offsite. This in itself protects confidentiality. Yet if two or more clients from the same company are scheduled too close together the probability is increased they will see each other. Even if neither employee cares who knows who uses the EAP, once word of this "chance encounter" gets back to the plant, credibility as to advertised confidentiality is lessened, if not destroyed. In any event, the EAP appointment secretary must take every precaution to make sure back-to-back appointments are avoided for employees from the same industry.

This problem becomes especially acute when the EAP contractor or coordinator gives service to several companies and is part of a large counseling team. Such an arrangement is helpful in that the contracting counselor or EAP coordinator has a pool of specialists nearby to whom he or she can refer employees and thereby match the client with a counselor having specifically needed expertise. When this occurs, over a period of time several clients from the same company may be in at least medium-term treatment. This means several clients may be coming to the EAP center to see several different counselors at the same time period, increasing the odds of clients from the same company being in the same waiting room at the same time. Someone has to be assigned to make sure this does not occur. This discussion could go on and on but the point remains clear: Don't let scheduling break the client's confidentiality. He or she may go back and tell the whole workforce—and some do!

2. Keep Rigid Intake/Counseling Hours

Another good way to break client confidentiality and credibility is to have a narrow nine-to-five intake schedule. This means the client has to ask for time off which usually requires telling someone to get excused from work. Since most (80–85%) EAP clients are self-referred, they require an appointment time when they are off work. This becomes complicated when work time is in shifts which run around the clock. Consequently, it is important for the EAP office to be open and appointments available at night. This is also true for ongoing counseling. The counselor with whom the client is eventually to work must have flexible hours.

3. Randomly Assign Clients to Groups

For many years the author has led after-care and ongoing recovery groups for alcoholic persons and their spouses. He has found this modality in conjunction with AA involvement an excellent one for ongoing treatment and generally stipulates this program for his substance abuse clients.

A good way to break confidentiality of a client, whether already in the groups (which are open-ended) or newly-entering, is to just "let it happen." Instead, when clients of the same industry are involved, each must be told he or she may see someone from his or her worksite without, of course, revealing who the someone is. Usually in the alcoholism field clients realize they are "in it together" and grant permission for the new person to come in and vice-versa. However, if there is any objection either way, other treatment opportunities must be identified.

4. Handle Insurance Locally

Most plants or sites have a person assigned to process insurance. This is helpful in that the fellow employee can expedite claims and usually takes a personal interest. However, when the client is seen by a therapist to whom a referral was made from the EAP office, or when the client is seen by someone in the EAP office, this procedure can jeopardize confidentiality. This problem can be resolved easily by arranging for a special (specific) person in the insurance office to process all EAP client claims. This author has found this to be a satisfactory way to solve this problem, and that the company and the insurance company readily comply with this method. Most importantly, clients report satisfaction and relief with this procedure.

5. Let Hospital Admittance Clerks Verify Employment

Hospitals and treatment centers are happy to get referrals but they often insist upon verifying current employment by calling the local plant. Since most EAP referrals are to mental health centers or alcoholism/ other drug treatment centers, a call to the switchboard, industrial relations, or the plant manager can be embarrassing to the employee. It is a simple matter for the EAP contractor to have a good enough relationship with the institution to pave the way for the client and eliminate this problem.

6. Plant (Site) Visitation

A good way to increase EAP visibility is for the coordinator/contractor to regularly visit the plant. However, if he or she seeks out only current or former clients, this activity can start rumors and people may shy away from being associated with the "shrink" or the plant "alcohol man." If care has been taken to do extensive supervisor and labor steward training, this problem can be meaningfully minimized as there is someone to see. And once some alcoholic persons are helped into recovery, this group (as a rule) is the best EAP advertiser. Alcoholic people, in this author's experience, once recovering, not only are not afraid to share their treatment and AA experience, but on the contrary—they tend to talk to everyone who will listen. This is a good nucleus to whom to say "Hi" while visiting. Actually this author's experience is that most employees are receptive to seeing the EAP person. Yet care must be maintained to protect the anonymity of clients.

7. Contacting Clients at Work

Sometimes appointments have to be changed and the client must be contacted. The general rule is to call at home if possible. If time does not allow this and the client must be contacted at work, caution is in order. It's best to have a first name, usually the secretary's, and a number rather than say "please have him call the EAP office as soon as possible."

8. Tell Referring Supervisors More Than Necessary

The usual procedure, spelled out in the policy statement, is for supervisors to be told three things when a supervisor referral is made:

a. The employee kept the appointment;
b. He or she does or does not need treatment (If he or she is to be hospitalized or referred to a treatment center, the supervisor is told approximately the time the employee will be away from work); and
c. He or she has accepted or rejected recommended treatment.

No other information is required and, as a matter of fact, any information about the nature of the problem is unethical and may be illegal.

Admittedly this section on confidentiality is detailed and perhaps tedious. Yet the message, hopefully, is clear. Every effort must be made to protect worker confidentiality or the program will falter. Keeping trust with the client is crucial.

V. Supervisor and Labor Steward Training. It is recommended that supervisor training be conducted at least once a year and certainly extensively as the program is initially instituted. Further, it is a helpful practice to have labor stewards and supervisors in training groups together (recommended size 15). This stresses the fact that the EAP is a joint management-labor venture. Likewise when top local management is oriented to the program, local labor executives should be included for the same reason.

Content of the sessions should include the following:

1. **Alcoholism Awareness:** Company policy typically states that alcoholism is a disease and that it is treatable. Other important concepts should include a thorough discussion of enabling behavior, effect on productivity, accidents, the family, etc.

The supervisor needs to be warned **not to diagnose** but to look for signs of trouble which include absenteeism, erratic behavior, tardiness, irritability, and a **drop in productivity.** The supervisor needs to know that what an employee does off time is his or her personal business. Yet, the supervisor needs to know that poor and erratic productivity often can be a sign of problems. He or she needs to be taught to more keenly observe work performance **only** and base referral on that alone. Large numbers of EAP studies evidence that this method of referral has rehabilitated more alcoholic persons than any other vehicle (Phillips, Purvis & Older, 1980).

2. **Family and Other Problems:** Problems hinder productivity and are human. No employee is immune. This is typically an EAP company policy. Again the supervisor/labor steward does not have to diagnose. Work performance alone is enough to refer an employee to the EAP.

3. **Drug Abuse:** Like alcoholism, drug abuse is a disease—company policy. Again the supervisor should be taught to act only on work performance with one exception. While alcohol is legal, drugs are not. Observing illegal drug consumption, therefore, is a different problem than observing an employee with a bottle. The supervisor should be advised to report this behavior. Nonetheless, an EAP referral is still in order.

4. **Any Problem a Referral Situation:** Often employees confide in supervisors or labor stewards. This can complicate their lives by trying to be "nice guys" and trying to do counseling "in house." They are not trained; neither do they have the time. They should be encouraged to use the EAP. That's what it is there for.

5. **No Problem Too Small:** This author has found that many employees believe they have to be "in crisis" to contact the EAP. Yet many of these "small" problems are, in reality, not so small. Supervisors and stewards need to hear (as do eventually the other employees) that a "little" problem can grow and that what bothers a person is important to him or her and therefore is important to EAP personnel.

6. **Policy Statement and Philosophy:** In essence, training should cover the content of the policy statement. If that statement is adequately complete, its elucidation will cover the content of the training.

7. **Practical Issues to be Covered:**

   (a) How to make a referral;
   (b) Off-hours practice;
   (c) Emergency calls—24-hour coverage;
   (d) Confidentiality of the program;
   (e) Cost to employers;
   (f) Insurance coverage of the company policy;
   (g) EAP consultation available; and
   (h) What feedback they can expect.

8. **Killing with Kindness:** A final word is required about "enabling." Many supervisors and stewards are from the ranks. They are friends of their employees. Hence, they may overlook behavior, cajole, counsel, and out-and-out cover up. They, like all of us, need to learn that you

don't help a friend with these behaviors. As a matter of fact, we "friends" will kill each other with "kindness." When this principle is understood, the EAP program is off the ground.

VI. Financial Aspects and Insurance Coverage. In each of the several local companies for which the author coordinates an EAP, the company pays for the first three visits. He has not escalated the cost of these visits for five years in an effort toward cost containment and to work with each company to make it easier for employees to make that first effort. Like most people, employees are fearful of counseling, psychotherapeutic, and psychiatric costs. When employees know that going to the EAP may cost them something but that it won't break them, they will be more apt to accept a referral or (as most do) refer themselves or members of their families.

In addition, insurance must be helpful in paying for any inpatient or ongoing outpatient visits they or their family may need. In each of the companies the author serves, the insurance has been arranged to cover at a rate of 80/20 percent which means the employee pays no more than 20 percent (or minimally) for treatment. Each of these programs has an 8–10 percent penetration rate for five years and this insurance arrangement certainly has proven to help. Preliminary evaluations tend to show that money is saved over a long period of time, especially in the treatment of alcoholism. Recovered alcoholic people use their insurance less, have fewer accidents, are sick less (fewer alcohol-related illnesses) (Asma, 1975; Pell & D'Alonzo, 1970). These same observations probably hold true for other strictly functional illnesses but have not been as well-tested.

Another important factor is that there should be an "okay to pay" list provided by the EAP coordinator and accepted by the insurance company. Typically and currently, insurance payments are made for services provided by a psychiatrist or psychologist. Yet some problems are better treated by other specialists, i.e., marriage and family counselors, alcoholism counselors, drug abuse specialists, sex therapists, rehabilitationists, social workers, nutrition specialists, and others. The EAP coordinator should have a list of such competent specialists to whom to refer, and the company (which pays the premiums) should urge the insurance company to accept a special "okay to pay" list of professionals.

Last, but most important, is the issue of third-party payments for the treatment of alcoholism. Since 1956, the American Medical Association has declared alcoholism a **primary, chronic, progressive disease.** Yet many insurance companies ignore this and **exclude** alcoholism and other drug abuse from treatment, especially outpatient treatment. Yet 40 percent of a good EAP caseload is for this disease and 7 out of 10 of these can be effectively treated with little or no time lost from work.

VII. Professional Personnel. The EAP Coordinator needs to possess expertise in the following general rehabilitation areas:

1. **Alcoholism and Alcohol Treatment.** It is important to note that the entire EAP movement began with efforts to rehabilitate alcoholic employees (Roman, 1981). This was so successful the movement was broadened to include other employee problems. However, occupational alcoholism (modern-day EAP) is still the best intervener in the treatment of alcoholism. To lose this thrust would be not only a blow to the national alcoholism treatment movement, but such loss would weaken the EAP (Dickman & Phillips, in press).

2. **Marriage and Family Counseling.** Relationship problems comprise the second largest expected EAP caseload (McClellan, 1982). It is important that the EAP personnel be knowledgeable in this area and have referral sources to remediate these problems.

3. **General Emotional Problems.** The EAP Coordinator needs to have a grasp of the more typical emotional syndromes such as depression, anxiety and stress reactions and have ready access to specialists relevant to rehabilitative treatment modalities in these areas.

4. **Other Typical Problems.** Financial, legal, trouble with other employees, etc. are but a few of the problems brought to the EAP. Again, ready referral sources need to be available.

5. **Basic Interview/Counseling Techniques, and Case Management.** The EAP Coordinator is the hub around which the services will be delivered. This specialist requires interviewing, diagnostic, counseling, and referral skills. Obviously he or she also needs to know the community and which are the good treatment facilities and who are the more appropriate or better specialists.

VIII. Broad Service Components. The EAP must be designed to helpfully respond to a wide variety of employees' problems (e.g., alcohol, drug abuse, personal, family, financial, grief, mental health, medical, legal, etc.). Such a concept is known as the "broad brush" approach to industrial counseling as distinct from the historically earlier occupational alcoholism programs (see chapter on history in Part I of this book). The advantage of the broad brush approach is obvious. More employees get help with problems which definitely have an effect on productivity and the employees' well-being (Dickman & Emener, 1982).

An obvious disadvantage is that practically such an approach attracts private practitioners who have little background in EAP and often no training in alcoholism and other drug abuse rehabilitation. There is supportive evidence that without these skills such a practitioner will not enhance alcoholism awareness nor will he or she properly diagnose alcoholism and other drug problems when confronted with them in an intake situation (Dahlhauser et al., 1983).

IX. Accessibility. Employees need to be able to get to their EAP site in a timely, convenient, and efficient manner. In the opinion of this author the off-site model is more effective in that such a model better protects the confidentiality of the client. (This issue is more deeply presented in Part II of this book). Along with accessibility, 24-hour service is critical.

X. EAP Awareness. The EAP requires constant marketing to be effective. Some of the ways this is done are the following:

1. Supervisor training;
2. Talks before shifts;
3. Home mailouts;
4. Plant (site) visitations; and
5. Presentations (such as union meetings, departmental meetings, and motivational meetings).

These opportunities to market the EAP are invaluable. In the author's experience every time one of the above occurs (mailout, visitation, supervisor seminar, etc.), calls for service increase.

XI. Program Evaluation. The entirety of Part IV of this book involves evaluation. Too much cannot be said about this endeavor; it is crucial to any effective program. The company and the EAP office need to know if the program is working and if it's doing what it purports to do. Some evaluation questions involve the following:

1. Penetration rates;
2. Cost effectiveness;
3. Nature of client populations;
4. Client satisfaction;
5. Management and union satisfactoriness;
6. Medical cost saving; and
7. Productivity gain.

Concluding Comments

These are critical attributes. If they are all in place the EAP will be effective and everybody wins—the employee, employee families, management, labor, and the human service personnel.

REFERENCES

Asma, F.E. (1975). Long-term experience with rehabilitation of alcoholic employees. In R. Williams & G. Moffat (Eds.) *Occupational Alcoholism Programs.* Springfield, IL: Charles C Thomas (175–193).

Beyer, J., & Trice, H. (1978). *Implementing Change: Alcoholism Policies in Work Organizations.* New York: Free Press, Division of Macmillan Publishing.

Beyer, J.M., Trice, H.M., & Hunt, R. (1980). Impact of federal sector unions on supervisor's use of personnel policies. *Industrial and Labor Relations Review, 33,* 212–231.

Dahlhauser, H.F., Dickman, F., Emener, W.G., & Yegidis-Lewis, B. (1982). Alcohol and drug abuse awareness: Implications for intake interviewing, submitted for publication.

Dickman, F., & Emener, W.G. (1982). Employee assistance programs: Basic concepts, critical attributes, and an evaluation. *Personnel Administrator, 27*(5), 55, 56, 58–62.

Dunkin, W.S. (1982). *The EAP Manual.* The National Council on Alcoholism, Inc.

McClellan, K. (1982). An overview of occupational alcoholism issues for the 80's. *Journal of Drug Education, 12*(1).

Pell, S., & D'Alonzo, C.A. (1980). Sickness absenteeism of alcoholics. *Journal of Occupational Medicine, 12,* 198–210.

Phillips, D.A., Purvis, A.J., & Older, H.J. (1980). *Turning Supervisors On (To Employee Counseling Programs),* Hazeldon Foundation, Inc.

U.S. National Institute on Alcohol Abuse and Alcoholism. Alcohol and health: technical support document. Third special report to Congress. (DHEW Pub. No. ADM-79-832).

COMMENT/UPDATE

ELOISE E. WILLIAMS

Employee Assistance Programs (EAP) continue to be a cost-effective mechanism for providing help to employees, employee family members and companies with issues that impact the performance of individuals within their respective organizations. Research findings have revealed that a total of 35.8 percent of the workers in an industrial setting experienced personal problems that were serious enough to cause a reduction in job performance or the use of one or more of the company benefits (Yamantani, 1988). Particularly in the past decade, EAPs have become an integral part of the management of public sector and private sector organizations (Cayer & Perry, 1988).

Many groups have supported the development of "broad brush" model EAPs that assist with alcohol/drug problems, legal/financial concerns, marital, family and medical problems (Mastrich & Beidel, 1987). In recent years, rising health care costs, increased EAP competition, increased cost containment efforts and the search for new or alternative delivery systems have resulted in new strategies for Employee Assistance Programs (Spicer, 1987). In a cost-effectiveness study conducted at the McDonnell Douglas Corporation, significant savings were found in treating employees through the EAP including fewer days of absenteeism, less turnover and lower medical claims (Smith & Mahoney, 1990). The initial decision to be made involves selection of an approach to delivering services; internal EAP, external provider of EAP services or a combination of both internal and external service provision. There are specific ingredients necessary for an effective program regardless of the variances in EAP goals, structure or personnel. Program Support, Program Plan, Policy Statement, Confidentiality, Training, Funding, Staffing, Service Components, Access, and EAP Awareness are the essential ingredients upon which this chapter will focus as well as upon Program Evaluation that includes outcome research.

Program Support: Support for the EAP must be gathered from key personnel within the organization during the development phase. Top level management as well as organized labor, where appropriate, must endorse and actively support the EAP concept. This will provide a labor-management cooperative effort that ensures the implementation of an effective EAP. Whenever the industry is union organized, it is crucial to the success of the EAP, through increased employee participation, that union cooperation with management on the EAP is explicitly expressed. This holds true for large and small organizations. Positive repercussions of top management and labor endorsement include:

- Adequate funding for the program
- Support for the EAP from all levels of management
- EAP personnel acceptance throughout the organization

Sufficient funding of the EAP allows for appropriate marketing to support the program start-up (e.g., employee mail-outs, supervisory training, employee orientation) and continued communications with employees and family members. Top level management and union support provides a model for middle and lower management to follow and allows the EAP personnel to function as a respected member of the organization. Research has reported that enthusiastic support of upper level management has been largely responsible for the achievement of an 8 percent penetration rate and high employee, management and labor satisfaction with EAPs (Dickman & Emener, 1982).

Policy Statement: Ideally, the development of the policy statement should occur prior to implementing the Employee Assistance Program. However, if it is not possible to have the completed policy statement, obtain a written communication from the President/CEO to be distributed to all employees that indicates the intent of the EAP (Spicer, 1987). The policy statement must clarify that (a) human problems are inevitable, (b) these problems often interfere with work performance, and (c) the company prefers to restore the employee to full capacity by providing the appropriate assistance in a confidential and professional manner (Dickman, Challenger, Emener & Hutchison, 1988). The policy should include: The purpose of the policy, organizational mandates and the source of authority for the program, eligibility of the employees for the EAP services, EAP location, integration of the EAP into the overall management systems of the organization, roles and responsibilities of various personnel in the organization, delineation of the EAP procedures, record-keeping procedures, criteria for EAP staff professionals, the importance of and procedures for supervisory training. EAP evaluations provisions, and a statement that employees' participation in the EAP will NOT jeopardize their future opportunities within the organization. A vital component of this document is the signature of the organization's top management and where appropriate include a joint union statement. The basic tenets that the EAP is a mechanism for the employee to receive help in an environment where confidentiality will be maintained, no employee will be coerced to use the EAP, and that the company considers its employees as its most valuable asset are necessary components of the policy statement (Spicer, 1987).

Confidentiality: Confidentiality is the cornerstone of an effective EAP (Dickman, Challenger, Emener, Hutchison, 1988). Employees have the right to seek assistance through their EAP, as mentioned in the EAP policy statement. In order to ensure that all employees will seek help, when needed, they must feel "safe" to disclose their problems to the EAP professional. All EAP records must be kept in a secure file with access only to EAP personnel. Individuals who seek assistance through the EAP need to know that their personal problems will be held in strictest confidence and that nothing of a personal nature will be discussed with anyone in the organization including their supervisor, unless the employee signs a release of information. In certain situations, a "duty to warn" will supersede the patient's confidentiality. Confidentiality must be maintained throughout the organization at all levels, or the EAP will not be successful.

Federal regulations against disclosure of records of clients with alcohol or other substance abuse problems are broad; each business entity should check with its own legal agent before making determinations of what applies to them. Federal law mandates that all records be kept confidential and be disclosed only as authorized by the regulations. Right to privacy is also addressed by federal regulation where individuals are granted a right of privacy against improper dissemination of personal information.

At this juncture, it is important to stress the legal implications of disclosing information. Invasion of privacy encompasses four primary causes of legal action.

1. Intrusion by prying into an employee's physical solitude or seclusion.

2. Appropriateness of a person's name or likeness for commercial gain.
3. False attribution of a statement or opinion to a person that results in harm to her/his reputation.
4. Public disclosure of private facts concerning a person (Spicer, 1987).

Following ethical as well as federal guidelines for confidentiality will assure success of the EAP and provide an environment where the employee feels "safe" to access EAP services.

Training: Prior to offering EAP services, all upper management, supervisory personnel and labor representatives (where applicable) should receive training pertinent to the functioning of the EAP: services to be offered including EAP consultation to supervisors and upper management, substance abuse and mental health, employee self-referrals, supervisory referrals, identification of employee workplace problems, and guidance to focus upon employee work performance not to diagnose the employee. In addition, the pragmatic components of the program (e.g., EAP policy, location, personnel, service hours, etc.) should be addressed. Importantly, this training should present an opportunity to stress the confidentiality of the program, the definition of confidentiality as it relates to the EAP, supervisors and management, and what feedback supervisors, labor representatives and management can expect to receive.

Funding: An EAP can be funded in a number of ways. The following types are not inclusive, but important to illustrate the variety of funding models for EAPs:

1. Organization assumes all expenses by maintaining in-house staff.
2. Organization performs all functions except Information and Referral (I&R) and/or short-term counseling which is contracted on a fee-for-service basis and is covered by the organization's insurance.
3. Flat administrative fee levied by the contractor to the employer in addition to the fee for service charges.
4. Organization contracts for a flat fee to the provider who is not reimbursed by an insurance carrier (Spicer, 1987).

Employee Assistance Programs instituted by the organization management provide initial visits to the EAP at no cost to the employee. Various session models are offered by organizations: The single session model which focuses primarily upon Assessment and Referral, 1-3/1-5/1-6/1-8 session models which provide assessment and short-term counseling. No matter what session type is used, the employee who may be reluctant to seek help due to financial implications, should be encouraged to use the EAP when the initial visits are at no cost to them.

Staffing:

The EAP industry has developed a standard by which to measure professionals involved in delivering EAP services, the Certified Employee Assistance Professional credential (CEAP). This certification is available through the Employee Assistance Professional Association and requires proof of years of experience in the field and completion of pertinent courses. Basic areas of knowledge must include:

1. Work Organizations—the principles and practices upon which organizations sustain themselves.
2. Human Resource Management—how human resources are organized, managed and financed.
3. EAP Policy and Administration—basic concepts and practices of EAP operations and the dynamics of policy, administration and programming in an evolving EAP profession.
4. EAP Direct Services—a critical component based upon interacting with individuals in the work organization.
5. Chemical Dependency and Other Addictions—dealing with addictions in the workplace has its own special demands and opportunities which can enhance or undermine treatment. It is necessary for the EAP to understand treatment issues and the workplace intervention issues as well.
6. Personal and Psychological Problems—understanding the characteristics associated with various problems and resources for assistance is of prime importance.

Continuing education must occur, on a routine basis, in these six functional areas in order to maintain the CEAP credential (*EAPA Recertification Guide, 1995*).

Staffing for the EAP must address the recommended employee/EAP staff ratio of one professional full-time staff person for every 3,500–4,000 employees. This ratio is for the Information and Referral (I&R) model. For the short-term counseling EAP model, it is recommended that the EAP staff members/employees ratio increase. When the family members of the employees are included in EAP service delivery the short-term counseling model ratio applies (Spicer, 1987).

Service Components: The "broad brush" approach is most prevalent within today's EAPs. These EAPs are designed to respond to a wide variety of employee's problems (e.g., substance abuse, personal, family, financial, stress, work related, medical, legal, etc.). The "broad brush" approach has the advantage of providing more employees with help that effects their productivity and well-being than the traditional industrial counseling programs which focused upon alcoholism (Dickman & Emener, 1982). In addition to delivering services to the employees, the EAPs offer consultation, coaching, constructive confrontation skill training to supervisors and labor representatives. The direct services which EAPs offer constitute the program's reason for existence (*EAPA Recertification Guide*, *1995*).

Access: The employee's ability to attain services in a timely, convenient and confidential manner is crucial for success of an EAP. The physical location of an EAP should be accessible to all employees, maximize confidentiality by being housed in an inconspicuous area so that employees can be identified as seeking EAP services, be well-furnished and located in good surroundings. All these factors communicate the company's commitment to and opinion of its EAP (Spicer, 1987).

EAP Awareness: EAP personnel must continually market the program beginning with the training of management, supervisors and labor representatives. The employees must be oriented to the EAP with information delineating services to be delivered, costs of services (or no cost), EAP process, confidentiality, location, and EAP personnel. Communication through a newsletter, payroll inserts or information mail-outs to employee homes are methods to promote the EAP. Other examples of opportunities to market the EAP include: (a) presentations at staff meetings and (b) workshops during lunch breaks. A typical occurrence following any of these marketing efforts is an increase in calls for service delivery.

Evaluation: No EAP can continue to exist without proof of the benefits of its services. The organization as well as the EAP need to know what impact the EAP is having among employees' functioning in the workplace and the savings related to employee benefit utilization. Evaluative measures have become more sophisticated in recent years. Previously, penetration rates, cost effectiveness, client population utilization, client satisfaction, management/labor satisfaction, medical cost savings and productivity gain were the areas that were evaluated. In recent years EAP evaluations also have documented results indicating major reductions in mental health and substance abuse treatment utilization and costs. Most recently, studies have taken into account the possible cost shifting within the employer benefit plan by conducting outcome research. A study conducted with Southern California Edison Company hypothesized that they might accrue hidden costs due to overutilization of primary medical services, increased disability and workers' compensation claims, increased disciplinary problems, greater termination and turnover due to reduced behavioral health care claims as a result of EAP service delivery. The conclusion of this outcome evaluation was that the organization's EAP could add value to its services by increasing its emphasis in the areas of risk management and early intervention (Conlin, Amaral & Harlow, 1995). Adding outcomes to the evaluation process serves not only to show cost-effectiveness of the EAP, but to identify areas for expansion of EAP services and potentially "best practices" for the EAP.

In summary, the processes necessary to establish and maintain an Employee Assistance Program have been described in this chapter. Most important of the information imparted is to provide client confidentiality; client confidentiality is pivotal to the viability of the EAP. If the EAP components mentioned are a genuine and integral part of the program, success will be ensured.

BIBLIOGRAPHY

Alander, R. & Campbell, T.W. (1975). An evaluative study of an alcohol and drug recovery program: A case study of the Oldsmobile experience. Human Resource Management, 14, 14–16.

Amaral, T.M. (1987b). Cost-effectiveness of EAPs. EAP Coordinator, 2(1), 1–3, 10–11.

Amaral, T.M., & Kelly, M.A. (1989). EAP cost-benefits analysis: Exploring assumptions. EAP Coordinator, 4(2), 1–9.

Asma, F.F., Hilker, R.R.J., Shevlin, J.J., & Golden, R.G. (1980). Twenty-five years of rehabilitation of employees with drinking problems. Journal of Occupational Medicine, 22(4), 241–244.

Blum, T.C., & Roman, P.M. (1995). Cost-effectiveness and preventative implications of employee assistance programs. Rockville, MD: U.S. Department of Health and Human Services.

Cayer, N.J., & Perry, R.W. (1988). A framework of reevaluating employee assistance programs. Employee Assistance Quarterly, 3(3/4), 151–168.

Chandler, R.G., Kroeker, B.J., Fuynn, M., & MacDonald, D.A. (1988). Establishing and evaluating an industrial social work programme. The Seagram, Amherstburg experience. Employee Assistance Quarterly, 3(3/4), 243–253.

Colantonio, A. (1989). Assessing the effects of employee assistance programs: A review of employee assistance program evaluations. Yale Journal of Biology and Medicine, 62(1), 13–22.

Conlin, P., Amaral, T., & Harlow, K. (1995). The value of EAP cases management. EAP Coordinator, 3, 1–8.

Dickman, F., Chandler, B.R., Emener, W.G., & Hutchison, W.S. (eds.) (1988). Employee assistance programs: A basic text. Springfield, IL: Charles C Thomas.

EAP Association Exchange (1992h). Outcome studies: Conoco, HAI release data. EAP Association Exchange, 22(10), 48–49.

Erfurt, J.C, & Foote, A. (1990b). Using an EAP information management system for EAP operation and evaluation. EAP Association Exchange, 20(10), 40–43.

Gaeta, E., Lynn, R., & Grey, L. (1982). AT&T looks at program evaluation. EAP Digest, 2(4), 22–31.

Grimes, C.H. (Ed.) (1984b). EAP research: An annual of research and research issues (Vol. 1). Troy, MI: Performance Resource Press.

Hilker, R.R.J., Asma, F.E., & Eggert, R.L. (1972). A company sponsored alcoholic rehabilitation program: Ten year evaluation. Journal of Occupational Medicine, 14(10), 769–772.

Kabb, G.M. (1992). Managed family care and EAPs. EAP Digest, 12(2), 40–43.

Kim, D.S. (1988). Assessing employee assistance programs: Evaluation typology and models. Employee Assistance Quarterly, 3(3/4), 168–188.

Knott, T.D. (1991). Costs and outcomes: Driving EA program decision making. Employee Assistance, 4(2), 35–37, 52.

Luthans, F., & Waldersee, R. (1989). What do we really know about EAPs? Human Resource Management, 28(3), 385–401.

Mastrich, J., & Beidel, B. (1987). Employee assistance programs cost-impact. ALMACAN, 17(6), 34–37.

Myers, D.W. (Ed.) (1984c). Establishing and building employee assistance programs. Westport, CT: Quorum.

Naditch, M.P. (1995). The new frontier: Moving beyond the black hole of outcome data collection. Employee Assistance, 7(10), 14–17.

Nadolski, J.N., & Sandonato, C.E. (1987). Evaluation of an employee assistance program. Journal of Occupational Medicine, 29(1), 32–37.

National Council on Alcoholism (1974b). PAR study yields cost savings data. Labor Management Alcoholism Journal, 3(6), 37–38.

Newman, P.R., & Duxbury, R. (1989). Hospital staff counseling, EAP Digest, 9(2), 27–31, 57–61.

Shain, M., & Groeneveld, J. (1980). Employee assistance programs: Philosophy, theory, and practice. Lexington, MA: D.D. Heath.

Smith, D.C., & Mahoney, J.J. (1990). McDonnell Douglas Corporation employee assistance program financial offset study 1985–1989. Westport, CT: Alexander & Alexander Consulting Group.

Spicer, J. (Ed.) (1987). The EAP Solution, Hazelden Foundation, 187–202.

Spicer, J., Owne, P., & Levine, D. (1982). Evaluating employee assistance programs: A sourcebook for the administrator and counselor. Center City, MN: Hazelden.

Van Wagner, R.W. (1978). A simple measure of program effectiveness. Labor-Management Alcoholism Journal, 8(2), 62–63.

Washousky, R.C., & Kruger, R.M. (1984). Evaluating employee assistance through supervisor follow-up. EAP Digest, 4(3), 32–35, 45.

Tamantani, H. (1988). Client assessment in an industrial setting: A cross-sectional method. Social Work 33(1), 34–37.

Chapter 6

UNION INVOLVEMENT: A KEY INGREDIENT TO SUCCESSFUL EMPLOYEE ASSISTANCE PROGRAMS

FRED DICKMAN AND WILLIAM G. EMENER

Indeed, no basic text on employee assistance programs would be complete without stressing the need for cooperative program involvement on behalf of both management and labor. Such cooperative involvement should occur all throughout an employee assistance program—its inception, planning, implementation, evaluation, program refinement, and continuation. By far, most employee assistance programs are management conceived, financed, and managed. Nonetheless, some employee assistance programs such as the Postal Workers Alcoholism Programs and Eastern Airlines Machinists Program are union managed. Whichever is the case, however, experience repeatedly had demonstrated that an employee assistance program's success ultimately is contingent upon **mutual cooperation** between the two—union and management. This concept and its importance was expounded as early as at the beginning of the 1960s when far-sighted union leaders like Leo Perlis, Director of Community Services for the AFL–CIO, pointed out that **more workers could be reached by union and management working together** than by either entity working alone (McWilliams, 1978). Other experts in the field also have stressed union and management cooperation: "Organized labor on a national level has wholeheartedly endorsed the EAP concept, and other experts in the field have expounded the value of labor-management cooperation in implementing an effective program (Beyer, Trice & Hunt, 1980; McWilliams, 1978)." (Dickman, 1985, p. 40) It is interesting to note, moreover, that some experts even have argued that an employee assistance program has no place in a company or business without labor-management cooperation:

This chapter is reprinted from *Counseling the Troubled Person in Industry* (1985) with permission of the author, the book's editors (Dickman, Emener, & Hutchison, Jr.) and the publisher (Charles C Thomas, Publisher).

96

However, we do not wish to imply that "cooperation" just means that management creates a program and the union endorses it. While it is true that management will have to do more work than the union, no results are likely to emerge unless the program is a *joint* one. Company management and company unions must be involved right from the start and must back each other up all the way through. Otherwise, the program may not be sold, and adversary situations—which are out of place where an individual's health or sickness is concerned—will be inevitable (Sadler & Horst, 1972, p. 5).

In addition to mutual involvement on behalf of both labor and management, a demonstrated and genuine genre of **trust** must exist between them in order for an employee assistance program to be successful. In his discussion regarding the initiation of a joint labor-management EAP, Corneil (1982) stated:

> Mutual trust and relative power are central issues to this step [starting an EAP]. If the trust level is low, perhaps due to a history of labor-management proposals that never quite worked out as planned, this step, and indeed the entire process to date, will have been characterized by suspicion and testing out of each others' motives. (p. 24)

Thus, an important a priori contention on behalf of the authors of this chapter is that these two elements on behalf of both union and management, **mutual involvement and trust,** can almost ensure an employee assistance program's success and create exceptional benefits for all concerned. Relevant to this contention, the remainder of this chapter will identify and discuss specific: (a) benefits to the union; (b) benefits to management; (c) benefits to the employee assistance program; and (d) benefits to employees. The chapter will then conclude with a recommended conceptualization of the interfacing linkages among these three critical employee assistance programming entities, the union, management and the EAP, **and** the employees.

Benefits to the Union

1. **Consistency with the Union's Mission.** Typically, a union's primary stated purpose is to help its workers (members). This is also the primary purpose of an employee assistance program. Thus, when a union supports the efforts of an EAP, it essentially is doing what it is primarily designed to do—help employees (its members). Sadler and Horst (1972) articulated this notion when they stated: "The unions, too [in addition to management] have a vital reason for cooperating. The program [the

EAP] is designed to help workers, and helping workers is the stated reason for the union's existence" (p. 5).

2. **Building of Cohesiveness.** In most instances, a union's strength and power, which comes from its members, is contingent upon the members' perceptions of the extent to which the union is "caring"—the extent to which it cares about the well-being and wellness of its members. An excellent way for a union to demonstrate its "caring" for its members (and also thereby communicating its "caring" message) is through meaningful involvement in a successful employee assistance program which is helpful to employees (the union's members). And as most unions appreciate, this is an important message to communicate.

3. **"Real Help" Versus "Sympathy."** To help initiate, plan, support, implement, evaluate, and improve an effective employee assistance program, is an excellent way for a union to say (figuratively): "We want to support each member's access to expert assistance." In his discussion of an EAP's responsiveness to substance abuse problems, McWilliams (1985) addressed the importance of not just being sympathetic: "Unions, because of their relationship with their members, can give understanding and a sympathetic offer of assistance, counseling, and treatment. Yet, there is overwhelming evidence that alcoholics rarely respond to sympathy" (p. 54). Almost all experts in the field of alcoholism rehabilitation proport that employee assistance programs are very effective interveners in stopping active alcoholic behavior and maintainers of long-term recovery. Simplistically stated, when a special tool is needed to repair a special piece of equipment, you engage the use of a specialist, e.g., a machinist; when a person or a family breaks down, you engage the use of a specialist, e.g., a licensed counselor.

4. **"Help" Versus "Arbitration": Another Option.** Arbitration is expensive—not only to management but to the union as well. For example, the business manager, the employee and the steward typically are all involved (usually on their own time). Too often the situation emerges as a "win—lose" situation, and frequently "to win" or "to lose" is not the solution for the employee. This is almost always true for the alcohol/drug abusing worker who needs "help" rather than "fairness"; this many times is also true in instances when employees have other kinds of problems as well. Recently, in discussing union-vs-management handling of employees problems, McWilliams (1985) stated: "No matter who wins, the employee is the loser. A union victory, in effect, kills the member with kindness. A management victory, in the absence of an enlightened joint program [an

EAP], might result in punitive action rather than in urgently needed treatment" (p. 54).

Reasons such as these above four offer compelling reasons for unions to play an active role in the initiation, planning, implementation, evaluation, and refinement of employee assistance programs. Moreover, a healthy workforce can enhance more overall productivity. Evidence is abundant that EAPs save the company money and thereby increase profits. The bottom line consideration for a union is that higher wages are more easily negotiated from a profitable than a nonprofitable company.

Benefits to Management

When mutual involvement and trust pervade the cooperative activities of both labor and management, there are specific benefits that can be realized by management. The following five are among such management benefits and tend to represent those found to be highly appreciated by management.

1. Increased Cooperation. Employee assistance programs involve key personnel in what is frequently called "supervisory training." This training typically focuses on intervention techniques, referral procedures, signs to look for in the troubled employee, and reviews and discussions of company policies and procedures, among others. Importantly, supervisors and management representatives and stewards and other labor representatives typically are trained together, and training experiences such as these facilitate closer cooperation and increased "togetherness" among leaders within the environment which is good for the company.

2. Enhanced Morale. "Low Morale" frequently is discussed on American business pages as being meaningfully related to reductions in productivity. Other related concerns include high absenteeism, high turnover, and apathy. Nonetheless, it has been experienced that when union and management cooperatively work together to help troubled employees and their families through the auspices of an effective employee assistance program, worker morale tends to increase and be more positive (Dickman & Emener, 1982). On behalf of the management of a company, this spin-off outcome would appear to be very appealing.

3. More Troubled Workers Are Helped. For numerous reasons (e.g., philosophical, utilitarian), companies want to help their troubled employees. Identifying them, convincing them that they need assistance, and then helping them, is easier said than done. Nonetheless, when union and management cooperatively work together with an employee assistance program, the likelihood of a higher penetration rate exists, and hence a greater likelihood of reaching more troubled workers who need help.

4. Enhanced Productivity. In the final analysis, helping workers toward being more fully functioning individuals will have a positive impact on productivity (Corneil, 1982; Dickman & Emener, 1982). The troubled on-the-line worker and others in the workforce, assuredly do not represent all of the variables related to less than potential productivity levels. On the other hand, however, a company's "happy and trouble free" workers do represent chief reasons for a fuller productive enterprise.

5. Increased Alternatives and Options to Problem Resolution. Surveys conducted by the authors of this chapter (e.g., Dickman & Emener, 1982), among others, clearly indicate that both high level managers and union officials alike do not enjoy disciplinary processes and procedures. Fittingly, one of their consistently reported areas of "satisfactoriness with" and "liking of" employee assistance programs is that the programs provide an option other than disciplinary action regarding a troubled employee. They are aware that the employee who requires disciplinary action and/or arbitration, often is troubled in some way, and that in many instances it is better, more effective, and cheaper to explore a "helping alternative" via the EAP than to go immediately to a disciplinary and/or arbitration alternative. Basically, it has been experienced that while it is not the only alternative, when appropriate, the "helping alternative via the EAP" is the preferred mode of action.

Reasons such as these above five, while not all inclusive, provide compelling rationale for management to work cooperatively and closely with labor in initiating, planning, implementing, evaluating, and refining employee assistance programming for workers. In effect, management has much to gain and very little (if anything) to lose.

Benefits to the Employee Assistance Program

As the leaders and developers of an employee assistance program plan, implement, evaluate, and refine their program, it is critical for them not only to involve union and management but also to facilitate cooperative and trusting relationships among all those involved. Identi-

fiable, mutual, and cooperative tasks and activities are not only beneficial to the union and management but to the EAP itself. The following
five are noteworthy and deserving of special attention.

1. Increased Probability of Success. As discussed earlier in this chapter,
the active, mutual, and cooperative involvement of both union and
management with an employee assistance program, increases the program's
probability for success. This, without a doubt, is important to the program.
Corneil (1982), for example, discussed six developmental stages of a joint
labor-management EAP [viz: (a) commitment; (b) policy; (c) procedure;
(d) communication; (e) training; and (f) evaluation)], and stated: "If the
site manager and supervisors and the membership of the local union do
not support the EAP and are not willing to be actively involved in
leadership, chances of success are limited" (p. 25).

2. Increased Referrals. A well-run and effective employee assistance
program will have an 8 to 10 percent penetration rate (Dickman &
Emener, 1982). More pointedly, this means that an effective EAP should
serve approximately 8 to 10 percent of the total number of individuals
who have access to it (e.g., employees and their immediate family
members). Achieving a penetration rate such as this without full labor
and management cooperation and involvement is very unlikely. An
employee assistance program must be postured to respond to the needs
of its constituancy group (i.e., the employees); moreover, it must facilitate the employees' **demands** for it (i.e., their use of it).

3. Freedom of Movement in the Plant and the Union Hall. The authors
of this chapter have had, and currently have, a variety of experiences in
working with employee assistance programs in companies with union
shops. In those situations in which the employee assistance program
enjoys active, mutual, wholehearted, and supportive involvement from
both the union and management, one important benefit is that the EAP
contractor or manager has free movement throughout the plant and
access to union meetings. This privilege of free and full visitation greatly
enhances many important aspects of the program such as marketing of
the EAP, follow-up, employee's perceptions of the program, and penetration rates.

4. Joint Training Sessions. The training sessions typically conducted
by employee assistance program staff are attended by representatives
from both labor and management. Not only does this provide serendipi-

tous opportunities for cooperative interaction on behalf of the union and management representatives, but on behalf of the EAP staff as well. For example, the EAP professional enjoys the opportunity: to work with both the supervisors from management and the union stewards in a noncrisis, nonproblem-oriented situation; to train mixed intervention teams focusing on employee concerns; to educate and market the program; and above all, to **assist critical plant leadership on knowing "how not to enable the troubled worker."** This is absolutely invaluable if seriously troubled employees are to be identified and helped. Frankel (1985), in his discussion of alcoholism treatment in the partial hospital or day program, addressed this issue very well:

> A labor-management employee assistance program helps eliminate many of the pitfalls characteristic of other types of intervention. Alcoholism is dealt with by labor and management under the same rules followed with other illness. It says that we are willing to help you deal with this illness by setting up the machinery to make it easy for you to get competent help and treatment. It confronts the employee with realistic and observable dimensions such as job performance and absenteeism. It eliminates cover-up and links one of a person's key worlds within which he or she operates (work world) with the treatment of his or her illness. (p. 133)

5. Early Intervention. Dickman and Emener (1982) conducted an evaluation research survey on one employee assistance program population with a focus on consumer satisfaction. In addition to finding a high degree of reported satisfaction with the employee assistance program, most participants also reported that they would not have tended to their problem as early as they did had it not been for the existence of, and the assistance they received from, the EAP. This particular EAP was strongly supported by both labor and management from its beginning and throughout, and it was concluded that this cooperation and involvement was a significant influence on the employees' reported early intervention experiences.

There are many more benefits of mutual involvement and trust on behalf of labor and management for an employee assistance program. These above five only scratch the surface. The important thing is for the professionals in an employee assistance program to not only remember that there are many, many benefits that result from fostering mutual cooperation and trust on behalf of labor and management, but also that there are no valid reasons for not fostering it.

Benefits to the Employee

In the ultimate sense, the vast majority of the previously discussed benefits of mutual cooperation and trust on behalf of labor and management (i.e., to the union, to management, and to the EAP), will directly and indirectly result in benefits to the employee. Nonetheless, there are numerous identifiable benefits to the employee, and the following five appear to be worthy of special attention.

1. A Well-Run EAP. First of all, it is important to remember that the mere existence of a good employee assistance program, in and of itself, is a meaningful employee benefit. Moreover, those that are joint labor-management supported tend to be more efficient, more effective, and helpful to a larger proportion of the employees and their families who have access to them (Corneil, 1982; Dickman & Emener, 1982; Emener & Dickman, 1983). Joint labor-management-supported EAPs also tend to facilitate the existence of other positive qualities within the workplace (e.g., high morale), and with the existence of joint labor-management support conditions the longevity and continuance of the EAP assuredly is on more solid ground. It can be quite comforting and assuring to all those concerned to see healthy labor-management relations supporting a company's EAP; on the contrary, fear and concern that labor and management may get into a hassle and kill the company's EAP can be very debilitating.

2. Real Help in Response to One's "Cry for Help." In most instances, it takes caring, trained and cooperating individuals to recognize and helpfully respond to a hurting employee's crying out for help. For example, many authorities in the field of alcoholism (consult Johnson, 1980) believe that the person troubled with alcohol or other drugs suffers from a "catch 22" situation: part of the person wants to hide and not be found out, and another part of the person wants to be identified and helped. When union and management cooperatively and in trusting ways work together with an effective employee assistance program, the latter alternative is more likely to be the affected outcome. Trice, Hunt, and Beyer (1977) articulated the key mechanisms operating in situations such as this:

> While the real objective of an industrialized alcoholism program is to assist the problem drinker, dealing with him/her in a unionized work setting requires overcoming the traditional advisory relationship between union and management. Problem drinkers usually seek to deny or rationalize their drinking

problem, often becoming effective manipulators. Should the drinker detect an opportunity to play off the union against management, he/she can "divide and conquer," thus seriously damaging the effectiveness of the confrontation. (p. 104)

Thus, as this illustrates, the importance of the union, the management and the EAP professionals cooperatively working together cannot be underscored enough.

3. Stigma Reduction. When both labor and management jointly communicate and demonstrate that "to be troubled is to be human," a much more trusting environment exists and employees tend to feel more comfortable asking for and accepting help and assistance. It is not easy for an employee and/or a family to admit that they need help. The cultural stigma that suggests that people should be able to solve their own problems without help from others can be a very powerful influence on a troubled employee and render him or her as being reluctant to seek assistance. However, when a person's **supervisor and labor steward** jointly recommend that he or she seek assistance from the employee assistance program, an altogether different atmosphere exists—one which is ultimately much more helpful to the troubled employee.

4. Feeling Cared For as a Person. No one advocates coddling, especially in the workplace. At the same time, however, a worker does not like to feel as if he or she is "a dispensable tool," "a number," or "a temporarily needed piece of machinery." When employees have feelings like these, morale tends to go down, job satisfaction dwindles, and quite often productivity suffers. Nonetheless, in environments where labor, management and the employee assistance program cooperatively, trustingly, and mutually work together, employees are more apt to feel that others (e.g., their union stewards, their supervisors) care about them as people. This environmental attitude, in turn, tends to enhance morale, job satisfaction and productivity.

5. Affordable Access to Help. One of the primary reasons why employees seek help and assistance early from an employee assistance program (e.g., before their problems get out of hand), is that they can afford to (Dickman & Emener, 1982). Effective EAPs are well-financed, at least to the extent that feared economic hardship is not an up-front deterrent to seeking help and assistance. "Affordability," in terms of the perceptions of troubled employees, also means that they can seek assistance and help without immediate fears that it could cost them their jobs (or benefits, opportunities for promotion, etc.). In an ideal employee assistance program environment, troubled employees do not consider whether or not they can afford to seek help and assistance, they consider why they cannot afford not to seek help and assistance. Hopefully, their considerations produce the conclusion, "I have a lot to gain and nothing to lose."

As suggested earlier, joint union-management-supported employee assistance programs produce numerous direct and indirect benefits for employees. These above five represent but a few of them.

Conclusion

In its purest form, an employee assistance program is the third arm of industry. As portrayed in Figure 9-1, labor, management, and the employee assistance program meaningfully interface with each other. The most important aspect of this conceptualization of the three arms of industry, however, is that **the employee is central to all three.** This assertion stems from the notion that the human being, the employee, is industry's most precious, valuable, and essential resource. Fittingly, labor (the union), management (the company), and the employee assistance program should feel compelled to cooperatively, mutually, and trustingly work together to have the best employee assistance program they can have—what better way is there to protect their most precious resource? Should this be the case, everyone wins! Emener and Dickman (1983) captured this valuable workplace genre with a quote from a company official:

> A business manager of one unionized plant has personally made appointments and brought several workers to the EAP. He stated: "The EAP is not a company or a union outfit. It is for the well-being of each of us. Let's support it for ourselves and our families." This is management backing of a high sort and exemplifies the role a well-run EAP can play in the morale of everyone. (p. 38)

As suggested throughout this chapter, when labor and management cooperatively support an employee assistance program, **everyone wins.**

REFERENCES

Beyer, J.M., Trice, H.M., & Hunt, R. (1980). Impact of federal sector unions on supervisor's use of personnel policies. *Industrial and Labor Relations Review, 33,* 212–231.

Corneil, W. (1982). Initiating a joint labor management EAP. *EAP Digest,* 2(5), 22–17.

Dickman, F. (1985). Ingredients of an effective EAP. In J.F. Dickman, W.G. Emener, &

W.S. Hutchison, Jr. (Eds.), *Counseling the troubled person in industry.* Springfield, IL: Charles C Thomas, Publisher.

Dickman, F., & Emener, W.G. (1982). Employee assistance programs: Basic concepts, attributes and an evaluation. *Personnel Administrator,* 27(8), 55–62.

Emener, W.G., & Dickman, F. (1983). Corporate caring: EAPs solve personal problems for business benefits. *Management World,* 12(1), 36–38.

Frankel, G. (1985). Alcoholism treatment in the partial hospital or day program. In J.F. Dickman, W.G. Emener, & W.S. Hutchison, Jr. (Eds.), *Counseling the troubled person in industry.* Springfield, IL: Charles C Thomas, Publisher.

Johnson, V.E. (1980). *I'll quit tomorrow.* San Francisco, CA: Harper & Row Publishers.

McWilliams, E.D. (1978). The values of a joint union-management program. *Labor-Management Alcoholism Journal,* 8(3).

McWilliams, E.D. (1985). The values of a joint union-management program. In J.F. Dickman, W.G. Emener, & W.S. Hutchison, Jr. (Eds.), *Counseling the troubled person in industry.* Springfield, IL: Charles C Thomas, Publisher.

Sadler, M., & Horst, J.F. (1972). Company/union programs for alcoholics. *Harvard Business Review,* 50(5), 1–8.

Sutermeister, M. (1963). *People and productivity.* New York: McGraw-Hill.

Trice, H.M., Hunt, R.E., & Beyer, J.M. (1977). Alcoholism programs in unionized work settings: Problems and prospects in union-management cooperation. *Journal of Drug Issues,* 7(2), 103–115.

Chapter 7

A NATIONAL EAP PROGRAM: AN EXAMPLE

DONALD W. MAGRUDER

Introduction

The Anheuser-Busch Companies Employee Assistance Program provides services for all of the company's employees and their family members. The program extends to all subsidiaries within the Anheuser-Busch Companies, Inc. This encompasses some 40,000 employees and their dependent family members.

The Anheuser-Busch Companies Employee Assistance Program has its corporate headquarters in St. Louis, Missouri where its director, manager, three clinical personnel, and other staff are housed. These staff members manage the program nationally as well as directly serve those employees in the St. Louis area. The remainder of the national program is staffed with contracted persons supervised by the corporate EAP staff in St. Louis.

The Anheuser-Busch EAP provides evaluation, referral and follow-up services only.

History and Philosophy

The overriding goal of the Anheuser-Busch EAP is to restore less than fully productive employees to fully productive status. Other goals such as saving money and improving morale, are important considerations.

This chapter is reprinted from *Employee Assistance Programs; A Basic Text* (1988) with permission of the author, the book's editors (Dickman, Emener, & Hutchison, Jr.) and the publisher (Charles C Thomas, Publisher).

This chapter was originally written by its author specifically for the first edition of this book, and is being reprinted in this second edition, unabridged and unedited. Over the past eight years, however, there indeed have been escalating changes in national Employee Assistance Programs (EAPs). Moreover, advancements in communications and computer technologies, couples with the over-arching "managed care" paradigm of health care, certainly have increased the rate of change in national EAPs. For purposes of preserving historical perspectives and the fact that the basic elements of the Anheuser-Busch EAP as discussed in this chapter assuredly are critical elements in any national EAP, the editors chose to reprint this chapter in its original version. Students and readers interested in recent advancements in particular national EAPs as well as their specialized features, fittingly are encouraged to contact such EAPs directly.

The program was started in April, 1978 following the recommenda-tions of a labor-management joint committee developed to establish policy, procedure and direction. Adhering to these recommendations the program was established in 1978. EAP staff reported to the Vice President of Human Resources.

The program was implemented in stages, first the Anheuser-Busch Breweries and secondly the various subsidiaries including Anheuser-Busch Wholesaler Employee Assistance Program.

Three regions were established: middle, eastern, and western, each overseen by administrators who supervise contractors in their various locations.

Organization

The program is headed by a member of top management who has the title, Director, Employee Assistance Program. This individual has responsibility for all Employee Assistance Programs in any Anheuser-Busch owned company. Consulting services are also provided to the independently owned wholesaler network.

The Manager of the Employee Assistance Program reports to the director and is responsible for the everyday operation of all the Anheuser-Busch EAPs throughout the country.

Reporting to the manager are three coordinators who are based in corporate headquarters. Their responsibilities are seeing clients in the home office and supervising contractors in locations other than corpo-rate headquarters. The coordinator, therefore, must have a clinical back-ground and appropriate education as well as clerical and administrative experience.

Contractors are selected by the director of the EAP for all locations away from corporate headquarters. All contractors must be experienced Employee Assistance Program practitioners with minimum of a masters level counseling degree. Most are private practitioners. However in some locations EAP companies are used.

Some of the skills looked for in contractors are knowledge of and experience in:

1. Chemical dependency
2. Family therapy
3. Psychological counseling
4. Community resources

All clients are uniformly assessed for chemical dependency and suicide ideation.

Each contractor is provided with orientation, training and a manual containing the following:

1. Statement of Policy.

   The policy statement illucidates who is eligible, how referrals are made and by whom, the general purpose of the program, how records are kept and by whom, that records are confidential except when self-released or by a court order, that assessment visits are free up to three, and that the EAP in no way is designed to interfere with disciplinary problems or job performance expectations. Various problems listed as appropriate for EAP assessment and referral include physical or mental illness, alcoholism, drug abuse, marital issues, compulsive gambling, and financial, legal, or other concerns. Expenses for treatment are to be reimbursed in accordance with group insurance programs, a community agency or wherever is an appropriate referral from the EAP.

2. Definitions.

   Client, coordinator, contractor, and counselor are clearly defined in the manual.

3. Eligibility.

   All employees and family members who are covered under the applicable insurance program.

4. Leave of Absence Procedures.

   Most employees are covered under a leave of absence policy. When this is not the case the contractor/assessor contacts his/her coordinator.

5. Code of Ethics.

   An extremely thorough list of ethical principles covers such topics as counselor areas of competency, need to know referral resource quality, assessor-client physical contact, rules of confidentiality, record-keeping and record safety, and the need to be clear with clients from the beginning what the EAP can and cannot do.

6. Referral Procedures.

   Four kinds of referrals; self, union, management, and medical are made to the EAP. Procedures to ethically and legally expedite referrals of each kind are clearly spelled out in the manual and communicated to management, union, and supervisors as well as rank and file employees and their eligible family members.

7. Responsibilities.

Responsibilities of both the contractor to the EAP and the EAP to the contractor are made clear within the contractual agreement between the EAP and each contractor. Each contractor is required to maintain ethical standards, and high professional standards. The EAP in turn provides training assistance, financial support, direction, guidance and counsel, psychiatric consultation support, and if necessary, corporate legal support.

In summary, organizationally the Anheuser-Busch Employee Assistance Program is both an in-house and contractual program.

Utilization

Utilization of the program has been encouraging from its inception. Figures 7-1 and 7-2 depict total participation cumulative by year, employee/family ratio, referral source and problem category.

Program Evaluation

There are a number of ways to evaluate a program including

1. Cost Benefit
2. Penetration rates
3. Absenteeism reduction
4. Problem category success
5. Client survey
6. Management/supervisor satisfactoriness
7. Utilization rates.

The Anheuser-Busch Employee Assistance Program has determined that utilization rate is its bottom line determination of success. That rate is 10 percent. Consistent with its philosophy, the Anheuser-Busch EAP is successful.

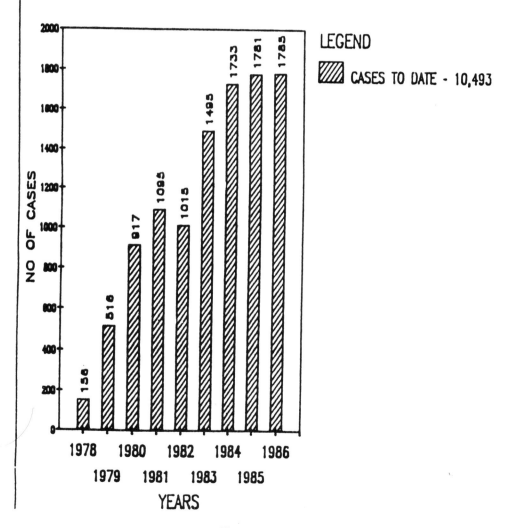

Figure 7-1.

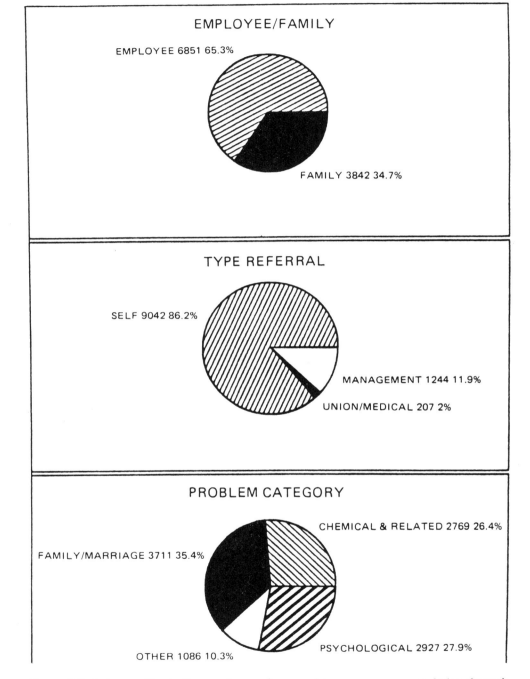

Figure 7-2. Anheuser-Busch Companies employee assistance program cumulative through fourth quarter 1986 all locations.

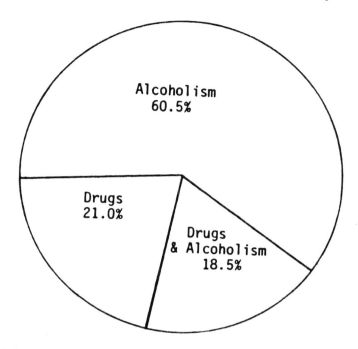

Figure 7-3. Anheuser-Busch Companies employee assistance program 1986—Chemical and related total 502.

PART III
CLIENT CHARACTERISTICS AND SERVICES

The four chapters in this Part are directed primarily to the EAP Coordinator. The basic theme is that the EAP Coordinator must be an expert in biopsychosocial assessment and case management. To this end, each chapter addresses contemporary knowledge, treatment methods and resources fundamental to the three primary problem areas clients present: (1) alcoholism and other chemical dependency; (2) marriage and family problems; and (3) mental health problems.

Emener and Dickman, in Chapter 8, introduce this Part with a detailed description of the roles and skills of the case management function of the EAP Coordinator. Additional attention is provided to time management of the caseload with four sample forms that facilitate this task. In Chapter 9, Dickman provides an in-depth discussion of the signs, symptoms and progressive nature of alcohol addiction. He also furnishes the reader with an excellent review of preferred treatments throughout the progression and concludes with a listing of the addresses of national alcoholism treatment resources such as Alcoholics Anonymous (AA).

Hutchison, in Chapter 10, provides a theoretical connection, e.g., family socialization to Employee Assistance and Wellness Programs. Additional contact elaborates methods of developing and delivering health promotion and wellness programs and concludes with implications for Employee Assistance Programs. In the last chapter in this Part, Chapter 11, Pinkard provides a broad overview of mental health problems and treatment methodologies. Of particular note is his citation of empirical evidence on critical characteristics of successful therapists. In addition, he links health promotion and wellness strategies to primary prevention of mental health problems.

Collectively, these four chapters offer a good, basic foundation for coordinators of employee assistance programs as well as EAP professionals working with and within them.

Chapter 8

CASE MANAGEMENT, CASELOAD MANAGEMENT, AND CASE RECORDING AND DOCUMENTATION IN PROFESSIONAL EAP SERVICE DELIVERY

WILLIAM G. EMENER AND FRED DICKMAN

The continuing emergence and development of employee assistance programs in modern industry has witnessed a growing enhancement and enrichment of the professionalism of employee assistance program service delivery. Contributing to this phenomenon is the fact that more and more professionally educated and trained human service professionals are being employed in employee assistance programs—for example, rehabilitation counselors (Desmond, 1985; Dickman & Emener, 1982) and social workers (Hutchison & Renick, 1985; Maiden & Hardcastle, 1986). Importantly, these human service professionals are being professionally prepared to perform the variety of human service roles and functions that are extremely relevant and necessary for successful employee assistance program service delivery (Dickman & Emener, 1982; Emener, 1986; Emener & Rubin, 1980; Hutchison, 1985). Three categories of professional service delivery which are critical entities of employee assistance programs, constitute the focus of this chapter: Case Management, Caseload Management, and Case Recording and Documentation. Utilizing relevant information from professional literature (e.g., Cassell & Mulkey, 1981; Henke, Connolly & Cox, 1975; Roessler & Rubin, 1982; Third Institute on Rehabilitation Services, 1965; Thompson, Kite & Bruyere, 1977) and examples and illustrations from their own professional experiences in employee assistance programs, in this chapter the authors: (a) provide a brief overview of important professional attributes critical to case management, caseload management, and case recording and documentation in employee assistance program service delivery; (b)

This chapter is reprinted from *Employee Assistance Programs; A Basic Text* (1988) with permission of the author, the book's editors (Dickman, Emener, & Hutchison, Jr.) and the publisher (Charles C Thomas, Publisher).

117

differentially present and discuss case management, caseload management, and case recording and documentation roles and functions in employee assistance program service delivery; and, (c) conclude with a brief discussion of the synergistic relationship among these three categories of EAP professionals' roles and functions.

Important Professional Attributes of the "Case Manager"

In the process of performing the variety of job tasks within the categories of case management, caseload management, and case recording and documentation, it is very important for the practitioner to possess and demonstrate identifiable attributes of a "professional." The primary purpose of the following is to identify, discuss, and illustrate selected important attributes of professionalism. As will be discussed in more detail later in the chapter, there are distinct differences between case management and caseload management. For the moment, however, it is important to acknowledge their differential distinctions: **Case Management** refers to the practitioner's managerial activities that facilitate the individual client's progress through the service process; **Caseload Management** refers to the responsibility of the practitioner for the progress of the whole group of clients who constitute the practitioner's caseload. For purposes of expediency, and in view of the fact that the following materials are designed to address generic attributes of professionalism, the following will use the terms practitioner, counselor, social worker, and case manager as generic constructs (viz, they can be considered interchangeable). Understandably, there are numerous important attributes of the professional service provider in an employee assistance program. The following four areas, nonetheless, were determined to be noteworthy of special address in this chapter: (a) community resource awareness; (b) clinical assessment; (c) caseflow expertise; and (d) professional behavior.

Community Resource Awareness. The effective case manager knows the community—both the "internal community" and the "external community." The internal community is comprised of the company which the employee assistance program serves and in which the employees are employed. The case manager must know the formal and informal infrastructure of the company. The external community, in effect, is comprised of the community surrounding the company—the community in which the employees live. The case manager has to know the community of available human services. For example, it is commonly known that approximately one-third of the employees who come to a well-run employee assistance program will have some form of alcohol or other substance abuse problem (Dickman, Emener & Hutchison, 1985). Knowing this, knowing that each individual needs individualized assistance and health care, and knowing that the larger the known available array of service centers, facilities, and professionals the higher the probabilities that "the right place or person" can be found for the individual client, case managers should feel compelled to know their community like the backs of their hands. When confronted with an employee with an alcohol or substance abuse problem, it is quite common for case managers to ask themselves questions such as: (a) For this particular client with these particular needs, where can I find the best professional, center, or facility? (b) Where is the most appropriate inpatient or outpatient, day care or night care, individual or group, and/or AA or NA facility or center? and (c) What are the differential costs of the treatment programs in the community, where are they located, are they available by public transportation, etc? As can be quickly seen, in order to find the right "fit" between the client's needs and the services available, the case manager has to know his or her community. To further illustrate, according to national figures, another one-third will come with marriage and/or family relationship problems. Some of these clients will have both alcoholism or substance abuse problems and marriage and/or family relationship problems. Again the questions arise: Where do they treat codependents, and/or children of alcoholics, etc. In view of the fact that the remaining approximate one-third of EAP referrals have a wide variety and combination of problems and difficulties, similar concerns also may arise when a client needs legal services, medical assistance, and/or financial services (among others). The bottom line is that when the troubled employee comes to the employee assistance program for help, he or she in many ways is handicapped—not only do they have problems, but they also do not know where to, or how to, get help. It is important for case managers to be sure that they aren't just as handicapped as their clients are!

Clinical Assessment. In order to identify and procure the "best" services in the community for a client, not only does an effective case manager have to know the community, but he or she also has to accurately assess the client's needs and the client's "readiness" for assistance. Employees frequently are defensive, scared, and threatened by the thought of "telling someone the truth" about their problems. Moreover, they can be very reticent about the thought of going somewhere for assistance. Thus, while in the role of a representative of the company and also while having to engage in detailed assessment, the case manager simultaneously has to establish a relationship of openness and trust with the employee so that (a) the assessments are based on accurate information, and (b) when the case manager suggests a treatment strategy and/or makes a referral the client will listen to him or her and follow through. For example, it is not uncommon for an individual who comes to an employee assistance program with a chemical dependency problem to present his or her difficulty as being anything but chemical dependency related—quite often, initial presenting problems are identified by the client as being related to job stress, marital or family difficulties, and/or financial problems. And while the individual indeed may have some real difficulties in these areas, the client with a chemical dependency problem may be very reluctant to discuss the possibility that he or she actually may be chemically dependent. More often than not, the "real problems" are beneath the surface. For reasons such as this, most employee assistance programs allow for three or four evaluation visits so that accurate and thorough assessments and accurate and relevant treatment strategies can be determined. These sessions also allow for the relationship building to take place (e.g., developing openness and trust). In addition to formal clinical assessments of the client (e.g., standardized personality testing), assessment interviews with "significant others" such as family members and supervisors can also be very beneficial to the case manager. Throughout these assessment sessions, however, because of the client's potential fears, denial, and subconscious attempts to mask the real issues, it is imperative for the case manager to communicate compassion, caring, and respect: **to relate—not challenge.** Even though the case manager may suspect the existence of a chemical dependency problem early in the first session, it is critical that during the history taking, relating with empathic understanding, and exploring and discussing further what the client is saying, that the case manager not challenge the client—this very easily could threaten the client, enhance their fears and defensiveness, and possibly even run them off. What is being suggested here is that with high level profession clinical and counseling skills, the truth will eventually emerge, and concurrently the client will trust the case manager and the client's "readiness for help" will be such that he or she not only will go for help but also be ready to benefit from it. In view of the critical importance of these clinical assessment issues for the case manager, the following case example, based on the authors' experiences, is designed to enhance the readers' understanding and appreciation of their magnitude.

A Case Example. A self-referred young couple arrived to see the employee assistance program counselor. They requested to come into the session together. The husband was 30 years old and the wife was 27, they had dated for four years before getting married, and at the time had been married for seven and one-half years and had one child, an eighteen-month-old son. The husband, a college graduate, was working as a junior executive for the company which sponsored the employee assistance program. The wife, who had a two-year junior college degree, was working as a medical secretary. When they sat down to talk with the counselor, they were both very nervous and uncomfortable. Nonetheless, after an atmosphere of trust and acceptance was established and the purpose of the assessment sessions was explained, toward the end of the first session the husband volunteered that he had had an affair. He stated that he felt relieved after he was "found out" (after about three months), but still felt guilty and responsible—responsible not only for his wife's pain and hurt but for the feelings of the other woman as well. The wife explained that she indeed did feel hurt and betrayed, and she also felt very indignant in view of the fact that the other woman was a friend and coworker in the same medical complex where she was working.

Two days later, each of them came in for individual, one-hour sessions. She revealed that before her husband's affair, she had been feeling down, caught in the trap of work and child care, and possibly not as attentive to herself as she had been previously. He expressed feelings of inadequacy as a provider. He believed that he should have been further along in his career, and generally felt quite frustrated. He also indicated that he had not shared these feelings with his wife (seeing them as his problems). At that juncture, it appeared quite clear to the counselor that in the absence of other possible coexisting and/or confounding problems, they needed to see a marriage counselor to help them learn to communicate with each other more meaningfully, and share with each other their feelings of inadequacy and being trapped. It is important to note that in view of their having had pulled apart from each other and that he had had a three-month affair, a premature and inaccurate assessment that they were having "sexual-boredom problems" could have been determined by the counselor. Had this been the case, inappropriate treatment could have been recommended, and that would have been very unfortunate. Nonetheless, an accurate assessment was gleaned, an appropriate referral was made, and the couple's readiness for help had been established by the counselor.

It was learned through follow-up (with appropriate signed releases for follow-up information), that the couple had seen a marriage therapist, had improved their interpersonal communications, and had regained the meaningfulness from their relationship that they both desired. Moreover, the husband was allowing himself to feel more adequate, and he was becoming more assertive as to his own needs. The wife became aware that she had not been taking care of herself nor being assertive to her own needs, joined an inexpensive spa, began feeling "less down and more attractive," was communicating her needs and feelings to her husband, was receiving more attention from her husband, and importantly was feeling more adequate.

This is somewhat of a typical marital situation case which an employee assistance program counselor may encounter. With clients who come to an employee assistance program with severe psychiatric problems, mental health concerns, and serious physical problems, the importance of thorough and accurate diagnosis, the appropriate utilization of appropriate medical and paramedical professionals, facilities and centers in the community, and the facilitation of "readiness for help" can be even more demanding of the professional assessment and counseling skills of the case manager.

Case Flow Expertise

From the moment the client appears for EAP assessment until his or her case is closed, the case manager is responsible for knowing what is happening. The case manager's responsibility includes much more than seeing someone for a few minutes, making an appropriate referral, and then thinking or assuming that his or her job is done. On the contrary, case managers retain responsibility for the client's progress throughout the process. As discussed previously, accurate and thorough clinical assessment (including relationship building) is critical—it is very important that the "real problems" receive appropriate and corrective attention. Two additionally important professional attribute/skill areas extremely relevant to case flow expertise are referral and follow-up.

The process of referring a client to someone else for treatment can be ticklish. Consider, for example, the following scenario. An employee comes to the employee assistance program, usually self-referred, but sometimes supervisor or union referred. He or she is understandably cautious, suspicious, fearful, apprehensive, and nervous. Essentially, he or she is coming to see someone he or she can trust—someone who will genuinely care. During the assessment interviews, the counselor is "real," "genuine," and "open," and the employee's hypothesis that the counselor will be trustworthy and caring is confirmed. Simultaneously, the client experiences the painful process of revealing himself or herself, sharing personal "secrets" with this caring person he or she trusts, and in effect a closeness, a rapport, develops. Then, just when the client really feels comfortable with this caring and trustable counselor, the client is told that he or she is to be referred to someone else. This is the litmus test of the counselor's art of referring. When handled properly and skillfully, most clients understand the reasons for referring, especially in an EAP setting. Nonetheless, the client can also feel rejected, betrayed, discouraged by the prospect of going through all of that again with someone else, or some other hurtful response. In view of this, the case manager needs to be sensitive to the client's processing and experiencing of the referring process, and compassionately attend to the client's feelings as they emerge. At times, a brief follow-up check with the referred professional is recommended to assure that there aren't any carry over concerns from the referral process that need to be attended to by the case manager.

Follow-up on behalf of the case manager is important, and it is helpful if it is done systematically. Most professionals to whom employee assistance program case managers refer clients, have busy practices and typically are not going to keep the case manager apprised of a referred client's progress (or lack of it). Nonetheless, it is the case manager's responsibility to know what is happening with and for his or her client until the case is closed either by successful resolution, rejection of treatment, improvement, or termination for a variety of reasons. The case manager is also busy, and therefore some systematic method of assuring follow-up is recommended. For example, it can be helpful to place the client's name and telephone number on a "tickler" (like a calendar) and a call can be made periodically (e.g., every month or two) to "see how things are going." With this procedure, it is also recommended that the client be made aware of the "tickler" follow-up call system so that he or she isn't surprised or misinterprets the calls. Likewise, it is a good idea to apprise professionals to whom referrals are made so that they also understand how the case manager will be operationalizing his or her follow-up responsibilities.

Professional Behavior. Case managers in employee assistance programs must behave like professionals at all times. There is no way, however, that all of the behaviors becoming a "professional" could be addressed in one section of one chapter. There are, nonetheless, some areas of professional behavior on behalf of employee assistance program case managers that deserve special attention. **First,** it is important for case managers to keep in close touch with: (a) professionals in their external professional communities; (b) supervisors, managers, and administrators in the internal communities of their companies; (c) union leaders; and (d) fellow professionals in their employee assistance programs. Maintaining "professional relationships," not being a nuisance, and simultaneously promoting the professional integrity of one's EAP requires skill, tact, constant vigilance of one's own behavior, and awareness of how one's behavior is perceived by others. **Second,** the case manager must remain cognizant of his or her multiple professional roles and the appropriate professional codes of conduct commensurate with each of them. For example, during the assessment stages of working with a client, the case manager is predominately a representative of the employee assistance program and his or her records are confidential to the EAP. However, if a case manager were to have a client referred to him or her from another case manager for individual treatment (e.g., counseling), he or she would be more in the role of an individual professional practitioner and his or her notes and files would be confidential to his or her own professional domain. In most situations like this latter one, he or she would rely on the code of ethical conduct commensurate with his or her professional preparation (e.g., rehabilitation counseling, social work, counseling psychology) for guidance and direction. And **third,** case managers should make very clear distinctions between their assessment-referral roles and their treatment-practitioner roles. For example, based on their experiences the authors of this chapter strongly recommend that when case managers (who typically are professionally prepared practitioners) conduct an assessment and are ready to recommend treatment, they do not refer the client to themselves. Among the many reasons why this is recommended are the possibilities that: (a) the case manager subconsciously could be less than professionally influenced by self-referral decisions; (b) such decisions may not be as objective as they should be (possible self-serving motives could exist); and (c) even if such decisions were objective and excellent decisions, others may question such processes and ultimately the case manager's perceived level of professionalism could become tarnished.

The bottom line is that **the client always comes first,** and this basic component of the professional's service ethic should guide and drive his or her every action. Moreover, when performing their case management and case load management roles and functions, employee assistance program professionals are epitomizing the basic integrity of their EAPs for everyone to see. Indeed, they should feel compelled to conduct themselves as professionals at all times.

Case Management, Caseload Management, and Case Recording and Documentation Roles and Functions

As discussed earlier in this chapter, professional service delivery in employee assistance programs is predicated upon the existence of numerous "professional" characteristics, attributes, and behaviors on behalf of the service deliverer. Moreover, the service deliverer (e.g., EAP counselor, social worker, case manager) is responsible for what happens to, and for, the client from the time the client enters the assessment session through closure of the case. Knowing what is going on with and for a client, on behalf of the professional, denotes also knowing what he or she is doing and the effects of what he or she is doing. More pointedly, professionals should know: (1) **what** they are doing (throughout all stages and phases of a case); (2) **how** to do what they are doing (with professional skill and expertise); and (3) **why** they are doing what they are doing (viz, knowing the effects of their actions and non-actions). These are three very important guiding challenges for the professional service deliverer. High level knowledge, skill, and expertise in case management, caseload management, and case recording and documentation, however, to a large extent are prerequisites for the professional practitioner committed to successfully responding to these three above guiding challenges. Case management, caseload management, and case recording and documentation are highly interrelated phenomena. For purposes of clarity, understanding, and appreciation, however, the following will present and discuss them separately. (Their synergistic interrelatedness, however, will be discussed and illustrated at the end of the chapter.)

Case Management

Case management refers to the practitioner's managerial activities that facilitate the individual client's progress through the service process. The social worker, psychologist, or EAP counselor, as a "manager" of the treatment process(es) of the client, is responsible for efficient and effective activity at each step or phase. In the overall carrying out of this responsibility, the case manager typically engages in identifiable job tasks and duties which collectively constitute the following 10 case management roles and functions:

1. **Case Finding** — activities that facilitate potential clients' awareness of the employee assistance program, as well as their potential utilization of it
2. **Intake** — upon referral, conducting intake interviews with clients and processing their initial contacts with the program
3. **Eligibility Determination** — active engagement in processes and activities designed to determine whether or not an individual is eligible to receive assistance from the program
4. **Assessment** — accurately determining the client's problems and establishing a recommended treatment plan, identifying recommended treatment sources, and determining the client's "readiness" for recommended treatment(s)
5. **Counseling** — providing necessary counseling services commensurate with appropriate assessment and referral services and activities
6. **Plan Development and Implementation** — working with the client in developing and determining a treatment plan
7. **Service Provision and Supervision** — appropriately providing, coordinating, monitoring, and supervising all services provided for and to the client
8. **Monitoring Service Effectiveness** — through systematic follow-up activities, monitoring the efficiency and effectiveness of services being provided to and for the client
9. **Closure Determination** — via contact with the client, relevant professionals providing services, and appropriate others (e.g., the client's family, supervisor, etc.), determining when the case should be closed and the closure status (e.g., successful resolution; incomplete — client refused treatment; etc.)
10. **Post Services Follow-up** — when appropriate, following-up on a client to evaluate the effectiveness of the services the client received, potential needs for additional services, etc.

In the process of performing these case management roles and functions, at times the counselor will be managing the client's treatment relevant activity and at times the counselor will be managing the client's clinical development activity. The following is designed to illustrate the differences between these two distinct categories of the case manager's roles and functions.

The client's **treatment relevant activity** includes those activities on behalf of the client that, by the design of the treatment plan, are directly and indirectly related to resolution of the client's problem(s). For example, in addition to other treatment resolution activities, a client with an alcoholism problem may agree to attend Alcoholics Anonymous meetings. A client with a weight control difficulty may agree to work out at a local gymnasium three times per week. In working with clients such as these, case management activities may include assisting the client in identifying a local AA group or an appropriate gymnasium, and/or keeping in touch with the client to monitor the client's attendance at the AA meetings or the regularity of his or her workouts at the gymnasium. Whatever the treatment-related activities may be for the client, it behooves the case manager to "manage" such activities. Among the many benefits of such management activities is that through activities such as these the counselor demonstrates to the client that the activities are important and that they should be taken seriously.

The client's **clinical development activity** includes a large variety of clinical actions (and nonactions) on behalf of the EAP counselor that are in keeping with the planned clinical development of the individual client. For example, if one of a client's goals is to become more self-directed and/or more independent, then when the client asks the counselor to answer a question such as, "Which gymnasium should I join?" or if the client asks the counselor to tell his supervisor at work that he would like to have a modification made in his job assignment, then the counselor should **not** answer the question (i.e., make the decision for the client) nor speak to the client's supervisor for him (i.e., to do for the client what he is capable of doing for himself). On the surface, answering a question such as this or talking to a client's supervisor for him could appear to be a helpful thing to do. Unfortunately, however, under circumstances such as those described in this example, actions such as these on behalf of the counselor would actually be counterproductive to the client's problem resolution goals (i.e., to become more self-directed and more independent).

Moreover, this even could be an excellent time for the counselor to process with the client why the client ostensibly is being reluctant to act on his own behalf. With skillful intervention, this could be an advantageous clinical opportunity to work with (e.g., "challenge") the client.

Case management includes a large variety of "managing" job tasks and roles and functions on behalf of the case manager. Of utmost importance, however, is that no matter "What?," "How?" or "Why?" the case manager does them, they should always be by design and they should be guided by what is best for the client.

Caseload Management

Caseload management refers to the responsibility of the practitioner for the progress of the whole group of clients who constitute the practitioner's caseload. Obviously, the most outstanding difference between case management and caseload management is that the former focuses the case manager's management energies on the individual client, and the latter focuses the case manager's energies on the aggregate group of clients with whom he or she is working. The understandable overlap between these two sets of "management activities" as well as this obvious distinguishing feature which separates them, are contained in Cassell and Mulkey's (1981) Functional Definitions of Caseload Management:

- the process of analyzing, planning, supervising, and administering the smooth flow of rehabilitation services to the number of clients for which you have responsibility and the coordination of other professionals and resources utilized.
- to effectively coordinate a system whereby the individual clients are provided services toward eventual rehabilitation by predicting through evaluation, setting objectives, processing, coordinating, and maintaining an equitable and just flow of clients toward individual goals.
- the ability to organize, coordinate, and effect the smooth flow of cases and services with maximum return from the services, to be utilized in returning clientele to the most independent status of which he is capable (p. 9).

As can be easily discerned from these above functional definitions, effective caseload management on behalf of EAP counselors maximizes the probabilities that smooth, equitable, efficient, and efficacious services will be provided to all clients served by the program. The number of specific job tasks and roles and functions under the rubric of caseload management is too large to receive presentation in this one section of one chapter. Nonetheless, the experiences of the authors repeatedly have indicated the following three to be paramount and therefore worthy of address and discussion.

Accurate Assessment of Caseload Service Demands. It is critical for the caseload manager to accurately assess the demands of providing services (especially caseload services) to each individual client as well as to the aggregate of all the clients on his or her caseload. In order to effectively plan, organize, coordinate, and manage one's work, the individual must be able to accurately assess and predict "what it will take" and "how long it will take" to do what needs to be done.

Planning, Organizing, and Coordinating Work Tasks. The effective case manager simply cannot wait until things need to be done before doing them. An approach such as this eventually would turn into nothing more than a minimally effective, crisis-oriented worklife. The effective case manager plans, organizes, and coordinates his or her work tasks, such as, for example: (a) plant visitations and "walk-throughs" (when supervisors, managers, and union officials are visited); (b) community contacts and visitations; (c) staff meetings and professional consultations; (d) paperwork; and (e) the scheduling of appointments with clients and times for intake assessment sessions. As one EAP case manager stated to one of the authors of this chapter: "I simply cannot be effective if I fly by the seat of my pants."

Time Management. The case manager's "time" could be considered his or her most precious commodity. It is a finite variable. And by planning, organizing, and coordinating their time, on a daily, weekly, monthly, and annual basis, case managers can maximize the potential benefits resulting from efficient use of their time.

Accurate assessments of caseload service demands, good planning, organizing, and coordinating, and efficient and effective use of time on behalf of case managers in employee assistance programs, produce numerous benefits. For example, it is important that clients receive services when they need them; unnecessary delays in service provision can be detrimental. Employee assistance programs are charged with the responsibility of efficiently and effectively utilizing their resources; the professional case manager is one of an EAP's most valuable resources. Moreover, effective caseload management also can minimize job stress and professional burnout on behalf of professional human service practitioners (Emener, 1979; Emener, Luck & Gohs, 1982; Krucoff, 1980; Maslach, 1976). These are just a few of the many reasons why caseload management constitutes an extremely important part of the effective EAP counselor's professional skills and expertise.

Case Recording and Documentation. From a global perspective, case recording and documentation involves three sets of professional activities on behalf of the case manager: (1) keeping client records; (2) reporting on client progress to appropriate persons within the employee assistance program, the company, the union, and within the community of professionals providing client services; and (3) preparing summary reports to describe aspects of a client's progress to professionals involved in a client's treatment. The specific job tasks on behalf of the case manager involved in these three sets of activities, constitute an exhaustive list. Nonetheless, the experiences of the authors repeatedly have demonstrated that among the extensive list there are three critical areas of job task functions worthy of presentation and discussion in this chapter: (a) recording and reporting; (b) case documentation and report writing; and (c) the use of forms.

Recording and Reporting. Among the variety of recording and reporting functions of professional case managers, the following five are especially relevant in an employee assistance program setting (with appropriate signed releases when necessary):

1. completing assessment and evaluation summaries, and forwarding them to one's supervisor for review and approval (especially during the case manager's training and/or probationary period).
2. recording the steps in a recommended treatment plan, as developed with the client, and forwarding them to one's supervisor for review and approval (especially during the case manager's training and/or probationary period).
3. preparing summary reports and letters regarding clients for cooperating professionals, facilities, agencies or centers.
4. reporting verbally and in writing on a client's progress to a treatment team or selected group of professionals.
5. writing case notes, and interim and summary reports (including analyses, reasoning, and comments) so that others clearly can understand the client's progress and experiences.

In the process of carrying out these above job functions, it is important for the case manager to have high level cognitive and organizational thinking abilities. Moreover, it is very important for the case manager to be able to write thoroughly, clearly, cogently, and with detail and accurate expression.

Case Documentation and Report Writing. There are many instances when the case manager has to record, document, and report specific aspects of a client's case. Individual employee assistance programs usually develop specific forms for such occasions in order to facilitate and systematize such activities [the use(s) of forms will be addressed in the next section of this chapter]. In the process of working with a client, nonetheless, there are four typical instances when a case manager will have to prepare a written record: (1) Intake Interviewing; (2) Services Planning; (3) Routine Contacts; and (4) Case Closure. For each of these four typical instances, the following provides a list of content which may be relevant to a client's case. (Each client's case obviously is unique, and as such, the specific content of each report will be different and unique to the individual client under consideration.)

1. Intake Interview

1. identification information on the referral, EAP counselor, and date
2. reason(s) why the referral came to the EAP (also, type of referral: self-, supervisor-, etc.)
3. description of the counselor's perception of the referral (noting that it is the counselor's perception)
4. an indication and discussion of the referral's assets, liabilities, problems, concerns, and difficulties
5. indications of the referral's experiences and perceptions of his or her problem(s)
6. an indication that the referral understands the employee assistance program (its policies, operations, services, etc.)
7. discussion of the referral's current circumstances (including family situation)
8. an indication of the referral's background, specifically: education, employment, and previous incidences with the problem(s) which brought the referral to the EAP
9. indications of the referral's social or leisure activities
10. justification(s) for accepting (opening) the case and providing services to the referral (and/or denying the referral)
11. indications of the referral's financial resources and ability to pay for services (if appropriate)
12. a list of the types of evaluations necessary to determine the individual's capacities, limitations and treatment needs
13. recommended action steps

2. Services Planning

1. identification of the client, counselor and date
2. review of the client's problem(s)
3. discussion of the client's "readiness" for services and treatment
4. justification, identification, and discussion of recommended treatment services (including availability and sources)
5. indication of the client's involvement in the planning process(es)
6. identification and justification of selected professionals, facilities or centers to who client will be referred
7. notation that all official releases and other appropriate forms have been signed by the client
8. a statement as to the client's prognosis for success (upon receipt of recommended treatment services)

3. Routine Contact

1. identification of the client, counselor and date
2. identification of the person(s), facility and/or center contacted
3. explanation of the reason(s) for the contact
4. discussion of what was accomplished
5. recommended action steps

4. Case Closure

1. identification of the client, counselor, and date
2. detailed description of services received by the client (types, sources, duration, etc.)
3. behavioral and emotive indications of the status of the client's resolution of his or her problems and difficulties (including appropriate information from others, e.g., family members, supervisor, etc.)
4. statement(s) as to why the case is being closed
5. an indication of recommended future follow-up (and with whom)

The actual format that case managers use for their report writing is typically contingent upon a combination of the individual policies and procedures of the employee assistance programs in which they are working and their own individual style. For some aspects of documentation, recording and reporting, however, the use of standardized forms can be very helpful in the overall operations of an employee assistance program.

Use of Forms. If an employee assistance program is going to use standardized forms for specific case services functions, it is highly recommended that all members of the staff of the EAP understand the forms, know how to use them, and know why they are important and related to the goals of the program. The following discusses three of the numerous benefits that can be derived from their effective use.

1. **Assessment and Planning.** The assessment and planning phases of EAP service delivery are highly reliant on the gathering and processing of data and information on clients. The intake assessment process and the effective use of the case manager's time can be facilitated if the referral completes a standardized Information Sheet (see Fig. 8-1) and a Health Statement (see Fig. 8-2) prior to entering the initial assessment session. Not only can this information be kept in the client's file for future reference, but the case manager can use the information from the forms as stimulus exploration sources for intake counseling with the client.

2. **Legal Protection.** Federal confidentiality laws prohibit the release of information on individuals without their written permission. In the event that the treatment plan for a client will necessitate the release of information, an advantageous time to have an Authorization of Release of Information Form (see Fig. 8-3) signed by the referral is during the initial assessment session (or even prior to it). Another important authorization to obtain from a referral is his or her signed Consent for Services (see Fig. 8-4). In most employee assistance program settings, clients are aware of the need for such forms and written releases and are quite willing to complete them.

3. **Program Evaluation and Documentation.** For a variety of reasons, as discussed in Chapter 26, employee assistance programs are compelled to document and evaluate their efficiency and effectiveness. Accurate and systematic case recording and documentation plays a critical role in an EAP's impact—not only in terms of being pivotal to its program evaluation efforts, but in the many ways it enhances the efficiency and effectiveness of the services provided by the program's professional practitioners.

Case recording and documentation unfortunately is perceived by some practitioners as a "necessary evil." On the contrary, case recording and documentation, when used effectively by the professional practitioner, not only enhances the overall efficiency and effectiveness of the employee assistance program, but it also plays a vital role in the quality and quantity of clinical treatment services provided to and for the program's clients.

PLEASE TAKE A FEW MOMENTS TO COMPLETE THIS INFORMATION SHEET

Client Name: _____   Spouse Name: _____

Address: _____   Spouse Address: _____

_____ Zip   _____ Zip

Phone: (Home) _____   Birth Date: _____

(Work) _____

Place of Employment: Client _____

Spouse _____

Social Security Number: Client _____ Spouse _____

Who can we notify in an emergency?

Name: _____ Phone: _____

Family Physician: _____

Do you have any medical condition(s) we should know about? If so, explain: _____

_____

If currently taking prescription medication, list here: _____

_____

Have you ever had psychological testing? If so, state where and when: _____

_____

Do you have medical insurance? _____ Policy Holder: _____

Name of company, address, and policy number: _____

_____

How did you hear about us? _____

PLEASE NOTE:

The above information as well as all information pertaining to your treatment is considered strictly confidential.

A fee may be charged for appointments not cancelled within 24 hours.

_____   _____

Client's Signature   Date

_____

Figure 8-1. Example of General Information Questionnaire used at intake.

HEALTH STATEMENT

NAME _____ DATE OF BIRTH _____ SEX _____

	YES	NO	REMARKS (re "YES" responses)
Have you ever applied for or received disability benefits, compensation or pensions for illness or injury?	____	____	
Were you ever rejected, deferred or released for physical or mental reasons?	____	____	
To the best of your knowledge and belief, have you suffered from or ever been treated for:			

a. Epilepsy, fainting spells, nervous or mental disorder?   _____ _____

b. Tuberculosis, asthma, pneumonia?   _____ _____

c. Heart disease or murmur, high or low blood pressure?   _____ _____

d. Stomach or duodenal ulcer, gall bladder, liver disease, colitis?   _____ _____

e. Kidney or prostatic problems, or albumin or blood in the urine?   _____ _____

f. Diabetes, sugar in urine?   _____ _____

g. Rheumatic fever, arthritis, gout, bone or joint disorder?   _____ _____

h. Cancer, tumor, polyp, goiter?   _____ _____

i. Hernia, hemorroids, varicose veins, appendicitis?   _____ _____

j. Venereal disease, blood or skin disorder?   _____ _____

To the best of your knowledge and beliefs:

a. Do you have any eye, ear, nose, or throat problems?   _____ _____

b. Have you ever had chest pains, shortness of breath, or palpitation of the heart?   _____ _____

c. Have you ever had back strain or back injury?   _____ _____

d. Have you ever had any physical examinations, x-rays, or EKG within past 5 years?   _____ _____

e. Are you addicted to or ever been treated for alcoholism or drug addiction?   _____ _____

f. Have you ever undergone or been advised to have surgical operation not included in above questions?   _____ _____

g. Any illness or injury requiring medical treatment or hospitalization within past 5 years?   _____ _____

h. Are you now taking any medication?   _____ _____

i. Any physical or mental impairments or any reason you think you are not in good health?   _____ _____

j. Were you absent from work (school) during past year?   _____ _____

k. Any of the following diseases:
      smallpox, diphtheria, scarlet fever, whooping cough, typhoid fever, influenza?   _____ _____

I hereby declare that to the best of my knowledge the statements and answers above are full, complete, and true.

Date _____ Signature _____

Figure 8-2. Example of Health Statement used at intake.

THE SYNERGISTIC RELATIONSHIP AMONG CASE MANAGEMENT, CASELOAD MANAGEMENT, AND CASE RECORDING AND DOCUMENTATION

Professional EAP counselors' working lives are typically very rapid-paced and hectic ones. They have many, many responsibilities, perform numerous important roles and functions, and are in very important positions in the lives of employees and clients who have a wide variety of problems, difficulties, and concerns. In addition to counseling with clients, they also coordinate and "manage" a variety of other professionals' services provided to their clients. Tantamount to their successfulness is their ability to be in control. **They have to know what's going on** — in the various treatment services being provided to their clients, in their relationships with their clients, in their client's experiences with what is happening to them, and in their own professional working lives. Furthermore, **professional EAP counselors have to influence what's going on, know how they impact such influences, and be able to predict and measure the impact of their influences.** From a macro or gestalt perspective, effective EAP counselors understand and appreciate the individual events in the clinical services and processes that their clients are experiencing, and also understand and appreciate the aggregate, collective, and overall impact of the individual events. Thus, the highly synergistic and interrelated relationships among effective EAP counselors' case management, case load management, and case recording and documentation roles and functions become glaringly evident. For the ultimate benefits of their clients, their employee assistance programs, and their own professional working lives, EAP counselors should give these roles and functions their utmost attention and constantly strive to improve them through continuous self-evaluation and professional continuing education and training. In doing so, they validate and verify the essence of their existence as "professionals."

Acknowledgment. Sincerest appreciation is extended to the Seminole Heights Counseling Center, Tampa, Florida for granting permission to reproduce (with minor modifications) the four examples of forms published in this chapter (Figures 8-1–8-4).

AUTHORIZATION OF RELEASE OF INFORMATION

I, the undersigned, hereby authorize _____

(name of agency)

_____

(address)

to disclose to _____

(name of person/agency to receive information)

the following information from records in its possession:

_____ Treatment and Discharge Summary   _____ Laboratory Reports

_____ Psychological Testing & Evaluation   _____ School Transcripts & Grades

_____ Medical History & Physical   _____ Other (specify)

The purpose or need for such disclosure is _____

_____

This authorization to disclose information may be revoked by me at any time except to the extent that action has been taken in reliance thereon.

This authorization shall expire upon: _____

_____

(specify date, event, or condition upon which it will expire)

_____   _____

Signature of Client   Date

_____   _____

Signature of Legal Guardian   Date

_____   _____

Signature of Witness   Date

NOTICE TO WHOMEVER DISCLOSURE IS MADE: This information has been disclosed to you from records whose confidentiality is protected by FEDERAL LAW. Federal regulations (42 CFR part 2) prohibits you from making any further disclosure of this information without the specific written consent of the person to whom it pertains, or as otherwise permitted by such regulations. A general authorization for the release of medical or other information is NOT sufficient for this purpose.

Figure 8-3. Example of Authorization of Release of Information form to be completed at intake.

CONSENT FOR SERVICES

Signed Consent is required before services can be rendered.

I, _____ hereby authorize and give
　　　　　　　　　(client's name)

consent to _____ to provide
　　　　　　(name of program providing services)

family therapy services. These services may consist of evaluation, counseling, individual and/or group therapy, and such other services as the _____
　　　　　　　　　　　　　　　　　　　　　　　　　(program)

believes are necessary and to which I agree.

I agree to pay for services received according to the _____
　　　　　　　　　　　　　　　　　　　　　　　　　(program)

approved fee structure. I understand I may be charged a fee for appointments not cancelled within 24 hours.

In the event that I become ill or am injured while on the premises, I authorize

_____ to provide or obtain emergency medical services
　　　　　　(program)

(i.e., call an ambulance).

_____	_____
Witness	Signature of Client
_____	_____
Date	Signature of Parent/Guardian
	_____
	(Relationship)
	_____
	Date

Figure 8-4. Example of Consent for Services form to be completed at intake.

REFERENCES

Cassell, J.L., & Mulkey, S.W. (1981). *Rehabilitation caseload management: Concepts and practice.* Austin: PRO-ED.

Desmond, R.E. (1985). Careers in employee assistance programs. *Journal of Applied Rehabilitation Counseling, 16*(2), 26–30.

Dickman, F., & Emener, W.G. (1982). Employee assistance programs: An emerging vista for rehabilitation counseling. *Journal of Applied Rehabilitation Counseling, 13*(3), 18–20.

Emener, W.G. (1979). Professional burnout: Rehabilitation's hidden handicap. *Journal of Rehabilitation, 45*(1), 55–58.

Emener, W.G., Luck, R.S., & Gohs, F.X. (1982). A theoretical investigation of the construct burnout. *Journal of Rehabilitation Administration, 6*(4), 188–196.

Emener, W.G., & Rubin, S.E. (1980). Rehabilitation counselor roles and functions and sources of role strain. *Journal of Applied Rehabilitation Counseling, 11*(2), 57–69.

Hastings, M.A. (1984). Employee assistance programs: A place for rehabilitation counselors? *Journal of Applied Rehabilitation Counseling, 15*(4), 29–30, 56.

Henke, R.O., Connolly, S.G., & Cox, J.G. (1975). Caseload management: The key to effectiveness. *Journal of Applied Rehabilitation Counseling, 6,* 217–227.

Hutchison, Jr., W.S. (1985). Personal and family problems in living: Implications for EAP service delivery. In J.F. Dickman, W.G. Emener & W.S. Hutchison, Jr. (Eds.), *Counseling the troubled person in industry.* Springfield, IL: Charles C Thomas, Publisher.

Hutchison, Jr., W.S., & Renick, J.C. (1985). Social work in an industrial setting: An idea whose time has finally come. In J.F. Dickman, W.G. Emener & W.S. Hutchison, Jr. (Eds.), *Counseling the troubled person in industry.* Springfield, IL: Charles C Thomas, Publisher.

Kaplan, H.I., & Sadock, B.J. (1981). *Modern synopsis of comprehensive textbooks of psychiatry III (3rd ed).* Baltimore: Williams & Wilkins.

Krucoff, C. (1980). Careers: Confronting on-the-job burnout. *Washington Post,* August 5, B-5. Maiden, R.P., & Hardcastle, D.A. (1986). Social work education: Professionalizing EAPs. *EAP Digest,* November/December, 63–66.

Maslach, C. (1976). Burn-out. *Human Behavior, 5,* 16–22.

Roessler, R.T., & Rubin, S.E. (1982). *Case management and rehabilitation counseling: Procedures and techniques.* Baltimore: University Park Press.

Third Institute on Rehabilitation Services. (1965). Training Guides in Caseload Management for Vocational Rehabilitation. Vocational Rehabilitation Administration, DHEW, Washington, DC.

Thompson, J.K., Kite, J.L., & Bruyere, S.M. (1977). Caseload management: Content and training perspective. Paper presented at the American Personnel and Guidance Association Annual Convention, Dallas.

Chapter 9

ALCOHOLISM AND EMPLOYEE ASSISTANCE PROGRAMS: ASSESSMENT AND TREATMENT

FRED DICKMAN

Alcoholism, alcohol-related problems (codependency), and alcohol and drug abuse (polydrug addiction) encompass a category of problems which comprise 30 to 40 percent of the cases entering an Employee Assistance Program for assessment, assistance, and follow-up. Consequently it is imperative that EAP coordinators, contractors, and assessors are thoroughly competent in the identification of alcoholism, its ramifications and its treatment. To follow is a general discussion on alcoholism, its pervasiveness, its definition, alcoholism as a disease, signs and symptoms, principles of intervention, treatment options, and implications for EAP practitioners.

Alcoholism has been universally recognized as at least the third leading health problem and disabling condition in the United States (National Center for Alcohol Education, 1978; U.S. Department of Health, Education, and Welfare, 1981). In addition to its status as the third most serious primary disabling condition, it is known to impact on and exacerbate many other disabling conditions, including some forms of heart disease and cancer, first and second in fatality causation respectively (American Medical Association, 1973; U.S. Department of Health, Education, and Welfare, 1981).

Conditions affected by alcohol abuse and alcoholism frequently encountered in Employee Assistance Programs are:

Pervasiveness

1. **Mental Illness.** It is estimated that up to 40% of persons diagnosed as mentally ill may be dually afflicted by alcoholism (Bachrach, 1976; Cotton, 1979; Leiber, 1982).

This chapter is reprinted from *Employee Assistance Programs; A Basic Text* (1988) with permission of the author, the book's editors (Dickman, Emener, & Hutchison, Jr.) and the publisher (Charles C Thomas, Publisher).

2. **Heart Disease.** Researchers contend that alcohol has a detrimental effect on the heart muscle and is significantly correlated with cardiomyopathy (Hamby, 1970; Schwartz, Sample & Wegle, 1975). Heart patients no longer are advised to have "a little glass of wine" (Schneider, 1980).

3. **Cancer.** While the research results on cancer are far from being conclusive, evidence is emerging to allow an inference of higher risk associated with alcoholism, alcohol abuse, and mere alcohol intake and some forms of cancer (Williams & Horn, 1977; Wynder, 1978; Wynder, Bross, & Feldman, 1957).

4. **Orthopedic Impairments and Amputations.** Since 40–60 percent of all accidents are reported to be alcohol-related (U.S. Department of Health, Education, and Welfare, 1981), an as yet untested hypothesis is that alcoholism may impede the rehabilitation progress of the victim.

5. **Birth Defects.** There is an abundance of new research available on fetal alcohol syndrome (FAS). FAS is the third leading cause of birth defective persons which adds significantly to the population of mentally retarded individuals (Clarren & Smith, 1978; Streissguth, Little, Herman, & Woodell, 1979).

6. **Other Disorders.** Characteristic disorders of rehabilitation populations related to alcohol abuse and alcoholism are gastrointestinal disorders (Leiber, 1982), genitourinary disorders (Fort, 1973), liver problems and disease (Leiber, 1982), diabetes (Kissin & Begleiter, 1977), and central nervous system problems (Parsons & Farr, 1981; Smith, 1977).

While the above disabilities tend to be most frequently encountered in public rehabilitation programs (Wright, 1980), the private sector rehabilitation focuses on workers' compensation cases (Rasch, in press). Many industrial accidents which are associated with a significant percent of these conditions are clearly alcohol-related (Manello & Seaman, 1979; Wolkenberg, Gold, & Tichauer, 1975). Other accidents covered by insurance, such as auto accidents and domestic falls (Haberman & Baden, 1978) are highly related to drinking alcohol.

When other rehabilitation issues and populations are addressed, i.e., divorce, spouse abuse, child abuse, runaways, school dropouts, suicide, and public offenders (Emerson, 1979; Hindman, 1977; Julian & Mohr, 1980; Kempe & Heller, 1972), and the clear relationship these have to alcoholism is noted, the magnitude of the problem is brought into focus. These stress only alcohol relatedness. When the identified alcohol client population is considered, the problem for rehabilitation is formidable. Clearly, the rehabilitation counselor requires tools for diagnosis (early and late) and state-of-the-art methods of treatment (Dickman & Phillips, 1985).

Alcoholism—A Definition

In general, treatment experts and scholars vary only minimally in defining alcoholism. E.M. Jellinek (1960) defined alcoholism as any use of alcoholic beverages that causes any damage to the individual or to society or both.

The Alcoholism Subcommittee of the World Health Organization (1952) defined alcoholism as any form of drinking which in extent goes beyond the traditional and customary "dietary" use, or the ordinary compliance with the social drinking customs of the community concerned, irrespective of etiological factors leading to such behavior, and irrespective also of the extent to which such etiological factors are dependent upon heredity, constitution, or acquired physiopathological and metabolic influences.

The following definition is from the American Medical Association (1973, p. 11):

> Alcoholism is an illness characterized by preoccupation with alcohol and loss of control over its consumption such as to lead usually to intoxication if drinking is begun; by chronicity; by progression; and by tendency toward relapse. It is typically associated with physical disability and impaired emotional, occupational, and/or social adjustments as a direct consequence of persistent and excessive use of alcohol.

The National Council on Alcoholism defined alcoholism as a chronic, progressive, and potentially fatal disease. It is characterized by tolerance and physical dependency, pathologic organ changes, or both, all of which are the direct consequences of the alcohol ingested.

Finally, Marty Mann, founder of the National Council on Alcoholism, defined the alcoholic as "a very sick person, victim of an insidious progressive disease, which all too often ends fatally. An alcoholic can be recognized, diagnosed, and treated successfully" (Mann, 1958, p. 17).

The diagnostic criteria for alcohol abuse published by the American Psychiatric Association (1980, p. 169) specifically addresses:

   a. pattern of pathological alcohol use;

   b. impairment in social or occupational functioning due to alcohol use; and

   c. duration of disturbance of at least one month.

The diagnostic criteria for alcohol abuse published by the American Psychiatric Association (1980, p. 170) are:

   a. either a pattern of pathological alcohol use of impairment in social or occupational functioning due to alcohol use; and

   b. either tolerance or withdrawal.

These definitions, a few among a myriad in the alcoholism literature, have a common theme which leads the author to define alcoholism as a phenomenon with three criteria:

   a. a drinking pattern;

   b. a loss of control due to the drinking pattern;

   c. a serious interference with one or more major areas of the drinking person's life, i.e., marriage and family, vocational, legal, financial, physical/medical, social, and intrapersonal areas.

Alcoholism—The Disease Concept

In addition to a growing consensus on the definition of alcoholism, the rapidly growing alcoholism treatment community is gaining agreement on the notion of alcoholism as a disease (American Medical Association, 1973; Blum & Blum, 1972; Forrest, 1978; Gitlow, 1973; Hunter, 1982; Jellenik, 1959; Johnson, 1980; King, Bissell, & O'Brien, 1979).

Inherent to the disease concept are the following:

1. **Chronicity.** Alcoholism once contracted is contracted unto death (Martin, 1972). This is the belief that alcoholism is incurable. This incurableness, however, had led many researchers (Armor, Polich, & Stambul, 1976; Sobell & Sobell, 1978) to hypothesize the opposite. Interestingly, to date no one has been able to prove that alcoholism recovery can be obtained with any treatment goal short of total abstinence (Fewell & Bissell, 1978; Gitlow, 1973; Johnson, 1980; Milam & Ketcham, 1981).

2. **Progressiveness.** Like any other disease, alcoholism has been thought of as having a "course" with definite, identifiable symptoms (Forrest,

1978; Jellinek, 1960; Johnson, 1980). This consideration is crucial to the rehabilitation counselor in that early identification is vital to successful intervention (Catanzaro, 1974; Johnson, 1980; Kinney & Leaton, 1978).

3. **Predictability.** Consequences of alcoholism are foreseeable, and as the progression of addiction continues, what is in the beginning a disparate and uniquely individual population (Catanzaro, 1974; Jellinek, 1960; Johnson, 1980).

4. **Primariness.** Alcoholism is a disease in and of itself and not a symptom of other more underlying disorders. In other words, alcoholism **causes** symptomatology—symptomatology does not cause alcoholism (American Medical Association, 1973; American Psychiatric Association, 1980; Estes, Smith-DeJulio & Heinemann, 1980; Forrest, 1978; Johnson, 1980; Milam & Ketcham, 1981; Murphy, 1980).

5. **Fatality.** Undiagnosed, untreated alcoholism results in early fatality estimated between 12 and 15 years off the average expected lifespan (American Medical Association, 1973; Kissin & Begleiter, 1972).

6. **Arrestableness.** Alcoholism is paradoxical in nature. It is the most destructive, pervasive, costly, and debilitative of the diseases; yet it is one of the most rehabilitative. Left alone, it is always fatal; diagnosed and successfully treated, the recovery is the most complete of all the diseases (Forrest, 1978; Glatt, 1974; Goldenson, Dunham, & Dunham, 1978; Milam & Ketcham, 1981).

Ironically, rehabilitation counselors, social workers, and other health professionals view the alcoholic as the least attractive, least acceptable client (Fewell & Bissell, 1978; Milam & Ketcham, 1981; Wechsler & Rohman, 1982).

A Model of Alcoholism: Diagnosis, Intervention, and Treatment

Figure 9-1 illustrates a theory of the alcohol addictive progression and its predictable consequences, the intervention process, and signs of recovery. This model provides the counselor with state-of-the-art knowledge of alcoholism and its symptomatology with implications for intervention and rehabilitation planning. The model reproduces signs of alcoholism from early to late stages in that alcoholism, like most other diseases, is treatable in proportion to its early identification.

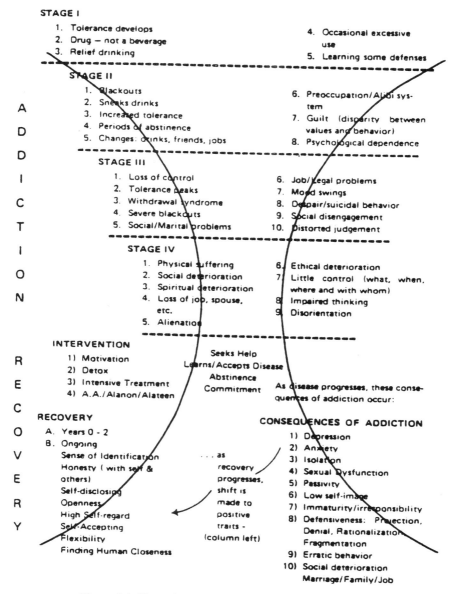

STAGE I
1. Tolerance develops
2. Drug — not a beverage
3. Relief drinking
4. Occasional excessive use
5. Learning some defenses

STAGE II
1. Blackouts
2. Sneaks drinks
3. Increased tolerance
4. Periods of abstinence
5. Changes: drinks, friends, jobs
6. Preoccupation/Alibi system
7. Guilt (disparity between values and behavior)
8. Psychological dependence

STAGE III
1. Loss of control
2. Tolerance peaks
3. Withdrawal syndrome
4. Severe blackouts
5. Social/Marital problems
6. Job/Legal problems
7. Mood swings
8. Despair/suicidal behavior
9. Social disengagement
10. Distorted judgement

STAGE IV
1. Physical suffering
2. Social deterioration
3. Spiritual deterioration
4. Loss of job, spouse, etc.
5. Alienation
6. Ethical deterioration
7. Little control (what, when, where and with whom)
8. Impaired thinking
9. Disorientation

INTERVENTION
1) Motivation
2) Detox
3) Intensive Treatment
4) A.A./Alanon/Alateen

Seeks Help
Learns/Accepts Disease
Abstinence
Commitment

As disease progresses, these consequences of addiction occur:

RECOVERY
A. Years 0 - 2
B. Ongoing
Sense of Identification
Honesty (with self & others)
Self-disclosing
Openness
High Self-regard
Self-Accepting
Flexibility
Finding Human Closeness

. . . as recovery progresses, shift is made to positive traits - (column left)

CONSEQUENCES OF ADDICTION
1) Depression
2) Anxiety
3) Isolation
4) Sexual Dysfunction
5) Passivity
6) Low self-image
7) Immaturity/irresponsibility
8) Defensiveness: Projection, Denial, Rationalization, Fragmentation
9) Erratic behavior
10) Social deterioration Marriage/Family/Job

A D D I C T I O N   R E C O V E R Y

Figure 9-1. Hourglass theory of addiction and recovery.

Symptoms Critical to Early Identification

The scope of this paper precludes a thorough discussion of all symptoms depicted in Figure 9-1, but following are the more common ways the EAP assessor/counselor can identify alcoholism early on in the progression.

1. **Has there been an increase in tolerance?** The concept of tolerance is considered a major indicator of addiction (American Psychiatric Association, 1980; Forrest, 1978; Jellenik, 1960; Kinney & Leaton, 1978). In the early stages tolerance increases and often is a source of pride for the progressing alcoholic. Yet increasing tolerance is indicative of heavy consumption as the "budding" alcoholic is adding acquired and metabolic tolerance to innate individual capacities. For example, a high blood alcohol content (BAC) has emerged from Driving While Intoxicated (DWI) Counterattack studies as a major early identifier.

2. **Has there been an arrest record, especially a DWI or driving while under the influence (DUI) charge?** U.S. Department of Transportation studies (1974) suggest that of those persons with one arrest, 60% are in some stage of alcoholism. Those with two or more arrests are within a 90% certainty of being alcoholic.

3. **Has the client experienced periods of forgetting events or blocks of time, even though not asleep, while drinking?** While blackouts occur all through many alcoholic individuals' drinking lives, in varying degrees, they definitely are a sign of neurological disturbance due to alcohol ingestion (Fort, 1973; Kissin & Begleiter, 1972; Milam & Ketcham, 1981).

4. **Has the client experienced signs of physical withdrawal indicative of some phase of physical addiction?** Butterflies in the stomach, shakiness, insomnia, and irritability are all signs of alcohol withdrawal in some phase. Signs can be less severe to severe, such as delirium tremens, convulsions, hallucinations (Fort, 1973).

5. **Does the client become defensive when asked about his drinking pattern?** Treatment personnel agree alcoholic persons build a predictable wall of defenses to protect their drinking. They tend to rationalize, deny, project, and repress their drinking-involved behavior, probably to protect a declining self-image (Fewell & Bissell, 1978; Forrest, 1978; Johnson, 1980; Murphy, 1980).

6. **What exists in the client's medical history with a probable relationship to an abusive drinking pattern?** Liver functioning, the gastrointestinal system, the pancreatic system (especially adult diabetes), and cardiomyopathy are particularly affected by alcohol abuse (Estes, et al., 1980; Hamby, 1980; Schneider, 1980).

7. **What in the client's marital and family history and present situation may point to alcoholism? Has there been child or spouse abuse reported? Is there alcoholism in their history/Have they been involved in frequent divorce?** Each of these has been correlated with alcohol abuse and alcoholism (Emerson, 1979; Filstead, 1977; Hindman, 1977; Krimmel, 1973).

8. **Is there any sign of loss-of-control drinking?** Progressing alcoholic persons cannot always predict how much they will drink, on which occasions they will drink, with whom they will drink, or what they will do when they drink. The insidiousness of this phenomenon is that often they can predict, but there are many times they cannot. This adds to their increasing fear which they attempt to build a defense against (Forrest, 1978; Jellinek, 1960; Johnson, 1980; Kissin & Begleiter, 1977).

9. **Do they project frequently rather than take responsibility for their behavior?** Progressing alcoholic persons quickly learn to defend a weakening ego by blaming their troubles on the outside world (Fewell & Bissell, 1978). The skilled rehabilitation counselor can typically recognize this in the initial interview.

10. **Have any of the problems presented to the counselor been accompanied by drinking or other drug use?** Often an aware and sensitive intake counselor can identify a problem with drinking by asking the client or significant others the appropriate questions about presenting problems, i.e., a family fight, trouble with a child, marital problems, problems with an employer, etc. (Dahlhauser, Dickman, Emener, & Lewis, 1982).

Intervention Strategy

A myth exists that implies alcoholic individuals have to "hit bottom" before they will seek help or be receptive to treatment. Quite often, they are unable to do this. Their defense system is too strong. They must be confronted before they can perceive the need for treatment (Catanzaro, 1974; Fewell & Bissell, 1978; Forrest, 1978; Johnson, 1980).

Essential to intervention strategy are: (1) significant others, (2) caring confrontation, and (3) a treatment plan.

Significant Others

People close to defended alcoholic individuals can penetrate their defense system so that they can see enough reality to enter treatment. Research indicates that well-trained confronters can increase the probability of entering treatment from 15 percent up to 70 percent (Dickman & Emener, 1982b; Emener & Dickman, 1983; Johnson, 1980). Also, research indicates that the best confronters are employers, spouse, other family members, and friends, in that order (Johnson, 1980).

The counselor is invaluable in this process in that they train the interveners to make successful confrontation on the basis of proven principles.

Caring Confrontation

The following principles of caring confrontation are generally recommended:

1. The goal is to get the alcoholic into treatment; to take a first step toward recovery. The goal is not to get him to see all the ramifications of his or her disease at once.
2. Significant others have to be involved. Only those who see the seriousness of the problem and have first-hand, observed data as to the addicted person's use can be helpful.
3. The significant others need to be trained:
   a. To present facts as to what they have seen and how they felt about what they saw.
   b. To present facts nonjudgmentally and with a minimum of emotion.
   c. To present facts as specifically as possible.
   d. To present data only related to drinking or use.
   e. To learn to feel comfortable about what they are doing; that they are trying to help the addicted person, not condemn him or her.
   f. To see that they too will be personally involved in a program of recovery, i.e., codependency, ACOA, and enhanced family/ employer/employee communication.
   g. To agree upon appropriate treatment modalities.
4. Present available, appropriate choices to the alcoholic (Johnson, 1980).

Treatment Plan

Treatment choice depends upon how far the addicted client has progressed. If they are clearly and well into Stages III or IV (see Fig. 9-1), they probably need medical attention and should be referred to an intensive, inpatient (usually 28-day) program. For this purpose, the practicing EAP assessor/counselor should have a directory of resources and treatment facilities. While the client is in his program, it is recommended that the EAP assessor/counselor:

1. Visit the client to secure the relationship as a caring one.
2. Arrange for outpatient follow-up.
3. Arrange for members of Alcoholics Anonymous to meet the client to secure a continuing program after inpatient treatment.
4. Arrange an appointment for weekly follow-up counseling with alcoholism specialists for the client and his/her family.
5. Continue frequent follow-up to check the progress of the client's recovery.
6. Make sure to provide needed family therapy.
7. Contact ACOA specialist counselors for an appointment with the family including small children.

If intervention is early enough, inpatient treatment may not be necessary. For instance, it was found that a good employee assistance program intervenes early enough so that 7 out of 10 alcoholic employees can recover without inpatient treatment (Dickman & Emener, 1982a). If such is the case, all the above recommendations hold with the addition of:

a. an immediate physical;
b. antabuse treatment (if medically feasible); and,
c. an intensive outpatient program to include individual, group, and family counseling.

Signs of Recovery

Commensurate with the progression of the disease, the process of recovery offers predictable indicators for the rehabilitation counselor. Although abstinence is critical to recovery (Gitlow, 1973; Milam & Ketcham, 1981), it must be considered as a first step on a journey of recovery along with other emotional and behavioral signs. Indeed, to get sober, the alcoholic individual cannot drink; to stay sober, alcoholic clients need to make changes in their lives. The process of recovery reverses the consequences of addiction (see Fig. 9-1).

The following are signs to look for, and to counsel toward, in following up the recovery of an alcoholic individual:

1. **Hope replaces despair.** Does the client believe the circumstances can change? Do they believe their lives can become more meaningful? Are they willing to take steps to effect these changes?

2. **Acceptance of alcoholism.** Has the client stopped blaming others for the drinking behaviors? Do they understand it was not outside circumstances and people which caused them to drink? The clients grow to accept their alcoholism and incorporate it as part of their self-image.

3. **Attendance at Alcoholics Anonymous meetings.** Is client attending AA meetings regularly and willingly? This can be vital to recovery, increasing chances for a successful recovery by as much as 75 percent by attending AA meetings (Gellman, 1964). Does the client go to a particular group on a regular basis? Has the client obtained a sponsor?

4. **General appearance.** The counselor may notice early on the alcoholic client's recovery a "glow" of health, i.e., improved personal appearance, with clients taking an interest in how they look. They begin to like the person they see in the mirror in the morning. For example, the rehabilitation counselor will notice improved eye contact and more open-body language.

5. **Responsibility.** Are the clients taking responsibility for themselves in all areas of their lives? Are they going to work regularly and arriving on time? Are they fulfilling obligations and commitments to family and friends?

6. **Communication.** Is the client communicating more freely with significant persons, i.e., employer, family, counselor? Is the client more willing to share feelings and risk self-disclosure? In this sense, the rehabilitation counselor will note increasing congruency in what the client feels and says, with appropriate voice tone and cadence.

7. **New interests.** To replace the time spent drinking, the client will develop interests in leisure activities, i.e., sports, hobbies, and social situations that do not involve drinking alcohol. They will

become less and less threatened by new experiences. Is the client experiencing socialization and integration in the community?

8. **Present-centeredness.** Is the client focusing on the here and how and on what is, rather than what has been or what might be? With increased self-worth and resultant self-acceptance, the recovering alcoholic client will experience "living in the here and now" more and more fully.

9. **Goal-directedness.** Has the client's life become purposeful? Does the client have short and long-term goals that are realistic? With increasing self-worth, the client can function more freely and work in the direction of fulfilling personal potentials.

10. **Spirituality.** On a continuing journey of recovery, the alcoholic individual gains a sense of identification, of oneness, a feeling of being a part of—rather than apart from. A sense of alienation and loneliness is replaced with a sense of belonging and purposefulness; and the client grows to accept and believe in a power greater than self. Fears are replaced with a faith, and an attitude of trust develops that things will work out as they should, not necessarily as the client wants them to be.

11. **Family growth.**

12. **Children's growth.**

The process of recovery is lifelong, beginning with abstinence, maintained by a support system of which Alcoholics Anonymous is crucial and of which the EAP assessor/counselor can be a powerful part.

Follow-up and Reentry

Follow-up by way of telephone calls, plant visitation or sessions every month or so is crucial. Is the recovering person active in AA/NA treatment center follow-up groups, other group counseling, and private alcoholism counseling designed for continuing recovery? Is he relating at work? Are supervisors aware of his reentry problems? If the absence for treatment (in the case of inpatient) were known by supervisors were they involved in the intervention and how can they help in the client's reentry? Are the family members in Alanon/Narcanon, ACOA, Alateen and other forms of recovery treatment? These are important questions to be answered by the assessor/coordinator/counselor in charge of overall case management (see Chapter 8).

Summary, Conclusions, Recommendations

The following conclusions and recommendations are offered.

1. Alcoholism is a hidden, serious factor in many other disabled populations and can easily sabotage the rehabilitation process if not detected.
2. Alcoholism is one of the most treatable of the major rehabilitation disabilities.
3. The stigma surrounding alcoholism still is the major barrier to treatment and rehabilitation of alcoholic persons and their families. Rehabilitation counselors themselves need more alcoholism awareness training to make sure that their own attitudes are nonjudgmental. Alcoholism education and awareness help in this regard.
4. Alcoholism is a disease in the most practical sense of the concept. Whether alcoholic individuals can learn to drink again or not is a major research issue. However, state-of-the-art treatment practice would dictate a program aimed at cessation of drinking and a definite recovery program.
5. Family involvement in alcoholism counseling and treatment is critically important.
6. Counselor education programs need to offer more courses and training in alcoholism and alcoholism counseling.
7. Counselor education needs to focus more on family counseling theory and practice or, at least, help the assessor/counselor become aware of these services in the community.
8. Alcoholic individuals, fully recovering, are among the most productive workers in industry (Dickman & Emener, 1982b).

No one doubts that alcoholism is a major disabling condition. Nor is there doubt that alcoholism seriously affects the rehabilitation process in many cases involving other disabilities. Therefore, the profession of counseling and EAP should feel compelled to consider the pervasiveness of alcoholism and all of its ramifications.

RESOURCES FOR THE REHABILITATION COUNSELOR ON ALCOHOLISM INFORMATION

Alcoholics Anonymous
P.O. Box 459, Grand Central Station
New York, NY 10017
(212) 686-1100

Al-Anon Family Groups
P.O. Box 182, Dept. G
Madison Square Garden Station
New York, NY 10010
(212) 475-6110

National Council on Alcoholism
733 Third Avenue
New York, NY 10017

National Institute on Alcohol Abuse & Alcoholism
Division of Resource Development
5600 Fishers Lane
Rockville, MD 20857
(301) 443-2570

National Clearinghouse for Alcohol Information
P.O. Box 2345
Rockville, MD 20852
(301) 948-4450

REFERENCES

American Medical Association. Manual on Alcoholism (Rev.). Chicago: Author, 1973.

American Psychiatric Association. *Diagnostic and statistical manual of mental disorders* (3rd ed.). Author, 1980.

Armor, D.J., Polich, J.M., & Stambul, H.B. *Alcoholism and treatment.* Report R-1739-NIAAA, Santa Monica, CA: Rand Corporation, 1976.

Bacharach, L. Characteristics of diagnosed and missed alcoholic male admissions to State and County mental hospitals in 1972. *Mental Health Statistical Note No. 124.* National Institute of Mental Health, 1976.

Blum, E., & Blum, R. *Alcoholism: Modern psychological approaches to treatment.* San Francisco: Jossey-Bass Publishers, 1972.

Catanzaro, R.J. The disease: Alcoholism. In R.J. Catanzaro (Ed.), *Alcoholism: The total treatment approach* (3rd printing). Springfield, IL: Charles C Thomas, 1974.

Clarren, S.K., & Smith, D.W. The fetal alcohol syndrome. *New England Journal of Medicine,* 1978, 298, 1063–1067.

Cotton, N.S. The familial incidence of alcoholism: A review. *Journal of Studies on Alcohol,* 1979, 40(1), 89–116.

Dahlhauser, H.F., Dickman, F., Emener, W.G., & Lewis, G.Y. *Alcohol and drug abuse awareness: Implications for intake interviewing.* Manuscript submitted for publication, 1982.

Dickman, F., & Emener, W.G. Employee assistance programs: An emerging vista for rehabilitation counseling. *Journal of Applied Rehabilitation,* 1982, 13(3), 18–20.

Dickman, F., & Phillips, E.A. Alcoholism: A pervasive rehabilitation counseling issue. *Journal of Applied Rehabilitation Counseling,* 1985.

Emener, W.G., & Dickman, F. Corporate caring. *Management World*, 1983; 12(1), 36–38.

Emerson, C.D. Family violence: A study by the Los Angeles County Sheriff's Department. *Police Chief*, 1979, *46*, 48–50.

Estes, N.J., Smith-DeJulio, J., & Heinemann, M.E. *Nursing diagnosis of the alcoholic person*. St. Louis: C.V. Mosby, 1980.

Fewell, C.H., & Bissell, L. The alcoholic denial syndrome: An alcohol-focused approach. *Social Casework*, 1978, 59(1), 6–13.

Filstead, W. The family, alcohol misuse and alcoholism: Priorities and proposals for intervention. *Journal of Studies on Alcohol*, 1977, 38, 1447–1454.

Forrest, G.C. *The diagnosis and treatment of alcoholism* (2nd ed.). Springfield, IL: Charles C Thomas, 1978.

Fort, J. *Alcohol: Our biggest drug problem*. New York: McGraw-Hill, 1973.

Gellman, I.P. *The sober alcoholic: An organizational analysis of Alcoholics Anonymous*. New Haven: College and University Press, 1964.

Gitlow, S.E. Alcoholism: A disease. In P.G. Bourne & R. Fox (Eds.), *Alcoholism progress in research and treatment*. New York: Academic Press, 1973.

Glatt, M.M. *A guide to addiction and its treatment*. New York: John Wiley & Sons, 1974.

Goldenson, R.M., Dunham, J.R., & Dunham, C.S. (Eds.). *Disability and rehabilitation handbook*. New York: McGraw-Hill, 1978.

Haberman, P.W., & Baden, M.M. *Alcohol, other drugs, and violent death*. New York: Oxford University Press, 1978.

Hamby, R.I. Primary myocardial disease. *Medicine*, 1970, *49*, 55–78.

Hindman, M. Child abuse and neglect: The alcohol connection. *Alcohol Health and Research World*, 1977, 2–7.

Hunter, C.W., Jr. Freestanding alcohol treatment centers—a new approach to an old problem. *Psychiatric Annals*, 1982, 12(4), 396–408.

Jellinek, E.M. Recent trends in alcoholism and in alcohol consumption. *Quarterly Journal Studies on Alcoholism*, 1959, *20*, 261–269.

Jellinek, E.M. *The disease concept of alcoholism*. New Haven, CT: Hill House Press, 1960.

Johnson, V.W. *I'll quit tomorrow* (Rev. Ed.). San Francisco: Harper & Row, 1980.

Julian, V., & Mohr, C. Father-daughter incest—profile of the offender. *Denver National Study on Child Neglect and Abuse Reporting*, 1980.

Kempe, H., & Heller, R.E. *Helping the battered child and his family*. New York: Lippincott, 1972.

King, B.K., Bissell, L., & O'Brien, P. AA, alcoholism counseling and social work treatment. *Health and Social Work*, 1974, 4(4), 181–198.

Kinney, J., & Leaton, G. *Loosening the grip: A handbook of alcohol information*. St. Louis: C.V. Mosby, 1978.

Kissin, B., & Begleiter, H. *The biology of alcoholism*. New York: Plenum Press, 1972.

Krimmel, H.E. The alcoholic and his family. In P.G. Bourne & R. Fox (Eds.), *Alcoholism progress in research and treatment*. New York: Academic Press, 1973.

Leiber, C.S. Medical issues: The disease of alcoholism. In E.L. Gomberg, H.R. White, & J.A. Carpenter (Eds.), *Alcohol, science, and society revisited*. New Brunswick:

Rutgers Center of Alcohol Studies, and Ann Arbor, MI: University Press of Michigan, 1982.

Manello, T.A., & Seaman, F.J. Prevalence, costs, and handling of drinking problems on seven railroads. *U.S. Department of Transportation Federal Railroad Administration.* Washington, D.C.: University Research Corporation, 1979.

Mann, M. *New primer on alcoholism: how people drink, how to recognize alcoholics, and what to do about them.* New York: Holt, Rinehart & Winston, 1958.

Martin, J. *Chalk talk on alcoholism.* National Audiovisual Center. Washington, D.C.: General Services Administration, 1972.

Milam, J.R., & Ketcham, K. *Under the influence.* Seattle: Madrona Publishers, 1981.

Murphy, H.B.M. Hidden barriers to the diagnosis and treatment of alcoholism and other alcohol misuse. *Journal of Studies on Alcohol,* 1980, 40(5).

National Center for Alcohol Education. *The community health nurse and alcohol-related problems.* Rockville, MD: National Institute on Alcohol Abuse and Alcoholism, 1978.

Parsons, O.A., & Farr, S.P. The neuropsychology of alcohol and drug use. In S.B. Filskov & T.J. Boll (Eds.), *Handbook of clinical neuropsychology.* New York: John Wiley & Sons, 1981.

Rasch, J.D. *Rehabilitation of workers' compensation and other insurance claimants: Case management, forensic and business aspects.* Springfield, IL: Charles C Thomas, 1985.

Schneider, M.A. Some medical aspects of alcohol and other drugs of abuse. (Film narrative), Rev. 1980.

Schwartz, L., Sample, K.A., & Wegle, E.D. Severe alcoholic cardiomyopathy reversed with abstention from alcohol. *American Journal of Cardiology,* 1975, 36(12), 963–966.

Smith, J.W. Neurological disorders in alcoholism. In N.J. Estes, & M.E. Heinemann (Eds.), *Alcoholism.* St. Louis: C.V. Mosby, 1977.

Sobell, M.B., & Sobell, L.C. *Behavioral treatment of alcohol problems: Individualized therapy and controlled drinking.* New York: Plenum Press, 1978.

Streissguth, A.P., Little, R.E., Herman, C.S., & Woodell, S. IQ in children of recovered alcoholic mothers compared to matched controls. *Alcoholism: Clinical and Experimental Research,* 1979, 3(2), 197.

U.S. Department of Health, Education, & Welfare. *Fourth special report to the U.S. Congress on alcohol and health from the Secretary of Health and Human Services.* January 1981. National Institute on Alcohol Abuse and Alcoholism. Washington, D.C.: U.S. Government Printing Office, 1981.

U.S. Department of Transportation. *Alcohol safety action projects: Evaluation of 1972 operations.* Vol. 1 NHTSA Technical Report. Washington, DC: The Department: 1974.

Wechsler, H., & Rohman, M. Future caregivers' views on alcoholism treatment—a poor prognosis. *Journal of Studies on Alcohol,* 1982, 43(9), 939–955.

Williams, R.R., & Horn, J.W. Association of cancer sites with tobacco and alcohol consumption and socioeconomic status of patients; interview study from the Third National Cancer Survey. *Journal of National Cancer Institute,* 1977, 58(3), 525–547.

Wolkenberg, R.C., Gold, C., & Tichauer, E.R. Delayed effects of acute alcoholic intoxication of performance with reference to work safety. *Journal of Safety Research,* 1975, 7, 104.

World Health Organization, Expert Committee on Mental Health (1952). *Alcohol Subcommittee Second report.* W.H.O. Technical Report Series, No. 48.

Wright, G.N. *Total rehabilitation.* Boston: Little, Brown, 1980.

Wynder, E.L. Epidemiology of cancers of the upper alimentary and upper respiratory tracts. *Laryngoscope,* 1978, *88*(1), 50–51.

Wynder, E.L., Bross, I.J., & Feldman, R.M. A study of the etiological factors in cancer of the mouth. *Cancer,* 1957, *10*, 1300–1323.

Chapter 10

WORKING WITH FAMILIES THROUGH EMPLOYEE ASSISTANCE AND WELLNESS PROGRAMS

WILLIAM S. HUTCHISON, JR.

Prevention of illness and promotion of health have become major values for America (Weiss, 1991). Two problems contributing to this development are increased longevity and the increasing costs of treating illness (Weiss, 1991). Employee assistance professionals have contributed approaches to these problems by emphasizing early treatment for human problems identified in the workplace as well as expanding health promotion programs in the workplace such as stress management and financial and retirement planning (Opatz, 1994).

In addition, Employee Assistance programs recognize a dual perspective, that a healthy workplace promotes healthy family and community living and conversely, healthy family living promotes healthier workplace performance (Keita, 1994). This article describes a theoretical framework to analyze selected wellness/health promotion programs and to draw implications for continued development of employee assistance and wellness programs.

The first part of this framework draws from the concept of family socialization, e.g., the fact that families are the primary teachers of health attitudes and behaviors (Anspaugh, 1994).

From the field of health come the concepts of health, wellness, and health promotion. Originally, health meant that the individual had no disease. However, in 1940, the World Health Organization proposed that health was "a state of physical, mental and social well-being and not merely the absence of disease" (Anspaugh, 1994). This definition has stimulated the development of the concept of wellness as engaging in attitudes and behaviors that enhance quality of life and maximize personal potential (Anspaugh, 1994). Health promotion consists of efforts

157

that help people change their lifestyles and thereby move toward a higher state of wellness (Anspaugh, 1994).

Health promotion methods include education, treatment and related organizations, and economic or political interventions designed to facilitate behavioral and environmental changes conducive to health (Klarreich, 1987).

Elements of a comprehensive health promotion program would include (Chenoweth, 1987):

Healthy Lifestyle Education

- Drug and alcohol awareness
- Exercise and physical fitness
- Lifting properly—body mechanics
- Nutrition
- Smoking cessation
- Stress management
- Weight control
- Sexuality

Screening, Monitoring, and Follow-Up

- Cancer screening (breast self-examination, testicular self-examination, colorectal screening)
- Diabetes, glaucoma, sickle cell anemia
- Heart disease risk
- Hypertension screening
- Immunization (tetanus, measles for example)

Safety Promotion and Accident Prevention

- Cardio-pulmonary resuscitation (CPR)
- Choke-saving techniques
- Emergency medical treatment and first-aid
- On-the-job safety
- Right to know education (potentially hazardous substances)
- Seat belt/shoulder strap usage

Employee Assistance Programs (EAP)

- Family Health Promotions
- Domestic counseling (families, marriage and family problems)
- Preparation for retirement
- Psychological counseling

There are a number of methods and techniques available to deliver the program. These include:

Print Materials: Two general categories of print materials exist for use in health promotion: Externally produced print materials such as posters, pamphlets, payroll stuffers, calendars, newsletters, magazines, and booklets on specific or general health issues; and internally produced publicity that can include but not be limited to, announcements or program summaries appearing in the form of flyers, posters, newsletter announcements, or newspaper articles.

Audio-Visual Materials: Due to the rise in popularity of "wellness," the production of audio-visual materials on various health themes has expanded. Films, videos, and slide/tape presentations are available in a wide variety of topics.

Management and Authority: The authority figures in the workplace convey a tremendous message to the employee population, both directly in what they say, and indirectly in what they do not say, and how they behave. Therefore, the program can be given a marvelous boost by managers who make a personal commitment to the program's goals.

Committees: Committees are made up of carefully appointed representative employee groups that are given a serious mandate to investigate, problem-solve, monitor, and/or plan in areas that may affect employee health. The use of employee committees in overall workplace intervention can be a powerful way to expand the legitimacy of employee health concern in areas beyond the traditional individual behavior change strategies.

Microcomputer Software: New software products are being developed continually for the health promotion market. Interactive programs are available for almost any behavior change strategy from psychotherapy to weight loss and quitting smoking.

Health Promotion Events: An excellent way to increase the visibility of the health promotion program in an organization is through the sponsorship of large, widely-publicized events. Because the objective here is cultural change, not health behavior change, they are ideal for launching a new program.

Lectures/Talks: There are two types of talks or lectures that are important in a workplace health promotion program; (1) a promotional talk in which staff members speak to internal groups about the program itself, and (2) a lecture by an expert on specific health or program-related topics.

Workshops/Skills Training: In a workplace health promotion program, the purpose of any skills training intervention essentially is to teach people the skills they need to reach the goal of physical and psychological well-being. Areas where workshops and training programs are beneficial include, but are not limited to, weight control, exercise, stress management, smoking cessation, blood pressure control, nutrition, cancer detection and prevention, cardiovascular fitness, communications, management, decision-making, and interpersonal skills.

Ongoing Programs: Facilitate the organization of all kinds of fitness activities, such as walking during lunch hour, running, biking, swimming, or aerobics. Set up a nutrition awareness in the company cafeteria, lunchroom, or vending machine to assist in food-choice and decision-making by employees. Organize regularly scheduled public meetings to discuss a particular work-related topic with an expert.

Self-Help/Support Groups: Self-help groups are extremely helpful in providing socioemotional support for health-related topics, addiction problems, and family issues.

Referral: Because no workplace will ever be able to serve all of the health and psychosocial needs of every employee, it is imperative that the health promotion program provide a source of referrals to community groups and agencies.

Health Risk Appraisals: (HRA) A HRA is a general questionnaire that compares individual personal characteristics and behavior patterns with factors believed to increase the risk of disease, injury, or death. HRA's are used in three ways (1) to identify clusters of risk-producing behaviors in large populations, (2) to evaluate health promotion activities through administration at fixed intervals over time, and (3) to educate participants about the relationship between their behavior and health risks, thereby motivating behavior change.

It is important to remember, whatever the organization does, it needs to make certain that it has selected as wide a variety of tools as possible. In addition, it needs to recognize that the use of these tools has at least two purposes: (1) to encourage awareness of the health promotion program and participation in it, and (2) to promote incremental changes in the organization's norms regarding health.

Further research regarding this topic, produced numerous companies that have incorporated wellness in their EAPs. Some are: (1) Johnson and Johnson, (2) Control Data, (3) A T & T, (4) Speed-call Corp., (5) New

York Telephone, (6) Great Salt Lake Minerals, (7) Volvo, (8) Union Carbide, (9) Tel-Med Program, (10) Robert Mason, (11) Lord Corp., and (12) Quaker Oats (Weiss, 1991; Sloan, 1987; Klarreich, 1987; Opatz, 1994). A more detailed look at Johnson & Johnson, Control Data, A T & T, and Union Carbide follows.

Johnson and Johnson: The name of the program this company established is "**Live for Life.**" The principal goals of this program are to provide the opportunity and encouragement for Johnson and Johnson employees to become the healthiest in the world and to control the corporate costs of employee ill health. It is a comprehensive effort aimed at helping all employees at a work site to improve and maintain their health by establishing good health habits. Standard components include: (1) a health screening, (2) communications programs, (3) a lifestyle seminar, and (4) a variety of behavior-change-oriented action programs on numerous topics (Weiss, 1991).

> "Our objectives (Johnson and Johnson) include measurable, sustained lifestyle improvement among the greatest number of employees possible in regular exercise, smoking cessation, weight control, stress management, health knowledge, and awareness of medical intervention programs" (Sloan, 1987, p. 105–6).

Control Data: The name of the program this company established is "**Stay Well.**" It is a comprehensive health-promotion program designed to manage health-care costs and improve productivity by reducing the level of lifestyle risk among employees and their families. StayWell was initially developed for Control Data's employees, however today, it is available to other organizations through a nationwide network of over 50 authorized distributors. The StayWell program is organized around the four key phases of the health-promotion process:

1. **awareness,**
2. **assessment,**
3. **behavior change, and**
4. **maintenance**

The StayWell program objectives fall into four broad categories:

1. To assess risk status in the eligible employee population initially subsequent time periods.
2. To evaluate StayWell components and the overall program to support further development and refinement, including;
   - participation rates and patterns;

- participation reactions to program activities; and
- changes in participant knowledge, attitudes, skills, and behaviors.

3. To assess the effect of the StayWell program on long-term risk reduction.
4. To determine the impact of the StayWell program on healthcare costs and productivity (e.g., absenteeism) (Weiss, 1991, p. 50).

The major components of the StayWell program include:

1. An Employee Health Survey (EHS) that provides a corporate-wide description of health risk status.
2. An orientation to the program for all employees, on company time.
3. The Health Risk Profile and screening, with interpretations of results in group sessions.
4. Availability of lifestyle change courses in the areas of fitness, weight control, smoking cessation, nutrition, back care, and stress management.
5. Action teams, employee-led groups that concentrate on specific activities and goals, such as work site changes or lifestyle changes.
6. Special events such as health fairs or hypertension screenings (Klarreich, 1987, p. 115).

The premise of StayWell is that if people know how to reduce preventable risks and then choose to do something about these risks, health care costs can be reduced and people can live longer, healthier, and more productive lives (Klarreich, 1987).

AT&T: The name of this company's program is "**Total Life Concept.**" AT&T communications conducts one of the most extensive and thoroughly evaluated workplace health promotion programs. Total Life Concept was initially proposed as a way of helping employees cope with the disruption caused by massive reorganization of their work environment (Sloan, 1987).

The planning stage of AT&T's "Total Life Concept" included the following:

- **Formulation of mission goals**
- **Objective setting**
- **Hypothesis development**
- **Analysis of health-care costs**

- **Assessment of corporate culture and norms and their impact on employees' health** (Weiss, 1991, p. 33).

The core components of Total Life Concept are as follows:

- **Exercise**
- **Back care**
- **Weight management**
- **Smoking cessation**
- **Blood pressure control**
- **Cholesterol/nutrition monitoring**
- **Cancer screening/awareness**
- **Stress management**
- **Interpersonal communications** (Weiss, 1991, p. 34).

Evaluation variables selected for Total Life Concept were:

- **Health and job attitudes**
- **Health risks**
- **Health behaviors**
- **Program process (participation)**
- **Cost-benefit analysis** (Weiss, 1991, p. 34).

The mission statement from AT&T regarding their Total Life Concept program is: "To create a corporate culture that is supportive of a healthy lifestyle" (Sloan, 1987, p. 105).

Union Carbide: "Health Plus" is Union Carbide Corporation's comprehensive health promotion and fitness program. This program includes the "Health Plus Fitness Program" and the "Health Plus Learning Center." The "Health Plus" program is designed to have a positive influence on individuals, the organization, and the work environment. This program provides its participants with the tools to manage their own health with an emphasis on understanding the dynamics of personal change and the environmental/organizational changes that support these changes (Klarreich, 1987).

The objectives of "Health Plus" stem from the program philosophy that endorses the prevention of health problems in a comprehensive fashion, addressing the entire person's health needs and habits in programs that contribute to Union Carbide's business objective and enhance personal quality of life and productivity (Klarreich, 1987).

The objectives relating to individuals are:

Prevention of cardiovascular disease (specifically heart attacks and strokes) through prevention and reduction of cardiovascular risk factors (tobacco smoking, elevated cholesterol, high blood pressure, physical inactivity, excessive stress, diabetes, obesity); prevention and early detection of cancer; prevention and rehabilitation of lower back pain; and the prevention of other health problems through programs that impart personal lifestyle management skills, actively involve participants in changing their lifestyles, and provide health self-management information.

Enhancement of personal effectiveness and quality of life through the development of health as defined by dynamic health rather than lack of symptoms. The objectives that support organizational business objectives are:

Economic: management and reduction of health care costs and costs resulting from disability, workman's compensation, and absenteeism as they relate to preventable, lifestyle-related causes.

Subjective employee relations parameters: recruiting and retaining high quality personnel and enhancing employee morale.

Promotion of a healthy work environment.

Promotion of organizational and personal changes to promote greater productivity.

Management of occupational health issues as they relate to lifestyle (Klarreich, 1987, p. 126).

Each of these programs provide core services designed to prevent illness, increase health and promote wellness. The attainment of these program goals will reduce health care costs and keep American companies competitive in the global economy (Opatz, 1994). As these programs continue their impact, family wellness and health will be a rich area for research. In addition, program elements that are made available to non-employee family members will allow further exploration of the potential interactive effects of family functioning and employee work performance measurers such as absenteeism, production quality and quantity, and accident rates. There is promising evidence now that Employee Assistance Programs, and health prevention and wellness programs are increasing health in the American workforce (Keita, 1994). The potential for expanding the availability of these programs to employee families is an exciting opportunity.

REFERENCES

Anspaugh, D.J., Hamrick, M.H., & Rosato, F.D. (1994). *Wellness.* St. Louis: Mosby-Year Book, Inc.

Chenoweth, D.H. (1987). *Planning Health Promotion at the Worksite.* Indianapolis, IN: Benchmark Press, Inc.

Jensen, D.W. (1987). *Worksite Wellness.* Paramus, NJ: Prentice Hall Information Services.

Keita, G. and Hurrell, J.J. (1994). *Job Stress in a Changing Workforce.* Washington, DC: American Psychological Association.

Keita, G.P., & Sauter, S.L. (Eds.) (1992). *Work and Wellbeing.* Washington, DC: American Psychological Association.

Klarreich, S.H. (1987). *Health and Fitness in the Workplace: Health Education in Business Organizations.* New York: Praeger Publishers.

Opatz, J.P. (1994). *Economic Impact of Worksite Health Promotion.* Champaign, IL: Human Kinetics Publishers.

Sloan, R.P. (1987). *Investing in Employee Health.* San Francisco: Jossey-Bass Publishers.

Weiss, S.M. (1991). *Perspectives in Behavioral Medicine.* Hillsdale, NJ: Lawrence Erlbaum Associates, Inc.

Chapter 11

THE MENTAL HEALTH COMPONENT
OF EMPLOYEE ASSISTANCE PROGRAMS

CALVIN M. PINKARD

Over the past quarter century mental health care requirements within our nation have shown an almost astronomical rise. The financial and human costs of mental illness escalate annually. Amelioration of mental illness and promotion of mental and emotional health now absorbs a large part of the more than $200 billion yearly expenditure for health care in the United States (Matarozzo, 1982). A continually burgeoning mental health care movement has been created to meet the need.

In the same 25-year period Employee Assistance Programs (EAPs) in American business settings have shown a similar tremendous growth and enlarged scope (Jerrell and Rightmyer, 1985). From their beginnings as industrial alcoholism programs (Dickman, 1985) EAPs have developed programs aimed at assisting employees with a wide range of mental health problems. The contemporary services of EAPs in the field of mental health can be better understood from a description of the historical development of America's mental health movement and its present-day features.

Historical Development

Western society's choice of response to members of society who show mental and emotional dysfunctions may be characterized as having progressed from sorcery to science. The decisive turn to a scientific approach began in the late nineteenth century when a number of influential European physicians and lay persons insisted that severe mental and emotional aberrations be treated medically. Beyond the humanitarian

This chapter is reprinted from *Employee Assistance Programs; A Basic Text* (1988) with permission of the author, the book's editors (Dickman, Emener, & Hutchison, Jr.) and the publisher (Charles C Thomas, Publisher).

benefit, this reform promoted scientific inquiry into the conditions newly designated "mental illness." Scientific theories of mental disorders could be developed and a foundation was laid for therapeutic approaches to disturbed persons.

Following the European initiative, the first years of the twentieth century saw the establishment of mental hospitals in the United States. At first private, and few in number, hospitals to serve those afflicted with severe mental illness came to be built throughout the country. Before mid-century, patient care in these institutions was primarily custodial since effective treatment was largely unknown. Patients frequently were confined for long periods of time, sometimes for life. Nevertheless the existence of mental hospitals provided opportunity for observation and research on the causes and manifestations of mental disorders. A beginning classification of mental disorders was made and there was progress toward differential treatment of identified forms of mental illness.

Another early and potent influence on the treatment of mental disorders was the introduction of Freudian psychoanalysis to the United States in the first decade of the 20th century. Freud's theory attributed mental and emotional disturbances to **psychological** causes and delineated a sophisticated **psychological** approach to treatment of mental disorders. His ideas were seminal in the development of the plethora of psychological explanations of mental and emotional problems which exist today: his contention that psychotherapy is the treatment of choice for disturbed individuals remains a dominant treatment principle today. However, the Freudian treatment method proved too costly and too time-consuming to meet the need for treatment of the nation's large and growing population of individuals manifesting a wide variety of psychopathologies.

Psychological methods of alleviating mental disturbance also received impetus from two discoveries: (1) research showed that psychosocial conditions within mental hospitals had significant influence on clinical outcomes and the behavior of patients, and (2) during World War II the U.S. army demonstrated that neurotic symptoms could arise out of psychological stress associated with combat and could be treated effectively with short-term psychological methods. These findings challenged the medical model of mental illness and physical methods of treatment for mental disturbance. The second half of the twentieth century has seen a blossoming of theories which hold that psychological elements are both cause and path to amelioration of mental and emotional pathologies.

Since 1950 the focus of the mental health movement has shifted from the mental hospital to the community (Bloom, 1977). Outpatient and nonmedically-oriented facilities for treatment of mental and emotional problems have been established throughout the country although some rural areas remain underserved. For most U.S. citizens, mental health treatment programs are available within their own communities.

Three additional developments after the 1950s produced changes in the content of mental health services. New programs and approaches were developed after demonstration that:

1. stress causes mental and emotional distress and pathology;
2. difficulties in interpersonal relationships and pathology-producing social conditions affect the onset, course, and severity of mental disorders;
3. enhancement of mental health and prevention of mental disorders are possible and necessary goals of a national mental health movement.

Current Status

The contemporary developments in mental health services surround EAPs and have exerted great influence on the diversification of EAP mental health services. In the 1980s, EAPs have assumed responsibility for identifying and treating mental and emotional problems of individuals in the nation's work force. They also have initiated efforts to prevent such problems and to promote mental health of employees. This chapter will be concerned with how EAPs are responding to workers who need assistance with the garden-variety of emotional and mental difficulties and dilemmas which beset the human person. It addresses what the typical modern EAP offers to assist employees faced with mental health problems. A second focus will concern how an EAP can contribute to preventing these kinds of difficulties.

The EAPs in operation today typically offer mental health services which embody three major therapeutic interventions. These are: (1) psychotherapy and counseling, (2) stress reduction programs, and (3) prevention of disorders and promotion of physical and mental health.

Before 1950	After 1950
illness model; organic hypothesis of cause of mental illness	psychosocial model psychological hypotheses of cause of mental and emotional dysfunction
largely custodial care in mental hospitals	community-based services in a variety of settings; wide range of short-term, problem focused psychotherapeutic interventions
emphasis on severe disorders such as psychoses, organic deterioration	focus on mild, limited problems in living; concern with family and work-centered difficulties and drug and alcohol abuse
assessment of symptoms; assigning diagnostic labels; understanding past history of individuals	understanding current interpersonal relations and social and cultural contributions to mental disturbance; relative disinterest in formal diagnosis
psychiatrist practitioners	variety of practitioners and researchers (psychiatrists, psychologists, social workers, educators, social scientists, holistic health workers, specialists in particular problems [e.g., rape counselors, family therapists])
Freudian or Neo-Freudian theory and therapy	multiple theories of mental disorder and multiple therapeutic methods
	stress regarded as important contributor to mental disturbances; assessment of stressors and attempt to reduce them by therapeutic interventions
	prevention emphasis; early treatment emphasis; psycho-educational programs for teaching behavior change and coping skills; promotion of psychological wellness
	recognition of association between emotional and mental functioning and physical health

Figure 11-1.

Psychotherapy and Counseling

Psychotherapy and counseling (According to Patterson [1973, p. xiii] there is no useful or actual distinction between them and so the term psychotherapy will be used for both) are labels for more or less formalized interpersonal exchanges between two or more persons. The predominantly verbal exchange is directed by a professionally-trained helper (therapist, counselor) who employs a systematic, theory-based helping approach. The goal is improvement in the mental health of one or more persons (clients, helpees, in medical settings-patients). The psychotherapeutic approach is the mainstay of remedial mental health practice in the country today. (The thrust of the pharmacotherapy approach, also nation-wide in scope, is principally palliative [Klerman, Weissman, Rounsaville and Chevron, 1984].)

Since Freud developed psychoanalysis at the turn of the century there has been a proliferation of theoretical systems of psychotherapy. This multiplicity of systems reflects the lack of agreement as to what constitutes the optimal human psychological functioning toward which the psychotherapeutic process aims. There is corresponding lack of agreement on the essential features of human personality, on how it functions, and of how change in functioning may be effected. Lacking a unified view of what people are, and what they ought to be, widely divergent therapeutic approaches have been created, the goals of psychotherapies differ, and the therapeutic methodologies are distinctly different. At present, then, psychotherapeutic services are available in the United States from practitioners of therapeutic systems which share no single conceptualization of mental health. Figure 11-2 describes seven current major therapeutic systems and illustrates the differences in goals and methods which characterize modern psychotherapies.

Contemporary psychotherapy systems employ their therapeutic approaches with groups of individuals as well as with individual clients. It is now accepted that group therapy experience can enrich the possibilities for therapeutic gains. For example, the group itself can provide a laboratory for the study of the quality of interpersonal transactions and an opportunity to try out new behavior and communication styles in a social setting. Psychotherapy with existing groups, especially the family and the marriage duo, has become increasingly common (Haley, 1971). Marital counseling and family therapy are a large part of therapeutic enterprise today. There is consensus that mental health services to groups fill a vital need in modern living.

Although modern psychotherapies have different theoretical underpinnings, and each therapeutic system is tied to a partially unique body of techniques, they also have commonalities. All are rooted in respect for the worth and dignity of the human individual. Further, all share the aim of promoting personal autonomy so that ultimate therapeutic gain lies in empowering the client to use his own inner resources in living the life of his enlightened choice. No psychotherapy is simply advice-giving nor is it brain-washing. It is basically a very complex facilitative and educative process regardless of the particular techniques used by the therapist and regardless of the specific therapeutic desiderata of the therapeutic system favored by the therapist.

Moreover, many (even most) psychotherapists choose to be eclectic in methodology and in therapeutic aims (Garfield and Bergin, 1986). While the training of a psychotherapist usually is centered around a particular therapeutic system, his clinical practice often encompasses techniques drawn from other approaches. Experienced therapists, in particular, have found that the needs of clients cannot be met by a narrow methodology and outlook. Research has demonstrated clearly that experienced therapists are kissing cousins in their therapeutic practice (Auerbach and Johnson, 1977).

In the 1980s there is not only eclectic orientation to modify the picture of many distinct therapy models, there is increasing evidence that difference in therapeutic models is no more powerful an influence on therapeutic outcome than certain personal characteristics of the individual psychotherapist. To date, among others, important attributes of the therapist which contribute to successful outcome have been identified as warmth, empathy, expressiveness, genuineness, expectations of improvement in the client, faith in the capacity of the client to help himself, basic regard and respect for the client as a human being (Barrett and Wright, 1984). There is movement, too, toward integration of therapeutic approaches based on the hope that clients will be better served by a unified and comprehensive theory of personality and therapy that spawns broadly-figured therapeutic methodology (Lazarus, 1976). At present there is no compelling evidence that one therapeutic system is much more efficacious than another (McGuire and Freseman, 1983), although this finding must be considered tentative in view of the great difficulty in measuring psychotherapy outcomes.

The state of the art in today's psychotherapy practice and research has implications for EAPs. An EAP may have staff members who are expert psychotherapists who can serve the needs of employees for psychotherapy. In view of the large number of current therapeutic approaches, and the large variety of problems which clients bring to psychotherapists, it is usually necessary that an EAP have a system of referral to community therapeutic programs and practitioners. Whatever the mechanics of the referral system which an EAP adopts, it should operate so that employees are put in touch with skilled and caring psychotherapists who are not too narrowly focused on a particular therapeutic model. Any referral system also should be modifiable in view of the shifting character of the therapeutic scene and the growing body of knowledge about the effectiveness and applicability of particular therapeutic systems. EAPs, of course, must operate within a budget. In view of what we know today about the

CONTEMPORARY PSYCHOTHERAPY SYSTEMS

System	Therapeutic Goals	Methodology
Psychoanalytic Therapy	to reconstruct the personality; to promote insight; to make the unconscious conscious; to resolve internal conflicts; to understand the effect of early experience on adult functioning	free association; dream analysis; interpretation; reconstruction of early experience and analysis of its present influence; study of client's feelings toward therapist as revelatory of current interpersonal difficulties
Person-Centered Therapy (Alternate Name: Client-Centered Therapy)	to experience and accept aspects of self formerly denied or distorted; to encourage personal growth; to trust the self and remain open to experience; to maximize self-awareness and self-actualization	creation of a safe climate in which client can explore self-functioning; communicate qualities of the therapist (warmth, respect, genuine regard for client) to the client to promote realistic self-appraisal and personal growth; communicate empathic understanding to client to promote self-awareness
Existential Therapy	to accept responsibility for one's own life and choices; to discover meaning in life; to gain freedom by removing blocks to self-awareness and fulfilling potential; to clarify values	elicit client's being-in-the-world; establish a genuine encounter between therapist and client; examine choices client has made; lead client to make independent choices and adopt own unique values
Transactional Analysis	to re-examine decisions and to make new decisions based on accurate perceptions; to recognize the influence on behavior and attitudes of parts of the personality; to improve interpersonal relationships	analyze social transactions between individuals, especially games people play; psychodrama and role playing; explore consequences of commitment to adopting a rigid life pattern (script)
Reality Therapy	to learn to appraise the self and the world realistically; to develop a success identity; to develop the capacity to make and carry out plans for reaching realistic goals	therapist requires client to face reality and to make value judgments about his own behavior; determine specific desirable behavior changes; commit client to following through on behavior changes; promote sense of personal competence in the client
Cognitive-Behavioral Therapy	to change irrational beliefs about the self, others, the world, to rational beliefs; to replace maladaptive behavior patterns with more appropriate ones; to resolve relatively simple, practical problems and learn methods of problem-solving	systematic programs for observable, measurable behavior changes; analysis of irrational beliefs; experiment with new behavior and new beliefs; homework, treatment contracts to work on specific problem areas

CONTEMPORARY PSYCHOTHERAPY SYSTEMS (Continued)

Systems Therapy	to develop effective and harmonious interpersonal relationships; to learn to play appropriate roles in social systems—especially family and the marriage relationship; to communicate clearly and honestly	social systems (family, marital, employee group) are targets of therapeutic intervention; analyze and improve communication within psychosocial groups; assign behaviors to precipitate desired changes in group process

Figure 11-2.

comparative efficacy of the various psychotherapies, limited EAP funds will be well invested in time-limited, problem-centered therapeutic approaches and in marital and family therapy.

Stress Reduction

Nowadays everyone seems to be talking about stress. You hear it not only in daily conversation but also through television, radio, the newspapers and the ever-increasing number of conferences, stress centers, and university courses devoted to the topic...The word **stress,** like **success, failure,** or **happiness** means different things to different people....Is it effort, fatigue, pain, fear, the need for concentration, the humiliation of censure, or even unexpected success that requires complete reformulation of one's life? The businessman thinks of it as frustration or emotional tension, the air traffic controller as a problem in concentration, the biochemist...as a chemical event, the athlete as muscular tension. The problems they face are totally different but research has shown that they respond (so as) to cope with any type of increased demand upon the human machinery.[1]

The statement by a distinguished pioneer in stress theory and research points up the growing importance of the concept that stress in its myriad forms significantly impacts human psychological and physical functioning.

Over the past thirty years an extensive body of research on stress and its effects has accumulated. For the mental health field an important research finding has been the identification of psychological factors as stressors. Among these are major life events and transitions (e.g., death of a spouse, divorce, onset of serious disease, retirement). These happenings and life landmarks are stress-producing in that they require adaptation to significant forced changes in the life of the individual (Dohrenwald, 1978; Brim & Ruff, 1980). Stress also has been identified as inherent in the chronic presence of daily hassles and demands (e.g., providing care to an elderly relative, performing uninteresting tasks repeatedly, pressure to meet high standards) (DeLongis et al., 1982).

Research, too, has demonstrated that stress has effects on body functioning and body systems. For example, the major contribution of chronic stress to the development of diseases (e.g., hypertension, asthma, cancer) and to reduction in the capacity to fight disease has been documented (Olbrisch, 1977). Further, research findings have shown the importance of psychological functioning within the individual (e.g., coping style, degree of emotional stability, perception of harm or threat in events) in dealing with stress and reducing degree of stress (Lazarus, 1981; McCrae, 1982; Rabkin & Struening, 1976).

The demonstration that stress is universal among citizens of the modern world and that it can be expected to occur and recur throughout the life of the average individual has fueled the enormous growth in therapeutic efforts to reduce stress and teach effective ways of coping with it. Stress reduction frequently is a therapeutic goal in individual psychotherapy. Group counseling and psychoeducational programs are devoted to understanding the nature of stressors and to mastery of healthy response to stress. Content of these programs usually includes (1) identifying stressors, (2) as far as possible removing stressors, (3) developing emotional, cognitive, and behavioral methods of coping with stress, and (4) explicating relationships between stress reactions and physical and mental health.

An EAP may draw from resources available in the larger mental health system in making stress reduction available to employees. A common approach is to employ a mental health professional, with the requisite training and skill, to lead group sessions concerned with presenting information about stress and developing coping skills. Inhouse programs may also be developed and they provide a logical setting for stress-reduction programs dealing with work-related stress. The need for them is evident in research findings which show that many elements of work situations can be stress-producing (e.g., doing meaningless or monotonous work, heavy workload, threat of unemployment, approach of retirement, lack of clear direction, depersonalization, inadequate reward systems, prejudice in the workplace toward women and minorities) (Cooper and Marshall, 1976; Siegel, 1984).

EAP programs which combat work-related and other stresses have the potential to improve the quality of life and mental and physical health of employees. Since stress reactions reduce the ability to function on the job, these programs also have the potential for substantial benefit to employers through increased worker efficiency and satisfaction. Overall, understanding stressors and stress mechanisms and identifying protective factors is of great importance to EAP staff.

Prevention Programs, Promoting Physical and Mental Health

The major goals of prevention programs in the health field are to block dysfunction in those who are currently healthy and to prevent existing problems from growing more serious (Albee and Jofee, 1977). Since the early 1950s, studies have explored how individuals can promote and protect their own health (Brandt, 1982). Today it is proven that changes in life-styles and habits are powerful aids to physical and mental health.

> The morbidity and mortality rates of Americans are no longer related to infectious diseases prevalent at the turn of the century: instead they are related to chronic disorders related to our lifestyles. Influenza, pneumonia, tuberculosis, gastroentiritis and diptheria have been replaced by heart disease, cerebrovascular disease, respiratory diseases and the various cancers—all of which are, in part, a product of how we live; that is, what and how much we eat and drink, how we exercise, how we deal with daily stresses, whether or not we smoke . . . In short, the most serious medical problems that today plague the majority of Americans are not medical problems at all; they are behavior problems . . . [2]

In present-day society there is both tremendous need and tremendous justification for prevention-oriented health programs, and for such programs to reach the bulk of the population. The workplace is well suited to offering preventive programs which are capable of reaching large numbers of people. By including efforts to prevent dysfunction and improve health in their services, EAPs can contribute to the nation's effort to mitigate a vast public health problem. And preventive programs which address the behavior/health relationship are far less costly than traditional medical care for sick individuals. Modern-day employers support very costly programs which provide traditional medical treatment for sick employees and their families. Prevention-oriented programs are far less costly. Further, they have the potential, in the long run, for substantial reduction in medical costs for both employers and employees. Effective prevention and health promotion programs are a good investment for businesses. Prevention programs offered by EAPs can prove of major benefit to employers and employees—and for the future as well as the present.

In the past two decades prevention-oriented approaches have been growing in number and variety (Brandt, 1982). They include programs in physical fitness, nutrition and weight control, eliminating smoking, avoiding alcohol and chemical abuse, and accident prevention (Davis, McKay, Eshelman, 1982; Farquhar, 1978). Obviously such programs are intended to have beneficial effects on immediate and long-term physical health. Inevitably effective programs of this sort also foster mental health since good physical functioning is associated with energy, capacity for full and active living, and positive self-concept. Other health promotion programs deal more obviously with mental health issues. These include group psychoeducational and counseling services to individuals suffering from similar disorders (e.g., cardiac disease, diabetes, phobias) or facing similar life crises and major difficulties (e.g., bereavement, serious illness of children, unemployment, job change or retirement) (O'Rourke and Friedman, 1972; Nobel, 1981).

Another focus of mental health promotion programs is development of a wide variety of coping skills. These may be in interpersonal areas (e.g., assertiveness training, parent effectiveness training, developing social skills) or be concerned with intrapsychic functioning (e.g., learning to control thoughts, anxiety and depression (Adkins, 1984; Deffenbacher, Mathis and Michaels, 1979; Mendonca and Seiss, 1976; Davis, McKay, Eshelman, 1982). Albee succinctly puts the rationale for promoting coping capacity: "As coping skills of individuals or groups increase, emotional distress decreases" (Albee, 1982, 1047).

Programs for bringing skills and capacities to high levels also exist. These are intended to enhance creativity, leadership, self-actualization and other components of full and productive living (Schutz, 1979; Green and Green, 1973). Employers have long promoted further education of already skilled, higher level employees. Psychoeducational programs of the sort described fit logically into this effort and can enlarge and enrich it.

Prevention and health promotion programs based on the health/behavior relationship are not entirely or even primarily a province of medical practice. Although there is a growing field of preventive medicine, the American system of health care usually does not come into play until people are sick. Increasing awareness of how behavior, thoughts, and feelings can promote one's physical and mental health, and assisting the individual to take and sustain the required actions, is an extremely difficult task. Developing successful preventive practices based on the behavioral approach requires "all the skills of the behavioral scientist, the social scientist, the social service professional and the educator" (Brandt, 1982, 1040). In order to assess the quality of the health promotion programs being offered by practitioners, EAP staff need to include highly trained professionals in the social and behavioral sciences. Similar training background and theoretical knowledge is needed if EAP staff devise programs for particular health needs of employees in its own setting. To help employees help themselves to better physical and mental health is an objective which an EAP can adopt and implement today from available resources. It is likely to become of larger importance to the EAP of tomorrow. How important will depend not only on allocation of funds but on the value accorded to attempts to reduce emotional and physical disorders and to foster human competence.

NOTES

[1]Selye, Hans. The stress concept: Past, present and future. In Cooper, Cary L., Ed., *Stress Research*, 1983, 1–2.

[2]Stachnik, Thomas J. Priorities for psychology in medical education and health care delivery. *American Psychologist*, 35, 1980, 8.

REFERENCES

Adkins, W.R. (1984). Life skills education. In Larson, D. ed., *Teaching Psychological Skills.* Monterey, CA: Brooks/Cole, 44–68.

Albee, G.W. (1982). Preventing psychopathology and promoting human potential. *American Psychologist*, 37, 1043–1050.

Albee, G.W. & J.M. Joffe, eds. (1977). *Primary Prevention of Psychopathology:* Vol. 1. *The Issues.* Hanover, N.H.: University Press of New England.

Auerbach, A.H. & M. Johnson (1977). Research on the therapist's level of experience. In Gurman, A.S. & A.M. Razin, eds., *Effective Psychotherapy.* New York: Pergamon, 84–102.

Barrett, C.L. & J.H. Wright. (1984). Therapist variables. In Hersen, M., L. Michelson & A.S. Bellak, eds., *Issues in Psychotherapy Research.* New York: Plenum, 361–391.

Bloom, B.L. (1977). *Community Mental Health: A General Introduction.* Monterey, Calif.: Brooks-Cole.

Brandt, E.N. (1982). Prevention policy and practice in the 1980s. *American Psychologist*, 37, 1038–1042.

Brim, O.G., Jr. & C.D. Ryff (1980). On the properties of life events. In Baltes, P.B. &

O.G. Brim, Jr., eds., *Life-span development and behavior* (Vol. 3). New York: Academic Press, 1980.

Cooper, C.L. & J. Marshall. (1976). Occupational sources of stress. *Journal of Occupational Psychology,* 49, 11–28.

Corey, G. (1982). *Theory and Practice of Counseling and Psychotherapy.* (2nd edition). Monterey, CA: Brooks/Cole.

Davis, M., M. McKay & E.R. Eshelman. (1982). *The Relaxation and Stress Reduction Workbook.* Oakland, CA: New Harbinger Publications.

Deffenbacher, J.L., H. Mathis & A.C. Michaels. (1979). Two self-control procedures in the reduction of targeted and nontargeted anxieties. *Journal of Counseling Psychology,* 26, 120–127.

DeLongis, A., J.C. Coyne, G. Dakof, S. Folkman, & R.S. Lazarus. (1982). Relationship of daily hassles, uplifts, and major life events to health status. *Health Psychology,* 1, 119–136.

Dickman, J.F. (1985). Employee assistance programs: History and philosophy. In Dickman, J.F., W.G. Emener, & W.H. Hutchison, Jr., eds. *Counseling the Troubled Person in Industry.* Springfield, Ill.: Charles C Thomas, 7–12.

Dohrenwald, B.S. & B.P. Dohrenwald. (1978). Some issues in research on stressful life events. *Journal of Nervous and Mental Disease,* 166, 7–15.

Farquhar, J.W. (1978). *The American Way of Life Need Not Be Hazardous to Your Health.* New York: W.W. Norton.

Garfield, S.L. & A.E. Bergin. (1986). Introduction and historical overview. In Garfield, S.L. & A.F. Bergin, eds., *Handbook of Psychotherapy and Behavior Change* (3rd edition). New York: John Wiley & Sons.

Green, E. & A. Green. (1973). Regulating our Mind-Body processes. Topeka, Kansas: Research Department, Menninger Foundation.

Haley, J. (1971). Family therapy. *International Journal of Psychiatry,* 9, 233–242.

Jerrell, J. & J.F. Rightmyer. (1985). Evaluating employee assistance programs: A review of methods, outcomes, and future directions. In Dickman, J.F., W.G. Emener & W.H. Hutchison, Jr., eds. *Counseling the Troubled Person in Industry.* Springfield, Ill.: Charles C Thomas, 161–190.

Klerman, G.L., M.W. Weissman, B.J. Rounsaville & E.S. Chevron. (1984). *Interpersonal Psychotherapy of Depression.* New York: Basic Books.

Lazarus, A. (1976). *Multimodal Behavior Therapy.* New York: Springer.

Lazarus, R.S. (1981). The stress and coping paradigm. In Esdorfer, C., D. Cohen, A. Kleinman & P. Marim, eds., *Models for Clinical Psychopathology.* Jamaica, N.Y.: Spectrum.

Matarozzo, J.D. (1982). Behavioral health's challenge to academic, scientific, and professional psychology. *American Psychologist,* 37, 1–14.

McCrae, R.R. (1982). Age differences in the use of coping mechanisms. *Journal of Gerontology,* 37, 454–460.

McGuire, T.G. & L.K. Freseman. (1983). Reimbursement policy and cost-effective mental health care. *American Psychologist,* 38, 935–940.

Mendonca, J.D. & T.F. Seiss. (1976). Counseling for indecisiveness: Problem solving and anxiety-management training. *Journal of Counseling Psychology,* 23, 339–347.

Nobel, M., ed. (1981). *Primary Prevention in Mental Health and Social Work.* New York: Council on Social Work Education.

Olbrisch, M.E. (1977). Psychotherapeutic interventions in physical health: Effectiveness and economic efficiency. *American Psychologist,* 32, 761–777.

O'Rourke, J.F. & H.L. Friedman. (1972). An inter-union preretirement training program. *Industrial Gerontology,* Spring, 49–64.

Patterson, C.H. (1973). *Theories of Counseling and Psychotherapy* (2nd edition). New York: Harper & Row.

Rabkin, J.G. & E.L. Struening. (1976). Life events, stress, and illness. *Science,* 194, 1013–1020.

Schutz, W. (1979). *Profound Simplicity.* New York: Bantam Books.

Selye, H. (1983). The stress concept: Past, present, and future. In Cooper, C.L., ed. *Stress Research: Issues for the Eighties.* New York: John Wiley & Sons, 1–20.

Siegel, A. (1984). Working mothers and their children. *Journal of the American Academy of Child Psychiatry,* 23, 486–488.

Stachnik, T.J. (1980). Priorities for psychology in medical education and health care delivery. *American Psychologist,* 35, 8–15.

PART IV
PROGRAM PLANNING AND EVALUATION

The importance of the synergistic relationship between program planning and evaluation of an employee assistance program cannot be underemphasized. The planning of a program sets the stage for its evaluation, and its evaluation enriches and enhances its planning. Fittingly, it is critical for employee assistance program professionals to be knowledgeable of the basics of program planning and evaluation—especially those special to employee assistance programs.

Emener and Yegidis, in Chapter 13, present and discuss basic foundations and concepts of program planning and evaluation. Moreover, they (a) present six reasons for conducting program evaluations, (b) discuss the cyclical nature of program planning, program evaluation and program refinement, and (c) discuss important aspects of effective utilization of program evaluation results. Following a brief review of the rationale for evaluating employee assistance programs and the importance of it being an integral part of the planning of employee assistance programs, Ligon and Yegidis (in Chapter 14) identify and discuss (a) five types of evaluations of employee assistance programs, and (b) critical issues pertinent to the utilization of evaluations of employee assistance programs. In Chapter 15, Dickman and Emener provide an example of a program evaluation. Importantly, their research evaluation data (e.g., their measures of "consumer satisfaction" and "satisfactoriness") document and verify important employee assistance program ingredients, organizational aspects, and professional service delivery components discussed throughout this book. Emener, in Chapter 16, focuses on the importance of the relationship between service delivery and program evaluation in view of the missions, goals and objectives of an employee assistance program. Moreover, following his brief review of the critical components of program evaluation, Emener also discusses important considerations of the basic nature of service delivery professionals, highlights critical aspects of the interface between professional service delivery and program evaluation, and concludes with recommendations regarding the relevance of these issues in view of the future growth and development of employee assistance programs.

The importance of program planning and evaluation probably is best illustrated in Chapter 13 by Emener and Yegidis, and in Chapter 14 by Ligon and Yegidis. Basically, it is an Aristotilian "If-Then" argument:

- **If,** when people plan a program they do not have specific outcomes or outcome objectives in mind (results);
- **If** they do not consider their expected outcomes to be important (stated goals);
- **If** the outcomes or outcome effects are not discernable (observable or measurable);
- **Then** why have the program in the first place?

It is the assumption of the editors of this book that conclusions to arguments such as this one will compel employee assistance program professionals to continuously strive to enhance their knowledge, skills and expertise in the area of program planning and evaluation.

Chapter 12

PROGRAM PLANNING AND EVALUATION OF EMPLOYEE ASSISTANCE PROGRAMS FOUNDATIONS AND CONCEPTS

WILLIAM G. EMENER AND BONNIE L. YEGIDIS

T he concept of evaluation can easily have different meanings to people. Generally speaking, "evaluation" includes a determination of the relative importance of something, an extent to which a predetermined goal or expectation has been attained, and the relative effectiveness or efficiency of specific activities or sets of activities. When individuals plan a program, they typically consider some entity (e.g., events, people, activities) to be important, they have some preconceived goals or expectations in mind, and they have relative expectations regarding the activities and outcomes of the activities under consideration. For reasons such as these, program planning and program evaluation are interrelated and their relationship to one another is, at times, equally or more important than they are by themselves.

Program evaluation and program planning of any quality, must include a relationship factor—consider, for example, Trantow's (1970) definition of program evaluation:

> Evaluation is essentially an effort to determine what changes occur as the result of a planned program by comparing actual changes (results) with desired changes (stated goals) and by identifying the degree to which the activity (planned program) is responsible for the changes (p. 3).

With some Aristotilian logic, the following "If-Then" argument concretizes the importance of the relationship between program planning and program evaluation:

This chapter is reprinted from *Employee Assistance Programs; A Basic Text* (1988) with permission of the author, the book's editors (Dickman, Emener, & Hutchison, Jr.) and the publisher (Charles C Thomas, Publisher).

183

- **If** when people plan a program they do not have specific outcomes or outcome effects in mind (results);
- **If** they do not consider their expected outcomes to be important (stated goals);
- **If** the outcomes or outcome effects are not discernible (observable or measureable);
- **Then** why have the program in the first place?

Thus, assuming that there are valid answers to this latter question, there are some general reasons for conducting program evaluations; for example:

1. **Vindication.** At times, it is important to collect facts (data) to illustrate and demonstrate that a program is worthwhile. Justifying a program's existence and its continuance can be a very important function (especially if resources are scarce or threatened).
2. **Salesmanship.** It may be desirable to expand or extend parts of a program into new areas. Activities such as these frequently require the convincing of others that expansion or extension is worthwhile, and program evaluation facts (data) can be very useful.
3. **Verification.** In an era of "high accountability," it is not uncommon for people to say, "It's not that I don't trust you, but could you show me some evidence . . . " Verifying worth and impact is important to a program's survival.
4. **Improvement.** In order to improve a program, program leaders typically attempt to minimize a program's weaknesses and maximize a program's strengths. Analyzing facts about a program can not only specify strengths and weaknesses, but also suggest their magnitude and overall impact on program outcomes (results and effects).
5. **Understanding.** Program improvement requires knowledge and understanding of **how** a program works and **why** a program works. Program evaluation activities cannot always totally answer questions such as these, but indeed it can enhance one's understanding of the **how?** and **why?** aspects of a program.
6. **Accountability.** Beyond the genuine commitment to excellence on behalf of a program's leaders, programs are frequently under much pressure to demonstrate effectiveness, "results that show a difference—an impact." Direct funding sources (e.g., governmental bodies, grant agencies) and indirect funders (e.g., taxpayers, insurance companies' premium-paying constituents), insist on hold-

ing programs accountable for producing results. This funding source reality can be responded to in an effective manner if a strong program evaluation component is part of the infrastructure of a program.

There are numerous programmatic interaction effects that also deserve recognition. For example, high quality program planning includes important attributes such as specificity, objectivity, awareness of detail, reality factors, and tempered (realistic) goal setting. Program evaluation facilitates program planners' attention to attributes such as these, and this aspect of program planning has been found to be critical to high quality programs.

Beyond Planning and Evaluation

Good, high quality, efficient and effective programs operationalize the tenet: "Every program should be continually striving for improvement." From a philosophical point of view, it is suggested that while ultimate program improvement is an important aspect of a program, the process of "continuous striving for program improvement" is an important aspect of a program in and of itself. Programs that are remedial, restorative, preventative and/or curative in nature (e.g., rehabilitation programs, employee assistance programs), occasionally suggest that in view of their preventative mission(s), their ultimate goal is to go out of business—viz, to ultimately establish a condition in which there is no longer a need for the program. It is important for such programs to remain cognizant of their "ultimate" goals, and utilize their program evaluation components to drive their program initiatives closer and closer toward their "ultimate" goals.

The Program Planning and Program Evaluation Cycle

There are alternative models of program evaluation. For example, there is the **goal attainment model** which focuses on measuring the extent to which a program achieves the objectives which it set out to achieve; also, there is the **systems analysis approach** which focuses on the extent to which a program's functional organizational units demonstrate their worth in accomplishing the program's objectives. (These two approaches typically are not mutually exclusive—most program evaluation systems designed for a specific program are composed of components of more than one program evaluation model or approach.) Nonetheless, no matter which model or approach, or combinations of models or approaches, is best for a given evaluation program, the assessment procedures must be linked to the program planning. The missions, goals, and objectives of a program are often a result of personal, subjective, philosophical and/or political initiatives. It is usually the case, however, that as program planners translate ambiguous mission, goal and objective statements into functional, operationally defined, and evaluative/measureable entities, resulting program plans gain greater potentials for success. The program planning and program evaluation processes typically follow a pattern of development, and a movement "from the general to the specific."

Program Mission. This is generally a nonspecific yet comprehensive statement regarding the purpose and rationale for the developing and continuing existence of a program. In effect, the program's mission is its **raison d'etre** — an indirect response to the "why?" question of the program's existence.

Program Goals. From the program's mission(s) emerge action statements related to the program's client-, customer- and/or consumer-related activities. While program goals have some attributes similar to a program's mission(s), for example they tend to be related to the program's intentions, they suggest directionality and are not time bound, they are dissimilar in that they can change and usually are responsive to changing program priorities.

Program Objectives. Pivotal to program planning is the determination of program objectives which clearly specify the specific "how's?" and "when's?" of program goal(s) attainment. As opposed to missions and goals, program objectives are specific, concrete, and time-limited. By their nature and character, program objectives are assessment related. Three key attributes of a program's objectives must exist—they must be **observable**, within or over a specific **time frame**, and they must be identified in **measurable** ways.

Overall, a program's mission statement(s), goals and objectives: (a) define the purpose of the program; (b) define the reason for the program's existence; and, (c) indicate how and by when the program's goals will be attained. The next logical part of this consideration of a program is program evaluation.

Program Evaluation. Later in this chapter, some of the alternative ways program evaluation responds to questions regarding a program's mission(s), goals and objectives, will be presented. Importantly, the program evaluation component responds to questions such as: "Is the program doing what it is supposed to be doing?" "Is the program having the effect it is supposed to have?" "Is the program doing what it is doing efficiently and effectively?" With reliable, valid, and objective responses to questions such as these, program planners can then engage in program review, program refinement, and program modification activities.

Thus, the program planning and program evaluation cycle continues— hopefully, it continues in such a way that as time goes on the program continues to improve. This cyclical process is displayed in Figure 1. A fuller and richer appreciation of the importance of program evaluation and its important influences on program planning and program refinement, can be enhanced by understanding the essential questions to be addressed by an evaluation. According to Mayer (1985) these are:

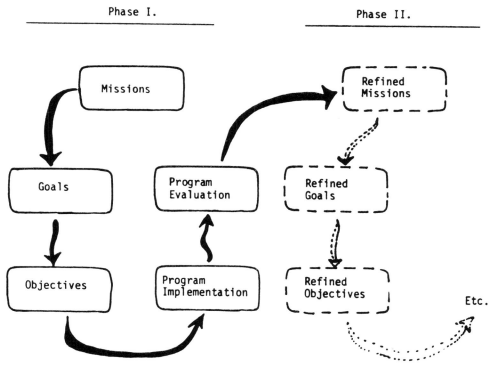

Figure 12-1. The cyclical development of program mission(s), goals, and objectives leading toward program refinement.

1. Was the program implemented as intended?
2. Were the program objectives achieved?

3. Was the program effective?
4. Was the program efficient?

Was the Program Implemented as Intended? This component of evaluation assesses whether a program was implemented according to plan.
This is important because a given operational program may function
very differently than how it was intended to and similarly may bring
about different outcomes than were planned. Therefore, an analysis that
examines the degree of consistency between program plans and actual
program activities is crucial. Evaluating these program plans, inputs and
activities is frequently termed process evaluation. Process evaluation
involves monitoring program inputs, resources, efforts and activities.

Were the Program Objectives Achieved? Key to a program evaluation is
the determination of whether specified program objectives were actually
achieved. A program may affect unintended consequences, but it is the
intended outcomes (objectives) that are of primary interest. This kind of
evaluation is known as outcome or product evaluation. In order to
determine whether program objectives were achieved, evaluators must
develop or locate measures that will tap the program objectives. Suchman
(1967) stated that the kinds of outcomes that may be measured include
knowledge, attitudes, skills, and behaviors.

Perhaps the most direct method of determining whether program
objectives were achieved is to compare before program measures with
after program measures on specific objectives. If the after program
measures reflect a change in the desired direction from the before program measures, then it could be concluded that the program objectives
have been met.

Was the Program Effective? One way to address whether or not a
program was effective is to conceptualize a model of the processes and
results of the program (Van Maaren, 1978). Thus, measuring the objectives of a program (as previously discussed) also provides an assessment
of program effectiveness. This is so because if program objectives were
achieved, then it can be inferred that the program activities brought
about the desired change in the measurement of objectives. This is
tantamount to concluding that the intervention caused the desired change.

In evaluation, we typically determine program effectiveness through
implementing some type of experimental design. The logic of experimental design enables the evaluator to make the kind of conclusions
about the program's effectiveness in which we are most interested. (For a

more indepth discussion of experimental designs, the reader may consult nearly any standard social science research text.)

Was the Program Efficient? The aspect of efficiency taps the relationship of outcome to efforts. Assessing program efficiency requires determining the costs of the program in terms of time, energy, and resources and relating these costs to the program's effects. Essentially, program efficiency is evaluated by cost-benefit or cost-effectiveness analyses, depending upon what types of objectives are the subject of evaluation.

Utilization of Evaluation Results

The Benefits of Program Evaluation

As outlined in an earlier section of this chapter, securing and disseminating evaluation findings is critical for the program planner/evaluator. Evaluation data enable one to demonstrate empirically what the program activities were (verification), what outcomes were achieved and at what costs (accountability). Appropriate utilization of evaluation findings allows one to tune up or modify program activities to improve and enhance program outcomes. Moreover, evaluation data permit planners and administrators to justify continued or enhanced program funding.

The Political Context of Evaluation

There is a political reality to program evaluation, though, that must be understood by planners and researchers. Part of this political context is determined by the nature of the decisions that may be made as a result of the evaluation. Such decisions are basically either: (a) to continue operating the program as planned and implemented; (b) to modify the program or some component of the program; or (c) to terminate the program or one or more of its components. The reality of these alternative decisions may create difficulties among staff members and administrators (the decision-makers), and between the evaluator and various constituent groups.

Additionally, there may be other political issues that the EAP evaluator is not even aware of—for example, the careers and egos of various personnel involved in, or affected by, the evaluation. While there are no cookbook responses on how to deal with these real and potential political issues, they are important considerations for the evaluator. The role of the evaluator, nonetheless, requires one to conduct him/herself in a professional and ethically responsible fashion.

Concluding Comment

Programs, typically, are designed, developed and implemented as a result of individuals' operationalized concern for the common good—for improving the existence and the essence of life for a targeted constituency group. For example, one of the primary reasons why companies and employers will institute employee assistance programs in their organizations and businesses is because they care about their employees and the quality of their lives. They want to be helpful to them. Assuring that program evaluation is an integral part of their programs, from the beginning and throughout, is an excellent way of assuring that their caring about their employees, viz helping them with their problems and difficulties, is what the program is doing. **Reasons such as this should compel us to be sure that our program evaluation components of our EAPs are the best they can be—that way, our EAPs can be the best they can be!**

REFERENCES

Mayer, Robert R. (1985). *Policy and program planning.* A developmental perspective. Englewood Cliffs, NJ: Prentice-Hall, Inc.

Suchman, Edward A. (1967). *Evaluative research.* New York: Russell Sage Foundation.

Trantow, D. (1970). An introduction to evaluation: Program effectiveness and community needs. *Rehabilitation Literature, 31,* 2–9.

Van Maaren, John. (1978). The process of program evaluation. Washington, D.C. National training and development service. The Grantmanship News. Jan.–Feb.

Chapter 13

PROGRAM PLANNING AND EVALUATION OF EMPLOYEE ASSISTANCE PROGRAMS: RATIONALE, TYPES, AND UTILIZATION

JAN LIGON AND BONNIE L. YEGIDIS

It has been reported that since the early 1990s, about 80 percent of organizations having over 250 workers offer employee assistance programs (White, McDuff, Schwartz, Tiegel & Judge, 1996) while 45 percent of all of those employed full-time have access to programs (French, Zarkin & Bray, 1995). Services offered by employee assistance programs (EAP) have greatly expanded from a focus on alcohol problems in the 1950s to providing services for financial problems, wellness programs, and stress management seminars (White et al., 1996).

At the same time, organizations have increasingly moved to managed care models to control and reduce their expenditures on behavioral health care services. In some programs, the EAP now functions as the gatekeeper to other mental health and substance abuse services (White et al., 1996) and large national service providers market both EAP and managed care products (Winegar, 1993). While more expansive information concerning managed behavioral health care is available elsewhere (Corcoran & Vandiver, 1996; Hoyt, 1995), increasing pressures to evaluate both practice (Corcoran & Vandiver, 1996) and programs (Chartier, 1995; Winegar, 1993) prevail.

While the intent of research is primarily to test hypotheses and develop new knowledge, program evaluation has a very different purpose. Program evaluations are charged with determining the worth or value of a program by assessing whether the program was effective or ineffective in reaching "a given action, process, or product" (Isaac & Michael, 1982, p. 2). Evaluations seek to determine if the target population was reached, whether or not the program was effective, and at what cost (Rossi & Freeman, 1993).

Reasons for Evaluating EAPs

1. **Vindication.** It is increasingly important to obtain data which will demonstrate that the EAP is worthwhile. Justifying a program's existence is essential to its continuance.
2. **Marketing.** As EAPs continue to broaden their services, it is important to be able to market the need for expansion in a persuasive and convincing manner.
3. **Verification.** EAPs cannot survive simply on faith that the services are beneficial. Instead, organizations are "calling for cold, hard data" (Landers, 1993, p. 3) to support the need for expending resources for EAPs.
4. **Improvement.** EAPs are subject to "the changing moods of the times" (Rossi & Freeman, 1993, p. 23) so it is important to understand the strengths and weaknesses of the EAP over time. Program evaluations provide input which is useful in modifying services on an ongoing basis.
5. **Understanding.** Evaluations help to provide a better understanding of how and why a program is working and this information may be invaluable when incorporating changes.
6. **Accountability.** Beyond a commitment to excellence on behalf of program leaders, funding sources hold programs accountable for producing results; evaluations can provide that accountability.

Steps in Planning the EAP

EAP planning and program development should begin with a *needs assessment* in order "to identify the requirements of the workforce prior to actually developing and implementing a program" (Csiernik, 1995, p. 26). Csiernik (1995) recommended several sources of information including personal interviews, surveys, and focus groups. Ideally, evaluation consultants should be included in this process unless this expertise is available in-house. It is important to assess all levels and functions of the organization in order that a thorough needs assessment is accomplished.

Next, a comprehensive *mission statement* is written to explicate the purpose and rationale for the development or continuation of the EAP followed by clearly formulating "a detailed and explicit statement of all program *goals* and *objectives* [emphasis added]" in order to "understand the nature of the phenomenon to be evaluated" (Albert, Smythe & Brook, 1985, p. 179). Therefore, from the mission will develop *goals* or action statements related to the EAP's activities followed by objectives which specify how the goals will be obtained. Program *objectives* should be specific, concrete, time-limited, and attainable. It is important that each objective can be observed and measured, and can occur within a specific period of time.

Finally, both the costs and outcome variables of the EAP are identified. French, Zarkin and Bray (1995) noted that both direct costs (personnel, supplies, contractors' fees, and office expenses) and indirect costs (office space and shared facilities or equipment) must be included to determine true costs of the EAP program. While EAP programs differ greatly, the authors identify a number of outcome variables which are frequently used including absenteeism, health care costs, workplace accidents, job performance, and numbers of grievances. Yamatani (1993) stressed the desirability to also include such intangible benefits as changes in worker attitudes and interpersonal relationships at work and home. It is important to secure both the sources of needed data and the support of those involved in providing the data prior to the EAPs implementation.

Types of EAP Evaluations

Because EAP evaluations will vary as much as the programs themselves, evaluators and program administrators may select from a combination of evaluation methods (Csiernik, 1995; French et al., 1995; Yamatani, 1993). The following examples, while not exhaustive, describe several approaches while potential obstacles are also noted which may be helpful in planning evaluations that will avoid the barriers indicated.

1. **Input evaluations** have been described by Csiernik (1995) as an internal method "that is of value in charting the evolution and development of an EAP" (p. 30) and consists of a simple audit "that takes an inventory of resources an EAP was intended to have and compares the list with those features the program actually has" (p. 28). This method is helpful in providing early information and no barriers are indicated.
2. **Utilization evaluations** provide programs with data concerning who is using what services and to what extent. For example,

White, et al. (1996) found that their EAP utilization rate increased from 5 percent to 12 percent in two years following the addition of staff, outreach efforts, and an off-site location. Such data are also helpful in determining if the target populations of the program have been reached and whether different aspects of the EAP are over or underutilized. A potential barrier is lack of access to data due to employee confidentiality which is easily remedied by coding data to eliminate any identifying information.

3. **Satisfaction evaluations** go beyond which services were utilized to a determination of the level of satisfaction employees have with the services received. The Client Satisfaction Questionnaire (Larsen, Attkisson, Hargreaves & Nguyen, 1979) is a brief, well-established instrument which has been used to measure satisfaction with EAP services (Ligon, 1996). There are other relevant short review instruments available to measure client satisfaction as well. Difficulty obtaining completed instruments is a potential barrier and can be addressed through the assurance of anonymity, by eliminating any personal identification, and by providing a secure method of collection such as a reply envelope mailed to an off-site address.

4. **Outcome evaluations** assess to what degree the EAP impacted the outcome variables identified at the onset of the program such as the level of absenteeism, the number of grievances filed and the number of workplace accidents. The primary obstacle to conducting outcome evaluations is the inability to obtain data which often crosses numerous organizational units as well as securing data from external resources (such as health insurance providers).

5. **Cost-benefit evaluations** are the most commonly published studies concerning EAPs (Csiernik, 1995; French, Zarkin & Bray, 1995; Yamatani, 1993) and involve summing the program's cost, determining savings to the organization on all outcome measures, then calculating a ratio of the costs to the benefits to reflect the "costworthiness" (Chartier, 1995, p. 18) of the program. Barriers to cost-benefit analyses include difficulty in determining costs and savings. Also, these studies often cover a relatively short timeframe while savings from some costs, such as health care, may not be evident for a longer period of time.

Utilization of Evaluation Results

The Benefits of Program Evaluation

As addressed earlier in this chapter, securing and disseminating evaluation findings is critical for the program planners and administrators. The obtained data can enable one to demonstrate empirically what the program activities were (verification), what outcomes were achieved and at what costs (accountability) to various stakeholders. Evaluation findings provide valuable input for use in the modification of program activities to improve and enhance the EAP. Moreover, evaluation data permit planners and administrators to justify continued or enhanced program funding.

The Political Context of EAP Evaluation

There is a political reality to EAP evaluation which must be recognized by both evaluators and administrators. EAPs involve many stakeholders within an organization (administration, finance, human resources, EAP staff, employees, etc.) and conflicting agendas are common. While Csiernik (1995) acknowledged that EAPs "actually do save companies some unspecified dollar amounts" (p. 32), French et al. (1995) noted that "many EAP evaluations tend to be in-house promotional efforts" (p. 453).

Albert et al. (1985) offered several suggestions that may facilitate the planning and evaluation of EAPs despite the complex political and organizational influences. First, "all of the different interest groups upon whom EAP activities may impinge" (p. 180) should be involved in determining program outcomes. Second, it is essential, during the planning and implementation stages, that goals and objectives are clear, specific, and realistic. Finally, evaluations should incorporate a team approach with all stakeholder groups to assure that "all of these relevant perspectives are employed" (p. 180).

CONCLUSION

Organizations implement employee assistance programs because they care about their employees and the quality of their lives. Employers are compelled to be sure that their EAPs are the best they can be and program evaluations play a critical role in making this determination. As EAPs continue to expand and broaden their scope, the demand by organizations for solid program evaluations will no doubt continue to increase. While the future of EAPs looks very bright, there is no greater assurance of their continued value than the ongoing evaluation, modification, and improvement of programs.

REFERENCES

Albert, W.C., Smythe, P.C., & Brook, R.C. (1985). An evaluator's perspective on employee assistance programs. *Evaluation and Program Planning, 8,* 175–182.

Chartier, B. (1995). EAP 2000: Leaders look at factors influencing EAPs in the year 2000 and beyond. *EAP Digest, 16*(1), 16–21.

Corcoran, K., & Vandiver, V. (1996). *Maneuvering the maze of managed care.* New York: Free Press.

Csiernik, R. (1995). A review of research methods used to examine employee assistance program delivery options. *Evaluation and Program Planning, 18,* 25–36.

French, M.T., Zarkin, G.A., & Bray, J.W. (1995). A methodology for evaluating the costs and benefits of employee assistance programs. *Journal of Drug Issues, 25,* 451–470.

Hoyt, M.F. (1995). *Brief therapy and managed care.* San Francisco: Jossey-Bass.

Isaac, S., & Michael, M.B. (1982). *Handbook in research and evaluation.* San Diego: Edits.

Landers, S. (1994). Managed care's challenge: 'Show me!' *NASW News,* September, 1994. Washington, DC: National Association of Social Workers.

Larsen, D.L., Atkisson, C.C., Hargreaves, W.A., & Nguyen, T.D. (1979). Assessment of client/patient satisfaction: Development of a general scale. *Evaluation and Program Planning, 6,* 211–236.

Ligon, J. (1996). Client satisfaction with brief therapy. *EAP Digest, 16*(5), 30–31.

Rossi, P.H., & Freeman, H.E. (1993). *Evaluation: A systematic approach* (5th ed.). Newbury Park, CA: Sage.

White, R.K., McDuff, D.R., Schwartz, R.P., Tiegal, S.A., & Judge, C.P. (1996). New developments in employee assistance programs. *Psychiatric Services, 47,* 387–391.

Winegar, N. (1993). Managed mental health care: Implications for administrators and managers of community-based agencies. *Families in Society, 74,* 171–177.

Yamatani, H. (1993). Suggested top ten evaluations for employee assistance programs: An overview. *Employee Assistance Quarterly, 9,* 65–82.

Chapter 14

EMPLOYEE ASSISTANCE PROGRAMS: BASIC CONCEPTS, ATTRIBUTES AND AN EVALUATION

FRED DICKMAN AND WILLIAM G. EMENER

Responding to Employee Problems and Their Effects on Industry

Over the past decade, Employee Assistance Programs (EAPs) in the United States have increased significantly in their quantity and importance to major industries. For example, Land[1] recently stated, "There are over 4,000 employee assistance programs in the U.S." Over half of the largest 500 industries in the United States currently have EAPs, over 5,500 American industries have EAPs and the Association of Labor and Management Administrators and Consultants (ALMACA) currently has 2,200 members.[2,3] Thus, it would appear that American industries are positively responding to their employees' problems and the effects these problems have on industry.

The EAP concept is rapidly expanding from an occupational alcoholism program concept to an EAP concept, which includes response to other problems of employees—including both psychological and physical difficulties known to impede overall productivity and hinder human well-being. Most EAPs today offer a variety of services for everything from marital problems to financial difficulties. The core of the current movement, as well as the largest part of the daily casework, is rooted in problem identification, intervention, treatment, and recovery.

Specific problems dealt with include depression, substance abuse, anxiety, domestic trauma, financial problems and psychiatric/medical problems. EAPs take into account the financial effects these problems can have on the company, plus "human cost factors" (loss of job, dignity,

This chapter is reprinted from *Counseling the Troubled Person in Industry* (1985) with permission of the author, the book's editors (Dickman, Emener, and Hutchison, Jr.) and the publisher (Charles C Thomas, Publisher).

197

family and sense of worth). Thus, it is not surprising that the EAP philosophy being adopted by industry embraces the tenet that workers, families, and the company all benefit by early identification and remediation of problems.

Vital Elements

The critical attributes of an EAP are central to its programmatic philosophy which was articulated by Busch: "An employee's personal problems are private **unless** they cause the employee's job performance to decline and deteriorate. When that happens, the personal problems become a matter of concern for the company. A trained employee is valuable and represents an asset to be protected if possible."[8]

Recent literature describing EAPs has addressed the key ingredients of a successful EAP. For example: "The most common ingredients, characterizing more than 75 percent of the programs in 1979, were assurance of confidentiality, written policy, written procedures and health insurance coverage for both inpatient and outpatient treatment of alcohol problems. A second set of ingredients was found in about 60 percent of the programs: management orientation, supervisory training, employee education and at least one full-time staff member."[5]

A General Motors study concluded that a program should have at least one full-time professional. Programs with such a person(s) "saw more clients with a greater variety of problems, dealt with more of the problems themselves and made more contacts relevant to the program than did programs with part-time staff only."[6] A review of related literature and the authors' experience strongly indicates 10 attributes of an EAP are critical for success:

1. **Management backing:** without it at the highest level, key ingredients and overall effect are seriously limited.
2. **Labor support:** the EAP cannot be meaningful if it is not backed by the employees' labor unit.
3. **Confidentiality:** anonymity and trust are crucial if employees are to use an EAP.
4. **Easy access:** for maximum use and benefit.
5. **Supervisor training:** is crucial to employees needing understanding and support during receipt of assistance.
6. **Labor steward training:** occasionally assistance alternatives are costly and insurance support is a must.

7. **Insurance involvement:** occasionally assistance alternatives are costly and insurance support is a must.
8. **Breadth of service components:** availability of assistance for a wide variety of problems (e.g., alcohol, family, personal, financial, grief, medical, etc.).
9. **Professional leadership:** from a skilled professional with expertise in helping. This person must have credibility in the eyes of the employee.
10. **Follow-up and evaluation:** to measure program effectiveness and overall improvement.

The specific importance of these 10 critical attributes as well as others, was experienced in the development and conduct of the EAP at Anheuser-Busch in Tampa, Florida.

EAP in Practice

In March 1979, Anheuser-Busch contracted with the Tampa Bay Neuropsychiatric Institute (then South Florida Mental Health Associates) to coordinate and implement its EAP in Tampa, Florida. EAP service was extended to all employees of the Tampa Brewery (about 350 employees), regular employees of Busch Gardens (about 350 employees) and their families.

The Tampa EAP office is not staffed with Anheuser-Busch employees, but is separate from both corporate management and labor. Moreover, a specific EAP coordinator and a medical director were designated to facilitate communication between the EAP, the company, and labor officials. Managerial supervision of the Tampa EAP office comes from the corporate EAP office in St. Louis through the Newark, NJ, Anheuser-Busch EAP. In essence, Anheuser-Busch uses corporate EAP professionals and contracted noncorporate EAP professionals to manage and supervise the entire corporate EAP program (52 sites).

The Tampa EAP office includes a variety of professionals: five psychiatrists, two clinical psychologists, two counseling psychologists, two clinical social workers, three rehabilitation counselors, two psychiatric nurses and support personnel. In addition, it has a 20-bed alcoholism treatment unit with accompanying qualified personnel. These trained professionals are of both genders. They include recovering alcoholics with long-term sobriety; generalists; and specialists in various aspects of alcoholism, marriage and family counseling, pain rehabilitation, child and adolescent therapy, etc. The professionals provide a vast resource for EAP referrals, since the Anheuser-Busch Program is "broad-brush." Thus the coordinator has the option to refer within or without the Tampa EAP office.

In addition to counseling and rehabilitative responsibility, the Tampa EAP coordinator consults with managers, supervisors, labor authorities and labor stewards. He participates in supervisor training and has free access to the company premises to make contacts and make presentations on the EAP. He enjoys the enthusiastic support of corporate and local management and labor leadership, all of which publicize the program throughout the workplace and in employees' homes via mailouts. This three-way cooperation between management, labor and the EAP office seems to ensure full participation; at the same time, absolute confidentiality is maintained.

Participation is encouraged by liberal company financial support. The first three diagnostic/evaluative visits are paid for by the company, then the company health insurance covers 80 percent of all outpatient costs and most hospital expenses. Separate colored insurance forms are sent directly to the insurance company so that no local insurance clerks can know who participates, thus safeguarding confidentiality.

In general the Anheuser-Busch EAP vigorously attempts to uphold all principles known to be vital to successful company programs, both corporately and locally. With this overall mission in mind, the following evaluation was conducted.

Evaluating the Program

Satisfaction estimates were determined by an **ex post facto** survey of the Anheuser-Busch, Tampa EAP participants who participated in the program over a 26-month period (March 1979 through May 1981). Endorsements of the survey were obtained from the company and the EAP staff. In August 1981, each of the 148 participants who participated in the program during the 26-month period were sent a cover letter confidentially soliciting their participation: a specifically-designed employee assistance program follow-up questionnaire; and a postage-paid self-addressed envelope. Of the 148 mailouts, 13 were returned "address unknown"; of the remaining 135, 45 usable returns were received for a 33.3 percent return rate. Frequencies, percentages, and measure of central tendency on the questionnaire data are displayed in Figure 1.

Results. As can be seen in Figure 14-1, analyses of the respondents' reported demographics reveal: (1) they ranged in age from 11 to 57; (b)

Part I. Demographic

1. *Age:* R = 11 − 57; x̄ = 38.48; sd = 12.34

2. *Highest grade in school completed:*

	f	%
1. elementary school	1	2
2. junior high school	—	—
3. some high school	4	9
4. high school graduate	14	31
5. some college	15	33
6. college graduate	8	18
7. graduate school	2	4
missing information	1	2
Total	45	99

3. *Sex:*

1. male	17	38
2. female	28	62
Total	45	100

4. Were you working at the time you came to the Employee Assistance Program?

1. yes	39	87
2. no	6	13
Total	45	100

5. If yes, what was your job title: _____

6. For what reason(s) did you seek assistance from the Employee Assistance Program—that is, what problem(s) or difficulty(s) did you have?

	f*	%
1. personal problem (e.g., depressed, nervous)	20	35
2. alcoholism (e.g., excessive drinking)	6	11
3. family or marital problem	24	43
4. other	6	11
Total	56	100

*seven responded with more than one answer indicating multiple reasons . . .

7. In your own words, how would you describe what your problem or difficulty was? _____

8. Was your problem or difficulty affecting your job (your ability to do your job)?

1	2	3	4	5	missing info	Total
no	probably no	maybe yes maybe no not sure	probably yes	yes		

f	11	5	7	9	11	2	45
%	24%	11%	16%	20%	24%	4%	99%

9. What services did you receive from the Employee Assistance Program?

	f*	%
1. medical evaluation	3	4
2. medical treatment	4	5
3. psychological evaluation (testing)	16	21
4. individual counseling	38	50
5. group counseling	9	12
6. referral to another program or service	5	6
7. other (explain)	—	—
missing info.	1	1%
Total	76	99

*seventeen responded with more than one answer indicating multiple services.

Part II. Evaluation

Scale used for items 10–13:

	1	2	3	4	5	missing info	Total
	no	probably no	maybe yes maybe no not sure	probably yes	yes		

10. Did you find the people you saw (doctors, psychologists) helpful to you?

	1	2	3	4	5	missing info	Total
f	1	2	3	8	31		45
%	2%	4%	7%	18%	69%		100%

11. In terms of confidentiality, did you feel that you could trust the people you saw?

	1	2	3	4	5	missing info	Total
f	1	—	2	4	37	1	45
%	2%	—	4%	9%	62%	2%	99%

12. If there had been no Employee Assistance Program like your company's, would you have sought assistance on your own?

	1	2	3	4	5	missing info	Total
f	7	14	12	5	7		45
%	15%	31%	27%	11%	15%		99%

13. If you knew of someone else (e.g., a fellow employee) who was having a problem or difficulty, would you recommend that they seek help from the Employee Assistance Program:

	1	2	3	4	5	missing info	Total

f	1	—	—	6	38	45
%	2%			13%	84%	99%

F14-1. Participants' (N = 45) Evaluations of an Employee Assistance Program

31 percent were high school graduates, 33 percent attended some college and 18 percent were college graduates; (c) there were more females (62%) than males (38%); (d) 87 percent were working when they sought assistance from EAP; (e) they sought assistance mostly for family or marital (43%) or personal (35%) problems; (f) 44 percent indicated their problems or difficulties were affecting their job; and (g) they received individual counseling (50%), psychological evaluation (21%) and/or group counseling (12%).

The respondents' reported evaluations of the EAP indicated that: 87 percent found the people they saw (doctors, psychologists) helpful; 91 percent felt they could trust the people they saw; almost half (46%) would not have or probably would not have sought assistance on their own if there hadn't been an EAP; and if they knew a fellow employee with a problem or difficulty, 84 percent would or probably would (13 percent) recommend they seek help from the EAP.

An estimate on how satisfactory the programs were was determined by conducting interviews with four individuals directly involved in the conduct and support of the Anheuser-Busch, Tampa, EAP. Their testimonial statements, in response to the question, "What is your evaluation of the EAP?" were as follows:

1. Frank R. Logan; Director of Personnel, Busch Gardens. "I feel the EAP offers the employee a new option to solving both work problems and personal problems that affect the job. In today's work environment stress is more prevalent than ever. The EAP helps us solve some of the employees' problems that we as employers helped to create."

2. William C. Bennett, Assistant Industrial Relations Manager, Plant Personnel Supervisor, Director of Plant Safety. "I've been able to witness some marked improvement in work performance in several persons known to be in the program. I've seen a change in the character and work performance of the many people I know who have used the EAP. It (the program) is a great benefit to the employees and the company in my opinion."

3. Fred J. Tarza, Plant Manager, Anheuser-Busch Brewery. "The EAP is a very valuable option in handling cases where job performance is involved. I've heard employees say it is the most valuable benefit the company offers."

4. Jimmy Dunlap, Business Agent, Teamsters and Brewer's Local No. 338. "At first some of our members were cautious but now the union is totally behind the program. A lot of our people and their families have been helped."

Overall Success

The responding participants seemed satisfied with the assistance they received. While it was hoped that a larger return rate would have been received, the extent to which the indices of satisfaction as indicated by the respondents was representative of the nonrespondents' is unknown. Nonetheless, the respondents' evaluations endorsed the key ingredients of an EAP:

1. **Confidentiality.** The respondents indicated satisfaction with this factor of the EAP. No EAP can expect to be worthwhile unless the individual anonymity of each participant and his family is protected.

2. **Referral.** It is crucial to an EAP that participants are willing to refer fellow employees when assistance is needed. Fellow employees are the best advocates of an EAP.

3. **Early Intervention.** The participants' evaluations validated the hypothesis that an industrial milieu is most suitable for each intervention into employees' mental, social, emotional, and substance abuse problems (among others).

4. **Effects on Job Performance.** The participants' responses strongly suggested employees are aware of the extent to which personal/social problems affect their job performance. Thus, the philosophical tenets of an EAP are substantiated—vis, when an industry helps its employees with their "personal" problems, the industry is ultimately helping itself.

5. **Problem Resolution.** It was refreshing to see that the EAP, designed and operated as described herein with the discussed critical attributes, was helpful to the participants and it actually assisted them in resolving their problems.

The indices of satisfactoriness demonstrated that if an EAP is designed and conducted properly, mutual benefits are realized by management (company officials) and labor (e.g., union officials). The importance of company and labor support is obvious.

Recommendations

Based on the outcomes of this project, it is recommended that the continuing development of EAPs in American industries would be enriched by:

1. Continuing evaluation components such as the areas in this project (e.g., measures of satisfaction).
2. An expansion of research methodologies to include pretest and postmeasures and other indices of effectiveness (e.g., supervisory ratings, absenteeism, safety records, productivity, etc.).
3. Differential evaluations of the critical attributes of an EAP to further document their importance.

In conclusion, it would seem fitting to assume that this study documented the importance, value and effectiveness of an employee assistance program. It could be suggested that everyone wins—the employee, the company and labor (e.g., the union). The essence of this conclusion is captured in an evaluative testimonial solicited from William H. Bohlinger, Director of Industrial Relations, Owens-Illinois, Inc., Glass Container Division, Lakeland, FL: "The EAP gives us more flexibility in dealing with problems which I believe industry used to cover up. People in industry have problems like everyone else and this new option is welcomed."

REFERENCES

1. Land, T. Global strategy: Confronting alcoholism at the workplace, *Alcoholism,* 1981, *1*(6), 41–42.
2. Roman, P.M. From employee alcoholism to employee assistance. *Journal of Studies on Alcohol,* 1981a, *42*(3), 244–272.
3. Land's (1981) estimation that there are over 4,000 Employee Assistance Programs and Roman's (1981a) estimation that over 5,500 American industries currently have an EAP, is accountable by the fact that some EAP's serve more than one industry.
4. Busch, E.J. Developing an employee assistance program, *Personnel Journal,* 1981, *60*(9), 708–711.
5. Roman, P.M. Corporate pacesetters making EAP progress, *Alcoholism,* 1981b, *1*(4), 37–41.

The authors thank Anheuser-Busch, Tampa EAP participants who returned the satisfaction questionnaires. Furthermore, the assistance and support from Frank Logan, Bill Bennett, Fred Tarza, Jimmy Dunlap and Bill Bohlinger was crucial to the conduct and outcome of this study. Also acknowledged is Thomas L. Porter, professor at Auburn University.

Chapter 15

SERVICE DELIVERY: IMPLICATIONS FOR THE UTILIZATION OF PROGRAM EVALUATION INFORMATION

WILLIAM G. EMENER

A s reflected throughout this book and other professional literature on employee assistance programs, pivotal to the efficiency and effectiveness of an employee assistance program (EAP) is the quality of its service delivery. In effect, programs, buildings, and policy manuals don't help people—**people help people.** Nonetheless, EAPs are purposeful, they have identified missions, purposes, and objectives. And as discussed in Chapter 19 of this book, program evaluation is a powerful program component that, if utilized to its fullest potential, can assure a program's attainment of its stated missions, purposes and objectives. Likewise, human service delivery professionals who work in EAPs (e.g., counselors, psychologists, social workers) have missions, purposes, and objectives in their efforts of helping employees (clients) who come to them for assistance. In Chapter 22 of this book, Cox discusses the importance of the relationship between managerial style and program evaluation in view of the missions, purposes, and objectives of an EAP. Toward similar ends, this chapter will focus on the importance of the relationship between service delivery and program evaluation in view of the missions, purposes, and objectives of an EAP. Specifically, this chapter will: (a) briefly review the critical components of program evaluation; (b) discuss important considerations regarding the basic nature of service delivery professionals; (c) highlight important aspects of the interface between professional service delivery and program evaluation; and (d) conclude with recommendations regarding the relevance of these issues in view of the future growth and development of employee assistance programs.

This chapter is reprinted from *Employee Assistance Programs; A Basic Text* (1988) with permission of the author, the book's editors (Dickman, Emener, & Hutchison, Jr.) and the publisher (Charles C Thomas, Publisher).

206

Critical Components of Program Evaluation

The importance of program evaluation to an employee assistance program is discussed by Emener and Yegidis in Chapter 19 of this text. They highlight six major reasons for conducting program evaluations: (a) vindication; (b) salesmanship; (c) verification; (d) improvement; (e) understanding; and (f) accountability. Moreover, in their presentation of the "cyclical nature" of program development and program evaluation, they demonstrate how program evaluation can enhance the refinement and enrichment of a program's future missions, purposes, and objectives. Toward outcome effects such as these, Emener and Yegidis (in Chapter 19) demonstrate how program evaluation is an extremely viable mechanism by which, as suggested by Mayer (1985), answers to important questions can be sought (such as: Was the program implemented as intended? Were the program objectives achieved? Was the program effective? Was the program efficient?) These issues are extremely important to the service delivery component of an employee assistance program. First, the service delivery professionals in an EAP, as an extension of their professionalism, are concerned about these same issues and want answers to these questions themselves. Second, they constitute a valuable source of information in the ultimate determination of answers to these program evaluation questions. And third, they many times are in the best positions to identify relevant and appropriate program modification responses to less than desirable program-evaluation-outcome-answers to questions such as these. Thus, for reasons such as these above three and as will be discussed later in this chapter, the service delivery professionals in an EAP should be an integral part of an EAP's program evaluation.

A Look at the Basic Nature of Service Delivery Professionals

As articulated earlier in this chapter (as well as throughout this book), the critical and most important services of an employee assistance program are provided by professionals. Professionals, by their very nature, have numerous characteristics and attributes that render them as unique types of members of a workforce. Likewise, employee assistance programs have numerous characteristics that render them as unique work environments. The "special" aspect of these two sets of unique attributes is that they are meaningfully divergent in numerous definable ways. For example, Emener (1978) discussed specific ways in which the unique features of state vocational rehabilitation agencies and the unique features of professionals working within them are discernably divergent: "With the existance of numerous conflicting and ambiguous goals, and antithetical principles and values, the professional is many times confronted with making choices between commitments to professional expectations and the organization of the agency (Goldner & Ritti, 1967; Scott, 1966)." (p. 167) The following is designed to illustrate some of the divergencies unique to an employee assistance program and the professionals working in them.

1. **Goals.** One of the goals of an employee assistance program is to get nonworking employees back to work and increase the efficiency and effectiveness of less-than-productive employees. Fittingly, it is not uncommon for an employee assistance program to emphasize and highlight outcome measures such as these. Commensurately, it is not uncommon for an employee assistance program to suggest that all employees who come to it for assistance receive "the same" high quality services. Uniformity, or at least perceived uniformity, can be very important to an EAP's perceived value and worth. On the other hand, human service professionals (e.g., counselors, social workers, psychologists) tend to operationalize a client-centered, holistic philosophy (e.g., every client is unique and should receive uniquely tailored services), and their genuine concern for the overall well-being of the individual as a person (i.e., not just an employee) can extend beyond the primary service-delivery-outcome-goals espoused by the program. Furthermore, there may be understandable pressure on the professionals to keep up with their case recording and documentation job tasks (e.g., "doing their paperwork") while the professionals are more concerned with working with their clients and performing their employee-contact job tasks (e.g., "doing counseling with their clients"). It is also important to note that discrepancies in expectations, perceptions and job roles such as these meaningfully can contribute to professional role strain and professional burnout (Emener, Luck & Gohs, 1982).

2. **Occupational Rewards.** As with most human service bureaucracies, the occupational rewards provided to employees who work in employee assistance programs tend to be salary (raises), promotion, prestige, and job stability. These are understandably important to employees. Nonetheless, professionals also tend to cherish professional and occupational autonomy; their sense of "autonomous functioning" is very important to

them. Thus, it is not uncommon for professionals to report that the greatest rewards that they get out of their work do not come from their employer per se, but from the intrinsic rewards from doing their jobs and the nature of the work environment in which they are able to work "as professionals."

3. **Occupational Punishments.** Somewhat similar to those phenomena above (in section 2), human service bureaucracies have understandable occupational punishments, for example: low merit increases (salary raises), lack of promotion, low recognition, loss of job, and required mobility or transfer. Professionals, on the other hand, tend to focus on additional occupational punishments consistant with their being professionals: perceived failure or feared failure in their working with their clients, and disrespect for their professional integrity. Occupational punishments such as these can be very potent to a professional, and in many ways they are not directly connected to the built-in occupational punishments of an employee assistance program (at least not in terms of the program's operating policies and procedures).

4. **Locus of Control.** As mentioned earlier, an employee assistance program understandably will make many efforts to provide high quality services to its clientele in a uniform, consistent, and similar manner. This is consistent with good program planning, management, and accountability. Nonetheless, as Friedson (1977) fittingly stated: "Virtually all writers, expertise and professions are equated with a flexible, creative, and equalitarian way of organizing work, while bureaucracy is associated with rigidity, and mechanical and authoritarian ways" (p. 429). Thus, while an employee assistance program may prefer that its professionals respond "externally" to the conformity and uniformity oriented guidelines and stated procedures of the program, its professionals may tend to prefer to respond "internally" to their own individual and professionally derived guidelines and procedures for working with their clients. It is not uncommon to hear a professional say, "I'm a professional—don't try to tell me how to do my job."

5. **Principles and Guidelines.** In most employee assistance programs, there are policies and procedures, rules and regulations, and formal and informal mandates and expectations regarding the work behaviors of the employees who work in them. Professionals typically are very aware of them. Nonetheless, professionals also have learned knowledge bases, values, and specific codes of ethical conduct (e.g., from their professional training) that strongly influence their work behavior. It is not all that

rare for a situation to arise in which there is a discrepancy between the guidelines of the program and the guidelines eminating from a professional's professional training and background.

6. **Targets of Attention.** In order for an employee assistance program to maintain ongoing and accurate record keeping and accountability measures, it is important for the professionals working within the program to keep their records, files, case notes, and their "paperwork" up to date. This is time consuming. And when a professional simultaneously senses a real need to spend his or her time seeing clients, role ambiguity and role strain sets in and the professional has to make a decision. It is not uncommon for a professional to assert, "I'll see my clients first and do my paperwork later.", while his or her supervisor is urging him or her to get their paperwork done. From a more generalized perspective, Hasenfeld and English (1977), in discussing the self-directing aspects of professionals working within a bureaucracy, suggested that an occupational group is in trouble " . . . if it cannot control the production and particularly the application of knowledge and skill to the work it performs" (p. 432).

Thus, as illustrated by the above six areas of examples, it is understandably expected that the nature of employee assistance programs and the nature of the professionals working within them will produce numerous operational divergencies and discrepancies. Fittingly, the existance of these characteristics and attributes has numerous important implications for the program evaluation of an EAP and the services it provides to its clientele.

The Interface Between Professional
Service Delivery and Program Evaluation

It is important for employee assistance programs and the professionals working within them: (a) to understand the nature of these above identified divergencies; (b) to think of them as being "good for the program" (e.g., they provide a helpful system of checks and balances); and (c) to seriously discuss and consider them in the planning, implementation, and evaluation of the program. It also is important to remember that these identifiable, understandable and potentially beneficial divergencies do exist and will inevitably surface. Fittingly, it simply makes sense to build them into the infrastructure of the program from the beginning. Importantly, this ultimately will allow the program evaluation component of the program to minimize the potential inflammatory nature of these divergencies and facilitate their potentially helpful contributions to the program's efficiency and effectiveness. For example, when an employee assistance program's planners, administrators and managers, program evaluators, and representatives from the program's professional staff who will be delivering the services to its clientele collectively and cooperatively plan, implement, and evaluate the program, there will be fewer times in which these discrepancies will be destructive and more times in which they will be helpful to the program. It can be very beneficial for all of these individuals to "walk through the program" and address questions such as: "What do I do when . . . ?", "What will happen when . . . ?", and, "If I encounter a situation in which the program's guidelines say . . . and the code of ethics for my profession says . . . , how should I handle it—what should I do in that situation?" Processing questions like these can also lead to upfront, preventative, program modification(s) which can prevent and/or minimize possible (or even inevitable) conflicts later on.

When program evaluation data are being collected and subsequently analyzed, the program then must consider what the data mean and if there is any need for program modification. When the professional staff are involved in such processes, very useful and helpful reality testing can take place. Moreover, the chances for truth being known are much greater. For example, one time when the author had an opportunity to experience a process such as this, the staff of an EAP were reviewing program evaluation data and focusing on the results of a client satisfaction questionnaire which had been sent out to former clients of the program. A literal translation of the data would have suggested that the clients (employees) merely were saying that they had solved their own problems. This could have promoted concern as to why the program needed (highly paid) counselors, psychologists, and social workers. The ensuing discussion, however, revealed that most of the professional staff, in practice, operationalized a "client-centered philosophy" in their work with clients (e.g., facilitating the client's solving his or her own problems), and as such, the data actually were a compliment to the quality of the professional services the clients had received (as opposed to an indictment of the need for their existence). Fortunately, this philosophical orientation was addressed in the description of the program's services from the beginning (an example of good planning); also, this explanation was included in the interpretation of the data in the program evaluation report (an example of good program evaluation reporting). Importantly, this highlighted the criticalness of having had professional service deliverers involved throughout. This kind of synergistic relationship among the program's basic components and the entire staff of the EAP is extremely important.

Another important reason for having an EAP's professional staff intricately involved in the program's evaluation is that the evaluation data provide concrete evidence of the benefits of the staff's efforts and hard work. As discussed earlier, many of the occupational rewards that professionals experience as being meaningful is the feeling that they are really being helpful to people who are in need of help. It is not uncommon for professionals to be so caught up in day-to-day job tasks and duties that they wonder if all of their hard work is making any difference. It sort of goes along with the "who cares?" kinds of emotions. Fittingly, it can be very rewarding for a professional to review program evaluation data and see, in a more global manner, the difference that he or she is accounting for. Likewise, program evaluation data meaningfully can assist a professional in evaluating and possibly modifying their professional services. For example, if program evaluation data reveal that certain services are more helpful than others, or if the way in which certain services are offered is more helpful than others, the professional accordingly can take such feedback into consideration as he or she continues to serve clients.

There are numerous ways in which program evaluation can facilitate high quality services to clients; likewise, involvement on behalf of professional service deliverers can enhance the value and worth of an EAP's program evaluation to the EAP. In a nutshell, meaningful involvement throughout is the key!

Recommendations for the Future of EAPs and the Interface of Professionals and Program Evaluation

All indicators relevant to the future of employee assistance programs in the United States provide compelling evidence that EAPs will continue to develop, grow and flourish (Dickman, Emener & Hutchison, 1985). Business and industry has enjoyed its operationalized caring philosophy—companies and businesses like the idea of being helpful to their employees. Moreover, the utilitarian benefits of having an employee assistance program also has added to this growing trend. For example, Dickman and Phillips (1985) stated:

> Although most companies have yet to realize the benefits of a fully functioning EAP, in companies where data on program cost effectiveness is kept, the least return is $3. back for each one dollar spent. One company reported a $17. return on one dollar of EAP funding (Fetterolf, 1983). (p. 264)

It would also appear that the current trend of addressing "the whole person" in health care services (Hollman, 1981), will continue to be the underlying genre of employee assistance programs (Emener & Dickman, 1983).

The variety of "whole person" services will continue to focus on aspects of addiction, alcoholism, stress, physical wellness, and mental and emotional wellness. Specifically in regard to this latter foci area, mental and emotional wellness, Dickman and Phillips (1985) identified eight areas of EAP service delivery that are expected to receive specialized and increased attention in the future: (a) Communications Skills Training; (b) Assertiveness Training; (c) Parenting; (d) Retirement Preparation; (e) Sexuality and Changing Sex Roles; (f) Loss and Death; (g) Victim Assistance; and, (h) Day Care (p. 263–264). The implications of these continuing developments of "specialized" service delivery areas in employee assistance programs are critical to the future of program evaluation in EAPs and the importance of professional service deliverers' involvement in such activities.

First, employee assistance programs will be wise to conduct **special service needs assessments** in order to predict the kinds of specialized professional services that their clients (employees) will be needing. This is good planning.

Second, employee assistance programs will be offering a widening variety of human services which will require **multifaceted program planning, implementation and evaluation.** Fittingly, EAPs will be employing the use of specialized professionals (e.g., child development specialists, sex therapists, gerontologists, etc.) in order to provide specialized services.

And **third, the program evaluation components of EAPs in the future will need to be multifaceted.** This, in turn, will add additional importance to the finite understanding and appreciation of the specialized program evaluation aspects of future EAPs "specialized service delivery" components (such as, for example, the eight whole-person, wellness areas discussed by Dickman & Phillips, 1985).

In conclusion, it assuredly would appear that employee assistance programs of the future will be providing a widening variety of services and utilizing a widening variety of professionals to provide such services. Commensurately, the program evaluation components of EAPs in the future will be multifaceted and necessitate enhanced synergy and coordination. The active involvement of service delivery professionals in the planning, implementation, and program evaluation aspects of EAPs in the future will be more critical and important than ever before.

REFERENCES

Dickman, J.F., Emener, W.G., & Hutchison, W.S. (1985). *Counseling the troubled person in industry.* Springfield, IL: Charles C Thomas, Publisher.

Dickman, F., & Phillips, E.A. (1985). Employee assistance programs: Future perspectives. In J.F. Dickman, W.G. Emener, & W.S. Hutchison (Eds.), *Counseling the troubled person in industry.* Springfield, IL: Charles C Thomas, Publisher.

Emener, W.G. (1978). Reconciling personal and professional values with agency goals and processes. *Journal of Rehabilitation Administration, 2*(4), 166–173.

Emener, W.G., & Dickman, F. (1983). Corporate caring: EAPs solve personal problems for business benefits. *Management World, 12*(1), 36–38.

Emener, W.G., Luck, R.S., & Gohs, F.X. (1982). A theoretical investigation of the construct burnout. *Journal of Rehabilitation Administration, 6*(4), 188–196.

Fetterolf, C.F. (1983). Acceptance remarks upon presentation of Ross Von Wiegand Award at the 12th Annual Meeting of ALMACA. *The Almacan, 13*(10), 6–7.

Freidson, E. (1977). Dominant professions, bureaucracy, and client services. In Y. Hasenfeld & R.A. English (Eds.), *Human service organizations.* Ann Arbor, MI: The University of Michigan Press.

Goldner, F.H., & Ritti, R.R. (1967). Professionalization as career immobility. *American Journal of Sociology, 72,* 489–502.

Hasenfeld, Y., & English, R.A. (Eds.) (1977). *Human service organizations.* Ann Arbor, MI: The University of Michigan Press.

Hollman, R.W. (1981). Beyond contemporary employee assistance programs. *Personnel Administrator, 26*(9), 37–41.

Mayer, R.R. (1985). *Policy and program planning: A developmental perspective.* Englewood Cliffs, NJ: Prentice-Hall.

Scott, W.R. (1966). Professional in bureaucracies—areas of conflict. In H.M. Vollmer & D.L. Mills (Eds.), *Professionalization.* Englewood Cliffs, NJ: Prentice-Hall.

PART V
PROFESSIONAL AND PARAPROFESSIONAL
TRAINING AND DEVELOPMENT

Human resource development (HRD) is a major philosophical underpinning of employee assistance and wellness programming. Nadler (1979) defined human resource development as a series of organized activities conducted within a specified period of time and designed to produce behavioral change. Further, for a HRD activity to exist, each individual participant must feel that the intended activities and overall outcomes are for his or her benefit and the activities must be organized with predetermined process and outcome goals (Nadler, 1979).

The five chapters in this section provide specific knowledge about HRD as a field of practice within organizations and how HRD relates to employee assistance and wellness programs. Chapter 16 by Dickman provides definitions of terms central to HRD practice such as Performance Appraisal Systems, affirmative action, OSHA, and discusses these terms and their relationship to unionized and nonunionized organizations, employee benefits, training and career development, and health and wellness. In his Comment/Update to Chapter 16, "Human Resources and the EAP: A H.R. Practitioner's Perspective," Evans highlights six critical issues related to modern day human resources and employee assistance programs: (1) the decline of unionism; (2) workers compensation/rehabilitation; (3) the Americans with Disabilities Act of 1990; (4) the Family Medical Leave Act of 1993; (5) health and wellness programs; and (6) violence in the workplace.

In Chapter 17, Emener defines HRD and elaborates on the three primary forms of HRD activities: (1) education; (2) training; and (3) development. The chapter concludes with a discussion of how these activities are translated as an "integral aspect of the infrastructure and the overall working environment of an employee assistance program."

Dahlhauser, Dickman, Emener, and Yegidis, in Chapter 18, illustrate how the need for knowledge can be transformed into HRD activities. As an example, their chapter discusses how counselors need information about alcohol and chemical dependency to become effective counselors. Furthermore, they illustrate how this knowledge can be transmitted through HRD activities within an organization including preservice, inservice, and academically-based education, training and development programs.

Continuing the theme of "application aspects of HRD activities," Emener, in Chapter 19, briefly discusses critical issues regarding educational preparation for employee assistance careers. Drawing from proposed ALMACA guidelines, he provides a framework that can guide both curriculum development in colleges and universities as well as individuals who wish to assess their current knowledge and skill and plan continuing education career development activities in the EAP and wellness field.

Chapter 20 concludes this part, and in it Wright and Norris discuss the application of HRD activities to paraprofessionals and support personnel who work in EAP and wellness settings. This perspective demonstrates both the pervasiveness of the HRD philosophy in EAP and wellness as well as elaborating on the criticalness of a team approach to EAP and wellness service delivery.

Chapter 16

HUMAN RESOURCES:
BASIC DEFINITIONS AND CONCEPTS
FOR THE EAP PROFESSIONALS

FRED DICKMAN

Introduction

The purpose of this chapter is to present basic human resources definitions and concepts to the EAP professional. There is no attempt to cover the vast array of knowledge pertaining to the complexity of human resources. As a matter of fact such would be not only a volume, but volumes, in itself. Neither does the chapter attempt to acquaint the EAP professional with personnel complexities however desirable that would be. Yet the basic rudiments of personnel issues and concepts do require the attention of EAP persons at all levels of endeavor. For instance, clients do get involved with EEO and affirmative action. The EAP assessor/counselor needs to be acquainted with these offices and endeavors within the government agency or corporation. Also he will see persons on workmen's compensation and who may be in some phase of rehabilitation. Just what does this involve and what is the process? The same would follow for ERISA, or COBRA, or OSHA. Just what is a policy of commitment to fair treatment? And what is the company's process of action where sexual harassment is alleged?

Undoubtably a professional with an EAP relationship with a company will have much to do with the department of human resources. It is the hope of the authors that a brief sketch of important personnel concepts and definitions will be of assistance.

This chapter is reprinted from *Employee Assistance Programs; A Basic Text* (1988) with permission of the author, the book's editors (Dickman, Emener, & Hutchison, Jr.) and the publisher (Charles C Thomas, Publisher).

Demographics

The Demographics (mix) of the workforce in most organizations is multifaceted.

Factors which need to be considered when evaluating new programs are age, sex, ethnic background, current income level and socioeconomic background. When these factors are complied and graphically displayed, then informed decisions can be made as to the method of program implementation.

Performance Appraisal Systems

Performance appraisal systems, although known by many names, are all intended to accomplish one goal. That is, to inform employees of their performance as it relates to the objectives of the organization. These appraisals may be as informal as a periodic conversational exchange between supervisor and subordinate relating to achievements and/or deficiencies or as complex as the completion of a multifactor rating form, a lengthy feedback session, and an ultimate performance rating. Many companies base salary adjustments on this rating, others use it strictly as a communication tool. No matter what technique is used, the purpose of performance review is to guide the employee toward becoming a more effective and productive member of the organization.

EEO and Affirmative Action

Companies employing fifteen or more employees and/or doing business with federal, state, or local government agencies are required to comply with federal guidelines for hiring, promoting, and discharging employees. These guidelines take into consideration race, sex, age, religion, handicap, and veteran status.

Major employers must develop and adhere to an affirmative action plan which provides, among other things, goals and timetables for attaining parity between the workforce and the community.

Most business organizations have recognized this as being a civic responsibility and companies that elect to disregard affirmative action are subject to loss of contracts and costly litigation.

Workers Compensation/Rehabilitation

All states through their Labor Departments administer an insurance program designed to protect workers that are injured on the job, or while carrying work-related duties. The extent of such coverage is specifically prescribed in the statutes of the state and each state is different in terms of payment for lost wages, fees schedules for doctors and hospitals and dollar values for permanent disability ratings. This insurance is provided to the employees at no charge. The company, unless self-insured, pays a premium to the state, based on past claims experience and the "level of risk" for that particular job. Workers whose injury precludes their returning to the same or a similar job are often times sent to rehabilitative training to provide new skills with which to earn a living. The cost of this training in most states is covered by the workers compensation insurance program.

ERISA/COBRA

The Employee Retirement Income Security Act (ERISA) is the federal agency that regulates pension funds, profit sharing plans and other contributory and noncontributory company sponsored savings plans.

This agency was formed in 1974 to prevent risky or sometimes even unscrupulous investments of the employees' pension fund money.

ERISA requires that detailed explanations on the status of these various plans is provided periodically to all participants. Once a plan is approved as ERISA qualified, no changes can be made without first obtaining additional approval.

COBRA

The Consolidated Omnibus Reconciliation Act of 1986 was formed during the Reagan administration in an effort to reduce the cost of social services. This act requires that employers that provide health insurance to their employees offer this insurance to resigning employees for an additional eighteen months and thirty-six months for employees who are discharged.

The employee must, however, bear the entire cost of the insurance, not just the contributory amount, plus a 2 percent administrative charge payable to the company.

OSHA

The Occupational Safety & Health Act of 1970 is a federal act intended to formulate and enforce standards that provide for a safe working environment for employees in private industry.

Annual reports are provided to this agency providing the statistical information on the number of accidents, the degree of seriousness and the number of lost time days due to employee accidents. OSHA publishes standards and codes which must be complied with and periodic inspection of worksites are conducted by this company.

Failure to comply with OSHA regulations can result in monetary fines or the closing of the worksite.

Supervision

The key individual in the attainment of the organization's goals is the first-line or front-line supervisor. This person in the link connects organizational management with employees that actually do the job. It should go without saying that the success of any new program or policy rests solely on the support of these supervisors.

Union and Nonunion Operations

The private sector workforce is either represented by a labor union or operated on a nonunion basis.

This section is not intended to discuss the pros and cons of either, but, only to demonstrate how each functions.

Union Shop

The employees in this situation are covered by a collective bargaining agreement, generally referred to as a contract. This contract generally spells out wages, type of work to be accomplished, hours to be worked and grievance procedures.

The employees are represented by a labor union and officials of that union negotiate with company management on behalf of the rank and file employees for increased wages and improved working conditions. Employees covered by this contract typically pay monthly dues which are used to fund the administration of the union.

One important aspect of the collective bargaining agreement, is the grievance procedure. Although this process varies with each contract, the intent is basically the same. The grievance procedure provides a step by step process that is used to settle employee complaints. The complaints vary but the most common relate to work being performed by an individual in an unauthorized classification or by a nonunion employee and disagreement with disciplinary measures.

Generally, a union shop steward will represent the employee to management and typically grievances are heard at the first line supervisors level, then to general foremen and last at the plant or location managers level.

If efforts to resolve the grievances are unsuccessful, the final decision can be made by a federal arbitrator. These individuals are appointed on the basis of their labor relations experience and their decisions in grievances are final and binding.

Nonunion Shop

If it is the objective of the company to maintain a union free organization, then the management must operate in a similar manner to that of a union organization. Supervisor here again is key in communicating the organization philosophy. Supervisors must maintain an equitable and fair application of the company's rules and regulations.

The two main issues that are generally associated with a union organizing campaign are job security and consistent treatment of employees. In order to deal with these issues, it is necessary to establish a process for appeal. This allows employees who feel that they were mistreated to discuss the issue with management. Another tool that is used in a nonunion environment is the periodic performance appraisal. This is the means by which an employee learns how management feels about the kind of job that he does.

Generally the supervisor evaluates the performance over the past period, reinforcing the positive achievements and coaches the employee on methods to improve weaknesses. Often a plan is established for future performance by setting measurable objectives.

The use of the performance appraisal can sometimes help to avoid disciplinary action by pointing out potential trouble areas. However, if it is necessary to take disciplinary action, this should be done in an objective, professional and well planned manner. Rules should be clearly stated so that they are easily understandable. The most important aspect of disciplinary action is that it is applied the same for all employees.

Employee Benefits

Employee benefits are generally thought of as nonmonetary compensation, as the value does not show up on the paycheck. There are however, costs associated with these benefits and management takes these costs into consideration when developing or adjusting the compensation package. The range of benefits varies according to the organization. Generally included in the "Fringe benefit" package are:

a. Medical insurance coverage sometimes including dental and vision coverage. This benefit can be given free to the employees or a payroll deducted premium can be charged.
b. Vacation, usually the amount of time is based upon years of service with the company.
c. Holidays, these are days that are paid but usually not worked by the employee.

Other benefits that are available in some organizations are: tuition reimbursement, free meals, free uniforms, stock purchase plan, pension, and profit-sharing plans.

Training and Career Development

Basic orientation and "on-the-job" training is usually a division of the Personnel department. Depending on the complexities of the organization, these training programs can be very structured or casual in nature.

Successful training programs equip individuals to perform specific functions. Results of such a program can be measured and modification made if the objectives are not met.

More sophisticated programs are developed to assist the employee in achieving his/her goals in the organizations. It should be noted that an honest evaluation be made and stated to individuals who have unrealistic ambitions. This approach, though sometimes uncomfortable, will help to avoid frustration and long term disgruntled employees.

Safety and Security

Although these two topics appear dissimilar at first glance, they are not so far apart in their interaction. Safety is a must for any organization. Depending on the type of the organization, the need for safety can vary. An active program with good participation at all levels can make a big difference on any company profit margin, not to mention how one views the company. On the other hand, you can give security the same connotation. A strong safety and security program can maintain employees at a level of fitness that is conducive to the goals of the organization. Screening is accomplished at all stages of employment by utilizing both safety and security techniques.

Health and Wellness

An out-clinic probably coins this concept, "Be Your Best." To be at your best, one must be fit both mentally and physically. This can be accomplished through nutrition and exercise programs.

These programs have demonstrated savings in insurance costs, lost work days due to illness and better productivity. (Also see Chapters 5 and 6 on Wellness.)

Conclusion

EAP professionals have constant contact with departments of Human Resources. Indeed most "in-house" (See Chapters 7 & 10) programs are organized within these departments. And while a major thrust of this goal is EAP "separateness," close cooperation with Human Resources is absolutely a necessity.

HUMAN RESOURCES AND THE EAP:
AN H.R. PRACTITIONER'S PERSPECTIVE

Mark W. Evans

The chapter previously written by Fred Dickman entitled, "HUMAN RESOURCES: BASIC DEFINITIONS AND CONCEPTS FOR THE EAP PROFESSIONAL" captured the essence on how the Human Resources function had evolved and how those significant changes impacted the role of the EAP in organizations. The notions Dr. Dickman discussed concerning the interface between the HR function and the various facets of its role are as true today as ever. Since that writing, a number of cultural and legal changes have occurred which have created significant challenges for the Human Resources and EAP professionals alike. As we explore these in this "update," it will become apparent that while the world of Human Resources and EAP professionals has become increasingly more complex in recent years, the opportunities to have a significant and positive affect on the organizations they serve has never been greater.

The Decline of Unionism

Companies continue to deal with union issues, although in some industry sectors unionism among employees has in fact declined, leaving employees in the position of having to trust the company to fill the role they once entrusted to their union leadership. The company was portrayed as the "adversary" and was not to be trusted. How, then, is the employee going to be heard when a real-life problem enters his or her life? Can the company be trusted to handle their concern with compassion, respect and dignity? This dilemma offers a real opportunity for the forward-thinking organization to provide professional EAP assistance to help build and maintain trust through confidentiality and respect for the individual.

Workers Compensation/Rehabilitation

The injured worker is supported by most companies with Workers Compensation insurance and in many cases, company-sponsored health insurance and disability income protection benefits in some form. While the employee usually has some measure of financial protection for these events, there can be a strong sense of a loss of self-worth the longer a person is unable to contribute due to their injuries. How does an injured employee "get back into the habit" of working, rather than being nonproductive? It may have taken weeks or months to "get out of the habit" of coming to work every day. In some cases, the relationship between the company and its employee can be strained depending on the nature and reasons for the injury. The EAP can be effectively used to help recovering employees prepare for their return to work with confidence and healthy anticipation rather than with fear and apprehension.

The Americans With Disabilities Act of 1990

This law was enacted to attempt to prevent people from feeling the effects of discrimination due to their disability status. Employers with 25 or more employees must comply with the law by adopting nondiscriminatory hiring practices and providing a "reasonable accommodation" to a person with a disabling condition so they can perform the "essential functions" of the job they are hired to perform.

In this act, there are strict definitions of what constitutes a "disability" and what practices and recordkeeping procedures must be implemented to comply with the ADA. For example, employers may not ask questions which are designed to ferret out or determine the extent of a real or perceived disability during the hiring process. Only after the offer of employment is made can a company use such means as a fitness-for-duty physical exam to determine suitability for employment in the position the employee has just been offered. Once evidence of a disabling condition is learned, whether by self-disclosure by the employee or through other means initiated by the company, the company is bound to explore the notion of what "reasonable accommodation" might be appropriate under the circumstances.

A job offer may not be rescinded until the evidence shows that it is due to "business necessity" or if the disability poses a "severe threat to the health or safety of others." As with many employment laws, the burden of proof lies solely on the company if challenged. The penalties for noncompliance or discrimination can be severe, and employee plaintiffs are entitled to a jury trial. It will be many years before the law is well-defined and will undoubtedly be the fertile ground for many lawsuits.

Employees with disabilities have legal protection which enables them to become productive members of society without discrimination by the company who hires them. How does an employee who has a disabling condition deal with the reality that will confront him or her on the shop floor? Laws cannot legislate employee perceptions of those who are, or who appear to be different from themselves. Employees with physical, mental or emotional conditions may be treated differently by many who do not have compassion or understanding for their plight. In these situations, the EAP counselor can intervene once the problem surfaces and help both the employee and the company understand the moral and legal implications of their behavior. The EAP can serve to assist the company by counseling employees affected by the presence of the disabled person in the work place to promote some measure of understanding and tolerance.

The human resource department is responsible for ensuring compliance with the ADA and similar laws in most companies, and it does so through training and education to employees and management as to the law and their respective rights and responsibilities under it. The EAP counselor who is connected to the efforts made by HR to educate and inform employees, as well as the corporate culture they are surviving in will be better equipped to deal with ADA issues in the work place when they surface.

Family and Medical Leave Act of 1993

This law has been said to be one of the most far-reaching and least-understood laws in employee relations by both employees and management. It is one of the most complex and difficult to administer and comply with for most companies. In some cases, companies are still learning how to fully comply with its mandates.

The goal of the Family and Medical Leave Act is basically simple — employees who experience certain life events and may need (or elect) some time away from work may request unpaid leave time. If the request meets FMLA criteria, the company must grant unpaid leave time and must preserve the employee's job, pay and benefit status until the leave period ends and the employee has returned to work. An employee may request up to twelve weeks of unpaid leave in a twelve-month period according to the rules and policies set up by the company in compliance with FMLA.

In the past, a female employee who was pregnant and gave birth to a child was considered to be "temporarily disabled" and was granted time off (often with some pay) to give birth and recover from the rigors of childbirth in order to return ready to work. What if she was not ready emotionally to leave the new baby with others? What if there are no others ready and willing to care for the child? Asking for more time off was sometimes looked upon unfavorably by many companies. She either returned to work or faced the possibility of losing her job.

What about the male employee (father) who wants, or may need some time off to help care for the mother, baby or other family members? What about the employee who must take off work to take care of a seriously ill child? Or perhaps a seriously ill parent? Many companies took a dim view of granting an employee more than a few days off without running a risk of having his future employment in possible jeopardy. This is not to say that companies were not compassionate toward their employees. In the practical world of deadlines, production quotas and customer demands, a company is forced into making hard choices in order to accomplish their mission. Employees who are not at work when they could be are hindering the ability of the company to meet its obligations.

The Family and Medical Leave Act addresses all of these potential situations and gives direction as to how the company and employees must handle them when they arise. The rules are complete with detailed forms, procedures, etc., to hopefully prevent abuse or disparate treatment by either the employee or the company.

Human Resource professionals know that while the law can be seen as a restrictive one, the reality seems to be that very few employees actually take unfair advantage of the FMLA law. They see it as a "safety net" if something bad happens to them and they need to take some time off. They know they will not be "fired" indiscriminately based on their need to take care of family concerns or serious medical conditions. In most cases, an employee cannot financially afford to take 12 weeks of unpaid time away from work every year. It is also likely that the need to take this much time off from work may not present itself every year.

While it can be debated as to whether the law addresses all concerns of all parties in its application, FMLA gives the EAP counselor a powerful tool, which if used appropriately, can help preserve and balance an employee's home and work life. If and when the need arises, however, an astute EAP professional can intervene to help the employee solve such a problem and suggest the use of FMLA leave when appropriate.

Health and Wellness Programs

Many larger companies have adopted the notion that employees who have more healthy lifestyles will live longer, be more productive employees and cost their employers less in terms of absenteeism, utilization of benefits, and fewer debilitating injuries. They were among the first to implement "wellness" programs offering encouragement, and in some cases, direct incentives to achieve a more healthy state by making lifestyle changes. The literature is full of stories about companies who have reduced their costs and improved their performance through the use of such programs.

But how does a smaller company with limited resources get involved? Smaller companies can get the same positive effects and potential cost savings that are available to the larger entities, but the costs of implementation may outweigh the benefits in the near term. What can the EAP professional do to help?

Most HR practitioners know that employees with hypertension; those who may be overweight, those who do not get enough exercise; those who smoke; or those who may have substance abuse problems, put their companies at significant financial risk, not to mention the risks to their own personal health. If they believed that they could provide support through a cost-effective effort to create positive change, many would be interested and would work to convince their executive management of the benefits of such a program and would seek their support to develop. This is where the EAP counselor could make a significant and long-lasting contribution to the future success of the enterprise.

An EAP counselor has access to an array of literature and educational materials concerning healthy lifestyles. In addition to dealing directly with employees who may have individual lifestyle concerns, a low-cost approach may be the sharing of such information with groups of employees at "wellness meetings" during or after work hours. Some companies offer such meetings during the normal lunch break.

Another tool that can be effectively used is the "health risk appraisal," an instrument which allows an employee to answer a series of lifestyle questions and have their "health risk" measured and plotted in light of their answers to the lifestyle questions. EAP professionals have access to such tools and knowing the culture of the organization can recommend various methods to communicate wellness information in an effective manner. While near-term results are hard to measure, there is no denying the long-term benefits in human terms from making positive changes in ones health and life.

Violence in the Workplace

While some may argue that the news media has made us somewhat immune to violence these days, the thought that we cannot feel safe where we live or work is foreign to many of us. Recent accounts of violence in the workplace have struck a fearful note with employees, HR professionals and managers at all levels alike. The thought of someone attempting to settle a dispute through violent means within the framework of the workplace can be unsettling at best, or downright scary at worst. What can we do to protect ourselves from such violence? How far do we responsibly go to protect employees from potential danger while remaining focused on our business objectives? Progressive companies have a resource in the EAP professional if they choose to take advantage of it.

What is the profile of the potentially violent person? Most HR practitioners, company managers, supervisors and employees do not know. Even if they know what to look for, they may not know what to do if confronted with the situation. Many companies are responding by establishing policies to address these issues. A policy is only as effective as the manner in which it is carried out. People must be trained to know when and how to act in such situations. The EAP counselor can assist in helping company officials understand the profile of the potentially violent person and what may drive them to this level. The counselor may recommend other resources at his or her disposal to assist in this training effort for the company. The organization should take full advantage of any information it can give to its employees so they can effectively act to protect themselves and their fellow employees from potential harm due to such violent behavior.

Conclusion

Most Human Resource professionals understand that there are direct benefits to having a work force that has achieved a higher level of balance between their personal lives and their work lives. They understand that obvious work-related problems can be symptoms of other problems occurring outside the workplace, perhaps much more serious in nature. They also understand that these employees can be rehabilitated through proactive intervention by Employee Assistance Programs and the professionals who run them.

One of the important roles that the EAP counselor should assume should be that of "management trainer" in behavior-related issues. The EAP counselor must work in tandem with the HR practitioners in recognizing when an employee may be "out of balance" by the obvious (or perhaps not too obvious) behaviors displayed. They must work together to effectively use the current laws and other tools at their disposal to allow the employee to learn to bring their lives back into balance. Recognizing the legal, moral and ethical boundaries that must be maintained between HR and EAP professionals, the more they can work together to resolve such problems in the early stages, the more effective they can be. In the business world, one of the measures of success is effectiveness.

Chapter 17

HUMAN RESOURCE DEVELOPMENT IN EMPLOYEE ASSISTANCE PROGRAMMING: AN OVERVIEW

WILLIAM G. EMENER

Important and critical to the concept, **Human Resource Development**, is Prather's (1970) observation: "When I outgrow my names and facts and theories, or when reality leaves them behind, I become dead if I don't go on to new ways of seeing things." Commensurate with this philosophical observation, Stephens and Kneipp (1981) stated, "We can consciously manage only that which we can perceive. If our perception of the world is limited, our ability to conceptualize and choose among alternative courses of action will be even more limited" (p. 87). It is generally agreed that the world and people are constantly changing; interestingly, it has been observed that in the past decade the most observable form of change has been the spiraling rate of change. People, especially those working in employee assistance programs, must remain appreciative of the constantly changing nature of the world and commensurately the constantly changing nature of experience. People are constantly involved in refining their perceptions and the interpretations they give to their experiences (Hultman, 1979). For those individuals working in employee assistance programs, perception of what is possible and the ability to go beyond what was once considered expected, acceptable, and preferred, is directly related to one's capacity for intellectual, emotional, and functional growth. One of the major goals of employee assistance programs is to assist individuals (employees) in maximizing their ability to grow—to become what they are potentially capable of becoming. It would appear fitting to assume that a helper's capacity to help another person grow is related to the extent to which he or she is

This chapter is reprinted from *Employee Assistance Programs; A Basic Text* (1988) with permission of the author, the book's editors (Dickman, Emener, & Hutchison, Jr.) and the publisher (Charles C Thomas, Publisher).

231

growing. If this is true, then it equally would make sense to assume that by systematically expanding our perception of the world and adding to our repertoire of knowledges, skills, and abilities (as a function of our lifestyles), our potential ability to meaningfully contribute to the lives of others and the programs in which we work will be realized. Basically, this represents the **a priori** rationale for the importance of having a "human resource development philosophy" meaningfully built into the infrastructure of employee assistance programming. Commensurately, this chapter will: (a) discuss the concepts of education, training and development; (b) concretize the importance of a human resource development component of employee assistance programming; and, (c) conclude with extensional and futuristic suggestions for the overall development of employee assistance programs with a focus on the continuing development of the personnel working in them.

Education, Training and Development

Tantamount to appreciating the ways in which a "human resource development philosophy" can be an integral part of the infrastructure of employee assistance programming, is the understanding of how this philosophy impacts the connotations and denotations of education, training and development for employee assistance program personnel. For example, the phrases, "We need trained staff" and "Our staff needs inservice training" frequently implies the traditional conceptualization of training. "Training" literally means the act or process of directing or forming, typically by instruction, formal discipline and/or drill. Implicit to the acts of formal discipline and drill is the implication that the recipient engages in a passive role and the provider engages in an active role. The "trainer" trains the "trainee." Human beings, however, tend to unfold and change gradually; moreover, their attitudes toward themselves and toward change play an integral role in their ultimate learning and potential change. People have even been known to resist training — for a number of understandable reasons. People tend to not like being treated like a "trainee." As one trainee stated to this author during an inservice training session, "I'm not a seal or a lion you know. Just because my boss made me come here and I am here, that doesn't mean that I will benefit from the program!" Obviously, this person's boss's attitude toward training and staff development had an important impact on this person's overall benefit (nonbenefit) from the program.

As developed by Nadler (1979), "human resource development" is a series of organized activities conducted within a specified period of time; importantly, it is designed to produce behavioral change. Two key ingredients, however, must exist; (a) the individual must feel that the intended activities and overall outcomes are for his or her benefit (along with the fact that the activities and outcomes are also intended to benefit the program and the program's clientele); and (b) the activities must be organized with predetermined specific processes and outcome goals. If there are no specific outcome goals of a human resource development program, or if there are no expected behavior changes, then it would appear reasonable to question the existence of the human resource development program in the first place. It is important to remember that when planning human resource development activities for employee assistance personnel, the releasing and maximizing of human potential is the ultimate goal, and outcome goals should be thought of in terms of behavior change.

The following three primary forms of human resource development activities will be discussed in order to demonstrate the influence of the "human resource development philosophy" and also relate them to human resource development in areas relevant to employee assistance programs.

1. **Education** includes those learning activities designed to increase and enhance the individual's overall learning and human potential over time. For example, a preservice education program for employee assistance professionals should be designed to prepare students for a **career** in employee assistance programming not just a specific job in an employee assistance program. This career orientation is an important attribute of a human resource development program that is educational in nature. Whereas training will typically focus on the needs of the employer, the program or the company, education focuses on the needs of the learner. Education is less concerned with maximizing compliance, uniformity and sameness among personnel; education is concerned with individuality, diversity, and future ability to function autonomously. By focusing on more generalized knowledges, skills and abilities, education also prepares an individual to be able to cope, adapt, and adjust to a variety of situations, settings, and circumstances. A counselor working in an employee assistance program enrolled in a business management course at a university, is a good example of continuing education from a human resource development perspective. Such a course would appropriately

involve theory (a general orientation); skill development aspects of the course for this individual would be future, career oriented (he or she is currently a counselor and could understandably be considering an upward mobility opportunity as a program manager or program director).

2. **Training** typically involves activities designed to assist an individual in improving a specific job task or set of job tasks. For example, a secretary-receptionist employed in an employee assistance program may attend an inservice training program on bookkeeping and filing. As this clearly indicates, such a program would be expected to enhance his or her bookkeeping and filing job tasks. Training also entails the connotative notion of minimizing individual differences among staff and enhancing uniformity. While the counselors working in an employee assistance program may work differently with their clients, which from a clinical perspective is very understandable, it would appear very important for the program's clerical staff to do their bookkeeping and filing in a very similar manner. Quite frequently program maintenance and accountability functions such as these have to be uniform for overall program efficiency purposes. Nonetheless, attributes of training programs such as these should be explained to employees prior to their participating in training programs so that their individual feelings (e.g., such as feelings emanating from their need to be considered unique individuals) do not detract from nor minimize their overall benefits from the training program.

3. **Development** is typically directed toward the future and may include education and/or training. A key element of "development" is the possible element of risk on behalf of the organization, the company or the program. Basically, development activities are designed to move the organization and the employees toward the future, toward new directions and frontiers, and toward the development of possible new program developments and activities. The risk factor emanates from the realization that such future possibilities could entail change, and as most people have experienced, change can be very scary. Nonetheless, it is very wise for employee assistance programs to assure that "development" is an ongoing part of their programs of operation. Nadler (1979) poignantly described the importance of development to an organization:

> As individuals seek to grow on jobs, they need a legitimate and available mechanism for growth and development. If the organization does not provide it, they will either take their creativity and potential off the job or leave the job. (p. 96)

Consistent with the underpinnings of human resource development addressed at the beginning of this chapter, the assumption herein is that human beings not only appreciate and value growth and development as a person, but they will seek it out if it is not available in their environment.

Concluding Comments

An excellent article by This (1980) addressed eight critical issues facing managers in the 1980s. Three of them are very relevant to the importance of assuring that "development" is an integral aspect of the infrastructure and the overall working environment of an employee assistance program. **First,** all the numerous issues regarding the constantly changing worker values and motivation are critical to highly intensive work environments. Employee assistance programs tend to be highly intensive in nature, and it is not uncommon for the employees (clients) seeking assistance from an employee assistance program to be working in a high intensive work environment themselves. As the world changes around us, as people who seek our assistance are amid constant changes, it only seems fitting for us to experience change and development ourselves and continually seek out ways to help our employee assistance programs to be maximally responsive to such changes. **Second,** quality definition, quality assurance and quality control have become increasingly important to human service programs in the past decade. And, there are many good reasons for this. Nonetheless, if the personnel of an employee assistance program perceive their organization from a "growth and development" perspective, there is a lesser likelihood that they will be resistant to change and more apt to be aware of growth and development needs and potentials on behalf of the organization. As one director of an employee assistance program once said to this author, "My only concern about the growth and development and improvement of our program, is being able to support all of the good ideas for improvement that I am constantly getting from my staff. They seem to always be looking for ways to improve our organization!" (That is a good concern to have!) **Third,** it is not uncommon for employee assistance programs to have more work to do than they have the time and the staff to do it with. Increasing the resources available to the program is typically easier said than done. Thus, in a resource stabilization mode, program efficiency and effectiveness can really become strained. When the personnel of a program are vigilant of potential ways of growing and expanding, they also tend to be vigilant of ways of enhancing the efficiency and effectiveness of currently existing program components and resources. People in a growth and development-oriented environment, tempered with a genuine appreciation for reality, can be very creative in discerning ways of doing more and doing better with what they have (as well as thinking about what else they could be doing if increased resources were available).

As addressed by Knowles (1980), we are no longer thinking of staff development in the traditional ways of having someone other than the employee deciding what the employee needs, hiring a trainer to didactically tell the employee what he or she needs to know and learn, and then expecting the employee to passively participate and learn, grow, benefit from and enjoy the experience. Our tasks as administrators, managers, supervisors, and human resource development specialists in employee assistance programs, are: (a) to assure that our employees working in our programs experience an internalized desire to develop and grow to their fullest; (b) to help them feel good about themselves when they sense that there may be ways that they could improve themselves and be better than they are and (c) to make available to them opportunities for them to maximize their potentials. In his discussion regarding the growth and development of rehabilitation counselors, Emener (1986) stated:

> While professional trainers and professional educators are challenged to assess, plan, develop, implement, and evaluate their programs to maximize their potentials, the professional rehabilitation counselor is reminded that the one person who is ultimately responsible for the continuing education and development of the rehabilitation counselor is the individual rehabilitation counselor! (p. 222)

Thus, it is suggested that within our human resource development programs for our employee assistance program personnel, e.g., preservice, inservice, and continuing education, that this "human resource development philosophy" be part of the infrastructure and the bloodstream of our organizations so that our most precious commodity—our human resources, our personnel—are genuinely concerned about their own growth and development. Commensurately, our employee assistance programs will therefore grow and develop, and our programs will provide better, higher quality, and growing and developing services to those who come to us for assistance.

REFERENCES

Emener, W.G. (1986). *Rehabilitation counselor preparation and development: Selected critical issues.* Springfield, IL: Charles C Thomas, Publisher.

Hultman, K.E. (1979). *The path of least resistance.* Austin, TX: Learning Concepts.

Knowles, M.S. (1980). Malcolm Knowles on the challenge of the '80's. *Training and Development Journal, 34*(1), 42–44.

Nadler, L. (1979). *Developing human resources* (2nd Ed.). Austin, TX: Learning Concepts.

Prather, H. (1970). *Notes to myself.* Moab, UT: Real People Press.

Stephens, J.E., & Kniepp, S. (1981). Managing human resource development in rehabilitation. In, W.G. Emener, R.L. Luck, & S.J. Smits (Eds.), *Rehabilitation administration and supervision,* Baltimore, MD: University Park Press.

This, L.E. (1980). Critical issues confronting managers in the '80's. *Training and Development Journal, 34*(1), 14–17.

Chapter 18

ALCOHOL AND DRUG ABUSE AWARENESS: IMPLICATIONS FOR INTAKE INTERVIEWING

HELEN FRYE DAHLHAUSER, FRED DICKMAN,
WILLIAM G. EMENER, AND BONNIE YEGIDIS-LEWIS

Abstract

The following highlights the importance and utilization of intake counselors in community-based counseling programs, documents reported relationships between alcohol and drug abuse and typically expressed problems for which clients come to community-based counseling centers, and supports the relevance and importance of intake counselors having high level alcohol and drug abuse awareness. Following a report of a pilot observation, conclusions and implications are offered as well as suggested recommendations for counselor education and research and demonstration projects.

American society's commitment to being responsive to the psychosocial health care needs of its citizens has been witnessed in the growth, expansion, and enrichment of counseling programs. Community-based counseling centers are typically designed to be responsive to persons with categorical difficulties, e.g., mental health, spouse abuse, marital and family problems, sexual dysfunction, and rape crisis, among others. Tantamount to the quality of service delivery at such centers has been a unique practitioner—the professional counselor. "The counseling practitioner is in a unique position to influence the behavior of others" (Galvin & Ivey, 1981, p. 536). Moreover, it must be remembered that this influence may be "for better or worse," for counseling and psychotherapy can help as well as harm (Hadley & Strupp, 1976). Helpful counseling is many times meaningfully influenced by the initial, intake interview.

Tyler (1969) stated that "the first interview is in many ways the hardest" (p. 40), and offered three major goals of the initial interview: " . . . the

This chapter is reprinted from *Counseling the Troubled Person in Industry* (1985) with permission of the author, the book's editors (Dickman, Emener, & Hutchison, Jr.) and the publisher (Charles C Thomas, Publisher).

foundation for a relationship between counselor and client will have been laid down . . . to open up all of the psychological realities in the client's situation . . . to 'structure' the situation for the client" (p. 53–55). Wolberg (1954) articulated several other goals including the gathering of pertinent information from the client to help establish the tentative dynamics and make a tentative diagnosis. Hollis and Woods (1981) identified four questions that should be answered during the intake interview: (a) can the agency provide the help the client needs? (b) length of treatment required? (c) location of the problem? and (d) who is to be seen? It is the contention of the authors that most of the goals and objectives of initial interviews are the same goals for intake counseling. Intake counseling is a critical aspect of community-based counseling programs, requires specialized expertise, and is more effective if clients perceive the intake counselor to be an expert—viz, "the clients belief that the counselor possesses information and means of interpreting information which allow the client to obtain valid conclusions about and to deal effectively with his problems" (Strong & Dixon, 1971, p. 562). The intake counselor's expertness is critical for numerous reasons. It is important for the accurate communication of empathic understanding and to influence the client's attitude toward counseling. Keefe (1976) believed empathy provides the impetus for change in clients. Altmann (1973) stated:

> The findings suggest that the dimension of accurate empathy plays a vital role in determining whether clients will continue or terminate counseling after the initial interview . . . empathy is almost exclusively related to terminating or continuing counseling after the first interview. (p. 227–228)

Empathy training, initial interviewing, and intake counseling have been and are critical components of counselor preparation programs (Gilmore, 1973; Ivey & Authier, 1978).

Given the importance of intake counseling to community-based counseling programs and the importance of empathy and expertness in the intake counseling process, the purposes of this paper are to: (a) highlight the relevance of alcohol and drug abuse to community-based counseling; (b) describe a pilot observation which demonstrates the relevance of alcohol and drug abuse awareness to community-based intake counseling; and, (c) offer recommendations for preservice and inservice counselor education and training, and suggested research and demonstration needs.

Relevance of Alcohol and Drug Abuse

Correlational findings among alcohol and other drug use and abuse and individual and family problems have been documented. Expressed individual and family problems, such a those that follow, are those typically encountered by intake counselors at community-based counseling centers.

Divorce

Studies summarized by Shuckit and Morrissey (1976) have indicated a significantly higher divorce rate among families experiencing alcohol problems than is true in the general population. (Divorce in American society has witnessed an escalating incidence rate over the past decade.)

Family Violence

A positive relationship appears to exist between alcohol and other drug use and family violence. For example, in Emerson's (1979) survey of all cases of family violence handled by the Los Angeles police department over a period of five years, over half the cases were associated with alcohol or other drug use.

Spouse Abuse

While spouse abuse is not directly linked with alcohol abuse, drinking and other drug use and spouse abuse are associated. For example, in a survey of women who sought emergency aid in Ann Arbor, Michigan, over half of the abusive husbands were excessive drinkers and drinking was involved in 66 percent of the incidents (**Congressional Record,** 1978). Langley and Levy (1977) reviewed several studies of drunkenness and physical abuse and estimated that 40–95 percent of spouse abuse cases are directly linked to alcohol abuse. Other studies have indicated a significant relationship between spouse abuse and drinking by both spouses (Carder, 1978; Hindman, 1979).

Child Abuse

As in spouse abuse, excessive alcohol and other drug usage are associated with child abuse. A study attempting early detection of family pathology in a medical outpatient clinic found relationships between alcohol abuse and child abuse (Bekling, 1978). The same study found a relationship between child abuse and spouse abuse. A summary of studies by Kempe and Helfer (1972) estimated that as many as one-third of all cases of reported child abuse are alcohol related. Alcohol has also been related to child sexual abuse. Several studies (Epstein, Cameron, & Room, 1977; Julian & Mohr, 1980; National Center on Child Abuse and Neglect, 1981) have reported alcohol as a factor in incestuous families.

Sexual Dysfunction

Alcohol abuse and alcoholism has been definitely associated with lower testosterone level in males (DeLucca, 1981). This would corroborate clinical findings (Forrest, 1976) that alcoholics of both genders have an unusually high rate of sexual dysfunction.

Interpersonal Communications

In a study of both alcoholic and nonalcoholic couples, Ritchey (1979) found that drinking increased negative affective responses in both couples. The author concluded that ethanol introduction into couple interaction enhances the probability of negative emotional interaction. The increase in negative affect was highly significant for alcoholic couples and, while less significant, marked for nonalcoholic couples. (It may be that couples seeking counseling in communication skills would enhance these skills simply by not drinking, or by at least being aware of a pattern.)

Relevance to Community-Based Counseling Centers

The complex problems listed above are common complaints brought to community-based counseling centers. Since the relationship between typical individual, marital, and family problems and alcohol and other drugs is well-documented, it follows that the more "alcohol and drugs aware" intake counselors are, the better their understanding of client problems. For example, it is unusual that the problem family will mention drinking as a factor unless alcoholism has developed to an advanced stage. Alcoholism authorities recognize denial as a universal defense mechanism (DeLucca, 1981; Hirsch, 1967; Kissin & Begleiter, 1977). Yet drinking may be associated with the presented problem and in need of attention. If drinking or drug use is a pattern in spouse abuse, child abuse, sexual dysfunction, or other difficulties, problems may be somewhat minimized, or in some cases eliminated, with the cessation of drug intake or at least in the recognition of its involvement. As rehabilitation counselors continue to seek and obtain employment in settings involving work with clientele having alcohol and drug abuse difficulties (consult Dickman & Emener, 1982), it is critical for them to be professionally prepared to see alcohol and drug abuse as potentially being meaningfully related to clients' problems. In her article on intake and referral in an alcoholism setting, Petropoulos (1978) concluded that accurate assessment and referral are essential for successful rehabilitation of clients. Being aware of alcohol and drug abuse, is sine qua non to accurate empathy, perceived expertness, and overall effectiveness in the intake counseling process. The authors conducted a pilot observation to explore the criticalness of this "awareness" phenomenon.

A Pilot Observation

The purpose of this investigation was to explore the extent to which an intake counselor would/could identify the relatedness of alcohol and drug abuse to client problems. A comparison was made between intake counseling conducted by an intake counselor "untrained" in alcohol and drug abuse and an intake counselor "trained" in alcohol and drug abuse. All intakes were conducted at a community-based counseling center — the Family Service Agency, Clearwater, Florida.[1]

The "untrained" intake counselor (female) had a B.A. and several years experience as a volunteer in a rape crisis center. It was reported that: (a) almost all interviews were conducted by telephone; (b) the purpose was to determine the present emotional state of the caller and solicit information relevant to the presented problem(s); and (c) callers were questioned about their motivation for calling and their expectations of services. At the conclusion of each interview, she would determine whether to refer the client to another agency or assign the client to one of the counselors at the receiving agency. If she determined that the client was appropriate for the receiving agency, she needed to get certain specific information for the agency's records, such as: (a) names; (b) sex; (c) dates of birth and ages of each member of the household; (d) home address and phone number; (e) work phone number; (f) marital status; (g) by whom the client was referred; and (h) previous counseling. If appropriate, an appointment was made and the information was written up on an agency form and given to the counselor to whom the client had been assigned.

The "trained" intake counselor (female) had a B.A. and was completing a Master's degree in Rehabilitation Counseling. She had had one introductory course in the theoretical aspects of alcohol and drug abuse. Similarities between the "untrained" and "trained" intakes included: (a) most interviews were conducted by telephone; and (b) recorded necessary data remained the same. At the beginning of the telephone conversation, the "trained" intake counselor volunteered that all information was confidential and that it would be helpful in meeting the client's needs. She also checked specifically for the relationship of alcohol and drugs, legal or illegal, to the presented problem(s). This was frequently handled indirectly during the intake interview with questions such as: (a) "Has there been a change in lifestyle for you and/or any member of your household?" and (b) "How do you and members of your household handle stress?" When appropriate, she directly asked if drinking or the use of drugs accompanied certain behavior(s). For example, a man called for help because he hit his girlfriend on several occasions. When asked if he drank, he responded that he rarely did. When asked if he had been drinking in each instance when he hit her, he reported that he had. Another example of a drug-related problem was in the referral by the police of a six-year-old rape victim to the agency. When the intake counselor asked if drugs or alcohol had been involved, the response was that the offender was picked up in the front yard of the victim's home unconscious from the intake of too much alcohol. In another example, a call was received from a woman who asked for help because she was having marital problems. When specifically asked how she and her husband coped with stress, she said her husband locked himself in a room and drank heavily till he was drunk enough to get to sleep.

Observed Data

When the "untrained" counselor's intakes for a six month period were analyzed, out of 343 intakes, 21 (6.1%) of the problems were recorded as alcohol and/or drug related. The pilot observation conducted by the "trained" intake counselor over a two-month period of time, revealed that out of 138 intakes, 84 (60.8%) were reported as alcohol and/or drug related.

Conclusions, Implications, and Recommendations

Individual, marital, and family problems appear to be associated with alcohol and other drug use and abuse. Unfortunately, intake counselors and therapists may not be aware of such associations or may give a low priority to the role of drugs and alcohol. This lack of awareness may cause counselors to focus on marginally relevant symptomatology rather than addressing primary aspects of presented problem(s). Community-based counseling centers are progressively utilizing intake counselors as part of the overall service delivery processing. It is critical that intake counselors accomplish the goals of initial contacts with clients (Altmann, 1973; Hollis & Woods, 1981; Strong & Dixon, 1971; Tyler, 1969; Wolberg, 1954). Thus, it is concluded that the documented association between alcohol and drug abuse and many of the problems for which clients typically come to community-based counseling centers, clearly illustrates the importance of intake counselors having high level alcohol and drug abuse awareness.

Implications such as these translate into numerous recommendations for the counseling profession—such as:

1. Preservice, inservice, and continuing education programs for counselors should include alcohol and drug abuse awareness content (e.g., to distinguish between alcohol and drug use and abuse, problem drinking and alcoholism, and how drinking and drug use patterns are associated and differentiated from abusing patterns); specific skill-building in intake counseling should sequentially be included as well;

2. Research and demonstration projects should be conducted to empirically test the findings and recommendations of the authors' pilot observation; and,

3. Where known associations between alcohol and/or drug abuse and individual, marital, and family problems exist, research and demonstration projects should be conducted to see if cessation of the associated alcohol and drug abuse reduces, minimizes, or remediates the client problems (e.g., spouse or child abuse, sexual dysfunction, interpersonal communications problems).

It is also suggested that the outcome findings of such research and demonstration investigations would have direct and indirect impact on accreditation, certification, and licensure issues.

American society's commitments to its troubled citizens connotes efficient, effective, and timely service delivery. And as was clearly delineated in the Fall, 1981 issue of the *Journal of Applied Rehabilitation Counseling* [12(3)] which featured a Special Section containing five solicited articles focusing on alternative job markets for rehabilitation counselors (pp. 145–149), rehabilitation counselors are championing this commitment on behalf of society in a variety of settings—including community-based counseling centers. The observations, suggestions, and recommendations herein, although interpolated and extrapolated in nature, call for specially prepared "alcohol and drug abuse aware" intake rehabilitation counselors—the proposed benefits to clients are too compelling to ignore.

Acknowledgment

[1]The authors express sincerest appreciation to the Family Service Agency, Clearwater, Florida, for the helpful cooperation and assistance received during the conduct of the pilot observation.

REFERENCES

Altmann, H.A. Effects of empathy, warmth, and genuineness in the initial counseling interview. *Counselor Education and Supervision,* 1973, *12*(3), 225–228.

Bekling, D.W. Comprehensive care clinic: Findings relative to domestic violence and alcohol abuse. Paper presented at National Council on Alcoholism Meeting, St. Louis, 1978.

Carder, J.H. Families in trouble. Paper presented at 24th International Institute on Prevention and Treatment of Alcoholism, Zurich, 1978.

Congressional Record. Hearings on domestic violence prevention and services act. *Congressional Record,* 1978.

Delucca, J.R. *Alcohol and health.* Fourth Special Report to the U.S. Congress, Washington, D.C.: U.S. Department of Health and Human Services, January 1981.

Dickman, F., & Emener, W.G. Employee assistance programs: An emerging vista for rehabilitation counseling. *Journal of Applied Rehabilitation Counseling,* 1982, *13*(3), 18–20, 24.

Emerson, C.D. Family violence: A study by the Los Angeles County Sheriff's Department. *Police Chief,* 1979, *46*(6), 48–50.

Epstein, T., Cameron, T., & Room, R. Alcohol and family abuse. In Aarens, M., Cameron, T., Roizen, J., Roizen, R., Room, R., Schneberk, D., & Wingard, D. *Alcohol, Casualties and Crime.* Special report prepared for the National Institute on Alcohol Abuse and Alcoholism under Contract No. (ADM) 281-76-0027. Berkeley, Calif.: Social Research Group, University of California, 1977.

Forrest, G.G. *The diagnosis and treatment of alcoholism.* Springfield, IL: Charles C Thomas, 1976.

Galvin, M., & Ivey, A.E. Researching one's own interviewing style: Does your theory of choice match your actual practice? *Personnel and Guidance Journal,* 1981, *59*(8), 536–539.

Gilmore, S.K. *The-counselor-in-training.* New York: Meredith Corporation, 1973.

Hadley, S., & Strupp, H. Contemporary views of negative effects in psychotherapy. *Archives of General Psychiatry,* 1976, *33,* 1291–1302.

Hindman, M. Family violence: An overview. *Alcohol Health Research World*, 1979, *4*(1), 2–11.

Hirsch, J. *Opportunities and limitations in the treatment of alcoholics.* Springfield, IL: Charles C Thomas, 1967.

Hollis, F., & Woods, M.E. *Casework: A psychosocial therapy.* New York: Random House, 1981.

Ivey, A.E., & Authier, J. *Microcounseling: Innovations in interviewing, counseling, psychotherapy, and psychoeducation* (2nd ed.). Springfield, IL: Charles C Thomas, 1978.

Julian, V., & Mohr, C. Father-daughter incest—profile of the offender. Denver: National Study on Child Neglect and Abuse Reporting, 1980.

Keefe, T. Empathy: The critical skill. *Social Work*, 1976, *21*, 10–14.

Kempe, H., & Helfer, R.E. *Helping the battered child and his family.* New York: Lippincott, 1972.

Kissin, J., & Begleiter, L. *The biology of alcoholism: Treatment and rehabilitation of the chronic alcoholic* (Vol. 5). New York: Plenum Press, 1977.

Langley, R., & Levy, R. *Wife-beating: The silent crisis.* New York: Dutton, 1977.

National Center on Child Abuse and Neglect. *Study of the incidence and severity of child abuse and neglect.* 1981, in press.

Petropoulos, A.W. Intake and referral in an alcoholism agency. *Social Casework*, 1978, *59*, 21–26.

Ritchey, D. Marital interaction of alcoholic couples: Changes in affective communication during experimental drinking. Doctoral dissertation, University of Pittsburgh, 1979. (University Microfilms No. 7924738).

Shuckit, M.A., & Morrissey, E.R. Alcoholism in women: Some clinical and social perspectives with an emphasis on possible subtypes. In Greenblatt, M., & Shuckit, M.A. (Eds.), *Alcoholism problems in women and children.* New York: Grune & Stratton, 1976.

Strong, S.R., & Dixon, D.N. Expertness, attractiveness, and influence in counseling. *Journal of Counseling Psychology*, 1971, *18*, 562–570.

Tyler, L.E. *The work of the counselor.* New York: Appleton-Century-Crofts, Inc., 1969.

Wolberg, L. *The techniques of psychotherapy.* New York: Grune & Stratton, 1954.

Chapter 19

THE PREPARATION AND DEVELOPMENT OF EMPLOYEE ASSISTANCE PROGRAM PROFESSIONALS

WILLIAM G. EMENER

An EAP education and development program's greatest strength is vested in its diversity and tolerance of difference.

The number of employee assistance programs (EAPs) throughout the United States, especially over the past three decades, has been escalating at a geometric rate (Dickman, Emener & Hutchison, 1985). Commensurately, increased attention and energy has been given to the staffing, professionalism, and personnel preparation issues relevant to the advancements and continued developments of employee assistance programs. Recently, for example, Maiden and Hardcastle (1986) stated:

> There are currently more than 8,000 EAPs in American work organizations, including 80 percent of the Fortune 500 companies. In light of this growth, the development of standards and professionalization of employee assistance programs is receiving increased attention. (p. 63)

Human service professionals increasingly have been seeking employment opportunities in the private sector human service arenas (consult Dickman & Emener, 1982; Emener, 1986; Lynch & Martin, 1982; and McMahon, Matkin, Growick, Mahaffey & Gianforte, 1983). More pointedly, recent surveys of graduates of rehabilitation counselor education programs (e.g., Janes & Emener, 1985) and social work education programs (e.g., Maiden & Hardcastle, 1986) have reported high percentages of rehabilitation counseling and social work graduates seeking and obtaining employment in employee assistance programs. From a clinical service delivery perspective, this makes sense in view of the fact that current EAPs are typically characterized by a helping/rehabilitative orientation

---

This chapter is reprinted from *Employee Assistance Programs; A Basic Text* (1988) with permission of the author, the book's editors (Dickman, Emener, & Hutchison, Jr.) and the publisher (Charles C Thomas, Publisher).

which operationalizes the philosophy that personal problems, whether caused by work-related or nonwork-related events or situations, do affect the individual as well as the organization and the environment in which the individual is working.

In addition to fostering a helping/rehabilitative orientation, professional preparation programs should also be sensitive to the importance of their "developmental" mission (as discussed in Chapter 28 of this text). In his recent book focusing on the professional preparation and development of the rehabilitation counselor, Emener (1986) articulated this career orientation attitude: "They (rehabilitation counselor education programs) should be committed not just to their students, in view of their students' jobs as rehabilitation counselors, but to their students, in view of their students' lifelong careers in the field of rehabilitation" (p. 176). Thus, it would appear equally important for professional preparation programs whose graduates are seeking and obtaining employment in EAPs, to be cognizant of their role(s) in preparing students not just for specific jobs in EAP's but for careers in EAP service delivery which may include the eventual holding of numerous job positions in EAP's during their future professional lives.

Along with the continuing developments in preservice, inservice, and continuing education programs for EAP professionals, the recent past has witnessed increased attention to employee assistance program data, knowledge and information in textbooks, magazines, journals, and other assorted forms of information dissemination media. For example, Desmond (1982) recently stated:

> The Performance Resource Press in Troy, Michigan, has established itself as a leading resource center for training materials in the EAP field, including the EAP Digest. Other helpful journals and magazines are Alcoholism: The National Magazine, published by Alcom, Inc., and Alcohol Health and Research World, published by the National Institute on Alcohol Abuse and Alcoholism (NIAAA). (p. 30)

The professional publications of national associations of professionals in the fields of rehabilitation, social work, psychology, medicine, etc. have also witnessed an increasing number of refereed articles and reports addressing aspects of employee assistance programming. The important aspect of this is that there is a growing body of knowledge in the EAP field, the knowledge is in appropriate repositories of knowledge, and are available to professional education and programs for their use.

This chapter will: (a) discuss important and critical aspects of educational programming development relevant to employee assistance programs; (b) present and discuss important educational constructs and content areas; (c) review and discuss alternative learning modules, prerequisites and sequencing; (d) present important curricula areas of study; and (e) conclude with recommendations for the future of professional preparation programs for EAP professionals.

Important Aspects of Educational Programming for EAP Professionals

Professional literature is replete with textbooks, monographs, journal articles and guides relevant to the important and critical aspects of professional education and development programming. The purpose of the following is not to repeat, duplicate, or review all of such existing material. Rather, the following is designed to address those attributes and aspects of professional preparation and development programming that are relevant and germane to EAP professionals.

Student-Trainee Issues

One of the numerous sets of critical issues related to students in a professional preparation program, is that involving student recruitment and selection. Program faculty constantly should be aware of the preferred attributes of the students who enter their programs. In turn, faculty should identify and activate as many recruitment possibilities available to them (e.g., personal visits and presentations to student groups in colleges and universities, to professional groups at meetings and conferences; the mailing out of recruitment information and materials to potential sources of students). Student selection is a very important function on behalf of the faculty. Typically, there are admissions standards and criteria which supercede those of an individual program (e.g., for a graduate program, there usually are minimum grade point average and graduate record examination criteria). Standards such as these can be established by the program's home institution (e.g., college or university) or by the program's relevant national, professional accreditation body associated with the program's individual discipline (e.g., for a rehabilitation counseling program, this would be the Council for Rehabilitation Education; for social work, the Council on Social Work Education; for psychology, the American Psychological Association). In addition to admissions standards and criteria such as these, the faculty should also consider admissions criteria relevant to professional practice in an employee assistance program. In this regard, some programs require all applicants to have a personal interview with members of the program's admissions committee. Quite frequently, a counselor, social worker or administrator from an EAP can interview applicants and provide very helpful and useful information and feedback to the program faculty. This also is a very helpful recruitment measure in that applicants can readily see that the program values and works closely with professional practitioners from the field.

Another important aspect of a professional education program for EAP professionals is the extent to which the program operationalizes a "career orientation" toward and with its students. In view of the suggested "developmental philosophy" of an EAP professional education program (as discussed in Chapter 28 of this book), students, prospective and current, should be cognizant of the importance of their developing themselves for a career—not just a job. Fittingly, recruitment materials and presentations, EAP orientation workshops and courses, and the overall attitude of the program's faculty and staff should reflect this orientation. In such activities, moreover, applicants and students should be encouraged to engage in reality testing with regard to their intended career in employee assistance programs. For example, it can be very exciting for an applicant or a student to see that beginning salaries in EAP's are in the $20,000 range and that EAP directors can earn up to $100,000 per year, plus expenses. The glamour and glisten of envisioning a plush office, a new company car, nice clothes, and a private secretary can be very appealing. Nonetheless, as Desmond (1985) pointed out, there are other realities too:

> The aspiring EAP counselor also will encounter other aspects of EAP work which will be different than what would be found in more traditional rehabilitation settings. The counselor in an EAP may be required to travel extensively. An EAP in a headquarters setting may provide services to distant branches or plants of the organization. Personnel from the home office may set up EAPs at satellites, and either deliver services directly to workers in those settings or train personnel in those sites to deliver services. In the latter case, the satellite EAP staff must be trained, monitored, and supervised. Counselors also will encounter the expectation in industry that referred employees should "get better soon." Thus, it is likely that an EAP counselor will be expected to "produce" the desired improvement more quickly than would a counselor in a public or private, non-profit agency. For the most part, EAP jobs are not 9 to 5 jobs. Counselors may be confronted with a crisis and be expected to produce results quickly. In serious situations attention may be needed nearly around the clock. Lastly, EAP personnel are expected to have good writing skills. Reports must be well-written since copies may go to medical directors, plant managers and other administrators. (p. 29)

Indeed, there are numerous intrinsic and extrinsic rewards for working in EAP programs. The importance of assuring that applicants and students are realistically aware of what professional EAP work activities and job tasks entail, however, should be a basic element of the infrastructure of a professional education and development program.

Students should also be encouraged to explore the details of their professional career orientation. It is important for a professional to understand the multiplicity of professional identities and appreciate the potential role ambiguity and role strain that such multiplicities can present. For example, an individual's professional self-concept is frequently related to the ways in which he or she responds to questions such as: "Am I a professional rehabilitation counselor (social worker, psychologist, etc.) who happens to be working in an employee assistance program?" OR, "Am I a professional EAP counselor who happened to be educated and trained in a rehabilitation counselor (social work, psychology, etc.) education program?" An individual's response to questions such as this, moreover, will have a meaningful impact on what professional associations he or she will join, what journals he or she will subscribe to and read, and what professional conferences and workshops he or she will most likely attend.

Educational Program Issues

There are numerous educational program issues which are critical and important to an EAP professional education and development program—too many to address in one part of one chapter of one book. Nonetheless, the experience of the author suggests that the following issues deserve special consideration. In his discussion of key constructs and contents of rehabilitation counselor education, Emener (1986) suggested what he considered to be the two pivotal questions confronting professional program educators:

1. What contents and constructs should be included in a rehabilitation counselor education program? and
2. How should such contents and constructs be determined? (p. 115).

Typically, an EAP education and development program's response to questions such as these will be a function of the basic discipline of the college, department, or program in which it is housed. For example, if the program is housed in a college of education OR a college of arts and sciences, OR if the program is housed in a department of rehabilitation counseling, guidance and counseling, OR social work, respective college degree requirements and departmental, disciplinary professional accreditation standards will dictate certain requirements of the program. This reality, however, is not a negative or "bad" condition. Predicated on the assumption that professional disciplines deserve educational program "departmental" or sanctioned "program" status within a college or university (in this configuration they also enjoy the safeguards provided by respective accreditation bodies), then "employee assistance programs" are considered employment settings in which a variety of professionals work and not professional disciplines unto themselves. Fittingly, employee assistance education and development programs are typically options, specializations, or tracks within rehabilitation counseling, social work, guidance and counseling, and psychology (to name a few) degree programs. When faculty develop an "EAP specialty" (track, option, etc.) within their department's or program's degree, the first activity is to identify the special knowledges, skills and expertise necessary for successful employment as a professional in an employee assistance program. Sources of such information are available in the literature. For example, using the critical competency areas identified by Sink and Porter (1978), Hastings (1984) developed a questionnaire with 60 skill statements relevant to the professional work tasks in an employee assistance program. The nine competency areas were: (a) locating persons in need of services; (b) determining eligibility; (c) using diverse community resources; (d) assisting clients with the development of a rehabilitation plan; (e) insuring community services; (f) determining diagnostic procedures needed; (g) interpreting data to clients; (h) developing and maintaining a counseling relationship; and (i) using appropriate techniques to effect the job placement and job retention of clients. For the purpose of determining the extent to which persons working in EAP's thought rehabilitation counselor skills were applicable to the EAP field, Hastings (1984) sent her questionnaires to .50 companies thought to have EAPs. Respondents were asked to indicate (a) whether each of the individual skills listed was important in terms of the respondent's job in the EAP in his or her company, and (b) whether each of the individual skills listed was important in terms of the field of EAPs. Among her results, Hastings (1984) reported:

> The competency areas on which these respondents agreed for both relevancy levels were: locating persons in need of services; determining eligibility; using

diverse community resources; insuring continuity of services; and, developing and maintaining a counseling relationship.

Specific skill statements [which had high response frequencies] in relevancy to the EAP field included: can identify varied strategies for effective referral of clients to specialists; utilizes efficient case management and recording techniques; can use a systematic problem solving approach in counseling with clients; can demonstrate empathy, genuineness, warmth, concreteness, and respect across a variety of clients; is able to set mutually agreeable goals with clients; and, demonstrates an understanding of the ethical considerations of confidentiality. (p. 30)

Thus, as demonstrated by this illustration, the first step is to identify outcome expectations of the EAP education and development program.

It is also important to identify available resources within the immediate, on-grounds proximity of the program, faculty and students (e.g., on campus) which are critical to a successful EAP education and development program. Such resources would include:

1. Adequate library holdings—textbooks, professional journals, films, audio and videotapes, and microfiche (among others). Basically, the program has to have an up-to-date knowledge base to draw from.

2. Counseling and learning laboratories—a counseling lab with two-way mirrors and accommodations for individual and group sessions (appropriate audio and video equipment can be very helpful for research and instructional purposes), learning laboratories with computer facilities and media equipment. The learning environment is very important to an EAP education and development program.

3. Cognate educational programs within the institution (e.g., departments of psychology, social work, rehabilitation counseling, guidance and counseling, schools of business and schools of continuing education) can provide opportunities for students to choose elective coursework, for faculty to consult and request presentations, and for the program to have an overall base of expertise not readily available within it.

Essentially, it is most desirable for an EAP education and development program to be located in an environment that will support, enhance, and challenge it.

The surrounding community is another important environment to an EAP education and development program. For example, in a surrounding community which has local industries and businesses which have flourishing and successful EAPs, there would tend to be numerous opportunities for the program to: (a) have a large selection of EAP professionals from whom guest lecturers, guest presenters, and adjunct faculty could be recruited and used in the presentation of coursework; (b) opportunities for field site visits, practica and internships for students to have real, in-the-field learning experiences could be formally developed; and (c) settings and populations for basic and applied research on behalf of faculty and students would be available. When there are EAPs in the surrounding community, it also is advisable for the faculty to ask nearby, practicing EAP professionals to help the EAP education and development program with its organizational and operational activities by serving on the program's Advisory Committee, Curriculum Committee, Admissions Committee, and other assorted task force groups charged with the design, implementation, and evaluation of the program. Likewise, it is not uncommon for nearby, community EAPs to ask faculty and students to assist them in designing, conducting, and evaluating their own inhouse staff development and continuing education programs. Arrangements like this allows for the sharing of information, educational and training materials, and equipment.

It has generally been accepted that the most important resource to an education and development program is its faculty. Organizationally, it has been suggested that no program will exceed the effectiveness of its leadership (Emener, Luck & Smits, 1981). Fittingly, while it is advisable to have collective wisdom involved in the planning, designing and conducting of an EAP education and development program (i.e., through the use of advisory, admissions and curriculum committees), it is very helpful if one member of the faculty who is committed to professional employee assistance programming be "in charge" of the program. Basically, it is recommended that the program have a program Director or Coordinator. It is also important for the remaining faculty to be appreciative of employee assistance programming and to be committed to the program's missions and objectives. Students typically take courses with a variety of faculty, and the overall faculty members' collective and individual attitudes toward EAPs represent a very critical influential force in the students' development as professionals.

As discussed earlier, some EAP education and development programs are separate programs within colleges and universities and others (most) are programs housed within one department or program having a traditional, professional disciplinary base (e.g., rehabilitation counseling, social work, etc.). Nonetheless, it is recommended that the EAP education and development program operationalize a multidisciplinary approach. For example, it is important for the program's organizational structure to include professionals (viz, faculty) from a variety of cognate departments and disciplines (e.g., psychology, business, etc.). Students should be encouraged to take elective coursework in other departments, with faculty from other disciplinary backgrounds. Here again, the value of the "development philosophy" can be appreciated; disciplinary incestuousness should be guarded against at all times. As comforting as it can be for everyone to tend to see things in similar ways, in the students' overall, long-term "development" it is very valuable for them to be exposed to a variety of approaches, understandings, and styles.

Curriculum Issues and Content

Employee assistance program educators and human resource development specialists, assuredly are aware that circa 1987 there are numerous colleges, universities, and continuing education programs that have established curriculum and coursework for employee assistance professionals. It can be very tempting to go to a library or contact a university or continuing education program and simply implement their "canned" curriculum. It is strongly suggested, however, that in the long run this is a very poor approach. People typically have great difficulty investing themselves and their energies into "someone else's" program. From an organizational development point of view, it is very helpful for the leadership and faculty of an EAP education and development program to review and study what others have done ("there is no need to reinvent the wheel"). At the same time, however, it is equally very important for the program's leadership and faculty to "build their own program." For example, a good place to start is for the faculty to work together to develop their responses (answers) to the two questions suggested by Emener (1986): (1) What contents and constructs should be included in the program? and (2) How should such contents and constructs be determined? When the leadership and faculty of a program work together and develop their program, for their students, and for their community, the probabilities of their investing themselves into their program will be enhanced tremendously. When the program is then implemented, the faculty will invest themselves into the programs more because they want to, not just because it is their job.

Curriculum Planning and Development Issues

In the process of planning and developing an EAP education and development program, there are numerous important issues to be considered. Identifying and operationalizing appropriate learning approaches, discerning appropriate learning module areas, and then developing specific coursework are three important areas of consideration.

Learning Approaches. Two sets of differential approaches to the students' learning outcomes are deserving of the faculty's attention and consideration. First, there are alternative "models" of education to consider. For example, there is the Arts and Science Model, and there is the Professional School Model. Emener and McFarlane (1985) discussed the uniqueness of these two models:

> Among other constructs, the arts and sciences approach encourages coursework in the traditional, basic disciplines (e.g., sociology, psychology, humanities). The professional school approach . . . encourages coursework in applied, within-the-specific-professional-discipline area (e.g., social work, rehabilitation counseling), and also emphasizes supervised clinical practice (practica and internship). The arts and sciences model is more basic and generic in nature; the professional school model is more focused and applied in nature and has a strong "practice" component. (p. 8)

It is important for the faculty to discuss the pros and cons of these two models and their relevance to the overall program and curriculum and the individual courses. In most EAP education and development programs, combinations of both models can be found. Second, coursework can be presented in (a) a formal, in class, didactic format (e.g., the instructor lectures and the students listen, ask questions and take notes) or in (b) an experiential, in-the-field, learn-by-doing format (e.g., in a practicum setting under supervision, the student learns about counseling by doing counseling). Here too, in most EAP education and development programs, combinations of both approaches can be found. Overall, in terms of these differential learning models and approaches, possibly the most important reason for the faculty to attend to them is so that the faculty know what they are doing and why they are doing what they are doing.

Learning Module Areas. As already underscored earlier in this chapter, the first step in developing an educational and development program is to identify the necessary knowledges, skills, and expertise that the program's students will need after they complete the program and practice their profession. For example, the faculty at East Texas State University developed the first interdisciplinary counseling and human resource management program emphasis at the doctoral level, and the first step of their five-step program development tasks was:

> 1. loose examination was made of the roles and duties of human resource training and development (HRD/T&D) professionals in business and industry. Studies such as the Pinto and Walker (1978) ASTD research were extremely helpful. (Smith, Piercy & Lutz, 1982, p. 108)

Likewise, rehabilitation counselor education program development efforts will consult rehabilitation counselor competencies such as the 12 competency areas developed by Emener and Rasch (1984); social work education development efforts will consult social worker competency areas such as the six major areas identified by Maiden and Hardcastle (1986); and, employee assistance program personnel development efforts should consult studies such as Hastings' (1985) in which at least 10 different types of competencies were identified as important and needed by EAP professionals. Interested professionals are encouraged to consult other sources of needed and important EAP professionals' competencies and their relationship to curriculum development; an excellent place to begin such an investigation would be to consult the July/August, 1986 issue of *EAP Digest* and the October and November, 1985 issues of **The ALMACAN** (the national publication of the Association of Labor/ Management Administrators and Consultants on Alcoholism [ALMACA]). It is interesting to note that ALMACA has developed and recommended coursework for the professional development of EAP professionals, and in doing so ALMACA identified three learning module areas within which recommended courses are listed: (A) Understanding the Worksite: Work Organization as EAP Client; (B) Employee as EAP Client; and (C) EAP Courses.

After studying published EAP professionals' competency studies (e.g., ALMACA's, and Hastings, 1985) and recommended curricula and coursework (e.g., ALMACA's), and after tempering such information with his own experiences as a human service practitioner, educator, and educational program developer and administrator, the author of this chapter identified four learning module areas in which EAP education and development coursework and course content are recommended. The following lists these four modular areas and discusses: (a) the nature of the coursework and the fundamental elements considered critical to the courses in each area; and (b) possible sources of courses that may be available in a college or university that could be used (as they already exist, or adapted or modified) by an EAP education and development program.

1. **Module 1—Work, Employment and Industry.**
Nature/Elements: psychology/sociology of occupations; basics of vocational guidance and career development; industrial and organizational psychology; industrial relations; structures and processes of work and work settings; the role(s) of work in society; the business side of industry.
Sources: courses with content such as these could be found in departments of guidance and counseling, psychology (viz, industrial/organizational psychology), sociology, rehabilitation counseling, vocational education, and assorted departments in business colleges.

2. **Module 2—Human Conditions: Employees and Clients.**
Nature/Elements: psychology of personality; abnormal psychology; addictions and chemical dependency; interpersonal problems and mental health; occupational stress; human relations; psychosocial aspects of disability; human development.
Sources: courses with content such as these could be found in departments of psychology, rehabilitation counseling, allied health, nursing, social work, educational psychology, home and family life, gerontology, and assorted departments in colleges of education, allied health, and social and behavioral sciences.

3. **Module 3—Employee Assistance Program Service Delivery.**
Nature/Elements: principles and procedures of training; assessment and evaluation of techniques; counseling skills and techniques; case management; EAP consultation and development; community analysis and intervention; industrial consultation; organizational development; vocational guidance; group counseling; the entrepreneurial side of human services; the business side of EAP service delivery.
Sources: courses with content and skill development such as these could be found in departments of human resource development, counseling, social work, occupational and vocational guidance, industrial and organizational psychology, and assorted departments in business colleges.

4. **Module 4—Organization, Administration, and Management.**
Nature/Elements: human resource management in business and industry; principles of human resource behavior, innovation and change; policy analysis and development; administration and supervision; principles of management and marketing.
Sources: courses with content and skill development such as these could be found in departments of administration, management, organization

and industrial psychology, public administration, counseling, social work, and assorted allied health programs.

The actual recommending of specific courses that should be included in an EAP education and development program was considered to be outside the scope of this chapter. For example, the coursework suggestions within the above four learning module areas are far from inclusive! Moreover, there are numerous and very important curriculum contents that transcend these four modular areas and specific courses—for example, research, ethics, and legal issues. Furthermore, as discussed earlier, it is more important for the faculty and instructors in an EAP education and development program to work with each other and their respective advisory groups and committees and develop their own curriculum and their own courses for their own program. Decisions such as these, as well as decisions regarding whether a program should teach its own courses or explore the possible use of existing appropriate courses in other departments within the program's college or university, represent important decisions that should be made at the local level by the people who ultimately will be responsible for the implementation of the program.

Curriculum Implementation Issues. Once the leadership and faculty have identified the program's curriculum, the courses and the necessary policies and procedures (e.g., standards for admission), the program is then ready to be implemented. (This could be a good time for faculty to visit an already existing EAP education and development program, or to "work out some of the minor bugs and details.") At the outset and during the implementation stage, especially, other decisions have to be made. For example:

- Who will be teaching what classes? What attributes, knowledges, skills, and abilities should the instructors for the specific courses have?
- Should there be any maximum class enrollment sizes established for any specific courses? Should there be any specific prerequisites for the individual courses? Should the courses that students take be sequenced in any special way?
- When and in what ways should students take their supervised field work? How should fieldwork sites (for practica and internships) be identified, approved and utilized?
- What exit requirements should be considered, e.g., should students have to pass a comprehensive examination? What kind of certificate, diploma, degree conferment should the students receive?

Questions such as these are very important to the overall veracity and integrity of an employee assistance program education and development program. It also should be appreciated that questions like these should never be finitely answered—questions like these deserve constant address by the program's leadership and faculty. The price of movement toward excellence is constant vigilance and questioning.

Recommendations for the Future of Education and Development Programs for EAP Professionals

In their forecasting of the future of employee assistance programs, Dickman and Phillips (1985) discussed future increased attention to stress and the expanding developments of "wellness" programs. Commensurately, they forecasted increases in the needs for targeted services and specialty program emphases such as: communication skills training, assertiveness training, parenting, retirement preparation, sexuality and changing sex roles, loss and death, victim assistance, and daycare (pp. 263–264). Furthermore, Dickman and Phillips (1985) envisioned future EAPs focusing not only on remediation and restoration, but, in concert with the increased "wellness" movement, focusing on prevention as well.

In the development, design, and implementation of an education and development program for EAP professionals, it is obviously critical for the program to prepare students "for what it is really like out there." Nonetheless, as discussed at the beginning of this chapter, the world is amid rapid, geometrically escalating change. Fittingly, the program must be ready to change itself: (a) to meet current changing demands; (b) to prepare professionals for the EAPs of the future; and (c) to prepare EAP professionals who will not only be a part of change in the future but who will play vital and proactive roles in the changes that will occur in the future. Obviously it would be very important for education and development programs for EAP professionals to build appropriate learning knowledges (content) and skills development components into their programs today so that when their students graduate they will be ready for tomorrow—"tomorrow when the world will be different than it is today"!

Acknowledgment. For her technical suggestions and critical reading of earlier drafts of this chapter, sincerest appreciation is extended to Margaret A. Darrow, a Masters degree candidate in the Department of Rehabilitation Counseling, University of South Florida, Tampa, Florida.

REFERENCES

Desmond, R.E. (1985). Careers in employee assistance programs. *Journal of Applied Rehabilitation Counseling, 16*(2), 26–30.

Dickman, F., & Emener, W.G. (1982). Employee assistance programs: Basic concepts, attributes and an evaluation. *Personnel Administrator, 27*(8), 56–62.

Dickman, F., & Phillips, E.A. (1985). Employee assistance programs: Future perspectives. In J.F. Dickman, W.G. Emener, & W.S. Hutchison (Eds.), *Counseling the Troubled Person in Industry: A Guide to the Organization, Implementation and Evaluation of Employee Assistance Programs* (pp. 262–267). Springfield, IL: Charles C Thomas, Publisher.

Emener, W.G. (Ed.) (1986). *Rehabilitation counselor preparation and development: Selected critical issues.* Springfield, IL: Charles C Thomas, Publisher.

Emener, W.G., Luck, R.S., & Smits, S.J. (Eds.) (1981). *Rehabilitation administration and supervision.* Baltimore: University Park Press.

Emener, W.G., & McFarlane, F.R. (1985). A futuristic model of rehabilitation education. *Journal of Applied Rehabilitation Counseling, 16*(4), 5–9.

Emener, W.G., & Rasch, J.D. (1984). Actual and preferred instructional areas in rehabilitation education. *Rehabilitation Counseling Bulletin, 27*(5), 269–280.

Hastings, M.A. (1984). Employee assistance programs: A place for rehabilitation counselors? *Journal of Applied Rehabilitation Counseling, 15*(4), 29–30, 56.

Janes, M.W., & Emener, W.G. (1985). Rehabilitation counselor education graduates' perceptions of their employment and career satisfaction. *Rehabilitation Counseling Bulletin, 29*(3), 182–189.

Lynch, R.K., & Martin, T. (1982). Rehabilitation counseling in the private sector: A training needs survey. *Journal of Rehabilitation, 48*(3), 51–53, 73.

Maiden, R.P., & Hardcastle, D.A. (1986). Social work education: Professionalizing EAPs. *EAP Digest,* November/December, 63–66.

McMahon, B., Matkin, R., Growick, B., Mahaffey, D., Gianforte, G. (1983). Recent trends in private sector rehabilitation. *Rehabilitation Counseling Bulletin, 27*(1), 32–47.

Sink, J.M., & Porter, T.L. (1978). Convergence and divergence in rehabilitation counseling and vocational evaluation. *Journal of Applied Rehabilitation Counseling, 9*(1), 5–20.

Smith, R.L., Piercy, F.P., & Lutz, P. (1982). Training counselors for human resource development positions in business and industry. *Counselor Education and Supervision, 22*(2), 107–112.

Chapter 20

TRAINING AND DEVELOPMENT OF PARAPROFESSIONALS AND SUPPORT PERSONNEL IN EMPLOYEE ASSISTANCE PROGRAMS

TENNYSON J. WRIGHT, PH.D. AND DIANA NORRIS, M.A.

Jerrell and Rightmyer (cited in Dickman, Emener & Hutchison, 1985) indicated that "the goals of EAPs typically include promotion of employee health, moral and productivity . . . the primary emphasis remains on improving the work performance of the employee and minimizing the costs associated with these problems [absenteeism, grievances, disciplinary actions, alcoholism, drug abuse, etc.]" (p. 163–164). This chapter will discuss the training and development of paraprofessionals and support personnel who assist professional staff in implementing EAPs. The type of training required in EAPs is a function of the composition, qualifications, roles and functions, and experience of paraprofessionals and support personnel. Paraprofessionals primarily include lay helpers, volunteers and students in undergraduate and graduate programs at the community college, university or vocational-technical level. They may be enrolled in degree programs in rehabilitation counseling, social work, psychology, marriage and family counseling or other helping professions. Paraprofessionals can provide EAP services under the direct supervision of a professional counselor, psychologist, social worker, or other qualified staff member. Those services might include co-leading a group, serving as a counselor aide, assisting with coordination of EAP services, referral, marketing, program evaluation, research or other valuable services. Support personnel consist of office managers, secretaries, bookkeepers, typists, accountants, clerks, receptionists, stenographers, and volunteers who maintain the day to day

This chapter is reprinted from *Employee Assistance Programs; A Basic Text* (1988) with permission of the author, the book's editors (Dickman, Emener, & Hutchison, Jr.) and the publisher (Charles C Thomas, Publisher).

operations of the EAP office. These staff members can free professional and paraprofessional staff from clerical and other routine duties. Training and development are those activities which constitute Human Resource Development (HRD) and are valuable in meeting professional staff, paraprofessionals, support personnel, EAP, contractors, and clients needs.

Human Resource Development

The philosophical frame work of HRD is the development of human potential. Craig (1976) described HRD as "the central goal of developing human potential in every aspect of lifelong learning" (p. xi). Pfeiffer and Jones (1981) viewed HRD as a way to expand people's work-related abilities systematically and help them focus on the attainment of both organizational goals and personal goals. Nadler (1980) defined HRD as those learning experiences that are organized, for a specified time, and designed to bring about the possibility of behavioral change. Others (Daly, 1976; Laird, 1978; Tracey, 1974) have offered similar definitions but use the terms **training** or **training and development** synonymously with HRD. Chalofsky and Lincoln (1983) stated that one way to view HRD and related words such as training, education, and development within an operational context is to see HRD as an umbrella concept that is concerned with the process of change through learning. These definitions and descriptions appear similar to the view of Miller (1979) who indicated that training is the process of affecting change in an individual's behavior often applied to the acquisition of limited, job-related skills. Otto and Glaser (1970) referred to training as the "teaching/learning activities carried on for the purpose of helping members of an organization to acquire and apply the knowledge, skills, abilities, and attitudes needed by the organization to carry on its mission" (pp. 3–4). Perhaps Chalofsky and Lincoln (1983) described the concepts best—they indicated that "training means HRD for present and near-future job/personal goals and education/development means HRD for future and/or overall personal growth" (p. 16). For the purposes of this chapter, training and development will be used synonymously with HRD.

Recent management and HRD practices have emphasized the effective use of employees in an organization (Gatewood & Field, 1987). Central to their effective use is to select, assign, and train employees who are suitably matched for the right job. If paraprofessionals and support personnel are well matched, EAPs that highlight employee strengths will likely be more successful. If they are not well matched, training and development may be introduced to achieve the desired performance (e.g., skill, attitude, knowledge, behavior, etc.). The content, length and nature of training and development are affected by their level of skills and abilities. If these skills and abilities are well developed for the right job, then minimal training should suffice. If necessary job skills and abilities are low, then training and development should be more extensive. Thus, the roles and functions of paraprofessionals and support personnel in EAPs should be directed by personal, professional, and organizational goals and limited by their own potential.

The goal of HRD of paraprofessionals and support personnel is to enhance their knowledge, behaviors, attitudes, and/or skills thereby improving the quality of services of EAPs. HRD is an appropriate activity when there is an actual deficiency or a potential deficiency in job performance. This can happen when new jobs are being created (e.g., marketing, program evaluation, referral), when old jobs will be performed in new ways (e.g., completing insurance forms, training contract supervisors, scheduling clients), when existing jobs are being performed in deficient ways by members of the present staff, or when new staff are hired or new volunteer enter the EAP. Miller (1979) has proposed three questions to answer when contemplating HRD: (a) Where are we now? (b) Where do we want to be? and (c) How do we get there? He has suggested avoiding extremely specific training (as opposed to education) prior to or unconnected with employment. Instead, he suggested that specific training should accompany entry into employment. He further suggested combinations of learning opportunities in classrooms, in teaching workshops and on-the-job. These learning opportunities should address (a) training specific to the job, (b) orientation to the job, (c) real work experiences, and (d) further education, both job-related and general. For the purposes of this chapter, the authors will define and describe methods of HRD of paraprofessionals and support personnel vis-a-vis (a) General Education Training, (b) In-service Training, and (c) On-the-job Training.

General Education Training

General education training is considered **formal training** via classrooms and contains subject matter which may or may not be necessarily directly related to the EAPs employee's job. It consists of voluntary educational programs of varying scope which is designed to further the personal development and special abilities of employees (De Carlo & Robinson, 1966). The instruction is designed to develop basic knowledge, skills, and personality traits broadly applicable in many life situations, including a wide range of occupations in which the individual might engage. Subject matter may include occupational guidance, communication skills, human relations training, learning theory, ethics, computation, alcoholism, cross-cultural training, and other topics related to liberal arts education. General education training is equally competent to provide specific occupational training, general or theoretical learning required by specific occupations, and the remedial instruction needed to acquire basic job skills and attitudes. In addition, paraprofessionals and support personnel may attend formal training programs offered through community colleges, universities, vocational-technical schools and business colleges. Sponsorship may or may not be provided by EAPs but is strongly encouraged for professional growth and development. Ideally, general education training will prepare the individual to meet the requirements for an associate degree, bachelor's degree, or postgraduate degree.

In-Service Training

In-service training is training given an individual while employed by an organization. It may be conducted by or under the auspices of an EAP usually for one of the following purposes: (a) to improve job skills, (b) to impart new job skills, (c) to provide orientation to the EAP, (d) to train for advancement, or (e) to provide general education (Brender, 1974). Orientation training, for example, can be utilized to provide the volunteer or newly hired employee with information concerning EAP operations such as employee benefit programs, rules and regulations, policies and procedures, EAP history, operations, and services. Orientation training in EAP is designed to provide volunteers or new employees with as much information about EAPs in as short a time as possible so that they can readily adjust to the environment and become productive (Tracey, 1971). Additional topics to be included in in-service training programs are confidentiality, intake/counseling hours, assigning clients to groups, insurance, plant (site) visitation, contacting clients at work, communication with supervisors clients and family, alcoholism, drug abuse, referral, program evaluation, marketing, and accessibility (consult Dickman, 1985).

On-the-Job Training

On-the-job training (OJT) predominately is conducted while the employee is at his/her work site. In OJT, both the "trainee" and the instructor operate in the actual job environment (e.g., EAP). To be effective, OJT must involve an analysis of the job (e.g., filing, referral) to be learned. The job must be broken down into its processes and steps including not only the doing of the specific task, but also the obtaining and preparation of materials. Standards of proficiency must be established for each job task to insure the proficiency of the paraprofessional and support personnel. OJT is considered the most frequently used training method and training staff must possess two qualifications: (a) an adequate skill in the job where the training is to be done, and (b) an adequate level of skill in training techniques to teach the job to the "trainee." The OJT system must provide sufficient time for the trainee to learn the job and to do so without undue time pressures to get the work completed. There must also be enough space provided for the "trainee" and the trainer to work together on the job. Some examples of job tasks to be addressed during OJT are screening, scheduling, training programs for supervisors, referral, recordkeeping, insurance billing, filing, etc. For additional guidelines on the use of OJT, its advantages and disadvantages, consult Miller (1979, pp. 133–135).[1]

Paraprofessionals

Paraprofessionals may include volunteers, undergraduate students, graduate students, or trained part-time telephone counselors. Whomever a company elects to use to meet the demands of a large caseload, they must be trained to fully understand the components of EAP and to meet the recordkeeping requirements (National Institute on Drug Abuse, 1978). Many EAP professionals maintain a list of volunteers who are members of Alcoholics Anonymous (AA), Narcotics Anonymous (NA), Al-Anon, and Nar-A–Non. These are persons who are active in the Fellowship and are willing to receive a call from a newcomer, discuss their own experience, and, often, meet the newcomer at their first meeting. Most treatment professionals share the belief that AA is the long-term primary care resource for alcoholics (Bernstein & Malloy, 1985). It is important that the volunteers be educated regarding the functions of EAP and be supportive of the EAP services. Paraprofessionals like support personnel must also be advised of confidentiality and its ethical and legal implications.

Support Personnel

As indicated previously support personnel consist of a variety of individuals who can free professional and paraprofessional staff from clerical or other routine duties. Past experiences indicate that characteristics of effective support personnel include intelligence, integrity, emotional stability, trustworthiness, empathy for the human condition, diplomacy, good verbal skills, and a willingness to interact with a group of people of radically different socioeconomic backgrounds. Since these characteristics are difficult to assess in an employment interview, and may emerge over a period of time, it is suggested that new personnel be hired with a 90-day evaluation (probation) period.

The following are some issues to be addressed during the training period. Since the secretary or office manager is often the first person that a troubled employee has contact with at an EAP, every effort should be made to assure a positive experience for the troubled employee. Office managers and secretaries, for example, need to be familiar with the functions of EAPs and with the organization and management personnel and labor standards of each company to which the EAP is providing services. Often there is a need to refer inappropriate inquiries to the appropriate office, such as the personnel office, industrial nurse, or benefits office. Office managers and secretaries need to be trained to screen calls to determine their urgency. They need to be adept at scheduling and arranging for hospital admissions, if necessary. They also need to be knowledgeable of the training programs for the company supervisors so that they become adept at assembling the required materials. Office personnel (e.g., secretaries, clerks, bookkeepers) need to be trained to promptly and accurately complete all required recordkeeping procedures. An understanding of insurance requirements, verification, and filing requirements is essential. Accurate data must be gathered to facilities meeting the requirements of the company (contractor) and to facilitate program evaluation.

Confidentialities and Ethics

Among the responsibilities of paraprofessionals and support personnel is confidentiality. Maintenance of confidentiality is a critical component of an effective EAP. Dickman (1985), stated that all employees have the right to seek help for their problems and know that their problems will be best in the strictest confidence. Maintaining confidentiality is one of the most complex and pervasive problems confronting the EAP provider and has both legal and ethical implications. All employees must be trained regarding their role in insuring confidentiality of the clients. Some specific instructions to support personnel regarding confidentiality would include, but not be limited to:

- All clients should be clearly identified in the master appointment book as to place of employment. Clients from the same place of employment should be prevented from encountering each other in the waiting area.
- Always determine the identity of callers on the telephone and confirm appointments directly with the client.
- All records are to be kept in a locked cabinet and unavailable for inadvertent sighting by persons visiting the facility. Care should be taken to safeguard any item that contains a clients name, such as telephone message forms.
- Do not use a client's name when it may be overheard by persons in the waiting area.
- In any situation in which you are uncertain, give a noncommittal response and inform the appropriate professional counselor or EAP Directory promptly.

In addition to confidentiality, paraprofessionals and support personnel must be informed of their ethical responsibility to the EAP, client, and other staff members. *Webster's Third New International Dictionary* (Gove, 1966) defined ethics as "the principles of conduct governing an individual or a profession" (p. 780).

Since most paraprofessionals and support personnel do not belong to a profession, it is the responsibility of the EAP director and professional staff to provide training, guidance, and advisement of appropriate ethical behavior. Training should insure that the major purposes and functions of an ethical code are known. An example of an ethical code is "Ethical Standards for Rehabilitation Counseling (National Rehabilitation

Counseling Association Ethics Sub-Committee, 1972). The major purposes and functions of an ethical code include: "(a) protecting clients, (b) providing guidance to professionals, (c) ensuring the autonomy of professionals, (d) increasing and enhancing the prestige of the profession, (e) increasing clients' and the public's trust and faith in the members of the profession, and (f) identifying desirable conduct between professionals" (cited in Emener, Wright, Klein, Lavender & Smith, in press, pp. 1–2).

Benefits of Training and Development

The benefits of training and development will be evident in the increased effectiveness and efficiency of EAPs. Trained staff will be better prepared to demonstrate increased skills and knowledge; positive attitudes, and appropriate behaviors. Trained staff are also likely to demonstrate increased satisfaction with their job tasks and reduced absenteeism and turnover. Clients, the focal point of EAPs, will receive the quality of services that are the foundation of a good EAP. Contractors and labor unions will likely experience greater satisfaction with the quality of services as well. Professional staff will likely experience increased confidence in the quality of job performance of paraprofessional and support staff, thereby relieving them of the need to oversee and monitor every detail of the many day to day office functions. Effective training and development will also increase the efficiency and effectiveness of selecting new staff for vacancies. As turnover decreases, staff replacement costs are also likely to decrease. In short, training and development assuredly will enhance the goals of an EAP.

Summary

Training and development, also known as Human Resource Development, can assist EAPs in preparing paraprofessionals and support personnel to meet the demands of improving the work performance of the troubled employee while minimizing the costs associated with employee problems. It can assist in matching the right person for the right job while enhancing knowledge, skills, behaviors, and attitudes in EAPs. Several training and development methods are available to achieve the desired results including general education training, in-service training, and on-the-job training. Program evaluation efforts should focus on paraprofessional staff because the benefits resulting from training and development indeed will be evident to EAP professional staff, contractors, labor unions, clients, and paraprofessionals and support staff, and documentation of such can be very helpful to an EAP.

Notes

[1]For additional information on designing and conducting effective training consult Caffarella (1985); Chalofsky and Lincoln (1983); Craig (1976); Davis (1974); Goad (1982); Jackson (1985); Kells (1986); Mager and Beach (1967); and Pfeiffer and Jones (1972–1981).

REFERENCES

Bernstein, M., & Molloy, D. (1985). Putting alcoholics anonymous to work in business and industry. *The ALMACAN, 15* (6), 8–10.

Brender, S.I. (1974). *An analysis of selected in-service training programs for non-management office personnel with implications for designing, conducting and testing an in-service training program.* Unpublished doctoral thesis, The University of Iowa.

Caffarella, R.S. (1985). A checklist for planning successful training programs. *Training and Development Journal, 39* (3), 81–83.

Chalofsky, N. & Lincoln, C.I. (1983). *Up the hrd ladder: A guide for professional growth.* Reading, MA: Addison-Wesley.

Craig, R.L. (Ed.). (1976). *Training and development handbook* (2nd ed.). New York: McGraw-Hill.

Daly, A.A. (1976). Management on supervisory development. In R.L. Craig (Ed.), *Training and development handbook.* New York: McGraw-Hill.

Davis, L.N. (1974). *Planning, conducting, and evaluating workshops.* San Diego: Learning Concepts.

De Carlo, C.R., & Robinson, O.W. (1966). *Education in business and industry.* New York: The Center for Applied Research in Education.

Dickman, J.F. (1985). Ingredients of an effective EAP. In J.F. Dickman, W.G. Emener & W.S. Hutchison (Eds.), *Counseling the troubled person in industry.* Springfield, IL: Charles C Thomas.

Emener, W.G., Wright, T.J., Klein, L.F., Lavender, L.A., & Smith, D.W. (in press). *Rules of ethical conduct and rehabilitation counseling: Results of a national survey. Journal of Applied Rehabilitation Counseling.*

Gatewood, R.D., & Field, H.S. (1987). *Human resource selection.* Chicago: The Dryden Press.

Goad, T.W. (1982). *Delivering effective training.* San Diego: University Associates.

Gove, P.B. (1966). *Webster's third new international dictionary of the English language* (unabridged). Springfield, MA: Merriam.

Jackson, C.N. (1985). Training's role in the process of planned change. *Training and Development Journal, 39* (2), 70–74.

Jerrell, J.M., & Rightmyer, J.F. (1985). Evaluating employee assistance programs: A review of methods, outcomes and future directions. In J.F. Dickman, W.G. Emener, W.S. Hutchison (Eds.), *Counseling the troubled person in industry.* Springfield, IL: Charles C Thomas.

Kells, J.E. (1986). Developing training step-by-step. *Training and Development Journal,* *40*(1), 50–52.

Laird, D. (1978). *Approaches to training and development.* Reading, MA: Addison-Wesley.

Mager, R.F., & Beach, K.M. (1967). *Developing vocational instruction.* Belmont, CA: Fearon Pitman.

Miller, V.A. (1979). *The guidebook for international trainers in business and industry.* New York: Van Nostrand Reinhold.

Nadler, L. (1980). A model for professional development. *Training and Development Journal,* *34* (5), 14–22.

National Institute on Drug Abuse. (1978). *Developing an occupational drug abuse program* (DHHS Publication No. ADM 82-692). Washington, D.C.: U.S. Government Printing Office.

National Rehabilitation Counseling Association Ethics Sub-Committee. (1971). Draft of proposed ethical standards for rehabilitation counselors. *Journal of Applied Rehabilitation Counseling, 2,* 74–84.

Otto, P.O., & Glaser, R.O. (1970). *The management of training.* Reading, MA: Addison-Wesley.

Pfeiffer, J.W., & Jones, J.E. (Eds.). (1972–1981). *The annual handbook for group facilitators (10 Vols.).* San Diego: University Associates.

Pfeiffer, J.W., & Jones, J.E. (Eds.). (1981). *The 1981 annual handbook for group facilitators.* San Diego: University Associates.

Tracey, W.R. (1974). *Management training and development systems.* New York: American Management Association.

Tracey, W.R. (1971). *Designing training and development systems.* New York: American Management Association.

PART VI
SPECIAL ISSUES

The overriding purpose of this book is to proclaim the belief that EAPs are a chief means in our society to help people. People, the editors believe, want to be their fully functioning, fully productive selves. Consistent with this belief is that the nation's industry wants this too. Therefore the philosophy of this book is basically humanistic. Part VI is consistent with this philosophy. If EAPs are to be even more effective they need to be permeated with a genre of professionalism and staffed by people of the highest degree of professionalism. In addition to the basic canons of professionalism, EAP professionals also must remain cognizant of legal channel markers as well as aware of other critical, special issues surrounding EAPs throughout the United States.

In Chapter 21, Camazine surfaces and discusses important confidentiality/privilege issues (as well as legal concerns and laws pertinent to them), provides and discusses relevant case studies, and offers notable malpractice and types of malpractice information. In the area of drug and alcohol testing, indeed an important special issue, Camazine, in Chapter 22, presents and discusses five areas of key aspects of drug and alcohol testing: (1) guidelines for a drug policy; (2) off duty use of drugs; (3) constitutional issues; (4) views from the arbitrator's point of view; and (5) EAP involvement in drug and alcohol testing. This chapter's accompanying Comment/Update by Andrews and Hutchison discusses the passage of the drug-free workplace law in 1988, the continued drain of substance use on the American economy and workplace and concludes with some recent court cases related to use and testing in business. Another very important component of a modern day EAP is its involvement in critical incident stress debriefing (CISD). In Chapter 23, Rank discusses critical incidence stress, CISD, and CISD protocol, all within a proactive focus on prevention.

The last two chapters in this Part focus on aspects of credentialing.

Chapter 25, by Challenger, highlights the importance of credentialing EAP professionals. Emener and Hutchison, in Chapter 24, discuss and present important information regarding: (1) recent, key developments in the emerging, overall professionalism of EAPs; (2) the certified employee assistance professional (CEAP) movement and its grounding in professional ethics; and (3) "EAP Program Standards."

EAP professionals' awareness of (a) "special issues" within and surrounding EAPs and (b) the continuing developments of professionalism within EAPs, is tantamount to the provision of efficient and effective EAP services to employees of businesses and industries throughout the United States.

Chapter 21

LEGAL ISSUES

Alisse C. Camazine

Introduction

When employee assistance programs began, their main role was to address problems relating to alcohol and drug abuse. Because of their perceived efficiency and cost-effectiveness, EAPs have expanded, both in number as well as in the breadth of services offered. Today, EAP practitioners have responsibility for identifying and assessing a wide variety of problems which may have an impact on job performance, such alcohol and drug abuse, depression, marital problems, and financial problems.

EAP counselors wear several hats. They identify and assess employee problems, make referrals to appropriate outside individuals or institutions, and provide resources, education, and information to assist in solving problems.

EAP programs are part of the benefit packages provided for employees. The programs are an inexpensive, convenient method for seeking aid for the troubled employee and/or family. The programs can either be in-house programs or external programs. But no matter where the program is physically located or whether the services are provided by a company employee or external provider, the employee's expectation is that the program is "safe" and the services confidential. This expectation of confidentiality is an essential element of the program.

Confidentiality/Privilege

It is important to understand two legal concepts which govern confidentiality. The first, privilege, belongs to clients and is their guarantee

---

This chapter is reprinted from *Employee Assistance Programs; A Basic Text* (1988) with permission of the author, the book's editors (Dickman, Emener, & Hutchison, Jr.) and the publisher (Charles C Thomas, Publisher).

that if they speak to a counselor, physician, or attorney, their words will not be repeated. The second legal concept, confidentiality, is imposed upon the professional whether or not the client invokes privilege. The client is entitled to have his or her EAP records kept privately, securely, and separately from other corporate and departmental records.

Source: Professional Ethical Codes

Privilege is created by statute. Each state has a statute which lists those professionals for whom privilege exists. The lists vary from state to state and many statutes protect the records of psychotherapists who do not have a Ph.D.

Confidentiality arises from the ethical code of the counselor's profession. A counselor's conduct is governed by the code of ethics of the profession or adopted by the licensing organization to which he or she belongs. Professional responsibilities of psychologists, social workers, and other professionals are regulated by rules of conduct for each organization. For example, the National Association of Social Workers has a code of ethics which states in pertinent part, "I respect the privacy of the people I serve. I use in a responsible manner information gained in professional relationships."

EAP counselors, like other professionals, are also governed by ethical standards. There are two national organizations to which many professionals in the EAP field belong: The Association of Labor-Management Administrators and Consultants on Alcoholism, Inc. (ALMACA) and the Employee Assistance Society of North American (EASNA). ALMACA in conjunction with the National Council on Alcoholism (NCA), the National Institute on Alcohol Abuse and Alcoholism (NIAAA) and the Occupational Program Consultants Association (OPCA), developed standards for employee alcoholism and/or assistance programs (hereinafter referred to as the EAP standards).

EASNA also has developed proposed ethical standards which state, in part, that "The EAP practitioner protects the client's right to privacy with reference both to confidentiality and anonymity. Anonymity refers to nondisclosure of the identity of the individual. Confidentiality refers to the private, nondisclosable nature of information obtained in the communication between a client and practitioner."

No specific privilege statute has been enacted for the EAP counselor as a separate professional, but other privilege statutes may apply, depending upon the credentials of the individual counselor. For example, some states have privileges for psychotherapists, social workers, and marriage counselors. The privilege statute in a state may include broad language covering the "certified professional" or "one whom the client believes" to be such a professional. When a state statute is written this broadly, communications with the EAP counselor may be privileged. Some EAP counselors are licensed professionals to whom the statutory privilege would apply directly, while others may fall within the purview of a privilege statute because the client/employee reasonably believes the counselor to be a licensed professional.

Federal Regulations

In addition to the various codes of ethics and state statutes governing confidentiality and privilege, other laws require maintaining the confidentiality of the client. Federal regulations may, under certain circumstances, apply to an employee assistance program. (See Appendix for selected text of federal confidentiality regulations.) The federal rules and regulations regarding confidentiality apply to all programs and activities that are:

- Related to alcohol abuse or drug abuse education, training, treatment, rehabilitation, or research, and which are conducted either in whole or in part, directly or by grant, contract or otherwise, by a U.S. department or agency.
- Require a license, registration, or other authorization from a U.S. department or agency.
- Assisted by federal funds, directly through grants or contracts, or indirectly by funds supplied to a state or local government unit.
- Assisted by the Internal Revenue Service through tax-exempt status or income tax deduction for contributions (42 CFR Part II, Paragraph 2.1 et seq.).

The types of records and information covered by federal regulations include the names of clients, their diagnoses, prognoses, treatment plans, attendance records, and patient status information.

Prior to release of confidential information, there must be written consent of the patient or his or her authorized legal representative. Certain items must be included in the consent forms:

- Name of the program that is to make the disclosure.
- Name or title of the person or organization to which disclosure is to be made.

- Name of the patient.
- Purpose or need for the disclosure.
- Extent or nature of the information to be disclosed.
- Statement that the consent can be revoked and a specific date, event, or condition upon which consent will expire.
- Date that the consent is signed.
- Signature of the patient (42 CFR, Part II, Paragraph 2.3(a)).

In special circumstances, disclosure may be permitted without written consent. When a patient commits or threatens to commit a crime on the premises of the program or against personnel of the program, program personnel are not prohibited by the regulations from reporting the crime to or seeking the aid of a law enforcement agency, but such reports shall not identify the suspect as a patient (42 CFR Part II, Paragraph 2.13).

Additionally, a court may, in appropriate circumstances, authorize disclosure which otherwise would be prohibited under the federal regulations. In doing so, the court will weigh the public interest and the need for disclosure against the injury to the patient and injury to the physician/patient relationship. The request for court orders to authorize disclosure of records or facts pertaining to a patient cannot use the name of the patient unless the consent of the patient is obtained or consent of court is obtained anonymously (42 CFR Part II, Paragraph 2.64). The real name of the patient should not be used. Additionally, notice must be given to the patient that such a request will be made in court.

All 50 states require certain individuals to report child abuse, but until recently, there has been some controversy regarding whether reporting was allowed when the program operated under federal regulations. On Aug. 27, 1986, the federal regulations were amended to add: "The prohibitions of this section do not apply to the reporting under state law of incidents of suspected child abuse and neglect to the appropriate state or local authorities" (42 USF Section 290dd-3 and ee-3).

Under current federal regulations, reporting is required but applies only to initial reports of child abuse or neglect. The regulations permit reporting only when there is a danger of harm to the child and do not necessitate reporting merely because a patient has abused alcohol or drugs.

The person who wrongfully discloses confidential information can be subject to a fine of up to $500 for the first offense and up to $5,000 for each subsequent offense (42 CFR Paragraph 2.14).

Implied Promise of Confidentiality

One area of concern for all EAPs is that implied promises may arise from promises made indirectly to the employee by the distribution of a company policy handbook. A court may find that the policy of confidentiality as outlined in an employee manual, is sufficient to allow the employee a cause of action for breaching that promise of confidentiality even though such confidentiality is not actually promised by the EAP counselor.

In *Pacific Telephone & Telegraph* (73 CA. 1185 BNA 1980) an employee was fired for drinking on the job. The arbitrator held that the company manual stated that the company "provides a policy whereby if a problem drinker is identified, the Company will attempt to assist the employee in remedying his problem." The court felt that the statement in the manual created a contract between the company and the alcoholic employee and it therefore ordered reinstatement.

Similarly, when a company manual promises confidentiality, this too can be an implied contract, the breach of which could form the basis for a lawsuit. (See also *Wooley v. Hoffman-LaRoche*, 491 A 2d 1257 NJ 1985.) The key to this concept of an implied promise of confidentiality lies in the expectation of the employee that the information he or she discloses to the EAP counselor remains confidential. Frequently, policies and manuals which the EAP distributes may improperly include absolute promises of confidentiality. These statements simply say "The EAP is a confidential program. No information will be disclosed without written consent." Since absolute confidentiality has no basis in the law, these policies should contain a statement regarding the circumstances under which there will be a disclosure without the employee's consent. Consideration should be given by all EAPs to the use of a statement similar to the following:

"No one will reveal information obtained during a counseling session without written permission, unless required by law. The law may require the release of such information where life or safety of an individual are seriously threatened."

This statement should be included in a form to be signed by the employee indicating that it has been read and understood. An attorney should be consulted to ascertain the status of the law in each case.

Maintaining Client Records

Many EAPs maintain extensive files which might create liability since EAP records may be subject to subpoena. Therefore, it is important to keep only those records which are necessary. The proposed EASNA code of ethics sets forth guidelines for what information should be maintained in client files. These include the following:

- Every item of information related to the purposes of the individual or agency providing the service.
- Only information that is necessary for optimum clinical service should be maintained.
- Personal values and judgments should be excluded.
- Only factual information should be maintained.
- Information which is no longer relevant is deleted. Records should not be kept that include gossip, psychiatric records, psychological tests, personal opinion and unnecessary details.

Before disclosing any information from a client's file it is important for the client to know what information is actually in the possession of the EAP. For example, many EAPs receive copies of a psychologist's or a psychiatrist's test known as the Minnesota Multiphasic Personality Inventory (MMPI). This test forms the basis of a psychological diagnosis and the results have personal information in the test. Many clients are unaware that an EAP may even have such information. Often a client will sign a general release authorizing disclosure of any and all information in the possession of the EAP. Thus, the MMPI may be released without the client's knowledge and may cause problems for the client if it comes into the hands of a potential employer or opposing divorce attorney.

Before disclosure, the EAP professionals should review the contents of the file with the client so that there can be no mistake regarding the information to be disclosed and no allegations regarding wrongful disclosure.

Disclosures of Confidential Information

An employee assumes that confidential information will not be disclosed without his or her written consent. Unfortunately—for the EAP counselor—the issues of confidentiality and privilege are complicated by numerous exceptions which require that confidentiality and privilege must be set aside for the best interests of society or for the protection of an individual.

Subpoena and Subpoena Duces Tecum

The first such exception occurs when an EAP professional is served with a subpoena or subpoena duces tecum. A subpoena requires an individual to appear in court. A subpoena duces tecum will compel the individual to appear in court and bring documents or notes which are specifically listed in the subpoena duces tecum. Often, the subpoena duces tecum will be general in nature and will require that the witness bring any and all documents, records, papers or notes relating to a particular individual or case. An EAP counselor should, whenever subpoenaed, seek legal advice before disclosing material, discussing the case or providing any confidential information.

State Laws

A second exception is provided for in some state statutes. All privilege statutes have exceptions which authorize disclosure under certain circumstances. These include but are not limited to situations in which:

- The patient's purpose in disclosing the information is to seek advice in furtherance of a crime or fraud.
- The patient has waived the privilege.
- The disclosure relates directly to facts or circumstances of a homicide or lawsuit for malpractice which has been filed against a professional.

Child Abuse

A third exception occurs when an EAP counselor believes or suspects that a child is being abused. Under these circumstances, the counselor may have the responsibility of reporting that information to a state abuse hotline. Most state statutes list the particular professionals who must report, but some state statutes mandate reporting by an individual who has information relating to the abuse of a child. Still other statutes allow, but do not require, reporting by any individual who has knowledge of abuse.

Although an EAP counselor may not be explicitly mentioned in a statute, an EAP counselor may be required to report abuse if the EAP counselor has the credentials of one of the individuals listed. For example, a state statute may mandate reporting for a social worker, or mental health practitioner. Many EAP counselors are social workers and therefore will be required to report. Arguably, EAP counselors are mental health practitioners. Therefore, if mental health practitioners are listed in the state statute, EAPs in that state may be required to report. An EAP practitioner may be liable for damages resulting from nonreporting if a child is injured.

Dangerous Client

Disclosure also may be required when a therapist knows or should know that a client is dangerous and that the behavior of the client represents an unreasonable risk of harm to others. This duty first developed in California in the case of *Tarasoff v. Regents of the United States of California* (529 P.2d 533 (Ca. 1974)). In this case, a graduate student at the University of California met a woman who was also a student. He courted her, but she did not return his affections. During a counseling session at the university-sponsored counseling service, the student confided to his psychologist his intentions to kill this woman. The psychologist considered the threats to be serious and called the campus police. The student was detained but released when he later appeared "rational." The psychologist reported his concerns to the director of the counseling service, a psychiatrist, who determined that no further action needed to be taken in the case. No one warned the woman, who was overseas for the summer, nor did anyone warn her family of the threat. Upon the woman's return from overseas she was murdered. A lawsuit was filed by the woman's parents against the university, the psychologist, the psychiatrist, and the police. The Supreme Court of California held as follows:

[W]hen a therapist determines, or pursuant to the standards of his profession should determine, that his patient presents a serious danger of violence to another, he incurs an obligation to use reasonable care to protect the intended victim against such danger. The discharge of this duty **may require the therapist to take one or more of various steps depending upon the nature of the case.** Thus, it may call for him to warn the intended victim or others likely to apprise the victim of the danger, to notify the police or to take whatever steps are reasonably necessary under the circumstances (Id. at 340) (emphasis added).

The court based its ruling upon a determination that the therapist/client relationship had special features. These features generated a level of knowledge that goes beyond common experience. Because of that special knowledge and because the therapist might be able to control the patient, the court held that the therapist must take **reasonable steps to protect** individuals that the therapist knows or should know might be the victim of serious intentional violence. This duty to warn has been upheld by several state courts, including Alaska, Florida, Minnesota, Nebraska, New Jersey, North Dakota, and Vermont. The fact that a state may not have litigated a Tarasoff-type case does not mean that such a duty will not be required.

After the Tarasoff case, a New Jersey Court followed the Tarasoff reasoning in the case of *McIntosh v. Milano* (403A. 2d 500 (N.J. 1979)). In this case, the plaintiff brought a wrongful death suit against a psychiatrist after his patient murdered the plaintiff's daughter. The patient was a 17-year-old male who was involved with the daughter. In therapy the patient expressed fears of others and advised the doctor that he carried a knife, which he brought to therapy sessions. The patient told the therapist that he had previously fired a gun into the car in which the victim was riding with her boyfriend. The therapist, nevertheless, denied that the patient expressed any violence toward the victim or made threats to kill or hurt her. In this case, the plaintiff alleged that the doctor owed a duty to protect the victim. The doctor's defense was that there was no duty to warn and that if he did warn the possible victim, it would interfere with therapy and breach confidentiality. The court held that the duty to warn did apply in this case because of the imminent danger to the patient or society. Furthermore, the court stated that the "considerations of confidentiality have no overriding influence here" (Id. at 513).

In a 1982 Georgia case, *Bradley Center, Inc., v. Wessner* (296 S.E. 2d 693 (Ga. 1982)), a voluntary patient in a mental hospital advised his doctor that he wanted to kill his wife and her boyfriend. The patient further advised that he had caught his wife with this man on numerous occasions. Subsequently, while out on a pass from the hospital the patient killed his wife and her boyfriend. The children filed suit against the hospital on the theory that their father's criminal act was reasonably foreseeable and that the death of their mother was the proximate result of negligence.

In the 1983 California case of *Hedlund v. Superior Court of Orange County* (699 P. 2d. 41 (Ca. 1983)), the California courts again found a therapist liable for a failure to warn. In this case, a therapist was seeing a patient who threatened to hurt the mother of a small child. This child was seated next to his mother when she was shot by the patient. The child suffered emotional trauma. The attorney for the child alleged that it was foreseeable that if the patient's threats were carried out, those in close relationship to the individual would be at risk. The court said it was not unreasonable to recognize the existence of a duty to persons in close relationship to the object of a patient's threat.

In 1985, the Supreme Court of Vermont decided the case of *Peck v. The Counseling Service of Addison* County, Inc. (499 A. 2d 422 (Vt. 1985)) (see appendix). This case is especially interesting to EAP practitioners since most of the earlier Tarasoff-type cases deal with psychiatrists and psychologists. The counselor in the *Peck* case was neither a psychiatrist nor a psychologist, but held a master's degree in counseling. Since many EAP counselors have similar credentials, this case may have a direct bearing on the possible obligations of the duty to protect.

In this case, an individual was an outpatient at a counseling service. He had been to this counseling service on several occasions. On June 20, 1979, the patient had a fight with his father and left home. He went to the counseling service and told his therapist that he had a fight with his father. At the next session, the patient told his therapist that he wanted to get back at his father and stated that he could burn down his father's barn. The therapist made the patient promise he would not burn down the barn. Believing the patient, the therapist did not disclose the threat to the patient's father. The patient did, however, burn down the barn. The trial court found that the therapist's failure to warn the identified victims constituted a breach of the duty to take reasonable steps to protect them.

The court stated that the reasonably prudent counselor would have taken steps to prevent the harm by doing one of the following:

- Consulting with a supervisor.
- Consulting with a doctor.

The court further stated that it is always necessary to have a complete previous mental health history in order to determine the likelihood that a patient would carry out a threat. The court also found that the counselor was negligent in not believing that the patient would carry out the threat. The trial court, however, found that under Vermont law no legal duty existed between defendants and plaintiff.

On appeal, the Supreme Court of Vermont reversed the trial court's decision and found that there was liability. The court specifically stated as follows:

[W]e hold that a mental health professional who knows, or based upon the standards of the mental health profession, should know that his or her patient poses a serious risk of danger to an identifiable victim, has a duty to exercise reasonable care to protect him or her from that danger (Id. at 427).

This case is important to show that any lawsuit may be the one which would set the precedent for a court to adopt the Tarasoff line of cases.

In a recent case from Alaska, *Division of Corrections, Department of Health and Social Service, et al. v. Neakok* (721 P 2d 1120 (Alaska 1986)), Clifford Nukapiagak, while highly intoxicated, shot and killed his step-daughter and her boyfriend and raped, beat, and strangled another woman. Neakok, the survivor and representative of one estate, brought suit. Nukapiagak had been mandatorily released from prison on parole six months before the murders, after having served a six-year sentence for assault and rape. The plaintiffs alleged negligence on the part of the parole officers and the Division of Corrections in failing to impose certain conditions on Nukapiagak's release, failure to supervise while on parole and in allowing him to return to a small isolated community without parole officers or alcohol counseling and in failing to warn his victims of his dangerous propensities. The court found that the state should have regulated Nukapiagak's movements and should have imposed special conditions of parole, including a requirement that he refrain from alcohol use. The court also held that the state should have foreseeably expected that this individual would have caused harm to their public, especially because he went to live in a small, isolated community with a population of approximately 100 persons.

In the case of *Buwa v. Smith* (Cir Ct. Co. of Berrien, Mich. 84-1905 NMT (Aug. 20, 1986)), an out-of-court settlement in the amount of $2.8 million was paid to four children whose mother was murdered by their father. The suit charged that the counselor, Roger Smith, failed to advise either the woman or the police that the father, who was a client, had threatened injury to his wife, including the threat to kill her and then commit suicide. The woman was not a client. The lawsuit alleged that the therapist, who was a licensed family and marriage counselor, should have referred the client to a staff psychiatrist, who was more qualified. After his third counseling session at the center, the client allegedly shot and killed his estranged wife and wounded his wife's brother-in-law.

It is important to realize that the Tarasoff-type cases may require breaking confidentiality or may require the therapist to exercise reasonable care to protect by taking steps other than reporting.

In addition to the precedent which has been established by the above cases, many states are beginning to pass laws which provide when there must be reporting in a Tarasoff-type situation. These laws have been passed in an attempt to limit the liability for the violent acts of patients. California is one state which has passed such a bill.

California's bill states as follows:

> SECTION 1. Section 43.92 is added to the Civil Code to read:
>
> 43.92. (a) There shall be no monetary liability on the part of, and no cause of action shall arise against, any person who is a psychotherapist as defined in Section 1010 of the Evidence Code in failing to warn of and protect from a patient's threatened violent behavior or failing to predict and warn of and protect from a patient's violent behavior except where the patient has communicated to the psychotherapist a serious threat of physical violence against a reasonably identifiable victim or victims.
>
> (b) If there is a duty to warn and protect under the limited circumstances specified above, the duty shall be discharged by the psychotherapist making reasonable efforts to communicate the threat to the victim or victims and to a law enforcement agency.

In early 1987, the American Psychological Association was considering the adoption of a similar Model Bill. The Model Bill requires that there be an **actual** threat of physical violence, while the California code requires simply a serious threat of physical violence. The California law provides that the duty shall be discharged by making reasonable efforts to communicate the threat to the victim and to a law enforcement agency.

Case Studies

In order to help the EAP professional determine judgment boundaries in *Tarasoff* cases, we have constructed the following illustrations and analysis. The *Tarasoff* case requires the therapist to "bear a duty to exercise reasonable care to protect the foreseeable victim." Reasonable care need not involve warning the potential victim but could include a wide range of other actions.

Case 1. A new client, a 23-year-old stock clerk, comes to the EAP office late one afternoon for a consultation. History taking proves difficult as the client weaves around the room, sniffs continuously, appears agitated and angry. The apparent target of anger is his father. He reports that he plans to kill his father but inquiry regarding the plan and method reveals little. As the clinician describes her duty to protect the father the client abruptly bolts out of the room. The clinician jotted the following note, "Seemed disturbed, angry at father, possible drug use?" Later it is learned that the young man left work immediately, drove the wrong way on the highway resulting in a head-on collision with a car bearing a family of four. All were killed including the client.

Analysis: More clinical sensitivity might have proved useful in establishing a therapeutic alliance and obtaining a detailed clinical history and an evaluation of drug ingestion and agitation level. Another person (parent, spouse, friend) could have been notified to come to work to retrieve the young man before the discussion of the duty to warn. He did seek assistance spontaneously. Documentation was marginal and there was no indication the clinician attempted to follow up by consulting a supervisor or checking the personnel records.

Case 2. A steady and reliable employee with an 8 year work history requested assistance from the EAP clinician when the employee's supervisor refused to transfer her from night shift to day shift. She reports that her husband is threatening her with divorce unless she works different hours. She is seen over several sessions where she describes her rage at the supervisor and her plan to kill him. In the last session she produces a knife and describes "cutting his gizzard out." The clinician reviews with the client the options of how to proceed. These include: (1) referral to a psychiatrist for medication; (2) voluntarily taking time off; (3) calling the supervisor and requesting that he join them for a session, or (4) warning the supervisor that his life is endangered. Together the client and the clinician decide to ask the supervisor to join them in a session scheduled for just before the start of work the following day. At the meeting the clinician mediated the dispute. The supervisor agreed to shift the hours at the end of the year. The clinician also contacted the consulting psychiatrist before the mediation session.

Analysis: The therapeutic alliance in this case is much stronger. The clinician is candid about the options and involves the client in the decision making process. There was apparently no informed consent permission signed which stated the client waived privilege. Additional sessions may need to be held with the client and the supervisor over the long time interval until the hours can change. The clinician should also consider involving the spouse as the threats against the supervisor may result from pressures applied by the spouse.

Case 3. Both mother and son are employed at the same company; the son in the comptroller's office and the mother as a receptionist. The mother had made infrequent but effective use of the EAP program over the years to deal with a divorce from an alcoholic husband and a daughter's problems. The son had come to the EAP years ago to deal with his alcoholic father. The mother reported today, to an EAP counselor with whom she had never worked, that her son had confided to her last evening that he planned to kill a former girlfriend so that she could not marry her new boyfriend. The mother indicated that her son had been in treatment with a psychologist who, when consulted early in the morning, laughingly dismissed the concerns and told the mother that her son was not dangerous. The EAP counselor reassured the mother as the counselor personally knows the son and privately agreed with the psychologist. The counselor focused the session on the mother's anxiety and suggested some stress reduction exercises. That evening the son killed his former girlfriend, and seriously injured the fiance, by hitting them with his car when they came out of a restaurant. The EAP counselor, the clinical supervisor, the consulting psychiatrist, the EAP program, and the company were all sued by the surviving fiance for failure to take reasonable care to protect the readily identifiable victim of a threat.

Analysis: This illustrates the conflict when one person reports what another has said. The "hearsay" nature of this type of information poses special problems for the EAP. In many such situations, it may be easier to obtain a release of information, allowing the EAP staff to contact the alleged victim or to contact the alleged perpetrator since the current client is not the one threatening injury. In the event a request for release of information is refused, the EAP counselor must consider the possibility of disclosure if, after obtaining detailed information, it appears that injury to another individual is a possibility. Other steps the counselor should have taken include taking a detailed history of previous assaultive behavior or threats by the son. The son's treating psychologist should have been contacted. Personnel records of the son should have been reviewed and the EAP supervisor consulted. Since the mother had been a client of the EAP her file should have been reviewed to determine if there was a question of reliability of her reporting. Documentation of all those steps and the plan for future steps must be done to insure a recorded trail of reasonable and proper behavior by the therapist.

Case 4. An employee's wife comes into the EAP program and indicates that she wants a divorce. During the course of the interview it is reported that her husband is an alcoholic and a pilot. The following facts are obtained. He drinks four to five times a week, even if he has a scheduled flight. He took a 30-day vacation and entered a treatment center under an assumed name, leaving before treatment was completed. The counselor knows that FAA regulations require that a pilot not drink for a certain number of hours before a flight.

During the interview the home situation is discussed with wife. Since other people might be endangered by this pilot, the counselor discusses the possibility of his reporting her husband to the FAA. Wife becomes outraged and says "You said this was all confidential. I do not want you to report my husband as he will lose his job and we will not be able to pay our bills." Wife then left the session prematurely.

Analysis: This illustrates the conflict when the danger may not be immediate and the spouse has no connection with the EAP program. Consideration should be given to talking to the husband. A better alternative would be to work with the wife to enable her to bring her husband to the session. Remember, to have a duty to warn, there must be a special relationship between the caregiver and the care receiver. Further, the individual likely to do the injury is not the "client of the EAP and therefore, there is little ability to control the other person's conduct."

Malpractice

There are only a few cases which have been litigated to conclusion regarding malpractice of EAP professionals. There are many other cases which settled prior to trial. Since the case law in this area is sketchy, the following discussion is based upon results from an extrapolation and interpretation of cases and claims made against other professionals.

To prove liability in a malpractice case, an individual must be able to show the following elements:

- An EAP practitioner had a duty to an employee.
- There was a breach of said duty.
- The therapist was negligent.
- There were damages to the victim.
- There was no interruption or intervening event between the behavior of the therapist and the subsequent injury. (This is defined as proximate cause) (*Bradley Center Inc. v. Wessner*, see above for citation).

In order to prove that the practitioner was negligent, the client must be able to show that the therapist departed from acceptable standards of care in the profession.

It must be determined that the therapist failed to do that which a reasonably prudent person would do. If an employee assistance counselor is governed by the ethics of his or her profession, such as a social worker or a psychologist, the acceptable standards are more readily available for comparison. However, because EAP personnel are often uncredentialed, the only standards for EAP practitioners may be the EAP standards and the proposed EASNA standards. The proposed EASNA standards state in pertinent part as follows:

"EAP practitioners are responsible for recognizing the limitations of their competency, and for making certain that all work is performed within those limitations. When providing services or using procedures in which s/he is not fully trained and/or experienced, the practitioner works only under the supervision of a fully qualified person who is recognized as competent in those services and procedures. It is evidence of poor judgements and may be unethical, for a practitioner to offer services or use procedures that are not generally accepted by professional colleagues as representing the prevailing standard of practice."

The EAP standards state that an EAP staff will have skills in identifying problems, interviewing, motivating, referring clients, and where appropriate, in counseling or other related fields. Experience and expertise in dealing with alcohol-related problems are essential. These standards provide the criteria against which an individual case might be judged and evaluated.

Types of Malpractice

Misdiagnosis

The first area of concern for an EAP practitioner is the area of misdiagnosis. Misdiagnosis can occur by the negligent failure to assess any problem, or by failure to assess the correct problem. An early detection program may create the risk of employer liability where an employee is approached about alcoholism and enrolled in a rehabilitation program when the individual claims not to have a drinking problem.

The situation of an EAP client who appears to be an alcoholic and is referred to an Alcoholics Anonymous program or to a drug rehabilitation program, and subsequently commits suicide, creates possible professional liability for the program. The surviving family may be able to sue the EAP professional for referral to the wrong type of treatment facility, such as a psychiatric hospital, rather than a program specializing in alcohol and chemical dependency. If an EAP practitioner is in doubt as to the specific nature of the client's problem, referral to a more experienced practitioner or institution for a more detailed assessment is necessary.

For example, in the case of *Doss v. United States* (476 F.Suppl (E.D. Mo. 1979)), the physician negligently failed to perform tests which would have allowed the physician to make a proper diagnosis. Tests were either not performed or the results were ignored. The court found that the doctors were therefore negligent in failing to properly examine patients.

In the Buwa case cited earlier, the lawsuit alleged that the therapist had committed malpractice because he did not refer the client to a psychiatrist, even though the case was clearly beyond the therapist's capabilities. In the Peck case, cited above, the court held that a reasonably prudent counselor, under the same or similar circumstances, would have consulted with an individual who was more experienced than the therapist.

The EASNA and EAP standards discussed above indicate that EAP practitioners are responsible for recognizing the limitations of their competence, and for making certain that all work is performed within those limitations. The ALMACA standards require that the EAP professionals have skill in identifying problems, in counseling, in referring clients and have experience and expertise in dealing with alcohol-related problems.

In an attempt to avoid liability for malpractice, a therapist should obtain complete information from all clients, in order to have all relevant information. If the EAP professional is unqualified to assess the problem, he or she should refer the individual to someone who is more experienced.

Negligent Referral

It is incumbent upon an EAP practitioner to refer employees only to those referral sources who have proven track records.

EASNA's proposed ethical standards state that "[e]fficiency and effectiveness of the referral process is a cornerstone of ethical EAP service. The practitioner is responsible for making himself/herself thoroughly familiar with the private and public service providers available in his or her area before attempting to offer EAP service to the public." An EAP practitioner must verify accreditation with other EAPs or with the licensing agency of the professionals to whom referrals are to be made. Referrals to specific individuals should be made only if an EAP practitioner is aware of the credentials of that individual. For example, in *Allegheny v. American Car and Foundry Company* (198 F 447 (MD Pa 1912)), the court found liability on the part of an employer for failure to exercise due care in choosing a competent doctor to whom the employer sent employees for treatment.

In this regard, there is a problem developing with the increased use of health maintenance organizations (HMOs) and preferred provider organizations (PPOs). Many companies are using HMOs and PPOs to curtail the rising health care costs. Oftentimes, HMOs and PPOs, however, do not include physicians who are familiar with alcoholism and drug dependency, and will not have a qualified doctor on staff who can make appropriate referrals or treatment plans for such problems. As a result, referrals may be made to unqualified individuals, thus creating a potential liability for negligent referral.

Abandonment

Abandonment occurs when an EAP practitioner improperly terminates a relationship with an employee/patient. A clinician cannot suddenly unilaterally terminate an employee's treatment or therapy when there is still a need for continued care. Before termination from an employee assistance program, a therapist must take the time to refer the employee to another referral source.

EAP practitioners may find themselves in a different situation when employment is terminated and the employee is prohibited from using the EAP following termination, even though the employee previously had been utilizing the counsel of the EAP. Good clinical practice would suggest that there be at least one followup session following termination of an employee to allow the EAP practitioner to refer the individual to another qualified source. The company policy regarding participation in the EAP upon termination should be established and distributed to all employees.

In *Katsetos v. Nolan* (368 A. 2d 172 (Conn. 1976)), a woman entered a hospital for the delivery of her fourth child. Following delivery there were complications and death resulted. The estate filed a suit alleging wrongful diagnosis and failure to remain in attendance while in a critical condition.

The court held that:

"A physician is under the duty to give his patient all necessary and continued attention as long as the case requires it and that he should not leave his patient at a critical stage without giving reasonable notice or making suitable arrangements for the attendance of another physician."

Abandonment also may occur if an employee attempts to make an appointment to see an EAP practitioner and is unable to do so for several weeks. In the event the employee would attempt suicide or, worse yet, be successful, liability could result due to the failure of the practitioner to be available.

Sexual Relations with a Client

Unfortunately, sexual involvement with a patient is becoming more and more widespread. Such conduct may result in a lawsuit for malpractice. Malpractice is not difficult to prove in such situations because the conduct is a departure from acceptable standards of one's profession. The result of such a suit will be the same: liability for damages and possible loss of license.

In *Kulick v. Gates* (CV0041624 Super.Ct. Conn (1985)), the plaintiff filed a lawsuit against her psychologist, alleging severe mental anguish, depression, suicide, impaired relationships, sex life, and marital discord. During treatment, the doctor stroked the patient's hair, hugged her, and commented on her personal appearance. The plaintiff advised the doctor that she was attracted to him, but this issue was never addressed. The plaintiff then terminated treatment, but began again a few months later when the doctor called her. A sexual relationship between the two began and continued approximately four months. The plaintiff then terminated the relationship. The doctor called her several times in an attempt to reestablish the relationship.

The jury awarded the plaintiff $180,000 reduced by 15 percent for comparative negligence (for plaintiff's contribution to her injuries) for a total of $153,000; $80,000 for plaintiff's husband; $20,000 for medical bills, and $60,000 for loss of consortium.

It is inexcusable and unethical for an EAP practitioner to become sexually involved with a client. Sexual acts performed under the guise of therapy may also constitute fraud. The EASNA proposed standards for EAP practitioners specifically state that any form of romantic involvement or sexual activity between a practitioner and a client is unethical.

Damages as a result of such conduct would likely be extensive. Because of the widespread nature of this practice, many insurance companies have excluded coverage for lawsuits filed against therapists for this type of conduct.

In addition to the damages which could result from such a case, there is the additional problem of loss of license of the EAP practitioner for unethical, immoral conduct.

Defamation

Defamation is a communication by one person that harms the reputation of another. Libel is a written communication and slander is an oral communication. One area where defamation may increase is in the area of drug problems. Since many companies are using drug screening and drug testing, the results of the tests are often being improperly disclosed. In *Strachan v. Union Oil Company* (768 F.2d 703 (5th Cir. 1985)), an employee at a unionized operations unit of a refinery had been accused by his supervisor of being a drug user. The management conducted a physical search of the employee's body, locker, and vehicle, and obtained blood and urine samples. The tests shows that there were no drugs. The employee sued, claiming defamation, assault, and invasion of privacy. The employee was unsuccessful in this case because the claims were, according to the law, to be brought under the collective bargaining contract under the National Labor Relations Act and therefore the state court was not a proper forum for such a suit. The conduct of the company in this case, however, shows the possibility of liability under other circumstances.

In the case of *Houston Belt and Terminal Railway v. Wherry* (548 S.W.2d 243 (Tex. 1977)), a plaintiff was injured on the job and fainted. The company doctor ordered drug screening, which showed a trace of methadone. The doctor reported this to the personnel officer, adding that methadone was a drug used in treatment of heroin addicts, but that the trace was not significant. Personnel sent internal memos to seven managers who normally receive accident reports. The memo did not say that the trace was meaningless. The plaintiff was discharged for violations of the employer's safety and accident reporting rules, not for use of drugs. The plaintiff filed suit and the court found that the memo and the letter were libelous. A $150,000 judgment was entered including $50,000 for punitive damages.

In the case of *Moyer v. Phillips* (341 A 2d.441 (Pa. 1975)), a man who was a tractor/trailer driver for more than 35 years, went to a doctor for a physical as required by Interstate Commerce Commission regulations. After the examination, the doctor wrote to Moyer's employer that he considered Moyer to be a chronic alcoholic and that although Moyer could return to work, he ought not be allowed to drive a truck. During the seven years in which the employee had been employed, he maintained a perfect driving record. A lawsuit against the physician was filed by the employee which alleged that he suffered, and continues to suffer, damages in the nature of deprivation of his professional status, employee, company and union benefits, retirement, health, welfare, and life insurance benefits, and his good name.

These cases show that a wrong, hasty diagnosis may well constitute libel. An EAP professional should document what clients were doing, what they said, and what they looked like, rather than making a diagnosis which may prove to be incorrect. EAP professionals also should make sure that no information is disclosed to any individuals other than those individuals who absolutely require receipt of this information.

Wrongful Death

Wrongful death cases may be filed when a negligent intentional act leads to the death of an individual. When death occurs from the failure to warn as required in the Tarasoff cases discussed above, the plaintiff may have an action for a wrongful death. Similarly, if the negligent diagnosis results in the death of an individual, a wrongful death claim may result.

Negligence

An employer may be responsible for the negligent death or injury of an individual. For instance in *Otis Engineering v. Clark* (668 S.W.2d 307(1983)), an automobile accident occurred when an intoxicated employee was sent home from work. The court said that the employer was liable and held that:

[W]hen, because of an employee's incapacity, an employer exercises control over the employee, the employer has a duty to take such action as a reasonably prudent employer under the same or similar circumstances would take to prevent the employee from causing an unreasonable risk of harm to others. Such a duty may be analogized to cases in which a defendant can exercise some measure of reasonable control over a dangerous person when there is a recognizable great danger of harm to third persons.

In *Brockett v. Kitchen Boyd Motor Company* (264 Ca. App. 2d69 (1968)), an employer hosted a Christmas party at which an employee became grossly intoxicated. The employer led the employee to his car so that he could drive home. An accident occurred and the court held that the employer was negligent because of the affirmative acts of placing him in his car and directing him to drive home. If an employee comes to an EAP office and is unable to work, due to an impaired condition, the EAP counselor should not allow the individual to drive home.

Intentional Infliction of Emotional Distress

In the case *Bulkin v Western Kraft East, Inc.* (422 F.Supp. 437 (E.D. Pa. 1976)), a plaintiff sued a former employer, claiming that he had been damaged by an employer's negligence in maintaining personnel records. The plaintiff was discharged from employment after cutbacks occurred. The employer furnished a potential employer with incorrect personnel information relating to the circumstances of plaintiff's severance, indicating the reason for termination was due to his sales record. Furthermore, the employer stated that by "mutual agreement" he would not be eligible for rehire.

The plaintiff sued for negligence in failing to maintain proper records and for mental pain and suffering and humiliation. Although this case did not reach the court on its merits, this case shows a situation which could easily occur and the resulting problems associated therewith.

Breach of Confidentiality

As discussed previously, it is necessary for EAP policies and brochures to specifically state that there is no absolute confidentiality and that there may be situations which require disclosure.

In the case of *Horne v. Patton* (287 So.2d 824 (Ala. 1974)), a lawsuit was filed by a patient against his physician for damages allegedly suffered by reason of the physician's revealing to the patient's employer, information concerning the patient which the physician had acquired during the patient's treatment. The trial court dismissed the case and the Supreme Court of Alabama reversed the decision. The Supreme Court held that there was a confidential relationship between the doctor and the patient which imposed a duty upon the doctor not to disclose information concerning his patient obtained in the course of treatment, and that the physician's release of the information to the patient's employer constituted an invasion of the patient's privacy. Furthermore, the court held that by entering into the physician/patient relationship, the physician impliedly contracted to keep confidential all personal information given by the patient.

In the case of *Bratt v. IBM* (785 F.2d 352 (1st Cir. 1986), the patient had many disputes with his supervisor. He complained about numerous medical problems and then requested a transfer. The supervisor had Bratt examined by a doctor. The IBM regulations restrict company access to medical information from outside doctors unless there is an emergency. The physician told Bratt's supervisor that the employee was paranoid and should see a psychiatrist. The information was conveyed to another supervisor who prepared an internal memo. There were also many discussions among members of the company staff.

Bratt alleged a violation of confidentiality and privacy. The court found that there was no invasion of privacy because the employer's legitimate business interest outweighed the intrusion into the employee's privacy. The court did find, however, that when a physician/patient privilege exists, the integrity of that relationship outweighs the interest of a third party and found that there was a breach of confidentiality.

The case of *Davis v. Monsanto* (627 F. Suppl. 418 (S.D.W.Va. 1986)), emphasizes the need for a proper disclaimer. In 1983 an employee of Monsanto who worked with potentially dangerous chemicals began experiencing marital problems. In March 1984 his wife left him and he began having problems sleeping, lost weight, and became nervous. He voluntarily made an appointment to see a counselor at Personal Performance Consultants, Inc. (PPC), a subcontractor who provided counseling services to Monsanto employees. The counselor, who had a master's degree in counseling, concluded that the employee was dangerous to himself and to others. The counselor also determined that his responsibility required him to break the employee's confidentiality in order to protect him. The counselor recommended to the employee's supervisor that the employee be removed from his job and that he be urged to seek medical treatment.

The employee sued, alleging invasion of privacy and breach of contract. The court found that the West Virginia statute under which this occurred, permitted disclosure during the course of psychological treatment to protect against imminent injury by a patient or client. Additionally, the employee statement of understanding as set forth in the *Davis* case permitted disclosure. This case shows that in order for an EAP to successfully litigate a breach of confidentiality claim, there must be proper disclosures in the EAP's policies and procedures. Again, absolute confidentiality cannot be promised. Policies and procedures must advise employees of those situations which will require an EAP to disclose certain information.

Invasion of Privacy

A patient has a right to privacy in the course of his relationship with his physician or therapist. Allegations of invasion of privacy often are added as a separate claim for damages in lawsuits involving other claims, as can be seen in the prior section on breach of confidentiality.

In *O'Brien v. Papa Gino's* (780 F.2d 1067 (1st Cir. 1986), the plaintiff alleged invasion of privacy and defamation. The plaintiff was hired in 1973 by Papa Gino's of America, Inc., where he worked for nine years. At that time he earned $37,000 per year. During 1982 he had a disagreement with management and was discharged on September 7, 1982. The plaintiff alleged he was fired for failing to promote an employee under his supervision who was the son of the defendant's superiors and godson to the president. The defendant said the plaintiff was dismissed for poor job performance.

The plaintiff was then confronted with rumors that he had been using drugs outside work. He said that he was forced to take a drug test or lose his job. He also said he was asked questions about matters unrelated to his drug use. The defendant said that the plaintiff took the drug test voluntarily. Plaintiff filed a lawsuit based on defamation and invasion of privacy. A judgment was entered for $398,230 on the invasion of privacy claim and $50,000 on the defamation claim.

Two recent cases claimed an invasion of privacy against Southern Pacific Transportation Company.

The first case was *Luck v. Southern Pacific Transportation Company* (San. Fran. Sup. Ct. 843230 Calif. (filed 8/85)). In July of 1985, Southern Pacific demanded that 489 of its employees undergo urine tests. Barbara Luck refused the drug test. Southern Pacific acknowledged that Luck was an excellent employee and was not suspected of drug abuse, but fired her for failure to comply with instructions of proper authority. This case was still pending as of January 1987.

In *Pettigrew v. Southern Pacific Transportation Company* (San Fran. Sup. Ct. 849343 Calif. (filed 11/85)), plaintiff also filed an invasion of privacy claim against Southern Pacific Transportation Company following what he claimed was a false positive test for cocaine use. He was told that he could submit to another test, but regardless of the outcome, he would have to be evaluated. The second test was negative.

Plaintiff then was forced to enter a 28-day hospital rehabilitation program and to attend two Alcoholics Anonymous meetings per week. After submitting to 10 drug tests, he filed suit. He obtained a preliminary injunction against the company pending resolution of the case. He was then demoted to a nonmanagement job and his pay and benefits were decreased.

Chapter 22

DRUG AND ALCOHOL TESTING: CURRENT EAP DILEMMAS

ALISSE C. CAMAZINE

Introduction

Recently, employers have become more aware of the impact which substance abuse has on the workplace. Increased accidents, absenteeism, workers' compensation claims, and other similar circumstances have made employers aware that substance abuse problems may exist in their workplace. Numerous companies have, as a result, taken steps to attack this growing problem. Many Fortune 500 and smaller companies alike have chosen to institute drug screening programs in an attempt to curtail substance abuse problems. Removing employees with substance abuse problems from the workplace reduces the risk of injury to co-employees and provides a safe workplace.

Basic Guidelines for a Drug Policy

If your company is planning to institute a drug screening policy, the policy must meet the objectives of the company and at the same time meet certain legal requirements. Additionally, the policy should be developed in conjunction with union representatives, personnel managers, management, security and legal advisors in order to avoid any inter-company conflicts regarding the procedures of the policy.

The policy should be clearly written, clearly communicated to employees and uniformly enforced. Each employee should receive a copy of the policy. Company manuals and bulletin boards should be updated and include the policy. Any policy statement regarding drug screening should address the following issues:

This chapter is reprinted from *Employee Assistance Programs; A Basic Text* (1988) with permission of the author, the book's editors (Dickman, Emener, & Hutchison, Jr.) and the publisher (Charles C Thomas, Publisher).

1. The company should demonstrate the need for a drug screening policy by making employees aware of the substance abuse problems in the workplace. The employees should also be advised about the company's concern for the health and safety of its employees, as well as the safety, productivity and security problems associated with substance abuse.

2. The company must provide clear, explicit notification of the policy to all employees. This policy should advise the employees of the company rules regarding the use of illegal drugs, alcohol and prescription drugs, both on and off the company property. The employees should be advised that they will be subject to drug testing under certain circumstances, and those circumstances should be set forth in the policy. The policy should also define the consequences for refusal to take a test.

3. Disciplinary action which will be taken as a result of a violation of the policy should be set forth. An employee should be aware that he may be removed from his job pending a drug screen, or that he may be discharged or terminated.

4. The policy should clearly state which employees are subject to the test and under what circumstances.

5. Notification to employees of positive test results must be provided. Employees should be given an opportunity to contest the results before disciplinary action is taken. A hearing should always be permitted before terminations. Hearing procedures should be specifically set forth in the policy.

6. The company should advise the employees that it is the intent of the company to help troubled employees in overcoming drug, alcohol and other problems which are or may affect job performance. In order to accomplish this goal, the policy should provide for referrals to the company EAP following a positive drug or alcohol screen. Employees should also be encouraged to seek assistance at the EAP on a voluntary basis before more severe problems develop.

7. If the policy is going to be effective and at the same time avoid civil liability, safeguards for protecting employee confidentiality must be established. Results of the tests must be kept confidential and disclosed to only limited people. These policies should include to whom the information will be released and what will happen to the information after released. No results should be disclosed until a second test has confirmed the positive results.

Who Should Be Tested?

The company must determine from the outset which groups of employees will be subject to testing. The potential legal problems involved in testing the different groups of employees have assisted companies in making their decisions about whom to test.

Many companies have chosen to limit testing to pre-employment screens only. The companies hope that this will discourage drug users from joining the workplace. At the same time there are few legal problems associated with preemployment drug and alcohol testing.

Employers have the right to require employees to be free from the use of drugs as a condition of employment, especially since those individuals who are abusing alcohol and drugs may cause danger to co-workers.

All applicants should be tested, rather than testing applicants randomly and prospective applicants should be advised that they will be tested for drugs as part of the preemployment process. Employers should obtain a consent from each applicant that acknowledges that there will be testing and that the applicant is providing his/her consent.

Some companies have chosen to perform testing on those employees whose actions create a reasonable suspicion of drug use, as a result of being involved in an accident or being unable to work. In order to have such testing "for cause" there must be suspicion based on specific facts that the employee is under the influence of alcohol or drugs. Such reasonable cause includes, but is not limited to deteriorating work performance, excessive tardiness, absenteeism, an accident on the job or suspect behavior. Documentation must be maintained to substantiate why an employer or supervisor believed circumstances justifying "for cause" testing existed.

Based on recent cases, it is clear that "for cause" testing has met constitutional challenges. In *McKechnie v. Dargan*, (E.D.N.Y., April 28, 1986, No. C.V. 84-4339), the testing of a police officer was upheld when the department has reasonable grounds to suspect that the officer was intoxicated or under the influence of alcohol. In this case the officer's gun was used by a friend in a crime. Additionally, there had been deteriorated work performance over an extended period of time. Similarly, firefighters who exhibit signs of intoxication and smell from alcohol, create a reasonable basis to require testing. *Korlick v. Lowery*, 26 N.Y. 2d 723 (1970). Refusal to take a drug test, if based on reasonable cause, can result in dismissal. *King v. McMickens*, 501 N.Y.S. 2d 679 (1st Cir. 1986).

In *Division 241 Amalgamated Transit Union v. Suscy,* 538 F. 2d 1264 (7th Cir. 1976) the bus operators' union filed a complaint attacking the constitutionality of a rule enacted by the Chicago Transit Authority. The rule provided that employees who were suspected of being under the influence of alcohol or drugs while on duty may be required to take a blood and urinalysis test. The United States Court of Appeals held that the state had a paramount interest in protecting the public by insuring that bus drivers were fit for duty. The court balanced the drivers' rights to privacy against the public's interest in safety. The court further said that before there could be testing, employees had to be involved in an accident or suspected of being under the influence. As a result the court found that there could be testing under the rules as enacted by the Chicago Transit Authority.

In *Fraternal Order of Police, Newark Lodge No. 12 v. City of Newark,* (N.J. Sup. Ct. Essex Co., Mar. 20, 1986), the court upheld a police department's order requiring all members of the narcotics bureau to submit to mandatory screening. The court required that the department take some steps to assure the accurateness of the tests and to insure the privacy of the officers. Similarly, in *Seeling v. McMickens,* (N.Y.L.J. August 7, 1986), a state court upheld urine testing for correction officers who were required to drive prison vans because of the safety-sensitive nature of the job.

Many companies have taken the drug screening one step further and have instituted drug tests which are performed randomly and unannounced. These companies have justified these screens based on the inherent danger to the employees from working with other employees who have substance abuse problems and who are working in safety-sensitive positions. There have been many recent conflicting cases regarding the legality of such random tests. For example, in *Shoemaker v. Handel,* 608 F.Supp. 1151 (D.C.N.J. 1985), the court held that New Jersey had a legitimate interest in testing jockeys for drugs and alcohol in order to reduce the possibility of accident and death while racing. The basis of this decision was that horseracing is a closely regulated industry, which has traditionally been subject to close supervision and regulation. Additionally, there were substantial safeguards to protect confidentiality. Results were considered confidential and access to positive results was limited to Commissioners of the New Jersey Racing Commission and the Executive Director or his designee, unless there is a contested matter. The Racing Commission also stated that no information would be shared with any state agency regarding criminal prosecution.

In Marietta, Georgia, employees of the Marietta Board of Lights and Water were asked to submit to random drug tests. This occurred after the manager began receiving reports of drug usage by board employees. The company thought that the drug use may have been responsible for what they believed to be a large number of injuries to employees. Because of the extremely hazardous nature of the work performed by the employees, the manager felt that such drug usage constituted a threat to the safety of the employees and the public. After the random drug tests were completed each of the employees tested showed positive for marijuana. The testing was challenged, but the court held that the tests were administered as part of the government's legitimate inquiry into the use of drugs by employees engaged in hazardous work. The court found, therefore, that the tests were not unreasonable. *Allen v. City of Marietta,* 601 F Supp. 482 (N.D. Ga. 1985).

In the case of *Jones v. McKenzie,* 638 F. Supp. 1500, (D.C. 1986) the court held that subjecting a school bus attendant to testing without probable cause violated the attendant's Fourth Amendment rights. In this case, there was no evidence that the individual in question ever used drugs or was under the influence of drugs either on or off the premises. Additionally, the employer did not confirm the positive test result with a second confirmation test. However, the court stated that its ruling might be different for school bus drivers or mechanics who are directly responsible for the operation and maintenance of buses and that those employees might reasonably be subjected to urine tests without suspicion.

Many other recent cases have held that public employees, even in safety-sensitive positions, may *not* be subject to urine tests unless there is reasonable suspicion that the employee is using drugs and/or alcohol. In *Capua v. City of Plainfield,* 1 IER Cases 625 (9/18/86), firefighters employed by the City of Plainfield were ordered to submit to a surprise urine test. In this case there was no notice, no collective bargaining with the union, immediate termination for positive test results, surveillance during urine collection, no reasonable cause or suspicion, and no confidentiality safeguards. As a result, the court found such testing to be unconstitutional.

In *Caurso v. Ward* (N.Y. Sup. Ct. July 2, 1986, No. 12632/86) the court invalidated a New York City Police Department rule requiring random drug testing. The Department argued that the police were serving in safety-sensitive positions. The court held, however, that there must be reasonable suspicion before an officer can be required to take a urine test. Courts have recently issued similar decisions relating to other police departments and firefighters. See also *Turner v. Fraternal Order of Police,* 500A. 2d 1005 (D.C. 1985).

It is clear from the recent court decisions regarding random drug tests that these cases will be decided on a case by case basis. It is difficult to predict what the United States Supreme Court will finally decide on this issue. Until there is more guidance from the courts, testing should be limited to preemployment screening and "for cause" testing, rather than utilizing random screening. This approach to testing should limit liability and law suits.

Off Duty Use of Drugs

Many employers would like to take disciplinary action if an employee is involved with drugs off duty or if an employee is involved in other off duty criminal conduct. Generally, the case law indicates that what an employee does on his or her time, outside of work, is not subject to workplace discipline. However, if the conduct of the employee could affect the business reputation of the company, render the employee unable to work or affect morale, then discipline is permissible.

In *Trailways Southeastern Lines, Inc.,* 81 Lab. Arb (BNA) 712 (Gibson, Arb. 1983) an employee pled guilty to breaking and entering with the intention of murdering his ex-wife. The driver was put on probation for the criminal offense. As part of the probation the driver had to attend an alcoholic rehabilitation program, as well as attending Alcoholics Anonymous. Additionally, he was ordered not to consume any alcoholic beverages. A news article appeared in a local paper reporting the plea and identifying the employee as a Trailways bus driver. Other newspaper articles identified the individual as a Trailways bus driver and included details of the charges, including the fact that the driver had been carrying a gun. The arbitrator held that the publicity of the case and of the defendant as an employee of the company justified discharge. *See also City of Wilkes Barre,* 74 Lab. Arb. (BNA) 33 (Dunn 1980).

Similarly, in *Martin-Marietta Aerospace,* 81 L.A. 695 (1983), an arbitrator upheld the termination of an employee who had been convicted of selling cocaine off company premises. The arbitrator felt that the employer had a legitimate concern that the employee might attempt to sell drugs to other employees at the workplace.

In a contrary decision, an arbitrator found that an employer had no right to force an employee to submit to a drug test when a marijuana cigarette was observed in the employee's car after work hours. The employee in this case was on company property when drugs were found in his possession although his presence on the property was not related to his employment. *Texas Utilities Generating Co.,* 82 Lab. Arb. (BNA) 6 (1983). This case may indicate that an employee's drug use does not extend to off-duty use of drugs, unless the employer can show that the employee was unable to work as a result of the drug use, that the employer's reputation was harmed, or that the employee poses a risk to coworkers.

Constitutional Issues

The state and federal constitutions do not generally apply to the actions of private employers because the requisite "state action" is not present. Therefore, most of the challenges to drug testing have been brought by those individuals employed in the public sector. Challenges to testing in the private sector will generally be based on different grounds than those in the public sector. If, however, private companies are subject to a high degree of governmental regulation, the companies should be aware of the possibility that they may be subject to constitutional limitations. The following addresses the most frequent bases for constitutional challenges.

Right to Privacy

The first legal challenge raised by those opposing drug screening is an allegation of a violation on one's right to privacy. Although this right is not specifically enumerated in our constitution, the courts have found that specific guarantees exist in the Bill of Rights, the right of privacy being one of them.

In *Treasury Employees v. Von Raab,* 1 IER cases 945, (Nov. 14, 1986), an injunction was filed in Federal Court seeking to block the United States Custom Service from further urine collection as part of a drug testing programs. The program required that the service workers who seek promotion into certain positions submit to drug screening, as a condition of employment for placement into these positions. A collector was physically present in the bathroom during the urination process. The representative placed dye in the urinal and then stepped back behind a partition. The court found that the testing "detracts from the dignity of each customs worker covered under the plan and invades the right of privacy such workers have under the United States Constitution. Excreting bodily wastes is a very personal bodily function normally done in private; it is accompanied by a legitimate expectation of privacy in both the process and the product. The Customs directive unconstitutionally interferes with the privacy rights of the Customs workers." It is important to note in this case that there was no evidence of drug problems among the workforce, nor was there any reasonable cause to suspect that the employees were using or selling drugs at the worksite. See also *McDonell v. Hunter,* 612 F.Supp. 1122 (D.C.Iowa 1985), below.

Unreasonable Search and Seizure

The next constitutional challenge raised is that the testing violates the fourth amendment right to be free from unreasonable searches and seizures. It must be remembered that the Fourth Amendment protects individuals from governmental searches and seizures. In determining whether an individual has a reasonable expectation of privacy and whether the governmental instructions are reasonable, the courts will balance the need to seize against the invasion.

In *McDonnel v. Hunter,* three correctional institution employees challenged the constitutionality of an Iowa Department of Corrections policy which subjected the employees to searches of their vehicles and persons, including urinalysis and blood tests. The court found that the testing was an unreasonable search because there was no reasonable suspicion, based on specific objective facts that the employee was under the influence of alcohol or controlled substances.

Similarly, a court prohibited a local school board from performing drug testing of teachers considered for tenure because there was no reasonable suspicion of drug usage. *Patchoque-Medford Congress of Teachers v. Board of Education,* Case No. C85-8759 (N.Y. Sup. Ct. Suffolk City 1985).

The constitutionality of a police department order was tested in *Turner v. Fraternal Order of Police,* 500 A. 2d 1005 (D.C. App. 1985). The department order provided that upon suspicion of drug abuse a Department Official may order any member of the force to submit to urinalysis testing. The Court held that the department may compel officers to submit to the testing based on suspected drug abuse. The court considered whether, under the circumstances, an officer has a legitimate expectation of privacy and whether the department's order is unnecessarily intrusive. The court further stated that the department had a paramount interest in protecting the public. Based on the type of work in which officers engage and the need to be alert to carry out such duties, the court believed that the use of controlled substances by police officers was a situation which created serious consequences to the public. Because the order required that there be suspected drug abuse, the court held that the intrusion was not unreasonable.

Due Process Rights

Opponents of drug testing argue that such testing violates an individual's due process rights. Such claims allege that the drug tests are inaccurate and insufficiently related to work performance. These allegations also relate to whether or not there is proper notice of the circumstances under which testing will be performed, and whether the employee had a right to contest the results. Due process requires that no adverse action be taken without a second confirmation test.

Many drug screening policies have been found to be unconstitutional based on Due Process challenges. These challenges have been brought based on the fact that the test results do not and cannot indicate impaired job performance. Many courts, however, have accepted the notion that any detectable use of drugs may impair job performance, especially in safety-sensitive positions. See *Turner v. Fraternal Order of Police,* above.

In *Brotherhood of Locomotive Engineers v. Burlington Northern,* 117 LRRM 2739 (D.C. Montana 1984) the court granted the union's request for an injunction against the employer's new policy of using drug tests to detect possession of controlled substances by its employees because the employer failed to bargain with the union. In a union-represented workplace, it is necessary to discuss drug screens and searches with the union representatives before an employer can unilaterally make changes in the workplace rules.

Courts have also found that drug testing violates due process rights because the drug testing plan was far from an infallible system and was fraught with dangers of false positives. See *Treasury Employees v. Von Raab,* above. There can also be a violation of due process rights if the employee is not provided with an opportunity for a hearing before discharge. See *Jones v. McKenzie,* above.

These cases emphasize the importance of the proper development of a drug testing program. Many legal problems can be avoided by consulting with legal counsel and following constitutional safeguards to protect an employee's basic rights.

The Arbitrator's Views

Arbitrators will look unfavorably upon those companies who perform testing and do not provide the rehabilitative services of an Employee Assistance Program. For example, in *Alleghany Lundlum Steel Corp*, 84 Lab. Arb. 476 (1985), an arbitrator held that where misconduct is alcohol-related and the company has an EAP, the employee must be allowed to seek assistance. This was true even though neither the company nor the union had any knowledge of the employee's problem before the discharge. The arbitrator felt that the grievant had not been provided with an opportunity to seek assistance from the EAP because the dissemination of information regarding the EAP was inadequate.

Arbitrators may also consider the consistency of the treatment of employees. In *Indianapolis Rubber co.*, 79 Lab. Arb. (BNA) 529 (1983) the arbitrator found that the employer had previously reinstated terminated employees who successfully completed a rehabilitation program. The arbitrator, therefore, believed that the company improperly discriminated against another employee by refusing to reinstate him when he completed the same program.

The arbitration decisions indicate that the arbitrators will consider whether progressive discipline was used, the length of employment, work history, the type of job involved and whether there is danger to the public or others because of an employee's conduct. Notice requirements must be met for an arbitration decision to be upheld and the company must bargain with the union regarding the drug testing. In *Gem City Chemical, Inc.*, 86 L.A. 1023 (1986) an employee refused to submit to a urine test during a physical examination. The arbitrator held that the employee had been improperly discharged because the request was not based on reasonable cause. Additionally, the testing was not discussed or incorporated into the union's collective bargaining agreement. The employer also did not provide notice of the test.

Arbitrators will expect that reputable laboratories, with accurate results be chosen to perform the tests. Disciplinary action should only be based on the second confirmation test. In *Washington Metropolitan Area Transit Authority*, 82 L.A. 151 (Bernhardt, 1983), an arbitrator upheld the discharge of a bus driver who was tested for drugs following an accident. The specimens were confirmed and positive results obtained both times. In a Federal Court of Appeals case, the court overturned the discipline of air traffic controllers who tested positive for drugs because the samples were not maintained for independent verification. *Banks v. Federal Aviation Administration,* 687 F.2d 92 (5th Cir. 1982).

It is clear that the arbitrators will scrutinize drug testing procedures. Employers should be aware of the principles considered by the arbitrators. Arbitrators will favor use of an EAP prior to discharge, but will generally not have much sympathy for an employee who fails to recover or follow a "last chance" agreement. Arbitrators will require uniformity in discipline and will consider whether progressive discipline was utilized. Constitutional safeguards must be maintained if a discharge is going to be upheld.

EAP Involvement in Testing

The EAP should not be required to do the testing itself because this creates a conflict for the EAP whose primary purpose is rehabilitation, not discipline. An EAP should be involved in setting up a "last chance" agreement which addresses and includes a plan for treatment, and requirements for continued employment. Employees should be advised that the use of the EAP represents a "last chance" and not a guarantee that the employment will be maintained. Further, the use of the EAP will not provide protection against discipline. Failure to improve deteriorated work performance or continued drug use following treatment may result in termination.

The plan should be in writing and should be signed by the employee. Those persons who will receive the follow-up information regarding whether or not there is improvement and/or recovery should be listed in the plan so that there will be no question regarding breach of confidentiality if information is disclosed.

The plan should be specific and should be clearly written so that there can be no subsequent disputes regarding what is and is not expected of the employee.

Conclusion

In summary, it is clear that there are many conflicting decisions regarding the legality of drug and alcohol testing. It is hopeful that in the near future, the United States Supreme Court will provide guidance on this subject. Until that time, if a company is going to institute a drug screening policy, certain constitutional safeguards must be followed.

Without these safeguards it is unlikely that the validity of the program will be upheld.

If preemployment testing is going to be performed, all applicants must be notified in advance. Testing on the basis of reasonable suspicion has, so far, met legal challenges, if the testing is performed in accordance with constitutional safeguards. In comparison, the validity of random testing is questionable at this time, even in safety sensitive positions. The lack of uniformity in the recent decisions indicates that the courts may invalidate these programs in the future. Further clarifying decisions are necessary in order to provide the answer to whether random testing will be allowed in the future.

COMMENT/UPDATE

CHERYL ANDREWS AND WILLIAM S. HUTCHISON

Substance abuse cost America over $238 billion dollars in 1991 or nearly $1,000 per capita to pay for unnecessary health care, auto accidents, crime, law enforcement and lost productivity (Rice, 1993). In addition, the impact on the family is immense since alcohol is implicated in one of three divorces and one in four American families report that alcohol has caused trouble in their family. At the workplace, one of three Americans are dependent on cigarettes and 8 percent drink alcohol daily. Seventy percent of illegal drug users are employed (Rice, 1993).

The specific costs to employees include:

1. *Greater absenteeism:* abusers are 8 times more absent and tardy than nonabusers.
2. *Theft:* Ten percent of abusers steal from employers and co-workers.
3. *Worker's Compensation Claims:* Five times more claims for abusers.
4. *Health insurance/sick leave:* Abusers use 3 times as much sick leave and up to twice as much health insurance than nonabusers.
5. *Decreased Productivity:* Abusers work at 20–30% less capacity than they would be capable if they did not abuse substances. This costs American industry $100 billion and decreased competitiveness in the global economy.
6. *Accidents:* 47% of workplace accidents are drug related and 49% of workplace deaths are drug related.

In order to combat the problems created at the workplace the Drug-Free Workplace Act of 1988 was passed (Ray et al., 1993). This legislation toughened federal criminal statutes and provided funding for drug education, treatment and prevention programs. It requires federal contractors and federal grant recipients with contracts of $25,000 to implement and administer a program for maintaining a drug-free workplace. Some of the specific requirements include:

312

1. Notification to employees that as a condition of employment on federal projects or grants each employee must not engage in unlawful manufacture, distribution, dispensation or use of controlled substances in the workplace and must notify the employer of any criminal drug statute conviction for a violation occurring in the workplace not less than five days after the conviction.
2. That the employer notify the contracting federal agency within 10 days of notification by an employee or any other person of the conviction, or face sanctions including loss of the grant or contract.

Since the inception of the Drug Free Workplace Act the U.S. Department of Transportation, U.S. Department of Defense, the National Labor Relations Act, Railway Labor Act and Americans with Disabilities Act have specified drug and alcohol testing and treatment laws for the workplace (Rice, 1993).

On February 15, 1994, the Department of Transportation issued its rules under the Omnibus Transportation Employee Testing Act of 1991 which requires alcohol testing in certain industries. The projected impact of these rules is approximately 8 million workers who perform "safety-sensitive" functions in transportation industries including airlines, railroads, trucking and commercial vehicles, mass transit, pipeline operators and maritime vessels at a cost of $200 million annually. These rules expand existing drug testing programs to cover 3 million employees involved intrastate trucking, school buses and motor coaches, government vehicles and mass transit. These rules took effect for employers of 50 or more on January 1, 1995 and will take effect for small employers on January 1, 1996. These rules require post-accident testing where alcohol could have been a factor; random testing; testing where the supervisor suspects employee misuse; and testing before returning to work.

Under the U.S. Department of Defense's (DOD's) rules, all defense contracts must contain a clause requiring a drug-free workplace whenever the work involved entails (1) access to classified information, (2) bears on national security concerns in some other way or (3) necessitates protecting the health and safety of those using—or affected by—the product or performance of the contract. DOD contractors must, *inter alia*, establish a drug testing program, including random testing, for employees in sensitive positions (that is, those with access to classified information or in positions involving national security, health or safety, or requiring a high degree of trust and confidence). DOD contractors may also establish drug testing programs for employees in nonsensitive positions for reasonable suspicion, after an accident, as a follow-up to drug rehabilitation or counseling and where employees volunteer to be tested.

The National Labor Relations Act and Railway Labor Act require unionized employers to bargain about terms and conditions of employment, a category that includes drug testing and the requirements that workers be "drug free." This means that before implementing a drug-free workplace policy, unionized employers must notify their union representatives of what they intend to do and bargain in good faith, either until an agreement is reached or until an impasse is declared.

The Vocational Rehabilitation Act of 1973 defines drug abuse as a protected handicap. However, the 1978 amendments exempts individuals whose abuse interferes with the performance of their duties or are threats to safety of others.

The Americans with Disabilities Act (ADA), which became effective July 26, 1992, for all employers with 25 or more employees and on July 26, 1994, for all employers with 15 or more employees, prohibits discriminations against "qualified people with disabilities" and severely limits an employer's ability to inquire into an employee's or job applicant's medical history. While under the ADA, the employer cannot require an applicant to undergo a *medical* examination *prior to making a conditional offer of employment;* a drug test (as opposed to an alcohol test) is *not* considered a medical examination under the ADA.

Individuals who have been rehabilitated, are in suspended treatment and not using drugs or are erroneously regarded as using drugs are protected by the Act. Thus, the major thrusts of these laws are to protect industry and nonabusers while promoting recovery of substance abusers. It is anticipated that this emphasis will continue to expand to include required treatment and Employee Assistance Programs to be offered at all Drug-Free Worksites.

REFERENCES

Ray, O. and Koir, C. (1993). *Drugs, Society, and Human Behavior.* St. Louis, MO: Mosby.

Rice, D. (1993). Substance Abuse: The Nation's Number One Health Problem. Brandeis University.

Chapter 23

CRITICAL INCIDENT STRESS DEBRIEFING

MICHAEL G. RANK, PH.D.

As you begin to read this chapter, pause for a second and recall an event or experience that changed your life. Positive events come to mind for some. Unfortunately, others recall negative and painful experiences. Just as we are quick to recall positive experiences, the negative ones never leave our memory either, despite our best efforts to keep them buried. Sometimes these memories "pop up" at the most inopportune moments. There is usually some type of environmental or situational cue that triggers the memory. It is usually something associated with the original event. The memory can bring a smile to our face or be so severe as to prevent us from participating in activities or interacting with others in routine situations. The point is, memories remain. We do not forget special or extraordinary experiences, for example, a birth, a death, a bank robbery, or a physical assault. If the event is not discussed with others within a few weeks, our recollection of what really happened may become distorted. In the case of distressing events, this distortion tendency may lead to a failure to resolve the incident successfully. Horowitz (1979) notes that humans have a "completion tendency" in which information is processed until reality and perception match.

Consider the following statements made by tellers following bank robberies:

- "His eyes stared right into mine. He was angry. I know he would recognize me again if he saw me. I am always frightened."
- "He held the gun to my face. I can't stop thinking about the gun. I dream about it every night."
- "I will quit my job and move away before I will testify. He may try to find me."
- "Since the robbery, every person that comes into the bank, I consider a potential robber. I don't know if I can ever trust anyone again. I am constantly on guard."

315

- "I know he had been in the bank before. I recognized his voice. I recognized his eyes through the mask. His presence haunts me. I don't know who he is, but I know I know him. I can't sleep. I constantly think about his eyes. I dream about his eyes. He will find me and kill me. His eyes told me that."

The important thing about all of these recollections is that they remain etched within our memories. Special or extraordinary events are replayed over and over again in our mind and do not lose their power until we integrate them into our understanding of life's experiences.

In an effort to help, significant others, coworkers, or friends may say to individuals working through these memories, "Just don't think about it or talk about it and you will get over it." As most of us have experienced, we just don't stop thinking about extraordinary events. Memories are not choices. We cannot choose what memories come into our conscious thoughts at any particular time.

Critical Incident Stress

Critical incident stress is a unique type of personal condition that occurs when an individual experiences or witnesses an event that is unusual, extraordinary, or violent. The reaction to a sudden, random, and senseless incident is called a critical incident response (Family Enterprises Inc., 1993). The critical incident response is the immediate reaction to the event and may or may not develop into posttraumatic stress disorder (PTSD). The chances of developing PTSD are greatly reduced by immediate intervention. It is estimated that 60 percent of individuals who observe or survive a distressing event report experiencing subsequent emotional consequences (Family Enterprises Inc., 1993). The immediate response usually involves a vacillation between numbness and hyperarousal, that is, feeling nothing because of the initial shock or feeling overwhelmed with emotions. It is natural for humans to want to block painful feelings. Unfortunately, stress has to be expressed somehow. In an effort to avoid the painful feelings associated with the event, some people self-medicate with alcohol or drugs. Some may exercise excessively. Other people develop high blood pressure, ulcers, eating disorders, panic and anxiety attacks, or other forms of problems.

In most cases, individuals are able to integrate the event or "make sense of it" within four weeks following the experience. Those individuals who have experienced an extreme stressor and are unable to integrate the experience within one month are at risk for developing PTSD. The four week and one month guidelines noted above are set by the American Psychiatric Association (1994) in the diagnostic criteria for PTSD and acute stress disorder (ASD).

The Diagnostic and Statistical Manual of Mental Disorders published by the American Psychiatric Association (1994) noted that PTSD, ASD, and the adjustment disorders all require the presence of a psychosocial stressor, however with PTSD and ASD, the stressor must be extreme (p. 626). An adjustment disorder is characterized by a stressor of any severity. Within two days to four weeks following a severe stressor, an individual can be diagnosed with ASD. This is usually the case for individuals immediately following a severe stressor. If the symptoms persist past one month, an individual may be diagnosed with PTSD. If an event is not severe enough to satisfy the definition of an extreme stressor, an individual would be most likely diagnosed with an adjustment disorder.

Critical incident stress may or may not be extreme or traumatic for a given individual. An individual's response to a stressor is highly unique, depending upon one's interpretation of the event, coping style, and support system. Some individuals are able to immediately place the experience in perspective, and with immediate and appropriate attention to their physiological and emotional reactions, will integrate the experience within one month. Other individuals may become debilitated by an experience that for most of us would be integrated as a natural circumstance of life. It is impossible to predict by the nature of an event whether any given individual will develop PTSD.

There is a lack of clarity as to when an event is a critical incident and when it is a traumatic incident. Critical incidents and traumatic events overlap and the boundaries between them are blurred (Frolkey, 1992). The *DSM-IV* (American Psychiatric Association, 1994, p. 424) listed a number of qualifying traumatic events that are experienced directly or witnessed. These events are prefaced with the phrase "but are not limited to." The diagnostic criteria for PTSD (p. 427) states that "the person must have experienced, witnessed, or was confronted with an event or events that involved actual or threatened death or serious injury, or a threat to the physical integrity of self or others" and "the person's response involved intense fear, helplessness, or horror."

Walker (1990) defined a critical incident as "any crisis situation that causes emergency personnel, family members, or bystanders to respond with immediate or delayed stress-altered physical, mental, emotional, psychological, or social coping mechanisms" (p. 122). Lewis defined a critical incident as an event which is extraordinary and produces significant reactions for the affected individual (EAPA Exchange, 1991). According to Gwaltney (1987), critical incident stress symptoms follow a basic principle: any environmental stimulus that is perceived as dangerous to life or limb, whether or not it produces physical injury, can be regarded as a trauma and can precipitate PTSD. Trauma can produce either physiological or psychiatric conditions. Van Fleet (1992) pointed out that many situations are stressful yet not necessarily traumatic. A potentially traumatizing event is generally referred to as a critical incident. However, the critical incident is usually defined in terms of its effects; that is, as an event leading to a traumatizing reaction. Frolkey (1992) stated that critical incidents occur in a work-related setting while traumatic events may occur anywhere. Frolkey added that another major difference between a traumatic event and a critical incident is in the degree of personalization. According to Frolkey, a critical incident does not involve victims personally, victims just happen to be in the wrong place at the wrong time. Using a bank robbery as an example, it is not the tellers but the bank and its money that are robbed. A burglary or robbery at one's home is a personal violation of the individual's place of refuge.

Van Fleet (1992) offered the following examples to help distinguish between traumatic stressors and those that fall into the subtraumatic category:

Example: *Industrial setting*

Traumatic: fatal accident at the work site; violent death through other means (e.g., shooting incident; serious injuries, amputations, etc.; and, dangerous working conditions precipitated by a crisis (e.g., chemical spills, threats of explosions, cave-ins, rescue attempts, etc.).

Stressful: death by natural causes; unsafe working conditions (e.g., scaffolding, need for shoring, severe weather conditions, etc.); equipment failures; the work environment itself (e.g., mines, oil-rigs, etc.); and, hostile encounters (e.g., loggers versus protestors).

Example: *Bank Robbery*

Traumatic: incidents resulting in violent death or severe injuries; a prolonged hostage situation; a shoot-out between perpetrators and police; and when weapons discharge in the bank.

Stressful: weapons in evidence; threats and/or mention of weapons; notes passed requesting tellers' cash; suspicious-looking or irate customers; and, use of racial slurs, profanity, or insults.

Natural responses to a critical incident are often confused with PTSD (Van Fleet, 1992). Depression, irritability, and withdrawal immediately following an industrial accident in which one's best friend died are normal. The same reactions 30 days, three months or three years later are not.

An informal survey of potentially traumatic events was administered to a group of graduate students in a clinical social work program (Rank, 1996). The students were provided a list of twenty events and asked to rank them in order of severity as if it had happened to them, with one being the most severe and twenty being the least. The results of this survey with the mean scores are as follows:

(4.1) — Physical Assault (i.e., rape, crime victim)
(5.2) — Unexpected Death in Family (i.e., suicide, accidents, illness)
(5.7) — Hostage Situations
(6.7) — Kidnapping (i.e., child, sociopolitical, criminal)
(6.8) — Plane Crash
(7.4) — Survivors of Abuse (i.e., sexual, physical, economic, psychological, emotional, neglect)
(8.1) — Being Diagnosed with a Life-Threatening Illness
(8.2) — Natural Disasters (i.e., hurricanes, earthquake)
(10.2) — Automobile Accident
(11.2) — Death of a Family Member following a long period of illness
(11.2) — Bank Robbery
(11.4) — A product of a Violent Neighborhood
(12.2) — Financial Loss/Bankruptcy
(12.3) — Industrial Accident (i.e., a chemical explosion, a forklift accident)
(12.8) — Suicide of a co-worker
(13.4) — Sociopolitical Oppression
(13.6) — Major Layoffs, Unemployment
(13.7) — Intimidation (i.e., harassments, stalking, extortion, blackmail)
(16.1) — Noncombat Veteran of a Foreign War
(18.3) — Embarrassment (i.e., social, professional)

These findings are not to be considered a definitive research study. The survey was administered to a cohort of clinically-minded graduate students simply to gain a perspective about the interpretation of traumatic events. What is difficult to ascertain, however, is at what point along the continuum of events does an event become extreme. As mentioned previously, the meaning an individual gives to an event and their coping style, work together to determine the reaction to the event. One could argue for or against many of the events on the above list as being potentially traumatic. Few would argue that physical assault, the unexpected death of a family member, hostage situations, kidnapping, and plane crashes have the potential to affect an individual seriously. However, some people might argue that being a survivor of abuse, being diagnosed with a life-threatening illness, experiencing a natural disaster, and auto accidents are events that are more easily integrated for most individuals.

Suppose an individual's livelihood depended upon the competent presentation of oneself to the public as with an entertainer or athlete. An embarrassing performance could produce a performance anxiety that might prevent that individual from ever performing again. As a result of the embarrassment, the individual loses their livelihood and becomes depressed and suicidal. Was this experience severely traumatic for this individual?

During the stock market crash of 1929, many individuals killed themselves as a result of their financial losses. Were these individuals traumatized as a result of those circumstances? In the case of "noncombat veterans" who might have been in a war zone and lived with the persistent threat of being killed, or knowing directly of people being killed, or actually seeing the carnage of war in the aftermath, could these veterans have been traumatized by these experiences? How about the nurse or the physician who treat the victims of violence; are these health care professionals at risk to be traumatized by these experiences?

Events that produce a stress disorder are considered to be extreme, directly life-threatening, and experienced with intense fear, helplessness, or horror. In addition to unusualness and severity, environmental stressors vary along a number of other dimensions that may influence the pattern of post event adjustment. According to Fairbank (1989) the following eight variables must also be taken into consideration when assessing an individual's response to a critical incident:

1. *danger* —the degree to which exposure to the event entails risk of bodily injury;
2. *degree of personal involvement* —the degree to which the event is personally experienced;
3. *frequency* —number of exposures to the event;
4. *duration* —length of exposure to the event;
5. *predictability* —the degree to which the stressor is anticipated;
6. *controllability* —the degree to which the victim or survivor can control the onset and termination of the event;

7. *origin* —human versus natural events and, in the case of human events, whether the event was accidental or deliberate;
8. *number of persons affected.*

It is impossible to know how individuals experience an event. To attempt to assess the degree to which an experience may be traumatizing for any given group of individuals is pointless. The important point is to treat one who has experienced a critical event very sensitively, recognizing that responses are unique and must be considered seriously. The individual's response to the event as a result of their interpretation of the meaning of the event and not the event itself is the critical factor that will determine how an individual adjusts and whether or not an individual develops PTSD. An unusual experience may be only stressful for some while debilitating for others.

Critical Incident Stress Debriefing

An effective treatment approach to avoid long-term emotional consequences, or the development of PTSD, is to participate in a critical incident stress debriefing (CISD). A critical incident stress debriefing is an intervention for two or more individuals experiencing or witnessing a common distressing phenomenon. CISD's are intended to normalize the experience and provide an opportunity for individuals to express their interpretations, thoughts, and feelings about the event.

Critical incident stress debriefings, also called critical incident debriefings (CID), traumatic event debriefings (TED), or posttrauma interventions (PTI), are the preferred intervention for any group of individuals experiencing a common stressful or traumatic event in any setting. The event may not necessarily be a traumatic event as defined by the *DSM-IV* (American Psychiatric Association, 1994); however, it could be considered stressful for almost anyone regardless of the subsequent reaction. The intervention is designed to prevent PTSD and teach effective skills for coping with the current situation and for subsequent traumatic incidents which may occur in the future.

CISDs are intended primarily to provide the opportunity for all the individuals experiencing the event to freely discuss their perceptions, interpretations, feelings, and recollections in a supportive environment.

They are to be conducted only by trained mental health professionals (MHPs). CISDs are usually conducted as a structured group process which combines elements of diagnostic assessment, education, and psychotherapeutic abreaction (the relieving of a repressed emotion by talking about it) (Polen-Bonitz & Morrison, 1993). The MHP usually begins with basic post-trauma education to establish a therapeutic context for the group work which follows. Within the group, the MHP assists participants to understand the nature of the critical incident response. Each participant is provided the opportunity to speak. The MHP encourages all participants to express their concerns as completely as possible. The MHP educates the participants as to the nature and course of critical incident stress and provides suggestions to avoid emotional and physiological consequences. The MHP emphasizes that the reactions to the event are normal and predictable responses to an unusual event. The phenomena of intrusive thoughts and denial are especially highlighted. Intrusive thoughts refer to the re-experiencing of the feelings and emotions that occurred during the critical incident. Denial is explained as the defense mechanism that allows us to block out emotional pain rather than be overwhelmed by it.

CISDs are intended to remove the mystery and fear associated with distressing events. Participants describe their feelings and the effects the experience has had on their lives. It is important that participants understand that there are a variety of responses and that there is no one "normal" response to extraordinary experiences. Participants in CISD debriefings are given suggestions and handouts on how to deal with their reactions to the event. This includes stress reduction techniques, avoiding alcohol and drugs, and maintaining reasonable exercise and diet regimens. They are also advised of the course of the distress and what to expect in the future.

A follow-up adjustment plan is created using the suggestions of all participants. This plan should include, at the very least, learning stress-coping skills that may help far beyond the resolution to the incident and an awareness of the potential damage of accumulating stress without release. During this process, the MHP needs to be alert to individuals that may require treatment beyond this group intervention.

To be most effective, CISDs are conducted in groups of six to ten. Some professionals will conduct a debriefing with up to 25 participants (Bell, 1995). With more than 12 participants, the process becomes counterproductive and much too time consuming. As every individual in the group is given time to relate their interpretation of the event and discuss their thoughts and feelings, the process can become labored with too many participants. Generally, the intervention is conducted two to five days after the occurrence of a traumatic incident. Some suggest conducting the debriefing 24 hours after exposure to a traumatic event (Bell, 1995). At least 24 hours should elapse before a CISD is conducted. Within the first 24 hours responses may still be numb and many of the individuals are still processing through the experience, trying to understand it. A debriefing held too soon will not achieve the desired results, rather, it may further confound the recovery process.

It is not advisable to have individuals who were not involved in the common experience included in the process. It is especially not advisable to have supervisors, managers, or police officers involved unless they were also a part of the experience. The participants have to feel free to talk about their feelings in these sessions. Often a participant may make statements that are emotionally charged, perhaps blaming others for negligence. The individual must feel safe in the debriefing. The individual should not feel that being candid would threaten their employment or family, or victimize them further. A defensive or insensitive individual not a part of the event may take these statements personally and actually further victimize the individual.

Often the responses of others add to an individual's troubles following a critical incident. This phenomenon is referred to as secondary victimization. Secondary victimization impedes the recovery process and is often the major cause of poor morale, conflicts between management and employees, time away from work, conflicts with significant others, and litigation after a traumatic event. Matsakis (1992) referred to the phenomenon as secondary wounding. Secondary victimization or secondary wounding occurs when employers, managers, employees, friends, family members, or loved ones respond in an uninformed, caustic, unempathetic, unsympathetic, or cruel manner.

The following list, adapted from Matsakis (1992), notes some of the ways secondary victimization may be expressed:

- *Disbelief and Denial* — the general description or specific details of the traumatic incident are not believed; "I don't believe you, you are exaggerating."
- *Discounting* — the magnitude of the event and its results are poorly

understood; "So what's the big deal. You're not the only person with problems."

- *Blaming the Victim* — responsibility for the incident is attributed to its victims; "Your reaction is a self-inflicted wound." "You could have done something to prevent it." "It's your fault this happened."
- *Ignorance* — when nonsurvivors have improper information about the psychological, social, economic and other results of exposure to trauma; "Just forget it and get over it. Stop making an issue of it."
- *Impatience* — when loved ones or friends tire of the retelling of the story; "What's wrong with you, why can't you stop talking about it. I'm tired of hearing about it." "I can understand you would feel that way at the time, but the trauma is over now, you aren't living in the past, just get on with your life."
- *Stigmatization* — judgment made by others concerning the psychological consequences of a traumatic event, i.e., ridicule for experiencing symptoms or a belief that symptoms result from predisposing factors, malingering, for attention or sympathy; "He is a head case now." "She is different since the event. She will never be the person I once knew." "He is only acting like this to get out of work."
- *Denial of Assistance* — necessary services are denied because they are perceived as unwarranted or undeserved. "You don't deserve any help. Do it on your own."

There are many anecdotal stories told between friends and colleagues about secondary victimization. The media routinely prints horror stories about victims who are further victimized by insensitive interrogation or treatment. Another example of secondary victimization is the negative treatment of Vietnam veterans following their return home from Vietnam. Secondary victimization can be more damaging and debilitating than the original event. Effective CISDs incorporate information about secondary victimization and provide suggestions about how to cope with these circumstances.

Critical incident stress debriefings basically involve the following five steps (Family Enterprises Inc., 1993):

- telling the "story;"
- sharing responses and reactions to the event;
- understanding the responses of survival;

- contracting for recovery;
- closure.

Bell (1995) outlined a seven-step debriefing model. The first phase involves introductions and rule-setting; the second phase is for fact-finding; the third phase is for the expression of thoughts; the fourth is the reaction or feeling phase; the fifth is the symptom phase; the sixth is for teaching; and, the seventh is for reentry. Each participant is encouraged to make a final comment. No participant is ever *required* to speak or remain in the group process.

Mitchell (1985, p. 110) identified ten major objectives of the critical incident debriefing process:

1. Ventilation of intense emotions;
2. Exploration of symbolic meanings;
3. Group support under catastrophic conditions;
4. Initiation of the grief process within a supportive environment;
5. Reduction of fallacies;
6. Reassurance that intense emotions under catastrophic conditions are normal;
7. Preparation for the continuation of the grief process over the months to come;
8. Warning of the possibility of the development of a variety of emotional, cognitive, and physical symptoms in the aftermath of a serious crisis;
9. Education regarding normal and abnormal stress response syndromes;
10. Encouragement for continued group support and/or professional assistance.

The Critical Incident Stress Debriefing Protocol

There are many protocols available for CISDs (American Red Cross, 1991; Bell, 1995; Family Enterprises Inc., 1993; Mitchell, 1985; National Organization for Victim Assistance; 1992). The following section combines many of the principles from the above noted protocols in addition to the author's own experience.

CISDs are not intended to be therapy or counseling. They are a forum for the ventilation of emotions and reactions with the goal of normalizing responses. They provide information so participants can develop a more complete understanding of the incident and develop survivor group support and cohesiveness. CISDs teach appropriate coping skills, assist in adjustment to post-event circumstances, and advise participants of available services and resources.

The CISD should be conducted as early as possible during the day, in a private room with comfortable chairs and a restroom nearby. The chairs should be positioned in a circle with no table in the center. It is advisable to provide ample boxes of tissues and some refreshments. Name tags are optional. A handout package is always advisable. This package should contain at the very least, the agenda, descriptions of emotional and physiological responses common following a critical incident, as well as information for follow-up, referral, and community resources. A comprehensive, educational handout package is recommended.

The debriefing begins with introductory comments made by the MHP about his or her background and an explanation of the agenda, ground rules, and what to expect. The handout package should be distributed at this time. This is a critical time as participants will make the decision during this introductory period whether they will trust the MHP or not. During the introduction, the issue of confidentiality needs to be discussed thoroughly. It is also important to establish that blaming is inappropriate and that the debriefing is intended to promote an atmosphere of understanding and support. Participants are advised that they are free to leave the room at any time, do not have to speak, and if requested to speak, have the freedom to pass.

Following the introductory phase, each participant is invited, in turn, to tell their interpretation of the event. Often individual accounts of what happened can be quite different. It is not appropriate to point out inconsistencies in individual interpretations of the event. The MHP should ask questions that focus on the facts and description of the event including smells, sounds, sights, actions, thoughts, and feelings associated with the event. Each account should be kept as succinct and to the point as possible by the MHP. In the case of a verbose or tangential participant, it is important to gently advise that everyone must get the chance to speak and that an opportunity for more discussion will occur later in the process.

After all participants have had the opportunity to speak, the debriefer (MHP) summarizes the event based upon what was stated. At this point the debriefer can refer to the handout package, focusing upon the emotional and physiological responses that can happen. Participants are invited to comment and relate to these responses. During this process, the debriefer should relate present symptoms to the event and explain that subsequent symptoms may occur in the future that are a result of the critical incident and what to do if this happens.

The next component of the debriefing is contracting for recovery. Participants are advised of community resources, referrals, and follow-up. The debriefer should provide his or her telephone number and a time that he or she can be reached. The possibility for a follow-up debriefing should be offered.

Closure must be brought to the CISD. Final comments are made by the debriefer and time is allowed for participants to make final comments of their own. It is helpful for the debriefer to state that no one should leave the process if something has not been said that should be said or if there is an issue that needs to be addressed or if someone has a comment that should be made.

CISDs should be a gentle, nonthreatening process. The process lasts a minimum of one hour and ideally should be three hours with two breaks.

Although small group debriefings should be used whenever possible, there are often large numbers of individuals (more than 15) who have experienced a critical event. If there are not several debriefers that can break the group into smaller groups, the MHP should consider a community debriefing. The primary goals of community debriefings are only to provide information about the critical incident response and provide for self-referral. Community debriefings should be used when there is a large group which must be debriefed in one session, when two or more appropriately trained mental health professionals per session are not available, and when there is a time limit that absolutely prevents a small group debriefing from taking place.

In the community model, one to a few participants are invited to share the details of the incident so that all present have more knowledge of what was experienced. Several participants with the help of the MHP are invited to discuss their emotional and physiological reactions. The time required is more easily controlled in these situations. As with small group debriefings, community debriefings usually last one to three hours, depending upon the number of participants invited to speak. Information regarding community resources, referral, and follow-up is essential.

Community debriefings should not be confused with multiple stressor debriefings (MSD) (Armstrong et al., 1995). MSDs are for disaster relief workers or critical incident response teams (firefighters, emergency squads, etc.). The debriefing strategy is generally the same, although somewhat more sophisticated in that the methods presuppose that these workers already know and understand the principles of critical incident stress.

Conclusion

The key to preventing posttraumatic stress disorder is quick intervention. Posttrauma counseling and critical incident debriefings are most effective when done two to five days after the incident (Squire, 1990). The small group counseling session that a critical incident debriefing involves helps to prevent individuals from developing posttraumatic stress disorder. The goals of the debriefing process are to reduce the probability of PTSD or other psychiatric disorders and to reduce the probability of accessing workers' compensation benefits or stress-related early retirements (Frolkey, 1992). As PTSD can be diagnosed one month after the traumatizing event, responding with a debriefing as soon as possible, or at least before one month is essential. Van Fleet (1992) stated that with immediate intervention, attention to detail, and common sense, it is possible to arrest the development of the more serious components of PTSD. According to Van Fleet, a failure to dissipate what Freud called "psychic energy" may result in the inhibition of one body system or another, and can lead to a variety of symptoms ranging from skin problems to respiratory disorders, even cancer. We become vulnerable to a myriad of disorders when our immune system is inhibited. Debriefings allow for expression and seek to return those affected to full productivity and their environments to normalcy.

The amount of time that passes between the event and the treatment intervention is a critical factor. Immediately following a trauma, a crisis intervention model similar to a critical incident stress debriefing would be most effective. After one month, however, critical details of the event begin to be buried and distorted and a CISD would no longer be effective. At this time, it is necessary to take into consideration the unique characteristics of the victim/survivor and choose a treatment intervention specific to their needs. If symptoms persist past one month, whether or not an individual has participated in a debriefing, acute PTSD must be suspected. If the full symptom picture endures for more than three months, chronic PTSD is possible.

PTSD is a painful struggle. The torment of PTSD has caused some to take their own lives and the lives of others. It has caused some to live a reclusive lifestyle or to withdraw so deeply within oneself as to make meaningful contact with another impossible. Many individuals experiencing a potentially traumatizing event will bury their trauma, some will resolve it successfully, others will feel the pain throughout their lives. CISDs are the first line of defense in preventing the progression of PTSD. They are a powerful and effective intervention when employed in an appropriate and timely manner.

REFERENCES

American Psychiatric Association. (1994). *Diagnostic and statistical manual of mental disorders*, (4th edition). Washington, DC: Author.

American Red Cross. (1991). *Introduction to disaster services.* Disaster services regulations and procedures. Washington, DC: The American National Red Cross.

Armstrong, K., Lund, P., McWright, L., & Tichenor, V. (1995). Multiple stressor debriefing and the American Red Cross: The East Bay Hills fire experience. *Social Work, 40*(1).

Bell, J. (1995). Traumatic event debriefing: Service delivery designs and the role of social work. *Social Work, 40*(1), 36–43.

EAPA Exchange (1991, August). Critical incident stress debriefing in the workplace. *EAPA Exchange,* 38–39.

Fairbank, J.A. (1989). Chronic combat related posttraumatic stress disorder. In Nezu, A.M., & Nezu, C.M. (Eds.). *Clinical decision making in behavior therapy: A problem-solving perspective.* Illinois: Research Press Company.

Family Enterprises Incorporated (1993). *Posttraumatic intervention institute.* Training manual. Milwaukee, WI: Author.

Frolkey, C. (1992). Critical incidents and traumatic events: The differences. *EAP Digest, 12*(4), 35–59.

Gwaltney, G. (1987). Posttraumatic stress and the EAP response. *EAP Digest, 7*(5), 57.

Horowitz, M.J. (1986). *Stress response syndromes* (2nd ed.). New York: Jason Aronsen.

Matsakis, A. (1992). *I can't get over it: A handbook for trauma survivors.* Oakland, CA: New Harbinger.

Mitchell, J.T. (1985). Healing the helpers. *Role stressors and supports for emergency workers.* Center for Mental Health Studies of Emergencies. Rockville, MD: National Institute of Mental Health.

National Organization for Victim Assistance. (1992). *Community crisis response team training institute.* Community crisis response team manual. Washington, DC: National Organization for Victim Assistance.

Polen-Bonitz, C., & Morrison, R.A. (1993). Posttrauma intervention. *Connections, 1*(2).

Rank, M. (1996). [University of South Florida]. Unpublished raw data.

Squire, M. (1990). Emotional injuries: Their cost and cure. *The Branch Manager.* 11(5).

Van Fleet, F. (1992). Debriefing and the critical incident. *EAP Digest, 12*(3), 28–33.

Walker, G. (1990). Crisis-care in critical incident debriefing. *Death Studies, 14,* 121–133.

Chapter 24

PROFESSIONAL, ETHICAL, AND PROGRAM DEVELOPMENTS IN EMPLOYEE ASSISTANCE PROGRAMS

WILLIAM G. EMENER AND WILLIAM S. HUTCHISON

Pivotal to any human service program or delivery system is its perceived credibility. In the case of employee assistance programs (EAPs), especially with the increased penchant for accountability and the burgeoning managed care models of the 1990s, companies and industries, as well as the public at large, are demanding assurance, culpability and accountability, all of which are cornerstones of credibility. In many ways and for numerous reasons, enhanced professionalism, adherence to ethical standards and the development of program standards on behalf of EAPs, have significantly contributed to their perceived credibility within the business and industry, and the public at large. The purposes of this chapter are three-fold: (1) to discuss the *importance of professionalism* in EAPs; (2) to illustrate the EAP movement's commitment to *adherence to ethical standards* on behalf of EAP practitioners; and (3) to illustrate how the EAP movement is striving for adherence to *professional program standards* on behalf of EAPs.

Professionalism

In the delivery of human services there are three critical attributes of professionalism: (a) *licensure;* (b) *certification;* and (c) *accreditation.* Basically, when professional practitioners are licensed or certified, recipients of their services enjoy an embellished and reliable sense of trust that the licensed or certified practitioners possess the knowledge, skills and attributes necessary for quality service delivery. In effect, licensure and certification connotes that "a credible group of professionals who know what they are looking for and know what they are doing is verifying that people can trust that this licensed or certified practitioner is good at what he or she is doing." Moreover, when programs are accredited, individuals receiving services from or through the auspices of the program enjoy an embellished and reliable sense of trust that the programs are designed, organized and operated in compliance with standards that have proven to be efficient and effective. In effect, accreditation connotes that "people can trust that an accredited program will do what it professes to do."

Professional Service Delivery and Ethical Standards

Most, if not all, EAPs exclusively utilize certified and licensed professionals (e.g., Certified Rehabilitation Counselors, Licensed Clinical Social Workers). Certification typically is awarded by a national certification body (e.g., the Commission on Rehabilitation Counselor Certification) which attests to the certificand's specialized credentials, knowledge, skills and areas of expertise. Licensure typically is awarded by a state licensing board (e.g., through the auspices of a state Department of Professional Regulation) which not only attests to the licensee's specialized credentials, knowledge, skills and areas of expertise but also allows the individual to practice independently and autonomously.

The EAP movement also has witnessed the inclusion of a certification process specifically for EAP professionals: the *Certified Employee Assistance Professional* (CEAP). As announced in the Fall, 1995 *CEAP Update*, the Employee Assistance Certification Commission (EACC) upgraded its CEAP examination eligibility requirements beginning in 1997:

CEAP EXAM ELIGIBILITY REQUIREMENTS CHANGE FOR 1997

Beginning in 1997, there will be new eligibility requirements to sit for the CEAP examination—Two options are provided to qualify for the exam, based on whether the candidate has a related graduate degree:

• **Graduate degree** in related discipline (area approved by EACC) or equivalent outside the U.S.; and
• **2000 hours** within 2 to 7 years of supervised work experience in an EAP setting. Supervision must be EACC-approved; and
• **15 PDHs** completed prior to taking the exam. PDH process to be phased in at 5 PDHs per year beginning in 1997 (i.e. 5 PDHs for those taking the exam in 1997, 10 in 1998, 15 in 1999 and thereafter).

> • *professional credential in psychology, social work, rehabilitation or a related field of study based upon the standards of professional practice in effect within the given country.*
>
> ---
>
> OR
>
> ---
>
> •• **3000 hours** within 2 to 7 years of supervised work experience in an EAP setting. Supervision must be EACC-approved; and
> •• **60 PDHs** completed prior to taking the exam. The PDH process will be phased in at 20 PDHs per year beginning in 1997 (i.e. 20 for those taking the exam in 1997, 40 in 1998, 60 in 1999 and thereafter).
>
> ---
>
> The EACC is continuing to define the terms of the supervision process, the PDH process and accepted degrees. Further details will be provided as these definitions and processes are determined. (p. 1)

Current and future EAP professionals are encouraged to read the *CEAP Updates* and stay in touch with the EACC to remain abreast of changes in CEAP requirements as well as the dates and locations of CEAP examination sites.

Most EAP professionals belong to the professional association, the Employee Assistance Program Association (EAPA). Among EAPA's numerous professional development activities, it has strongly encouraged and enforced its members' adherence to its professional codes of ethics. This is very important because one of the marks of a professional is that he or she adheres to a code of ethics (Emener & Cottone, 1989). "The Oath of Hippocrates provided an early philosophical source for contemporary codes of ethics in the helping professions" (Davis & Yasak, 1996, p. 11). The Hippocratic principles that guide human service professionals' relations with their patients and clients include: (a) *autonomy* — respect for the consumer's right to free choice; (b) *nonmaleficence* — the injunction to do no harm to others; (c) *beneficence* — the duty to help others and do good; (d) *justice* — the obligation to attempt to achieve equality of resource distribution; and (e) fidelity — the duty to honor obligations (Beauchamp & Childress, 1983; Emener & Cottone, 1989). An example of encouraged and facilitated adherence to ethical standards on behalf of EAP professionals is observed in the following formal document which was approved by EAPA's Board of Directors on April 10, 1988:

EAPA CODE OF ETHICS
R*E*V*I*S*E*D

This document was drafted in final form on December 4, 1987 and approved by EAPA's Board of Directors on April 10, 1988.

Preamble

The EAPA Code of Ethics serves as a code of professional conduct for EAPA members. In cooperation with labor and management, EAPA members' primary objective is to provide the most effective employee assistance services to individuals and their families suffering from emotional, behavioral, alcohol and drug-related problems. The following principles are in accord with this goal and serve as guidelines for duly-constituted national and local ethics committees in their efforts to educate EAPA members regarding ethical professional conduct. Members of EAPA Affirm their endorsement of the Code of Ethics and acknowledge commitment to uphold its principles by signing the membership application and subsequent renewals.

Professional Responsibility

EAPA members help protect labor, management and the community against unethical practices by an individual or organization engaged in employee assistance programs, direct treatment, or consultation activities. When an EAPA member knows of an apparent ethical violation by another EAPA member, it becomes his/her ethical responsibility to attempt to resolve the matter by bringing that alleged unethical behavior to the other member's attention. If a resolution of ethical matters between members is not achieved, further informal consultation with colleagues and/or the local chapter's ethics committee is recommended, prior to any formalized national Ethics Committee review of a member's complaint.

Procedures for Review of Member Conduct

Per Article III—Section XI of Bylaws

Members of EAPA shall comply with its Bylaws and with its Code of Ethics. *Any member* who shall be found in violation thereof shall be subject to the action of the EAPA Board of Directors.

(A) To be considered, a complaint against a member from any source shall be submitted in writing to the National President. The National President shall designate an appropriate investigating committee. If in the judgement of the appropriate committee the complaint warrants a hearing, the committee will prepare a formal charge and request that a hearing be scheduled. The charge shall state clearly the section or sections under which the violation is charged, as well as the alleged conduct of the member constituting the violation.

(B) A copy of the formal charge shall be delivered to the member either in person or by registered or certified mail, and the member shall be given not less than thirty (30) days' notice by registered or certified mail of the time and place of the hearing on the charge. A closed hearing shall be conducted by the member's Regional Representative and the Chairperson of either the National Bylaws or Ethics Committee as appropriate. The member is entitled to be present at such a hearing and any continuation thereof, and may present oral or written evidence. The member may be represented in the closed proceedings by any voting member of EAPA in good standing. A written summary of the proceedings shall be made. Technical rules of evidence shall not apply.

(C) When the hearings have concluded, the Committee Chairperson and the Regional Representative shall in executive session determine if a violation has occurred and prepare a written confidential report for the Bylaws or Ethics Committee with their findings. The Bylaws or Ethics Committee upon receipt of the report shall within thirty (30) days prepare a recommended action to dismiss the complaint, to refer the individual for a professional assessment and treatment if appropriate, to request a letter of resignation, to censure, suspend or expel the member, or any combination of these actions.

(D) The Board shall no later than its next scheduled meeting act upon the report and the recommendations of the Bylaws or Ethics Committee. The member shall be informed promptly by registered or certified mail of the action of the Board.

(E) The findings of fact of the Regional Representative and Committee Chairperson shall be conclusive. However, the member may appeal to the Board of Directors concerning the interpretation of the facts or the proposed penalty. The member may request permission to appear before the Board and, if such permission is granted, the member may be accompanied by a voting member of EAPA if so desired, to present arguments. The Board shall have the right to impose reasonable time limitation upon such a presentation. The Board's final decision shall be conveyed promptly by registered or certified mail to the member.

Confidentiality

EAPA members treat client information as confidential. Members inform clients fully about their rights regarding the scope and limitations of confidential communications elicited during the assessment, referral, and treatment process. They do not disclose information without client consent except where failure to disclose would likely result in imminent threat of serious bodily harm to the client or others.

Professional Competency

EAPA members who are Employee Assistance Program (EAP) providers are expected to possess knowledge of work organizations, human resources management, EAP policy and administration, and EAP direct services. All members are expected to have knowledge of chemical dependency, addictions and emotional disorders, and acknowledge the necessity of continuing experience, education and training to maintain and enhance proficiency. While membership in EAPA may not be used to suggest professional competency, attaining the status of a Certified Employee Assistance Professional (CEAP) does attest to meeting the requisite standard of knowledge for competency in EAP practice.

Consumer Protection

EAPA members do not discriminate because of a client's race, religion, national origin, physical handicap, gender or sexual preference. They conduct research that respects and safeguards the welfare of research participants. EAPA members make full disclosure of the functions and purposes of the Employee Assistance Program as well as of any affiliation with a proposed therapist or treatment program, do not give or receive financial consideration for referring clients to particular therapists or treatment programs; do not engage in sexual conduct with clients; and do not act in any manner which compromises a professional relationship.

Assessment and Referral

Members are to make assessment and referral decisions only within their area of specific competency and to seek consultation or supervision when clinically indicated. To avoid appearances of conflicts of interest, it is recommended that members who do the initial assessment refer clients to individuals or entities not affiliated with the referring EAP or original referral source. Should a treatment decision be made to refer to the initial evaluator or an affiliated program, that disposition is to be done only if the client and contracting organization is informed of any financial interest in such a referral and it can be demonstrated that the referral is in the client's best interest.

Public Responsibility and Professional Relations

EAPA members agree that practitioners, both nondegreed recovering persons, as well as other professionals, form a partnership in providing employee assistance services. As such, members: are responsible for educating and fostering the professional development of trainees; are encouraged to promote EAPA to the public and to provide public statements based on objective information; and are expected to work cooperatively within their professional communities. Cooperation within a professional community precludes denigrating other professionals to promote one's own interests, as well as fraudulent or grossly misleading advertising practices, and requires that one's professional qualifications be presented to the public in an accurate and truthful manner.

EAPA members are encouraged to assist another member to seek treatment if that member's professional functioning becomes impaired through the use of alcohol, drugs, and/or mental illness.

(F) Any member who resigns, fails to maintain his membership during the pendency of these procedures or is expelled, shall be eligible to reapply for membership *only* upon conditions, if any, specified by the Board.

(G) For the convenience of EAPA, the National President may agree to accept the member's resignation as an alternative to these procedures. (pp. 2–5)

Thus, it is clear that the EAP movement, especially over the past few years, has strongly encouraged and worked hard to ensure continuing professionalism in EAP service delivery.

EAP "Program Standards"

EAPs currently are not accredited. Nonetheless, it remains critical for EAPs to be designed, organized and operated in accordance with currently accepted EAP program standards. The following are the "Program Standards" which provide the spirit, intention and guidance for efficient and effective EAPs and EAP service delivery:

INTRODUCTION

Purpose

The purpose of these Employee Assistance Program (EAP) Standards are to:
- Define the EAP field as a profession
- Describe the scope of EAP services
- Educate the community regarding EAP services
- Suggest applications for program standards, guidelines and definitions
- Serve the needs of the EAPA membership

History and Background

The Standards for Employee Alcoholism and/or Assistance Programs were originally drafted in 1981 by a joint committee representing these national groups:

- The Association of Labor/Management Administrators and Consultants on Alcoholism (ALMACA)
- The National Council on Alcoholism (NCA)
- Occupational Program Consultants Association (OPCA)
- The National Institute on Alcohol Abuse and Alcoholism (NIAAA)
- The American Federation of Labor and Congress of Industrial Organizations (AFL–CIO)

At that time, there were approximately 8,000 programs and 2,800 EAP professionals who belonged to EAPA. By 1990, the number of EAPs had increased substantially to an estimated 20,000, and EAPA membership had grown to more than 6,000 professionals.

In 1988, EAPA recognized the need for more detailed standards reflecting advancements in the EAP field. The EAP Association appointed a Program Standards Committee to develop revised Program Standards. The Committee developed a two-part document.

Part One sets forth specific Program Standards each of which is accompanied by a statement of Intent. These Program Standards identify the core ingredients of employee assistance programs and professional standards for carrying them out. The Program Standards are organized into six general areas:

- Design
- Implementation
- Management and Administration
- Direct Services
- Linkages
- Evaluation

**Part Two, The Consumer Guide, consists of recommendations for applying these Program Standards in the EAP field. The recommendations provide organizations and EAP providers with practical guidelines for the development, implementation, maintenance, and evaluation of an employee assistance program in accordance with professional program standards.

It is hoped that the availability of this two-part document will encourage and assist management and union leaders in establishing EAPs in accordance with EAPA's Program Standards.

EAPA thanks the National Institute on Drug Abuse for the use of its documents relating to employee assistance programs within federal agencies.

NOTE: Part Two of this document, *The Consumer's Guide,* is not included in this chapter. Interested readers, however, can obtain a copy of the *Guide* directly from the Employee Assistance Program Association.

I. DEFINITION

Standard:

An employee assistance program (EAP) is a worksite-based program designed to assist in the identification and resolution of productivity problems associated with employees impaired by personal concerns including, but not limited to: health, marital, family, financial, alcohol, drug, legal, emotional, stress, or other personal concerns which may adversely affect employee job performance.

The specific core activities of EAPs include (1) expert consultation and training to appropriate persons in the identification and resolution of job-performance issues related to the aforementioned employee personal concerns, and (2) confidential, appropriate and timely problem-assessment services; referrals for appropriate diagnosis, treatment and assistance; the formation of linkages between workplace and community resources that provide such services; and follow-up services for employees who use those services.

(NOTE: This definition was approved by the EAPA Board of Directors in 1988 and has been written into a number of state statutes.)

II. SIGNIFICANCE AND USE

The objectives of an employee assistance program are these:

- To serve the organization, its employees, and their families by providing a comprehensive system from which employees can obtain assistance addressing personal problems which may affect their work performance;
- To serve as a resource for management and labor when they intervene with employees whose personal problems affect their job performance;
- To effectively, efficiently, and professionally provide assessment, referral, and follow-up services for mental health, alcohol, and other drug related problems in the workforce.

This document identifies a coordinated set of policies, procedures, services, and consultation activities designed to ensure that EAPs effectively meet these objectives. Adherence to professional standards and policies will ensure a viable program which earns the respect and support of employers and employees. Effective programs are comprehensive enough in scope to respond to a wide range of employee problems, whether they are brought to the attention of the EAP by the employee, labor, or management.

When designing its EAP, each organization may apply these standards based on its own unique mission, operation and culture. In union-organized settings, union representatives should be included in the development, implementation, and monitoring of the EAP.

EAP services can be provided internally, by contract with external service-providers, or by some combination of these methods. Smaller organizations often provide EAP services by participating in a community consortium. Regardless of the exact structure of the EAP, ethical considerations are present in every aspect of the design, implementation, delivery and evaluation of the program.

III. PROGRAM DESIGN

A. Advisory Committee

Standard:

There shall be an advisory function at a high level within the organization involving representatives of all segments of the workforce.

Intent:

Program acceptance and utilization is directly related to the degree of support from top management and involvement by employees, supervisors, management, and unions. One technique for maximizing the potential for a highly effective program is to form, at the earliest opportunity, an Advisory Committee representing all the various labor and management groups. To ensure that the EAP is supported by and located at the highest possible organizational level, committee membership should include top management and union/ employee association officials as well as representatives from the following groups: medical, personnel/human resources, benefits, safety and occupational health, finance, legal, training and development, and EAP operations. This Committee can formulate a policy statement as well as specific strategies and procedures for implementing an EAP and criteria for evaluating its performance.

B. Needs Assessment:

Standard:

Program design shall be based on an assessment of organizational and employee needs as they relate to EAP utilization. The background information and organizational data to be factored into program design will include at least:

- an organizational profile
- an employee needs assessment
- surveys of supervisors and union representatives
- a review of service delivery models

Intent:

Program planning and development should always include an assessment of the needs of the employee population and the organization for which they work.

This assessment will help the advisory committee determine the most appropriate methods of providing EAP services.

C. Service Delivery Systems

Standard:

Employee assistance program services shall be provided through a comprehensive, formal delivery system.

Intent:

Employee assistance professionals and/or an advisory committee shall develop service delivery methods consistent with organizational and employee needs. Professional guidance is available through EAPA National, local chapters, or professional EAP consultants. There are a number of service delivery models, including:

- Internal programs through which services are delivered by EAP professionals employed by the organization;
- External programs (known as "service centers") through which services are delivered by EAP professionals under contract with the organization;
- Combined programs through which services are delivered by a core group of EAP professionals employed by the organization and contracts with external EAP vendors for certain services;
- Consortia of smaller organizations that jointly contract with an independent EAP vendor to provide services.

IV. IMPLEMENTATION

A. Policy Statement

Standard:

The policy statement defines the EAP's relationship to the organization as well as describes the EAP as a confidential resource for the organization and its employees. Additionally, it shall state the scope of the program's services as well as the program's limitations. The policy statement shall include at least the following concepts:

- The organization providing EAP services to its employees recognizes that a mentally and physically healthy employee is an organizational asset and that the availability of appropriate EAP services is beneficial to both labor and management
- Alcohol and other drug abuse, emotional, marital, family and other

related problems affect job performance, employee health and quality of life. Such problems are treatable and are the legitimate concern of employers. Employees who experience these problems may be unable to function efficiently, effectively, and safely on the job.

- Employees who need EAP services can voluntarily seek assistance, or they can be referred through constructive intervention. Job security will not be jeopardized as a consequence of seeking EAP services, except where mandated by law. However, employees who use an EAP are expected to adhere to the job performance requirements of the employing organization

- All EAP records will be kept strictly confidential and will not be noted in any official record or in the employee's personnel file. Information from the EAP may be released only with the written permission of the employee, or in response to the organizational EAP policy or from a court or other legal order (e.g., a subpoena)

Intent:

Program implementation will be preceded by the development of a policy statement clearly communicating the organization's rationale for instituting an EAP. The policy statement should not be confused with operating procedures or with any contractual agreements with an external EAP provider. Because operating procedures may need to be adjusted in response to emerging needs, they should not be incorporated into a policy document that is difficult to modify.

B. Implementation Plan

Standard:

An implementation plan shall outline the actions needed to establish a fully functioning EAP and set forth a timeline for their completion. The program implementation plan shall establish the EAP as a distinct service within the organization.

The implementation plan shall cover the following:

1. Policies, procedures, and objectives
2. Logistics of service delivery, including:
   - location
   - staffing ratio
3. An operations plan, including:
   - program promotion and employee communications, orientation, and education
   - training of supervisors and union representatives
   - review of health/mental health benefits coverage and possible benefits redesign
   - identification of community resources

- strategies for program integration
4. A management plan, including:
   - budget projections
   - record-keeping
   - reporting procedures
   - quality assurance
   - liability coverage
5. An evaluation system, including:
   - measurable objectives
   - appropriateness
   - efficiency
   - progress
   - outcomes

Intent:

An implementation plan should articulate the responsibilities of the organization and the EAP professionals. It should include realistic objectives and criteria for ongoing evaluation and, if necessary, program modification. Successful implementation encourages "ownership" by all sectors of the workforce. Special provisions may be needed for program implementation in worksites geographically distant from organization headquarters.

V. MANAGEMENT AND ADMINISTRATION

A. Policies and Procedures

Standard:

To achieve consistent and effective delivery of services, standardized policies and procedures for program administration and operation shall be developed in response to program objectives and organizational needs.

Intent:

The intent of this standard is to develop clearly defined administrative policies and procedures to insure a smoothly functioning and effective EAP. Standardized systems for program management and administration, combined with clear cut definitions of the program's scope, help delineate the program activities and guide the amount of resources dedicated to them. A clearly defined program may be better received and more frequently used. Standardized procedures are easier to monitor and adapt to changing needs, and may protect program staff from becoming overextended.

B. Staffing Levels

Standard:

An adequate number of EAP professionals shall be available to achieve the stated goals and objectives of the program. Organizations that choose to contract for EAP services shall have at least one liaison person with formal responsibility for coordinating the delivery of services and monitoring contract performance.

Intent:

EAP staffing patterns, and the number of professionals, vary according to the type of program and the scope of services provided. Whether the EAP is internal or delivered by external contractors, the number and qualifications of EAP professionals should match program needs.

C. Staff Qualifications

Standard:

Each EAP shall retain professionals qualified to perform their duties. Measures of qualifications should include evidence of specialized understanding of alcohol and other drug problems and certification in employee assistance programming (CEAP). EAP professionals shall adhere to all government regulations regarding their scope of practice.

Intent:

Staff competence is critical to program success. Depending upon the type of services provided, various levels of experience, education, certification, credentialing and licensure may be required.

Individual EAP professionals are responsible for recognizing the limitations of their competence and making certain that all work is performed within those limitations. Those individuals who are called upon to provide services for which they are not fully trained and experienced should be supervised by a person who is qualified in those areas. Consultation and referral can also supplement practitioner capability.

D. Community Networks

Standard:

The EAP shall identify, foster, create, utilize, and evaluate community resources which provide the best quality care at the most reasonable cost.

Intent:

Delivery of quality services responsive to the individual needs of employees requires that the EAP develop and maintain an effective community network of local treatment resources, health organizations, and self-help groups. This activity is required on an ongoing basis.

E. Confidentiality

Standard:

The EAP professional shall prepare and implement a confidentiality policy consistent with all professional standards and ethics, and adhere to all other regulations that may apply to information in the possession of the EAP. Disclosures specified by government guidelines and EAP policy will be communicated to users of EAP services. The limits of the confidentiality policy shall be disclosed in writing to those who use the EAP.

Intent:

Program success and credibility may hinge, to a large extent, on employee confidence that the EAP respects individual privacy and adheres to confidentiality requirements and procedures.

F. Liability

Standard:

All EAP professionals shall have adequate professional and other appropriate liability coverage.

Intent:

The EAP needs to have resources to answer legal challenges to its delivery of services. The organizations should demonstrate financial responsibility to ensure continuation of the program during and following any litigation.

G. Ethics

Standard:

EAP professionals shall adhere to the codes of ethics espoused by their professional organizations and by appropriate licensing and certifying bodies. Any actual or perceived conflict of interest among EAP professionals and service providers shall be avoided. Conflict of interest statements shall be filed when appropriate.

Intent:

The intent is to ensure professional behavior and provide consumer protection. EAP professionals are responsible for the consequences of their actions.

A potential conflict may arise when an EAP provides ancillary services beyond the core EAP services. This should be clearly addressed in the contract and/or internal philosophy of the EAP.

VI. DIRECT SERVICES

NOTE: EAPs deliver comprehensive, quality services to three target groups: employees and covered family members, supervisory and union personnel, and the organization as a whole.

A. Crisis Intervention

Standard:

The EAP shall offer responsive intervention services for employees, covered family members, or the organization in acute crisis situations.

Intent:

The EAP must be prepared to respond to emergencies and urgent situations in a timely fashion, consistent with organizational policies. Timely intervention may prevent or lessen long-term dysfunction.

B. Assessment and Referral

Standard:

EAP professionals, or an assessment service under contract to the organization, shall 1) conduct an assessment to identify employee or family member problems, 2) develop a plan of action, and 3) recommend or refer the individual(s) to an appropriate resource for problem resolution.

Intent:

The intent is to match the identified problems with the appropriate care. Accurate assessment and appropriate referral should result in improved job performance and employee well-being. In the course of assessment and referral, EAP professionals may offer short-term problem resolution services so as to assure timely and effective help for the individual.

C. Short-Term Problem Resolution

Standard:

EAP professionals shall determine when it may be appropriate to provide short-term problem resolution services, and when to make a referral to community resources. Long-term, on-going treatment is not part of the EAP model.

Intent:

In accordance with program policy, there are occasions when it may be more efficient and effective for the EAP professional to provide short-term problem resolution services than to refer to an outside resource. At no time will the EAP professional operate outside his/her scope of expertise and licensure or accept financial reimbursement other than that allowed by EAP design or contractual arrangement.

D. Progress Monitoring

Standard:

The EAP shall review and monitor the progress of referrals. This shall include assisting in reintegration to the worksite if the employee is taken off the job for treatment.

Intent:

The EAP is in a unique position to monitor and review the progress of referrals; ensure quality assurance; provide ongoing support to the treatment professional, the supervisor and the employee; and assist the employee with reintegration into the worksite if the employee is taken off the job for treatment. Progress monitoring and the reintegration process will vary depending on the individual employee's needs.

E. Follow-Up

Standard:

The EAP shall provide follow-up services to employees, covered family members, supervisory and union personnel, and the organization to monitor and support progress in the resolution of personal problems and improvement of job performance.

Intent:

The availability of follow-up services can enhance EAP credibility and ensure timely problem resolution. By providing ongoing follow-up services, the EAP demonstrates a commitment to the well-being of individuals and organizations.

F. Training

Standard:

The EAP shall provide training for supervisory, management, and union personnel to give them an understanding of EAP objectives, procedures for referring employees experiencing job performance problems to the program, and the impact of the program on the organization.

The following subjects shall be covered:

1. Understanding EAP
   * impact of employee well-being on job performance
   * management of employees with problems
2. Consultation
   * recognition of an employee's need for assistance
   * methods of referral to the EAP
3. Program operation
   * relationship of EAP to personnel actions
   * confidentiality
   * reintegration
   * relationship to federally mandated drug testing and training

The EAP shall ask those who attend the training to provide written feedback after taking the course.

Intent:

The intent of regularly scheduled training sessions is to encourage early recognition, intervention, and appropriate referral to the EAP.

G. Supervisor/Union Consultation

Standard:

EAP professionals shall provide individual consultation to supervisors and union representatives regarding the management and referral to the EAP of employees with job performance and other behavioral/medical problems.

Intent:

The purpose of such consultation is to ensure that EAP professionals provide technical support and policy-based advice to supervisors charged with monitoring job performance and taking appropriate action in dealing with problem employees.

H. Organization Consultation

Standard:

EAPs shall be both proactive and responsive when organizational developments and events impact employee well-being and fall within the EAP professional's areas of expertise.

Intent:

The intent is to ensure that the EAP functions as an integral part of the organization. EAP professionals can offer a valuable perspective as part of the organizational team confronting external and internal developments and changes.

I. Program Promotion

Standard:

EAPs shall ensure the availability and use of promotional materials and activities which encourage the use of the program by supervisors, union representatives, peers, employees, and covered family members.

Intent:

The EAP should be highly visible and presented in a positive light to encourage members of the organization to fully utilize the program services. Program promotion should be ongoing and should be directed to all levels of the organization.

J. Education

Standard:

Information about the EAP and its services shall be part of new employee orientation and ongoing employee education.

Intent:

Employee education is an essential EAP function and should emphasize primary prevention and self-care. Regularly offered presentations should include information designed to develop or increase employee awareness of factors that affect their personal well-being and impact on job performance.

VII. LINKAGES

A. Internal Organizational Activities

Standard:

The EAP shall be positioned at an organizational level where it can be most effective with linkage to the executive office. The EAP should establish working relationships with a variety of internal departments and committees, including:

- Human Resources/Personnel
- Benefits
- Safety
- Equal Employment Opportunity
- Medical
- Security
- Risk Management
- Legal
- Training
- Organizational Development
- Employee Relations
- Union

Intent:

The EAP operates at its optimal level when it is fully integrated with internal organizational activities. Close involvement and collaboration improves EAP visibility and increases its ability to have an impact. Linkages within the organization should maximize program effectiveness and decrease potential liabilities. Adaptations may be necessary in response to changes in organizational dynamics.

B. External Community Organizations and Resources

Standard:

The EAP shall develop and maintain relationships with the external health care delivery system and other community resources which provide EAP-relevant services.

Intent:

The EAP operates at its optimal level when it is fully acquainted and maintains working relationships with the referral and support resources available in the community.

C. Professional Organizations

Standard:

EAP professionals shall maintain and upgrade their knowledge through such activities as belong to one or more organizations specifically designed for EAP professionals, such as the Employee Assistance Professionals Association (EAPA), attending training and/or continuing education programs, and maintaining regular, ongoing contact with other employee assistance program professionals.

Intent:

The intent is to enhance the knowledge and skills of EAP professionals and ensure that they are aware of new developments and technologies in EAP service delivery.

VIII. EVALUATION

Standard:

An EAP shall evaluate the appropriateness, effectiveness, and efficiency of its internal operations. Measurable objectives shall be stated for both process and outcome evaluation.

Intent:

Meaningful evaluation of an EAP depends upon having measurable program objectives and data collection mechanisms. These should be developed early in the program planning process.

In addition to guiding the implementation and operations of the EAP, measurable objectives allow the organization to judge the program's progress and usefulness and to identify the need for program modifications. The procedures for achieving each objective should be reviewed periodically to assure that the objectives are obtainable.

Data that measure program effectiveness should be gathered routinely and analyzed to evaluate progress toward achieving each objective. Components for which data could be collected for program evaluation may include:

- Design effectiveness
- Implementation
- Management and administration
- Completeness of the program
- Direct services
- Linkages

A review of the daily operation of the program does not necessarily measure its total impact on the organization and the effectiveness with which it reassesses the needs of the organization.

As can readily be seen, these Standards are rather specific and rigorous, and clearly are designed to maximize an EAP's potentials for efficient and effective EAP service delivery to its identified primary consumer group.

Concluding Comment

It is predicted that EAPs will continue to be a viable, integral and significant humanistic component of business and industry in the decades ahead. EAPs' continued positive impact is assured because of (1) the continuing, developing professionalism on behalf of EAP practitioners and (2) the continuing developments in EAPs' program and operational standards. As EAPs proceed in these ways, everyone will win—unions, management, and especially labor.

REFERENCES

Beauchamp, T.L., & Childress, J.F. (1983). *Principles of biomedical ethics.* Oxford: Oxford University Press.

Davis, A., & Yasak, D. (1996). Supporting a colleague in ethical conflict: Resolving problems of common sense. *Journal of Applied Rehabilitation Counseling, 27*(3), 11–16.

Emener, W.G., & Cottone, R.R. (1989). Professionalization, deprofessionalization, and reprofessionalization of rehabilitation counseling according to criteria of professions. *Journal of Counseling and Development, 67,* 576–581.

PART VII
SELECTED EXAMPLES

In Part VII, the text endeavors to look at a sample of "special populations" of the world of work. Although demonstrated cost reductions could be most meaningful, programs in bureaucratic settings, such as governments and school districts, usually are based on the high rehabilitation rate and humanness ("the thing to do"). The minimized profit motive probably has led to the reluctant acceptance of the EAP concept in these settings and professional disciplines and associations. Three other factors to be considered in the rationale for programs in these groups are:

1. Fear of public knowledge and judgment.
2. Loss of earning power and professional standing.
3. Possible loss of licensure.

Common to many of the professions covered in the eight chapters in Part VII is the absence of a normally supervised workplace. In contrast to the closely supervised and measured job performance of most industrial workers, many professionals are loosely supervised, if at all, and usually are assigned little responsibility in accounting for their job actions, hours of work, and standards of performance. An additional unique feature is illustrated in Bromley and Blount's statement in Chapter 34 regarding criminal justice practitioners, "the occupational world of the criminal justice professional is both emotionally and psychologically demanding." On a day-to-day basis, most professionals such as those discussed in Part VII are "their own boss" therefore making any confrontation and intervention based on poor performance very difficult. In many instances, this readily requires the positive action of the governing professional associations, regulatory and licensing bodies, and public pressure on "boards" and elected officials to provide the impetus for these groups to police their own.

Chapter 25

NURSES

B. ROBERT CHALLENGER

The "Impaired Professional," in its broadest connotation, can include and refer to any physical or mental condition that prohibits or curtails a professional from performing normal duties. Where the term "impaired" came from, as it relates to EAPs is not really clear: It does not, however, usually denote dependency on chemicals or the abuse of same.

The Problem

As reported on numerous occasions in many articles, alcoholism and drug addiction strike young and old, rich and poor, and educated and uneducated alike. The nursing profession is **not** exempt. How many chemically-dependent nurses there are is not known, since denial is a typical characteristic of defense. The numbers of chemically-dependent nurses is more difficult to determine, primarily due to the fear of loss of licensure. It is commonly accepted that the rate of alcoholism and drug abuse among nurses (male and female) is 12–18 percent.

Needless to say, working in the health care profession can itself be:

1. Taxing, mentally and physically.
2. An open arena for the procurement of chemicals of all types.
3. Less rewarding in the recognition of a "job well done." The Nurse of the Year Award is not enough.

In the hospital setting, work regimen, changes of shifts, hours of work, relocation of duties, can lead to a group of workers "at risk" for chemical dependency.

This chapter is reprinted from *Employee Assistance Programs; A Basic Text* (1988) with permission of the author, the book's editors (Dickman, Emener, & Hutchison, Jr.) and the publisher (Charles C Thomas, Publisher).

Secondly, the training undertaken by nurses instills certain beliefs and attitudes that make it most difficult to recognize and accept their dependency. This manifests itself in:

a. This can't happen to me; I know too much.
b. Nurses can't get sick.
c. I can handle it.

Until recent years, the stigma and negative attitudes toward the alcoholic and alcoholism have delayed an understanding of the disease and its progression. The treatment of alcoholics as weak, immoral, lacking will power, and not deserving treatment has required a *major* educational blitz in all professions.

Possible Solution

As attitudes have changed and the recognition of the benefits derived from employee and family assistance programs has grown, nurses, as well as other professionals, have looked for ways to police and assist their own. This has resulted in the beginning of a series of moves that, if continued, will go a long way in providing the necessary structures to combat the problem.

1. Nursing and medical schools are expanding their curricula to include additional exposure and education to the field of "addictions and dependencies."
2. There are more and more hospitals adopting the EAP concept and implementing the programs, both internally and contractually.
3. Health administration curricula is including subjects concerned with EAPs as a profession and courses are now available for all involved in health and social care field that will emphasize the benefits that are available.
4. Nursing associations at the local, state, and national level are implementing assistance programs. In most cases, these programs are in conjunction with steps being taken by regulatory agencies in an attempt to put "teeth" into their actions.
5. Outside of the association's efforts, there are peer assistance programs and support groups in place in many states. These types of programs not only play a role in the identification and intervention process, but provide the much needed support in the recovery process; identical to self-help groups.

Necessary Trends

If continued progress is to be made, the following must take place.

a. Continuation of the effort to remove stigmas, wherever they are found, so that those afflicted with these addictions can seek treatment openly and without fear of being labelled.

b. Additional education and training for *all* medical/hospital administration and staff in the development of policies and procedures dealing with personal/behavioral/medical problems in order to ease the avenue for recovery.

c. The expansion of existing programs to include those employed in clinics, doctor's offices, nursing homes, visiting nurses associations, private duty, hospices, occupational health, social services, etc.

d. A recognition by nurses, as well as *all* professionals in the health care field, of their responsibility to accept the fact that the base problem is prevalent and to confront it constructively and compassionately. To begin to become leaders, rather than followers, in the overall effort to combat the addiction dilemma; who else is better prepared.

e. The continuation of the development and implementation of *comprehensive* Employee Assistance Programs in the work setting and professional organizations and associations.

f. A discontinuance of efforts aimed at reinventing the wheel, but instead

g. The establishment of adequate resources to record and research the existing core technology to provide updated findings aimed at improving current techniques and methods that are innovative and unique in dealing with the problems, using the past as a foundation for these efforts.

Chapter 26

ELEMENTS OF THE
IMPAIRED PHYSICIANS PROGRAM

G. Douglas Talbott

M ag's Impaired Physicians Program (IPP) consists of four elements which have evolved from experience over the past 10 years: identification, intervention, treatment, and reentry. All four elements are essential to the successful rehabilitation of Georgia's impaired physician.

Identification

The identification of impaired physicians is profoundly affected by their characteristic massive denial. Their almost phobic inability to reach out for help, combined with the conspiracy of silence evidenced by family, peers, friends, and even patients, makes identification very difficult. After analysis of the progression of the disease in the first 100 patients in the IPP, it became apparent that the signs and symptoms used as identification criteria occurred first in the home and family setting, then sequentially in the community and the church and in financial, legal, and health problems. Symptoms were apparent last at the office or the hospital. When impaired physicians arrive in an altered state of consciousness at their job, it is usually very late in the disease and the rest of their lives are already in turmoil.

Symptom inventories in the form of checklists have been prepared[1] and are utilized for early identification of the impaired physician. Inherent in identification is verification which is accomplished by confirming

Reprinted with permission from *Journal of the Medical Association of Georgia*, Vol. 73, pp. 749–751, copyright 1984.

This chapter is reprinted from *Employee Assistance Programs; A Basic Text* (1988) with permission of the author, the book's editors (Dickman, Emener, & Hutchison, Jr.) and the publisher (Charles C Thomas, Publisher).

the diagnosis with the IPP network of recovering physicians, spouses, administrators of hospitals, medical society staff, nurses, and friends in the self-help groups. Such verification is possible because of extensive educational efforts throughout the states to establish this program as a nonunitive, advocacy, disease model.

Intervention

The second element of the program, intervention, is dictated by the denial characteristic of impaired physicians and their inability to reach out for help. In the vast majority of physicians, motivation for treatment is dependent upon intervention. Following hundreds of interventions with impaired physicians, guidelines have been established,[2] the use of which has recently been demonstrated in a videotape. Basic to this approach is the requirement that this intervention be implemented by at least two physician intervenors; ideally, one of these is recovering from the disease of chemical dependence. The intervenors, who are carefully trained in the facts of this psychosocial biogenetic disease, must also be carefully instructed and practiced in dealing with denial, anger, and hostility.

Representing the Medical Association of Georgia, these intervenors, who are selected because of absence of personal or professional relations with the impaired physician, must have also carefully done their homework. This homework consists mainly of careful documentation of evidence of the disease and is accomplished by interviewing and mobilizing for the intervention the support systems of that particular impaired physician. In addition, intervenors prepare specific goals and objectives of the intervention with particular attention to the assessment and treatment plans to be presented.

When such homework is accomplished, then the support systems are brought together for instruction on the disease, for definition of their roles at intervention, and for role playing and rehearsal of the actual events. Attention to a realistic assessment of the situation and to likely responses by the physician to the intervention helps participants make a tough-minded commitment to follow through with whatever agreements have been made for negative sanctions if the person refuses help. It also helps them unequivocally accept the physician's decision to go into treatment. Careful attention is given to the selection of participants and of the time and place for the structured intervention. Adequate time is allowed in the intervention for meeting the physician's objections and for dealing with extenuating circumstances so that the goal of getting the physician into immediate assessment or treatment is accomplished. In the Georgia program, repeated interventions are utilized if the primary confrontation fails. Intervention without the implied authority and consequences of the MAG and/or the licensing board is usually doomed to failure.

Treatment

The treatment element of the Georgia Impaired Physicians Program is divided into an initial 72-hour assessment followed by four phases of treatment. The initial assessment has been found to be a very effective goal of intervention. This allows the intervention team, rather than play the role of judge and jury for the impaired physician, to emphasize that they want the impaired physician to see the "experts" who will define the problem and recommend the specific treatment course.

Five-member teams of medical specialists, psychologists and neuro-psychologists, psychiatrists, family therapists, and addictionologists consult to establish the diagnosis. They differentiate chemical dependence from primary psychiatric disease and assess other medical problems; then they present specific treatment plans to the impaired physician and the family. Various treatment options are utilized for patients in the Georgia program. These include referral to their community Alcoholics Anonymous/Narcotics Anonymous program and the prescribed plan for attending "90 meetings in 90 days," referral to outpatient alcohol and/or drug treatment only, referral to a psychiatric rather than a chemical dependence program, referral to counseling, and return to their practice or, as is true of the majority of assessment cases in the Georgia Program, referral to full treatment in the MAG Impaired Physicians Program.

With the signing of a treatment contract, all impaired physicians are regarded as entering into a 2-year treatment program, including aftercare, monitoring, and surveillance upon returning home. IPP's treatment regimen consists of four phases. Phase 1 is a 4–6 week intensive inpatient treatment program which may or may not be completed at Ridgeview Institute, where the majority of the treatment team is located. The Ridgeview model (as do other approved programs) stresses the disease precept of chemical dependence and emphasizes family therapy, AA/NA, a strong personal spiritual program, group therapy, nonchemical coping skills training, and detailed education on the psychosocial, biogenetic characteristics of the disease of alcoholism and drug addiction. In Phase 1, true peer group therapy is initiated to deal with special problems and influences that uniquely affect those in the medical profession (dealt with in detail in the other articles of this issue of the *Journal*). In the peer groups, physicians meet with physicians, dentists with dentists, pharmacists with pharmacists, and nurses with nurses. They consist of people in various phases of treatment. These special peer groups continue throughout the 4 months and beyond for those people in the area.

Following Phase 1, the impaired physician enters into Phase 2, which consists of outpatient therapy and supervised living in a recovery residence. The outpatient program at a SAFE (Substance Abuse Free Existence) Center is an extension of the medical model established at Ridgeview. Determined by the severity of an individual's disease, this phase lasts 1–2 months and provides further practice in nonchemical coping, development of a stronger spiritual program, and deeper involvement in AA/NA with intense family therapy. Caduceus Outpatient Recovery Residences (CORR) utilize rented apartments and houses in the metropolitan Atlanta area, and these recovery residences serve as a site for surrogate family living. For 90 days, impaired physicians live there, going to 90 meetings of AA/NA, participating in supervised group therapy four times a week, and learning in that ambience to care again, to trust, to socialize, to communicate, and to assume personal accountability for their own behavior.

Phase 3 is completed when impaired physicians, while continuing to live in the recovery residence, are judged able to move from strict patient status to that of counselor-trainees under strict supervision. As they become frustrated and try forcefully to get the addict or alcoholic they are supervising to break through denial, to deal with depression, anger, or hostility, or to mend family wounds, they can see themselves. This "mirror image" therapy is a very constructive experience lasting for a minimum of 2 months. Concomitant with this work, impaired physicians also teach, dialogue, and interact with medical students at Emory University School of Medicine. Dealing with these students in a variety of seminars, lectures, and workshops restores professional dignity while cleansing the impaired physician of the embarrassment, shame, and guilt that society assigns to this disease. In turn, the medical students acquire a new dimension regarding this disease—that indeed it could happen to them.[3]

Reentry

The last phase of the treatment process, reentry, is considered a separate element. Having already signed a treatment contract and having completed the 4 months of treatment, impaired physicians enter into a 20-month aftercare contract which provides for a primary monitoring physician and for random drug screens. It also states the agreed on schedule of AA/NA meetings and choice of "sponsor" in the AA/NA program. In addition, the elements of a personal spiritual program and further recommendations for a family therapy program are carefully detailed.

Another document, called "Relapse Guidelines," is also signed (see pp. 767–768). Rather than a firm contract, the Guidelines give certain suggestions to guard against relapse and to interrupt it if it does occur. Georgia's Program recognizes that chemical dependence is a relapsing disease and, while the Program does not give permission for relapse to occur, it recognizes that possibility. Procedures such as obtaining drug screens, calling the primary monitoring physician, calling the treatment center, and mobilizing the impaired physician's support systems are outlined for physicians to utilize before, and certainly after, using a mood-altering chemical. The guidelines also suggest procedures for families or supervisors to use when they are concerned about the physician's relapse.

Just as the effectiveness of the initial phase of treatment is dependent on its intensity to break through denial, the value of the aftercare phase lies in its extension to provide support during transition to community-based support. Twenty months allows for structured contacts to be maintained through the first 2 years after which, according to our data, the risk of relapse drops significantly.[4]

In addition to the aftercare contract and the relapse guidelines, the reentry phase is ideally characterized by continuous contact with the Caduceus Club network, the primary care physician, and the treatment center. In actuality, many physicians are miles from other recovering physicians. Other than frequent calls to contacts at IPP, they rely on AA/NA networks and sponsors for the support they need to stay sober. International Doctors in Alcoholics Anonymous (IDAA) offers further personal and professional support. Composed of physicians and Ph.D. psychologists, IDAA has an annual meeting and other informal meetings in conjunction with various conferences.

The long-term goal of Georgia's Impaired Physicians Program is that each physician who completes the treatment regimen will have acquired an emotional and spiritual commitment to "any lengths" to stay sober and live a productive and rewarding life 24 hours at a time. The tools for preventing relapse or for turning it into a higher quality recovery program are provided in the four elements of the Program discussed in this chapter.

REFERENCES

1. Talbott, G.D., & Benson, E.B. Impaired physicians: The dilemmas of identification. *Postgrad Med* 1980:68:56–64.
2. Talbott, G.D. The impaired physician and intervention: A key to recovery *J. Fla. Med. Assoc.* 1982:69:793–797.
3. Talbott, G.D. The role of the medical student in the treatment of impaired physicians. *J. Med. Assn. Ga.* 1982:11:275–277.
4. Unpublished study.

Chapter 27

THE BAR AND THE BAR

RICHARD E. GENTRY

The primary concerns of state Bar Associations are protection of the public from impaired conduct and protection of the integrity of the court system. As officers of the court, judges, clerks, and other court and professional personnel must be able to rely upon the representations of attorneys. Attorneys handle funds without daily scrutiny and to a large extent, the future of many members of the public.

Although drug/alcohol addictions are medical problems affecting numerous individual members of the Bar, until quite recently state Bar Associations viewed addiction only in its regulatory role. Therefore prevention, intervention, supervision, and aftercare were not within the scope of lawyers' regulation. In the past, attorneys who engaged in inappropriate conduct due to the addiction process, have been suspended or disbarred, and no measures were taken to reach the source of the conduct.

Attorneys and Bar Associations have always been leery of looking too deeply into their fellow attorneys' private lives. Merely "accusing" someone of being addicted could result in slander actions.

However, most state Bar Associations insure their members' escrowed funds. This self-interest has led to prevention efforts which try to avert actions requiring draconian punishments. In the State of Washington the Bar's prevention measures are supervised by the self-insurance fund. The prevention measures may include education, a hot line, referral network, or actual intervention.

The education efforts routinely include information about addiction as a disease, symptoms and the state Bar's attitude. This information is published in state Bar journals, newspapers and local Bar publications.

This chapter is reprinted from *Employee Assistance Programs; A Basic Text* (1988) with permission of the author, the book's editors (Dickman, Emener, & Hutchison, Jr.) and the publisher (Charles C Thomas, Publisher).

The state Bar's attitude about addiction seriously affects the willingness of its members to admit addiction prior to violating one of the rules. If the Bar is supportive, the result will be a better attitude about reporting impaired attorneys prior to disaster, or as is rarely the case, self-reporting.

In the 1970s the only mechanism for reporting impaired conduct was after noticeable misconduct occurred. Showing up drunk in court was not always reported, as sometimes it affected no one adversely; missed court dates were rescheduled. A simple denial was taken at face value. Once the disease had begun its active deterioration phase, local Bar committees simply waited for disaster to strike, then they stepped in to prevent further abuse of the public.

With the advent of the 1980s, programs such as California's "Other Bar," Florida's "Impaired Attorneys' Program," and others were instituted. These programs go into the area of referral prior to misconduct. Basically the systems call for confidential peer referral, followed by an investigation by the appropriate persons. With the well-justified assumption that lawyers are litigious, these are nonprofit corporations separate from the Bar itself.

One state has all attorneys arrested for driving while intoxicated referred directly by the police agency. The arrest process is generally a good time for intervention as denial is significantly lowered. In all other states outside of discipline, referral is a casual process in which the impaired attorney will be fortunate if referred by friends or other compatriots prior to discipline.

Intervention on nondisciplined attorneys takes great skill and patience. Attorneys are trained in avoidance, debate, cross-examination, and verbal self-defense. In my experience it is the brave intervener who comes out of the intervention understanding why he impuned the integrity of this attorney. Preparation must be exhaustive, facts presented (under the Johnson model) must be nonarguable, and the intervention site chosen to minimize avoidance techniques.

The Florida Bar utilizes one full-time intervenor and should expand in 1987–88 to include several part-time assistants. The response from Bar members has been appropriate and helpful although there is a long way to go before acceptance is total. Currently the Bar's intervenor confronts the member and refers for assessment by the appropriate agency. The member then enters into a private contract with the Impaired Attorney Program which states what the member will do to prevent further drug/alcohol abuse.

Normally an addicted attorney will have come to the attention of the regulatory process prior to intervention. Impairment does not constitute a defense for lawyer misconduct, although "voluntary" assessment and treatment will mitigate punishment. The Florida Supreme Court has recognized that a lawyer has a better chance at recovery, and any restitution to clients (unearned fees, missing funds, etc.) be paid by the attorneys on probation rather than while suspended or disbarred.

It is important that an individual attorney take responsibility for his actions while addicted and that he/she will be given a chance to make other victims of his/her disease whole. Any other course of conduct would breach the duty of the Bar to protect the public.

Most state Bar Associations are currently developing programs for detection and treatment of drug-impaired attorneys within the framework of peer reporting. A better approach would be through a statewide "Employee Assistance Program" which would direct education and prevention efforts to the home environment where the effects are noticeable prior to on the job.

Attorneys develop a thick skin and often do not identify clients' problems with their own. A family is in a better position to see developing problems, and if they could solve the problem without adversely affecting the breadwinner, they should be given the chance.

There are currently no programs to reach the families of attorneys for earlier detection. By the time the referral process has begun, the family denial is a necessary adjunct to family survival and the walls are effectively erected.

Chapter 28

PROFESSIONAL SPORTS AND EMPLOYEE ASSISTANCE PROGRAMS

Fred Dickman and Ben Hayes

Introduction

This chapter is designed to show how an Employee Assistance Program can be effective throughout the system of a Professional Sports organization. The example used is the minor league system of a professional baseball club. The program has been in operation about four years.

The baseball organization used as a model has teams of various levels located in seven different locations and comprises approximately two hundred players, managers, coaches and trainers.

The chapter's intent is to explain how and why the EAP was begun, to trace the development over four years, to describe the kinds of issues brought to the EAP for assessment, counseling, and follow-up and to discuss its evolution or utilization rate.

History

Minor league organizations have not been constrained by labor/management contract from performing drug testing on its personnel. Consequently the organization discussed decided a little over four years ago that players under contract with the organization would be drug-free. Tests were mandatory and given to all personnel universally. This was done during spring training when all personnel were together. Out of two hundred persons tested, twelve (or 6%) were positive. Consistent with the club's policy, an evaluator was called to assess each of the twelve persons so as to determine what treatment was needed if any. Out of

This chapter is reprinted from *Employee Assistance Programs; A Basic Text* (1988) with permission of the author, the book's editors (Dickman, Emener, & Hutchison, Jr.) and the publisher (Charles C Thomas, Publisher).

these evaluations it became evident that problems other than drugs existed in most cases and, in those cases, general counseling was recommended. Testing was done several other times during that season and where a positive was found the same result was found. A few needed substance abuse counseling; most needed and wanted assistance for other problems; problems such as performance anxiety, general stress, family issues, life-style stress, etc.

At the next spring training, in a general all-day session and small seminars, more was done than drug testing and alcohol and other drug education. Topics such as handling pressure, performance anxiety, and family relationships were offered with an enthusiastic response. Managers, coaches, and trainers were given special seminars on identifying the "troubled" player and players performing below their ability. During that season a "hot line" was installed for persons to call collect to get help for a problem or a feeling. Management could and did call for the EAP counselor to come to that city to see a specific player. Spring training instruction as to life-style and psychological issues has gotten bigger and alcohol and other drug use has gotten less attention. At the last drug testing, only four were identified, and total positives continue to be less and less. Either the message has gotten across or use is down even among the (each year) new players. The average of 2–3 percent is far less than the general population. Spring training EAP sessions have gotten more elaborate with national speakers on topics of interest chosen by the players. The EAP counselor goes on three to four day trips to each city and his time is used confidentially by the players and managers, whom coaches and trainers refer freely.

Issues Brought to the EAP

The most frequent concerns brought to EAP counseling/assessment session were the following:

1. **Insomnia:** A surprising finding (but logical when thought about) was that a considerable number of players had trouble going to sleep. This was not due to going out and staying out for long hours after the game. The great majority of players try to go to sleep reasonably soon after the game, especially on the road, but tend to toss and turn. It is difficult to stop obsessing about the game

whether mistakes were made or success enjoyed. An attempt was made to teach relaxation techniques and for those who came for a session (or sessions) with this problem a tape was made and sent to him with relaxation on one side and visualization (for either a hitter or a pitcher) on the other.

2. **Enhancing Performance:** Players came with a desire to utilize visualization to enhance concentration, focus, relaxation, and to "hold" the ball or "slow" the ball through mind control. Many athletes have the sense of being so grounded at times that everything seems in slow motion. Other times they have a sense of time acceleration and play seems actually faster than reality. Techniques of visualization often assist in more often capturing the former state.

3. **Family Problems:** Relationships: parents, wives, or girlfriends were a concern. Some were counseled and referred to family service centers if severe. These young people have relationships back home and when they are away, they worry. Then too, some are married and long road trips put a severe strain on the marriage. The life-style involving games every night, sometimes up to midnight, takes a special kind of tolerance and understanding to survive a marital or any other close relationship.

4. **Patience:** Many players, especially in the lower leagues, have trouble waiting for a chance to play. This entails learning patience, developing trust that they will be given a chance, dealing with resentment, keeping a positive attitude about themselves and continuing to work hard in practice.

5. **Anxiety:** Believing in themselves, staying too much in the (immediate) past or future, feeling "light" or "not here" are problems of deeper, nonperceived anxiety. Practice in proper breathing, relaxation, and grounding appeared to help. However, when a self image problem clearly created a marked discrepancy between ability and function, a referral to a psychologist for weekly sessions was in order.

6. **Life-Style Problems:** There is a temptation to sleep until noon or beyond. Players don't have to report for pregame practice until 2:30 p.m. The game is over around 10:00 p.m. unless it's a double header. Then midnight or later is the average. Players who can get

to sleep soon after the game and get up at least by midmorning usually feel less sluggish. Diet is another problem in this life-style. Past 11 or 12 p.m. only fast food places are open. Those who learn to keep fruit around and find some way to balance diets fare much better in the long run. Turning this around is not easy but worth it to the dedicated players.

7. **Substance Abuse Issues:** This part of the life-style requires special attention, more by management and the EAP philosophy (to assist players reach their potential), than the players themselves. While drug use is not to be permitted, and checks are made, drinking is an accepted part of the life-style. Hence, there is apt to be more denial and enabling than attentive caring confrontation and intervention. Some players are concerned and resist peer pressure. The majority do not. The effects of overuse and abuse and alcohol's effect on the nervous system has to be addressed in workshops, management training, and in counseling sessions. It is especially an appropriate issue when the problem is underperforming or performance associated with undue anxiety.

Mini-Workshops

Opportunity is given on road trips to present thirty-minute workshops each day in the clubhouse. These elaborated on spring training workshop themes in addition to problems learned about during the formal and informal sessions.

Among the topics were:

1. "Performance Anxiety"
2. "Relaxation Training"
3. "Insomnia—Causes and Remedies"
4. "Diet"
5. "Thinking Positive—Rational Emotive Therapy"
6. "Being in the Now"
7. "Learn From, Rather than Ruminate Past Mistakes"
8. "Being Grounded—Breathing, Listening, to Your Body"
9. "Visualization—Making the ball bigger and slower for the hitters; the reverse for the pitchers"
10. "Sitting on the Bench and Still Being Involved"

Informal Counseling Sessions

During the three-to-four-day team visitation, the EAP counselor/assessor had an opportunity to just "be around" during practice and the game, in the dugout or bullpen during a game, and going for the late meal after the game with several players and/or managers. These periods provided the opportunity for helpful contacts and even short counseling encounters.

1986 Statistics

During spring training and the three to four day trips to various sites, the following statistics were accumulated for the 1986 season:

1. **Formal Interviews:** Twenty-one persons made formal appointments about various issues (discussed later in the report). These persons were seen in a clubhouse office; the contractor's motel room; over lunch, dinner or coffee—tea; or isolated locales on the practice field.

2. **Informal Contacts:**
   (a) Five to ten-minute sessions were possible behind the batting cage during practice, in the dugout just before a game, visiting the bullpen during a game, between practice and dressing for the game, running-jogging in the mornings from the on-the-road-motel, and sitting by the pool at the motel from 11:00 a.m. to 1:00 p.m. It is difficult to be accurate about the number of these contacts, but a conservative estimate is fifty.
   (b) After the game, suppers with managers, workers, and trainers were enjoyed at every visited locale. These were found to be extremely helpful in getting better acquainted with these gentlemen and a more indepth perspective of the problems, both general and specific. As an aside, each person's grasp of the emotional aspect of the players was greatly admired.

Evaluation

The ultimate evaluation, of course, is how well a player does in relation to his ability. Some work is being done on this aspect of evaluation but the results will be long term. Some players who entered the program are already in the major leagues, but not enough evidence exists to infer the EAP program was a significant variable.

Another means of evaluation is utilization rate. So far 90 persons have entered the EAP program for at least one session. This is nearly a 50 percent utilization rate taken at face value of 180 plus players. Adjusting this down for trades, new players from the draft, releases and trades to other organizations the utilization rate is approximately 30 percent. This type interest alone demonstrates the value of an EAP program for a minor league organization and maybe to all other sports organizations as well.

Chapter 29

GOVERNMENT

B. ROBERT CHALLENGER

The disastrous results of chemical dependency have been well chronicled. Estimates ranging from $50 billion to $145 billion have been cited. "Problem employees" have been estimated to cost their employers between $1500 and $4000 annually, over and beyond their salary or wages. In addition, the majority of these individuals have considerable lengths of service; usually 10 to 15 years on the job and thereby represent a sizeable corporate investment.

Recognizing this gigantic economic and human drain, the private sector of our economy and business life has made some moderate strides in identifying and combatting the problem. Employee Assistance Programs are designed to provide intervention during the initial stages of an employee's problem; preferably prior to its affecting his ability to perform his job and/or the interruption of others. But as job performance is affected, the programs require a coercive confrontation, based on this poor performance record which offers the problem employee an opportunity to seek help in most cases, avoid the disciplinary measures called for in company policy. Success with this system, hopefully, returns the employee to health and provides the company with a productive human being.

The passage of the "Federal Comprehensive Alcohol Abuse and Alcoholism Treatment and Rehabilitation Act" in 1970 provided our governments with the tools to tackle this ever-increasing problem. The Act provided for the following:

1. As an effort to provide an example and some leadership, the Civil Service Commission was required to establish and operate occupational alcoholism programs for federal employees.

This chapter is reprinted from *Employee Assistance Programs; A Basic Text* (1988) with permission of the author, the book's editors (Dickman, Emener, & Hutchison, Jr.) and the publisher (Charles C Thomas, Publisher).

373

2. All of the states (50) were provided monies to fund two occupational program consultants, commonly known as OPCs. The initial group was known as the Thundering One Hundred and their responsibilities included the lead role in designing and implementing Occupational Alcoholism Programs (OAPs) in their respective states.

OAPs generated moderate interest at the local level, but through persistent efforts and additional funding, the number of programs steadily grew. Cost reductions, human features, and high rehabilitation rates provided the incentive for organizations to initiate these new programs in the public sector. Since the OPCs' charge included private sector companies as well as public employers, much of the early effort was placed in the private sector, where additional funding could be obtained through modest charges.

Unfortunately, there are still some states that have not fully recognized the benefits to be derived from such programs and lack the impetus and knowledge to install comprehensive programs for all their employees and family members. This has led to slow growth in this area. Even though these employers are not profit-oriented, the cost reduction aspect should surely provide the incentive to pursue their implementation.

In order to provide the reader with an example of what can be done, we have selected the program currently in place in New York state as an example. The following will spell out in some detail the steps taken, beginning in early 1970s, that resulted in one of the most comprehensive Employee Assistance Programs in a government setting. We would be remiss if we did not recognize the efforts of a special few, whose perseverance, patience, and empathy served as the backbone of this effort. Although we will probably miss some, we recall John Quinn, Gerry Rooney, Miriam Aaron, and Alden Asbornsen. Those who quickly joined our select group were the initial EAP Coordinators and Committee Chairpersons from the many Psychiatric and Developmental Centers in the Department of Mental Hygiene.

The state's commitment to the *Alcoholism Control Program* of the early seventies was successful in creating an awareness and recognition of the alcoholism problem among the workforce. In 1973 the New York State Division of Alcoholism distributed a questionnaire to personnel officers who were members of the New York State Personnel Council. The survey indicated that state personnel officers preferred a program designed to offer assistance to all employees who were not performing **regardless** of the nature of their problem, versus a program designed to offer assistance only to employees with alcohol abuse or alcoholism.

In early 1974 a planning body representing unions and several state agencies took as their principal task, the development of the state employee program. It initially functioned within the Employee Health Service under the auspices of the interagency committee.

This Health Maintenance Program recognized that:

- With no exceptions, in any sizable work population there will be people who have health-related job performance problems.
- Ignored, both the job performance problem and the health problem worsens.
- Health-related job performance problems when identified early and constructively, respond favorably to intervention and assistance.

With these principles in mind, a department wishing to develop a program would do as follows:

1. Contract the Employee Health Service requesting consultation.
2. With assistance from the Employee Health Service Consultant, develop a Health Maintenance Program policy and procedure. (The chances for a function program improved substantially when the policy and procedure were developed by a joint labor/management committee.)
3. Conduct a training and orientation program for top management, all supervisors, and union representatives.
4. Designate as resource people, personnel administrators whom employees can communicate with and trust.
5. Reinforce the original training with periodic articles in newsletters, with special preventive health programs, exhibits, etc.
6. Develop a monitoring and evaluation design to determine the impact of the program.

A report on the implementation and yield of the demonstration program was submitted to the administrative leadership of the specific department by the Employee Health Service. The report attempted to analyze the impact the Health Maintenance Program was having on the department employees. The general conclusion was that the program was not working very well. The intent of the report was to identify what the Employee Health Service Consultant believed to be the problem areas.

The following problem areas were reported:

1. It appeared that only chronic problem employees were being identified and referred. All of the employees examined by the Employee Health Service were people whose problems had been known and tolerated by the department for more than two years.
2. The number of referrals was far below program expectations. The yield did not justify the time and money put into the program.
3. The program was not being used by, or to refer, managers and top-level administrators.
4. The union was playing a passive role at best in supporting the program's development.
5. The program did not appear to be a priority with the administrative leadership of the department.

Therefore, the Health Maintenance Program was not perceived as a mutually beneficial program by either labor or management. The union leadership for the most part was not involved in the planning or development of the program. Union endorsement was given reluctantly, when given at all.

The implementation efforts, however, resulted in one functional program with minimal impact on 1,600 central office employees.

In 1976, the State launched an Employee Assistance Pilot Program for 13,000 state employees within the Department of Mental Hygiene's Mid-Hudson Region. During the previous year, the New York State Division of Alcoholism and Alcohol Abuse launched the most intensive "pre-implementation" work ever attempted with such a program. Upon concluding site visits to public sector programs in Illinois, California, New Jersey, Kentucky, and private sector programs such as ITT, AT&T, and Eastman Kodak, the major core characteristics of the project were identified. The primary goals of the project were to:

• Promote the **joint** labor/management approach in the development, design, planning, and implementation and evaluation of local Employee Assistance Programs.
• Provide statewide EAP Network with an understanding of the basic core elements of the Employee Assistance Program.
• Develop appropriate and adequate policy guidelines and procedures, endorsed by all participating parties.

- Reinforce the belief that the Employee Assistance Program is an effective method to assist troubled employees who account for inefficiency, lost client services, worker dissatisfaction, and friction within the work group.
- Develop an effective and durable helping network designed to promote interchange and cooperation between the labor, management, and treatment community.
- Deliver ongoing training and educational programs designed to inform and develop those skills necessary to develop quality programs and services.

An agreement was reached with the largest public employee union in the state, to base any further expansion of these services upon successful implementation and evaluation of the program in the Mid-Hudson area.

In 1976, the New York State Division of Alcoholism and Alcohol Abuse provided funds to deliver the first Employee Assistance Program Coordinators Institute.

The objectives of the Institute were:

- To provide the workshop participants with an understanding of the basic elements of a comprehensive Employee Assistance Program.
- To develop the participants' ability to motivate and refer the employee with a personal problem to the appropriate helping community resource.
- To train the participants to effectively coordinate their local programs.
- To reinforce the participants' belief in the importance of the role of the Employee Assistance Program Coordinator.
- To develop an appreciation on the part of each coordinator for the maintenance of program quality control and assurance through ongoing evaluation and feedback.
- To motivate the coordinator to market the Program concept, not only on behalf of the organization, but also the community.
- To become actively involved in professional organizations such as ALMACA, to proliferate the concept.
- To stress the inherent need for confidentiality.

In the Fall of 1987, a report was prepared by the Occupational Division of the New York State Division of Alcoholism and Alcohol Abuse, utilizing the results of the Mid-Hudson region project and submitted to the Commissioner of the Department of Mental Hygiene. The reports summarized the background of the project, its beneficial results, and recommended expansion of the project services to other areas of the state.

During the first fourteen (14) months of the Mid-Hudson operation, over 1,800 referrals were reported by participating worksites. The program design was cited as a highly functional model by key representatives of the labor and management communities at the local level.

On February 25, 1979, Governor Carey, in the **State of the Health Message**, emphasized the important role which the EAP concept would play in providing "New Paths to Better Health." The Governor requested the Director of the New York State Division of Alcoholism and Alcohol Abuse to implement workplace programs in cooperation with unions and public employees. This growing awareness was put forward as a far broader enterprise than merely providing clinical services. The interest shown in the EAP concept clearly recognized the state's role in promoting preventative health programs by providing employee assistance information and services to local worksites thereby enhancing the "quality of life" for state workers.

The *Employee Assistance Program,* which presently services most state employees at a majority of the job sites, is comprised of thousands of employee assistance committee members and hundreds of coordinators involving most state agencies, and remains evolutionary and developmental in nature since its inception during the Spring of 1976. This observation is reinforced when one understands the history and emergence of EAP within the public sector in New York. The EAP is based upon the recognition and commitment to

1. The joint labor/management approach as a proven way to establish workplace programs which have as their purpose, the early identification and referral of employees experiencing personal/behavioral/medical problems.
2. The workplace is the most effective arena to deal with these problems because of their steady and noticeable effect on work performance.
3. The EAP potential for early identification utilizes the employee's job as a motivating factor to seek assistance.

The present model provides for the: Formation of a local EAP advisory committee, trained/committed coordinators, policy development and dissemination, concurrent supervisor/steward training, program procedures, resource networking, quality treatment and aftercare resources, employee and family education, and program assessment.

In the development of these programs a working understanding of the EAP complex as well as the relationship between the structures and functions of the labor/management system was accounted for through the promotion of a constituent network based upon interchange and cooperation. Of primary importance was the development of this state-wide network to insure that case finding, referral activities, communications, and planning were carried out as part of an integrated and comprehensive plan consistent with the overall human services plan.

The 1980s continued the trend of further growth and structural evolution of EAP within New York State government. Program growth strategists provided for centralized review, coordination, research, evaluation and planning aimed at refining those characteristics of the existing model(s) which are aimed at providing effective primary and secondary prevention programs for state employees.

Currently, members of this "established" network, in conjunction with private EAP providers, are encouraging and assisting other governmental agencies (counties, cities, towns, villages and school districts) in the consideration and implementation of their own EAP.

More than any other area of work, an effective and viable EAP in the public sector requires:

a. Commitment to the EAP concept by all concerned.
b. A dedicated network of coordinators.
c. Support, financially, vocally, and actively, of the union and **all** levels of management.
d. Constant assessment and updating.
e. Coordinated planning and administration.

Chapter 30

THE CLERGY

FRED DICKMAN

Introduction

Clergy present a unique problem and opportunity to the Employee Assistance Professional. This is particularly true regarding alcoholism. The problem is that clergy too often are forced to deny personal problems, especially problems of addiction. Consequently the problems are apt to mushroom and be subjected to effective intervention much too far into the progression. The opportunity is that as a denomination is educated to the nature of personal problems in general, and addiction in particular, the clergy (both those who are recovering and those who are not) can, in turn, reach many more persons who are ill but in denial.

The purpose of this chapter is to focus on clergy and alcoholism. However as more churches embrace the EAP approach to early intervention, many more "EAP type problems," i.e., marriage and family, alcoholism, adult children of alcoholic parents, other drug addiction and general psychological issues will be identified and ameliorated at a much earlier time in each's progression.

The Clergy's Unique Problem

Not only is the clergy alcoholic person and his family subjected to the stigma of alcoholism as is the general population, he has a deeper stigma as well. He is led to believe that were he to have enough faith he would not become alcoholic. Conversely if he is an alcoholic, his faith must be either too weak or nonexistent. This "deeper" stigma is noticed anecdotally by the author as well as implied by survey type research (Moss, 1975). This phenomenon may well explain the often lack of interest in alcohol-

This chapter is reprinted from *Employee Assistance Programs; A Basic Text* (1988) with permission of the author, the book's editors (Dickman, Emener, & Hutchison, Jr.) and the publisher (Charles C Thomas, Publisher).

ism among pastors and in the churches noticed by researchers (Banks, 1983). If it is true that clergy believe alcoholism (and mental illness as well) to be an indication of low or absence of a living faith, then the problem of reaching the alcoholic clergyman and his family is doubly difficult. Hence the challenge and opportunity for the EAP professional who can penetrate the denial of church structures. Not only will the ill clergyman receive help sooner, but those whom he can reach early will be multiplied in that he is on the frontline of families approaching the church for help.

Paradoxical History

The double stigma felt by the clergy is all the more strange when viewed in the light of the history of Alcoholics Anonymous. Clergy and churches have been involved with AA since its beginnings in 1935 (Kurtz, 1979).

A prime example is the Reverend Doctor Samuel Shoemaker who was Bill Wilson's (Co-founder of AA) spiritual advisor in the early years of the latter's recovery (Kurtz, 1979). The Rev. Fr. Ernest Dowling is another example. With this shrewd Jesuit's early counsel, Bill and the early AA members kept Alcoholics Anonymous efficiently unattached from any form of organized religion.

In the early years churches of all faiths opened halls to AA groups for their "closed" and "open" meetings. To this day only a cursory glance in any city will list well over half the meeting places as in the halls of churches.

A Growing Reversal

Increasingly mainline Protestant denominations and the Roman Catholic Church are breaking the double stigma; in that to have the disease of alcoholism is tantamount to having no faith.

The Episcopal Church under the leadership of Vernon Johnson of Johnson Institute and the Catholic Church with good experience with Guest House (a Catholic treatment center outside Detroit) have issued policy statements that alcoholism is a disease and not a sin. With this kind of growing atmosphere an EAP for each diocese, district or presbytry can make a significant contribution to the clergy, nuns, lay brothers and the people to whom they are servants.

Church EAP's

As described above the climate may be appropriate for an Employee Assistance Program for the various church bodies for the following reasons:

1. **The Disease Concept.** A growing acceptance of the disease notion of alcoholism has filtered to many church leaders (Kellermann, 1958). Rather than viewing alcoholism as continuing sinfulness, there is a growing awareness that while faith is a necessary ingredient in alcoholism recovery (Roessler, 1982), the lack of faith does not cause alcoholism.

2. **History of Pastoral Concern.** Churches have long been involved in and sympathetic to the movement of Alcoholics Anonymous and alcoholism recovery in general. Early on (1932–1950) this support was spotty and evolved around pioneers such as Rev. Dr. Shoemaker and Fr. Dowling. And as early as 1948 was the Hazelden experiment and by 1952 the Lutherans sponsored a hospital-based treatment center in Chicago. More recently churches sponsor treatment and training awareness throughout the community.

3. **Church Policy Statements.** As stated earlier the Episcopal Church and various Catholic Dioceses have issued policy statements adhering to the disease concept of alcoholism. These clearly offer treatment rather than discipline and punishment and are actively engaged in the rehabilitation of clergy alcoholics.

4. **Recovering Examples.** Each diocese, district and many congregations have found, as has industry, that recovering persons are productive and fruitful workers and stewards. On a national level, some of the most noted and successful teachers of alcoholic recovery are members of the clergy.

5. **Public Acceptance.** Eighteen years ago in the author's diocese he found it nearly impossible to return to an active parish ministry as a recent recovering alcoholic. Today that is changed. He has been offered many parishes in the past ten years and experiences no obvious rejection as he speaks to church groups about alcoholism. Many parishes and other diocesan positions are filled by recovering persons.

The EAP Approach

The clergy may be approached to get early assistance for alcoholism and other problems just as have persons in industry since the 1940s—through an EAP.

Once the bishop of the diocese, president of the conference, or district secretary is convinced, a healthy or EAP committee comprised of knowledgeable lay and clerical members may be established. This committee agrees upon a policy statement that alcoholism is a disease and that other incapacitating problems are "human" and not antithetical to faith. Then the committee speaks at conferences and in small groups to raise awareness to: (1) clergy can have problems, (2) to early (or late, for that matter) rehabilitate is highly likely with an EAP, and (3) it is to the best interest of all concerned to face and ameliorate the problem(s) rather than deny to the point of destructiveness.

On this atmosphere intervention teams can be trained, adequate medical insurance provided, counseling/evaluation centers organized and treatment and follow-up plans initiated. The EAP coordinator, lay or clerical, is selected and the program can be launched. Not only does such a program work for those to whom it is intended, but the whole climate of the diocese/district is changed so that lay people who have the disease of alcoholism and their families are more apt to seek help faster.

Conclusion

This chapter has attempted to demonstrate that clergy face a unique situation when they "catch" the disease of alcoholism. They too often blame themselves and are blamed for lack of faith or they would not have contracted the disease. It was pointed out that such an attitude is strange in view of the close and helpful history the churches have in the historical progression of the alcoholism recovery movement.

It was recommended that:

1. Various church organizations initiate EAP's to reach and rehabilitate clergy alcoholic persons, and
2. The time and spiritual atmosphere is ripe for such a movement.

Finally, clergy are well-trained and necessary persons to the community. When one clergyman and his family accepts his or her alcoholism, gets treatment and returns to the active pastorate everyone gains; the church, the clergyperson and his/her family and the parishioners, especially those who have problems themselves.

REFERENCES

Albers, R.H. (1982). The theological and psychological dynamics of transformation in the recovery from the disease of alcoholism. *Dissertation Abstracts International, 43* (4-A) 1198.

Banks, R.E. (1983). Attitudes and alcohol: The use of the semantic differential with different professional and drinking populations in east Tennessee. *Dissertation Abstracts International, 43* (9-A) 2896.

Desilets, R. (1968). Alcoholism and actual pastoral approaches. *Toxicomanies, 1* (1) 51–60.

Drummond, T. (1982). The alcoholic and the church: A pastoral response. *International Journal of Offender Therapy & Comparative Criminology, 26* (3) 275–280.

Fappiano, E.R. (1984). The alcoholic priest and Alcoholics Anonymous: A study of stigma and the management of spoiled identity. *Dissertation Abstracts International, 45* (4-A) 1211.

Fitzgerald, M.C. (1982). Correlates of alcoholism among Roman Catholic nuns: Psychological and attitudinal variables. *Dissertation Abstracts International, 43* (1-B) 246.

Kellermann, J.L. (1958). *Alcoholism a guide for the clergy.* New York: National Council on Alcoholism.

Kurtz, E. (1979). *Not — God a History of Alcoholics Anonymous.* Center City, MN: Hazelden.

Mann, K.W. (1972). The mission of the church in a drugs culture. *Journal of Religion & Health, 11* (4) 329–348.

Merrigan, D.M. (1983). Pastoral gatekeeper participation in community alcohol abuse prevention. *Dissertation Abstracts International, 44* (6-A) 1700.

Moss, D.M. (1975). Parochial ministry, the Episcopal Church, and alcoholism. *Journal of Religion & Health, 14* (3) 192–197.

Roessler, S.J. (1982). *The role of spiritual values in the recovery of alcoholics.* Wesley Theological Seminary.

Sorensen, A.A. (1973). Need for power among alcoholic and nonalcoholic clergy. *Journal for the Scientific Study of Religion, 12* (1) 101–108.

Chapter 31

EMPLOYEE ASSISTANCE PROGRAMS FOR SCHOOL TEACHERS AND SCHOOL PERSONNEL

WILLIAM G. EMENER

There is a serious crisis in teaching in the United States. It jeopardizes this nation's ability to conduct its own public affairs through the workings of an informed electorate. It endangers the nation's capacity to compete effectively in a shrinking world where technological skill and inventiveness will determine leadership. (Feistritzer, 1983, p. 59)

Indeed, in the recent past there has been increased public attention to our schools in the United States. Observations and concerns such as Feistritzer's (1983) abound not only among professionals but among the general public as well. "A variety of factors have contributed to the crisis in teaching, including population shifts, increased professional opportunities for women outside the teaching profession, and the declining caliber of those entering the teaching profession." (Raschke, Dedrick, Strathe & Hawkes, 1985). Within our schools and their environments, and within the working lives of educators and especially the working lives of teachers, there are identifiable attributes and characteristics which meaningfully contribute to our present teaching crisis. Evidence of these "special" aspects of the teaching profession(s), provide compelling reasons for school systems to have employee assistance programs for their personnel—especially for their teachers. The remainder of this chapter will: (a) discuss some of the identified "problems" of school personnel (with a focus on teachers); (b) present convincing rationale for having employee assistance programs in our school systems; (c) discuss important service delivery components of EAPs for school personnel; (d) address special concerns in need of attention in school system EAPs; (e) provide an example of a successful school system EAP; and (f) offer a

This chapter is reprinted from *Employee Assistance Programs; A Basic Text* (1988) with permission of the author, the book's editors (Dickman, Emener, & Hutchison, Jr.) and the publisher (Charles C Thomas, Publisher).

385

concluding comment regarding the design, development and implementation of an EAP in a school system.

Job-Related Problems of School Personnel (Teachers)

Over the past few years, our highly technological and complex society has added to people's pressures and stresses—especially on our educational systems and the professionals working in them. The president of a leading teachers' organization articulated these phenomena: "The dynamics of our society and increased public demands on education have produced adverse and stressful classroom and school conditions. These conditions have led to increased emotional and physical disabilities among teachers and other school personnel" (Moe, 1979, p. 36). Some attention recently has been focused on the new, beginning teacher in terms of helping him or her to quickly develop and learn "basic survival skills" and hopefully avoid some of the deleterious effects articulated by Moe (1979). Boynton, DiGeronimo and Gustafson (1985) stated: "Experienced and successful teachers appear to have an inexhaustible bag full of [necessary, personal survival] techniques, strategies, and methods going for them. Pity the first-year teacher. The new teacher comes to the profession with a nearly empty bag of experiences" (p. 101).

Recent studies have identified unique aspects of teaching that contribute to occupational difficulties and job-related problems. "Teacher isolation," for example, appears to have deleterious effects on classroom teachers. Goodlad (1983) reported that teachers are typically separated from one another in the schools and little is done to facilitate their coming together (e.g. to work on their curricula and instruction). Tye and Tye (1984) found that even though "sharing" is necessary and desired by teachers, most of them work alone in self-contained classrooms and have very little time to observe each other at work and to work together. Interestingly, Rothberg (1986) surveyed 196 teachers enrolled in graduate programs and in his findings he stated:

> Over 80 percent of each group (elementary, junior/middle, and senior high) felt, "Your classroom is a private world which no one besides you and your students enter." Senior high school teachers' perceptions were higher than others.
>
> In response to the question, "Do you feel your good work goes unnoticed?" over 85 percent of the elementary and middle/junior high school teachers

said, "sometimes" or "frequently," while 85 percent of the senior high school teachers said, "frequently" or "always." (p. 320)

Feelings akin to "separation" have also been reported by teachers. Cox and Wood (1980), for example, found teachers to report feeling "alienated" within the school with little opportunity to be involved in decision-making. Unfortunately, emotive reactions to the classroom and the school environment such as these also contribute to the stress that teachers experience.

There is a dearth of systematic research on stress in teachers, especially elementary teachers (Pellegrew & Wolfe, 1982). Professional literature in this area appears to be limited to personal reports, anecdotal observations and problem resolution techniques (Quick & Quick, 1979; Weiskopf, 1980; Werner, 1980). Even though daily stresses, student disruptions, verbal abuse from students, and less than preferable levels of administrative support have been associated with teacher stress (Chichon & Koff, 1978), there unfortunately remains very little systematic evidence that schools are attempting to rectify such conditions. It would appear reasonable to conclude, nonetheless, that some of these identified debilitative conditions are the types of conditions which schools could address. For example, Raschke, Dedrick, Strathe and Hawkes (1985) studied 300 K–6 teachers from school districts of various sizes in the central Midwest and reported: "When asked to list three things they did not like about their job, 70% of the teachers cited excessive paperwork and nonteaching duties as two major concerns." (p. 562) The existence of these conditions, per se, is not necessarily the problem in and of itself; the prolonged existence of these conditions is what tends to contribute to the debilitating effects and the eventual "teacher burnout" discussed in professional literature.

Freudenberger and Richelson (1980) offered an understanding of burnout that would appear to be very relevant to teaching: "...state of fatigue or frustration brought about by devotion to a cause, a way of life, or a relationship that failed to produce the expected reward" (p. 26). In her review of literature, viz on burnout related to teachers, Weiskopf (1980) summarized six categories of stress which contribute to teacher burnout: program structure, work overload, amount of direct contact with children, staff-child ratio, lack of perceived success, and responsibility for others.

Thus, as revealed in this cursory review of available, related professional literature, while teachers experience the types of pressures and stresses that many people experience as a result of societal conditions (Gold, 1985), there are also special and unique conditions of teaching and working in our schools that add to the pressures and stresses experienced by teachers. It is also important to note that in our society over the recent past, there have been increases in alcohol and drug abuse, increases in marital and family problems (e.g., the rise in divorce rates), and increases in reported problems in daily living (Dickman, Emener & Hutchison, 1985). Furthermore, employees can have work-related problems (as discussed above), and all of these potential difficulties and problems on behalf of employees, e.g., teachers, have effects on their work performance (Dickman & Emener, 1982). The fact that teachers play an extremely important role in the development of our children, our future generations (Moe, 1979), we should feel energized to proactively attend to such matters.

Rationale for EAPs in Our Schools

As portrayed in current popular media (e.g., newspapers, television), professional publications (e.g., journals) and in reports from assorted national commissions (consult Griesmer & Butler, 1983), teaching is a beleaguered profession. In a nutshell, to a great extent "teaching" is not meeting important, human needs of our teachers. Kreis and Milstein (1985) recently stated:

> There is a growing realization that our school boards and administrators who want teacher performance to improve will have to answer the age-old teacher question, "What's in it for me?". . . . Satisfying teachers' needs is complex, but is essential to improving the performance of our schools. (pp. 75 & 77)

As discussed in Chapter 28 of this book (i.e., the importance of "development"), if teachers are consumed with attending to their own needs, it will be difficult for them to attend to the needs of their students. And, it must be remembered that this involves large numbers of individuals. For example, the U.S. Department of Education's (1982) "Estimates of School Statistics: 1982–1983" revealed that over 1.1 million of the classroom teachers employed during the 1982–1983 academic year were elementary teachers—importantly, they were responsible for the education of almost 24 million children. Apropos of these data, Raschke, et al. (1985) stated:

Administrators, school board members, and taxpayers need to play a more decisive and responsive role in reducing some of the sources of stress that lie beyond the immediate control of the elementary school teacher. When one considers the vital role elementary teachers play in nurturing the psychological, physical, and intellectual competencies of young children, it becomes patently clear that these teachers need more time to teach and plan innovative and enriched instructional programs. (p. 563)

Considering the numerous difficulties and problems that school teachers and other professional school personnel can have, considering the deleterious impact of such problems on the school experiences of school children, and considering the positive impact that an employee assistance program can have when made available to employees with the types of difficulties and problems teachers can have, it indeed would appear imperative for school systems to have employee assistance programs.

Service Needs Provided by EAPs in School Systems

Employee assistance programs in school systems should be able to provide a full compliment of services typically provided by EAPs (consult Dickman, Emener & Hutchison, 1985; and other chapters in this book). For example, services in the areas of personal, marital and family concerns, financial planning, substance abuse and addiction, among others, are usually considered "must" service areas. The following, nonetheless, is designed to illustrate some of the school-oriented service delivery areas that EAPs for school systems should consider. (Specific service needs should be determined via evaluation research surveys within the specific school system the EAP is going to serve.) Services provided by school system EAPs can be categorized into four groups: (a) direct services— those provided to employees on an individually need-determined basis; (b) indirect services—those provided to employees on an "available to everyone" participation basis; (c) professionally oriented—those focusing on work (e.g., teaching) oriented problems; and (d) personally oriented— those focusing on problems unique to the employee's personal life. (In most instances, there is much overlap among these areas of distinction.) The following, however, will illustrate some of the services among these four groupings.

I. Direct Service Delivery

A. **Professionally-Oriented.** Based upon positive feedback from recipients, Boynton et al. (1985) offer 45 helpful suggestions for first-year teachers to help them adjust to some of the realities of classroom teaching. Their 45 suggestions, in four categories (16 in "classroom management"; five in "classroom discipline"; nine in "instruction"; and 15 labeled "professional"), can be offered to a teacher whose difficulties and problems are related to his or her classroom experiences.

B. **Personally-Oriented.** Quite frequently personnel will have a presenting personal problem that requires an individual service response. For example, Youngs (1985) analyzed questionnaires returned by 3,470 (69.4%) respondents from a population of U.S. superintendents and principals in a study of drug abuse. Among her findings she reported that "nearly 60% of the respondents knew of others who used drugs while on the job in the listed classifications." (p. 41). Her study also identified specific suggestions designed to help school professionals with drug and drug-related problems.

II. System-Service Delivery

A. **Professionally-Oriented.** There are numerous activities that EAPs in school systems can initiate, or encourage the staff to initiate, that can help minimize feelings of alienation and help facilitate a sense of community and professionalism. For example, Rothberg (1986) suggested activities designed to reduce teacher isolation: "Anything to improve and increase social interaction with and among staff would be meaningful . . . Attendance at professional meetings . . . Retreats at the beginning and/or at the end of the school year . . . " (p. 322)

B. **Personally-Oriented.** Examples of these kinds of activities were suggested by Gold (1985) in her descriptions of Stress Reduction Programs: "Inservice workshops, self-help groups, and stress clinics at teacher centers can help teachers make some necessary changes in their personal lives." (p. 211)

Employee assistance programs in school systems, as can be appreciated by these above illustrations, face the challenge of providing the "typical" array of EAP services provided by most EAPs and also providing and facilitating "school-system-specific" kinds of services that can be very helpful to personnel working in schools (especially teachers). Obviously, many of these service delivery components are more "wellness-oriented" (vis-à-vis remedial); nonetheless, their benefits have been documented and they certainly have demonstrated their worth.

Special Concerns of School System EAPs

As indicated in EAP literature (e.g., Dickman, Emener & Hutchison, 1985; and chapters in this book), there are numerous concerns and sensitivities of which an EAP must be aware if the program is to be successful. School system employees, management and labor, each have their individual and unique concerns about the operations and activities of an employee assistance program. There are unique characteristics of the teaching profession and of school systems that deserve special consideration.

Verification. When a school system plans, develops and implements an EAP, there are usually some skeptics in the community, on the school board, in the administration and among the staff who have concerns about, and are against, the program. It is critical for all operations and procedures of the program to be carefully monitored and appropriately documented. Furthermore, a high quality program evaluation component should be built into the infrastructure of the EAP. In these ways, the criticisms of the program's skeptics can be allayed, and the program's veracity and continuance can be assured.

Confidentiality. Similar to numerous other professions in our society (e.g., professional athletics, law enforcement, clergy), there are public expectations regarding the lifestyles of teachers and school officials—on and off the job. School personnel tend to be very concerned about what others think about them, how they act and what they do. Moreover, public opinion regarding teachers assuredly can influence their employment since they tend to be "in the public eye." This is especially true in small-town, rural areas. Thus, assuring the employees of the EAP's confidentiality is crucial.

Marketing/Trust. Establishing trust with an expectedly suspicious and fearful group should be a high priority in the EAP's marketing strategy. For example, it can be very helpful for EAP staff and school officials to attend faculty meetings and in "face to face" interactions explain the specific policies and procedures of the program. The bottom line is to convince the staff (especially the professional staff) that the program will respond to them and be helpful to them, and that they do not have to worry about being found out and/or punished because they come to the program for assistance.

Being sensitive and responsive to the uniquenesses of the teaching profession, school system attributes and community attitudes, is critical to the effectiveness of an EAP in a school system. Sensitivity to these special considerations, such as the ones discussed above, should be an integral part of the EAP and the mindsets of all of the personnel associated with the EAP.

An Example of a Successful School System EAP

For the purpose of providing an illustration of the important considerations involved in the planning, development, and implementation of an employee assistance program for a school system, the following describes and discusses the Employee Assistance and Wellness Program of the Hernando County School System in Hernando County, Florida. Key aspects of the Program's activities and experiences are highlighted.

Planning, Development and Implementation. Following numerous discussions among members of the school board, school officials and selected members of the professional staff, a contractual agreement between the school system and an independent provider was developed and enacted. Basically, the school system's EAP is an "outhouse" program (vis-à-vis the "inhouse" type of program). The Program began on November 1, 1985. Early implementation activities included multiple marketing strategies. For example: brochures describing the Program and its features and benefits were included with employees' paychecks on a periodic basis; members of the EAP staff and representatives from the school system attended meetings with personnel groups (e.g., at teachers' meetings) in order to discuss the Program in a face-to-face manner; and supervisory training sessions were conducted to assure that supervisors knew how they were to "work with the Program." Program evaluation activities included contract compliance monitoring and formal and informal observations of the Program's activities and their subsequent impacts and outcomes.

Program Evaluation Measures. Formal evaluation of the Program and its developmental activities was contracted out to a program evaluation consultant. The Program's "Six Month Preliminary Report" (Hutchison, Jr., 1986) includes foci on the five major areas of the contractual agreement: (a) Referral and Assessment; (b) Program Evaluation; (c) Case Management; (d) Ongoing Treatment; and (e) Training and Consultation. Data from the "Report's" Fact Sheet reveal that: (a) the total number of persons covered by the Program was 1,629 (1,150 employees and 386 family members); (b) 89 sessions had been held with the 49 EAP cases; and (c) the Program's utilization rate during the first six months was .085 (49/1150 × 2). The Summary of the evaluation "Report" includes the following:

> Findings support full contract compliance by HCEAP [the contractor]. The process evaluation indicates that the EAP service is being utilized at almost a 9% level by employees and their families. The utilization rate is almost double the national average of 5% for similar programs and is a strong indicator of client satisfaction. In addition, direct service costs have run almost as projected for this time period.
>
> The process evaluation provides additional support of client satisfaction with the EAP service as indicated by the fact that 100% of the clients responding to the survey [the Program's EAP Survey] felt they had been helped and would refer other persons to the program. In addition, clients feel they have been helped to decrease anxiety and depression as well as increase their work performance. The wellness program has served 65 employees and has been well-received. Participants indicate they were helped in a variety of areas including increased ability to relax, manage their time, and improve their work performance.
>
> In conclusion, the EAP and Wellness program has been well-utilized by employees and their families. The services are helping them solve important life problems which is improving both personal and work performance. The services are efficiently administered and program costs are well within budget projections. (Hutchison, Jr., 1986, p. 8)

Indeed, the Program's formal evaluation, thus far, is very complimentary to its efficiency and effectiveness.

The clinical staff's records from the employees' initial contacts to the EAP ("call ins"), indicate interesting data regarding the employees' initially, self-reported, presenting problem areas: (a) family relationships — 40%; (b) marital — 26%; (c) personal — 23%; (d) legal — 3%; (e) financial — 2%; (f) substance abuse — 1%; and (g) job stress — 1%. The EAP's Wellness Program, nonetheless, provided cardiovascular screening tests and the tests revealed that between 2/3 to 3/4 of the employees who were tested indicated some above-normal levels of stress (Landers, 1987). While these observations are casual and not conclusive, they do underscore the importance of an EAP's providing a complete complement of services and the apparent cautiousness with which employees describe their concerns, difficulties and problems to an employee assistance program at intake.

All indications are that this Program is doing very well, and there are no apparent reasons as to why it should not continue to be a meaningful component of the Hernando County School System.

Concluding Comment

Our schools play an extremely important role in our society—especially in terms of tomorrow's society. Currently, there are numerous problems in our schools, and the working lives of our schools' most precious resources—**our teachers and administrators,** are experiencing difficulties and problems. To a large degree, one very unfortunate result of this is that the quality of education in our schools is not what it could, or should be. Employee assistance programs have demonstrated their abilities to positively impact on the efficiency and effectiveness of employees' work. Likewise, EAPs in school systems also have demonstrated such positive outcomes. There would not appear to be any "acceptable" reason as to why a school system would not have an employee assistance program. And, with careful and professional planning, development and implementation, such as discussed in this chapter and as experienced in the Hernando County School System, employee assistance programs in our schools should do what they ultimately are designed to do—enhance the quality of education for our youth. Interestingly, when the author of this chapter was talking with officials from the Hernando County School System about the costs of their Employee Assistance Program, Landers (1987) poignantly stated: "It is not a question of whether or not we can afford our employee assistance program; in view of the outcome benefits to our school children, we cannot afford not to."

Acknowledgment. For his technical insights and suggestions, and his critical reading of an earlier version of this chapter, sincerest appreciation is extended to Dr. Roger R. Landers, Director of Health and Student Services, Hernando County Schools, Brooksville, Florida.

REFERENCES

Boynton, P., Di Geronimo, J.D., & Gustafson, G. (1985). A basic survival guide for new teachers. *The Clearing House, 59,* 101–103.

Chichon, D.J., & Koff, R.H. (1978, March). The Teaching Events Inventory. Paper presented at the annual meeting of the American Educational Research Association, Toronto.

Cox, H., & Wood, J.R. (1980). Organizational structure and professional alienation: The case of public school teachers. *Peabody Journal of Education, 58*(1).

Dickman, F., & Emener, W.G. (1982). Employee assistance programs: Basic concepts, attributes, and an evaluation. *Personnel Administrator, 27,* 8, 55–62.

Dickman, J.F., Emener, W.G., & Hutchison, W.S. (Eds.) (1985). *Counseling the troubled person in industry: A guide to the organization, implementation, and evaluation of employee assistance programs.* Springfield, IL: Charles C Thomas, Publisher.

Feistritzer Associates. (1983). *The American teacher.* Washington, D.C. Author.

Freudenberger, H.S., & Richelson, G. (1980). *Burnout: The high cost of achievement.* Garden City, NY: Anchor Press.

Gold, Y. (1985). Burnout: causes and solutions. *The Clearing House, 58,* 210–212.

Goodlad, J.I. (1975). *The dynamics of educational change.* New York: McGraw-Hill.

Goodlad, J.I. (1983). A study of schooling: Some implications for school improvement. *Phi Delta Kappan, 64*(8), 555.

Griesmer, J.L., & Butler, C. (1983). *Education under study.* Chelmsford, MA: Northeast Regional Exchange, Inc.

Griffin, W.D. (1984). Teacher alienation and isolation. Unpublished Master's Report, University of Central Florida.

Hutchison, Jr., W.G. (1986). Six month preliminary report: District school board of Hernando County—Employee assistance & wellness program. Unpublished report. Department of Social Work, University of South Florida, Tampa, Florida.

Kreis, K., & Milstein, M. (1985). Satisfying teachers' needs: It's time to get out of the hierarchical needs satisfaction trap. *The Clearing House, 59,* 75–77.

Landers, R.R. (1987). Personal communication. Brooksville, Florida. (January 30, 1987).

Lortie, D. (1975). *Schoolteacher: A sociological study.* Chicago: University of Chicago Press.

Maslach, C. (1976). Burnout. *Human Behavior, 5*(9), 16–22.

Moe, D. (1979). Teacher burnout—A prescription. *Today's Education, 68*(4), 36.

Pagel, S., & Price, J. (1980). Strategies to alleviate teacher stress. *Pointer, 24,* 45–53.

Pellegrew, L.S., & Wolfe, G.E. (1982). Validating measures of teacher stress. *American Educational Research Journal, 19,* 373–393.

Quick, J., & Quick, J. (1979). Reducing stress through preventive management. *Human Resources Management, 18,* 15–22.

Raschke, D.B., Dedrick, C.V., Strathe, M.I., & Hawkes, R.R. (1985). *The Elementary School Journal, 85*(4), 559–564.

Rothberg, R.A. (1986). Dealing with the problems of teacher isolation. *The Clearing House, 59,* 320–322.

Sparks, D. (1979). A teacher center tackles the issues. *Today's Education, 68*(4), 254.

U.S. Department of Education National Center for Education Statistics. (1982). Estimates of school statistics 1982–1983. *Digest of Educational Statistics,* Volume 34.

Weiskopf, P.E. (1980). Burnout among teachers of exceptional children. *Exceptional Children, 47*(1), 18–23.

Werner, A. (1980). The principal's role: Support for teachers in stress. *Pointer, 24,* 54–60.

Youngs, B. (1985). Drug abuse among superintendents and principals. *EAP Digest,* January/February, 41–46.

Chapter 32

CRIMINAL JUSTICE PRACTITIONERS

Max L. Bromley and William Blount

This chapter focuses on the effects of job-related stress on practitioners within the criminal justice system, specifically police, correctional officers, and probation officers. It also includes a brief review of documented sources of stress in criminal justice agencies, and suggests the types of employee assistance program services and strategies that might be most useful to assist workers in the criminal justice system.

Criminal Justice Practitioners at Risk

Approximately 1.8 million persons are employed at the federal, state and local levels within the justice system (*Bureau of Justice Statistics Sourcebook,* 1995). Over the last 25 years, criminal justice administrators have come to realize that many of their personnel face personal problems beyond those experienced by individuals in the general population. Criminal justice employees have had to deal with substance abuse, marital problems, job burnout and other stress-related issues on the job.

Numerous studies have been conducted that review stress within the context of criminal justice organizations. In the area of policing, for example, early stress-related research was conducted by Aldig and Brief (1975); Eisenberg (1975); Kroes et al. (1974); and Reiser (1974, 1976). Furthermore, Graupman (1983), Kroes (1985), Sewell (1981, 1983), and Spielberger et al. (1981) conducted investigations into stress issues within the police occupational world. A composite of work done by some of these researchers will be described later in this chapter.

More recently, according to McCafferty et al. (1992), police officers are at risk to develop posttraumatic stress disorders during their careers either as a result of a single horrible experience or as the result of an accumulation of a series of stressors over the span of a career. Specialized officers such as homicide detectives may feel additional stressors given the pressures inherent in solving murders (Sewell, 1993).

With regard to probation officer occupational stress issues, for example, Smith (1982), Sigler and McGraw (1984), Sigler (1988), Whitehead (1985) and Whitehead and Lindquest (1985) focused primarily on the occupational characteristics of burnout and role conflict as experienced by probation officers. The populations studied included both federal and state level probation officers.

Stress experienced by correctional officers also has been the subject of empirical research. There is little question that working in a jail, prison or other correctional setting is both psychologically and emotionally demanding. In many ways, correctional employees are as confined as the inmates they supervise. Individual and organizational stress experienced by correctional officers has been studied by Cheek and Miller (1983), Flannery (1986), Horowitz and Baker (1987), Siegel (1986), Ganster and Schaubroeck (1991), Whisler (1994), and Simmons (1996).

Sources of Stress for the Criminal Justice Professional

As noted by Ayres (1990), Stratton (1978) found it useful to develop a composite of the sources of stress drawn from the works of a variety of researchers including Eisenberg (1975), Reiser (1976) and Roberts (1975). These categories are identified as follows:

1. External stressors (stressors from outside the law enforcement organization)
   a. Frustration with the United States judicial system
   b. Lack of consideration by the courts in scheduling police officers for court appearance
   c. The public's lack of support and negative attitudes towards law enforcement
   d. Negative or distorted media coverage of law enforcement
   e. Police officers' dislike of the decisions of administrative bodies affecting law enforcement functions
2. Internal stressors (stressors from within the police agency)
   a. Policies and procedures that are offensive to officers
   b. Poor or inadequate training and inadequate career development opportunities
   c. Lack of identity and recognition for good performance
   d. Poor economic benefits and working conditions

   e. Excessive paperwork
   f. Inconsistent discipline
   g. Perceived favoritism regarding promotions and assignments
  3. Stressors in law enforcement work itself (stressors originating from within police work)
   a. Difficulties associated with shift work, especially rotating shifts
   b. Role conflicts between enforcing the law and serving the community
   c. Frequent exposure to life's miseries and brutalities
   d. Boredom, ultimately interrupted by the need for sudden alertness and mobilized energy
   e. Fear and dangers of the job
   f. Constant responsibility for protecting other people
   g. The fragmented nature of the job in which one person rarely follows a case to its conclusion
   h. Work overload
  4. Stressors confronting the individual officer (stressors confronting the officer as an individual)
   a. Fears regarding job competence, individual success and safety
   b. Necessity to conform
   c. Necessity to take a second job or to further education
   d. Altered status in the community due to attitude changes regarding a person because he or she is a police officer (pp. 4 & 5).

As mentioned earlier, considerable research also has examined the sources of stress for probation officers and correctional officials. Champion (1990) noted that stress among probation officers is derived from a number of sources including the following:

  1. job dissatisfaction
  2. role conflict
  3. role ambiguity
  4. client–officer interactions
  5. excessive paperwork
  6. performance pressures
  7. low self-esteem and public image
  8. job risk
  9. liability

Holegate and Clegg (1991), described the correlation between high turnover among probation officers and job burnout. Problems identified by probation officers in their research included inadequate resources, relatively low pay and status, low mobility opportunity, role conflicts and role ambiguity.

Whisler (1994) found that major sources of stress for probation officers were not inherent in the job itself, but tended to generate from within the organization and its procedures. For example, inadequate salary, lack of promotion opportunities, job conflict, lack of participation in policymaking decisions, and inadequate support from the department, illustrated that the most significant stressors were administrative or internal to the organization. In a study examining the influence of job-related stress and job satisfaction on probation officers' intent to quit, Simmons (1996) also found that the major job stressors derived from the organization, and included inadequate salary, incompetent supervisors, and excessive paperwork. Job satisfaction, inversely related to job stress, was directly related to the intention to terminate.

Several authorities also have investigated causes of stress among correctional officers working in jails or prisons. According to Dahl (1981), for example, the two most significant stressors for correctional officers were found to be management ambiguity and inmate contact. Lombardo (1981) noted that poor communication between correctional officers and their administrators was one of the top three sources of stress in their work setting. Fear of inmates and feeling that they did not participate in decision-making also were noted by correctional officers in this study. In a study by Brodsky (1982), it was reported that correctional officers cited role conflict as a major stressor in their jobs. That is, society expects them to rehabilitate inmates when they were often unable to do so. Whitehead and Lindquist (1986) noted that administrative practices and poor communication led to stress and burnout among correctional officers. In another study by Lindquist and Whitehead (1986), correctional officers cited inconsistent instruction from supervisors as a major stressor in their jobs. Furthermore, younger officers seemed to experience job burnout at a higher rate when compared to older officers.

Finally, Whisler (1994) found that the comparison of probation officers' stressors with police officers' stressors indicated that while the most significant stressors for probation officers were internal to the organization, police officers emphasized job/task-related stressors such as fellow officers killed in the line of duty, killing someone in the line of duty, exposure to battered or dead children, physical attacks, etc. These dissimilarities appear to be the result of distinctly different job requirements for each group.

While the majority of research has been conducted on law enforcement officers and correctional officers, there are other groups associated with criminal justice agencies that experience similar kinds of stress such as ambulance and emergency service personnel. Firefighters, for example, have been found to have similar sources of stress as police officers (Pendleton, Stotland, Spiers, & Kirsch, 1989). More closely related to the daily operations of law enforcement officers are telecommunicators, those individuals responsible for receiving emergency calls to the police and dispatching assistance. Whether they work within a police organization or within a 911 framework, Roberg, Hayhurst and Allen (1988) reported that dispatch personnel experience a significant amount of occupational stress similar to and often greater than that of sworn law enforcement personnel, and Decker, 1991, found a significant reduction in telecommunicator stress with an improvement in the work environment.

The Need for Employee Assistance Programs to Serve Criminal Justice Practitioners

Although the evolution has been slow in its development, a variety of employee assistant services are currently available for practitioners in the criminal justice field. Reese (1987) traced the growth of assistance programs in the law enforcement field back to the early 1950s. Many programs, such as those initiated in Boston, New York, and Chicago, were created to deal primarily with alcohol abuse problems.

In the 1970s, agencies such as the Los Angeles Sheriff's Office, the Chicago Police Department and the San Francisco Police Department expanded their programs to include nonalcohol-related problems. In 1980, mental health professionals began providing personal and job-related counseling services to FBI personnel. Mental health professionals also were used to assist FBI managers with a variety of employee-related matters (Reese, 1987). By 1986, many of the largest police departments in the United States had formed "stress units" or other sections to provide help for officers having personal or occupational difficulties. In the early 1990s, the United States Customs Service provided stress management training for both its supervisory and nonsupervisory personnel throughout the country (Milofsky et al., 1994). According to Reaves and Smith (1995), the majority of law enforcement agencies with 100 or more officers now have written policies regarding providing counseling assistance services for their officers. Today, in many law enforcement agencies formalized programs in place to provide critical incident stress debriefings (Mitchell, 1988; Mitchell & Bray, 1990).

Based on the research cited earlier in this chapter, probation officers and correctional officials also are in need of additional services in order to effectively deal with personal and occupational problems. While there may be some unique differences between problems experienced by police officers, correctional officials and probation officers, there are definite similarities among these criminal justice professionals. A few examples are offered to illustrate this point. Each of these professional groups are generally part of larger bureaucracies that tends to emphasize rather rigid rule-oriented approaches to policy matters. In addition, professionals in each of these groups are exposed to the suffering of others and often find themselves in personal danger. Frequently the public views their occupational roles in different ways than those held by the criminal justice professionals themselves. Prolonged work hours and difficult shift work are commonplace in the criminal justice occupational milieu. Additionally, these criminal justice professionals may be subject to post-traumatic stress disorder based upon their exposure to a variety of situations.

Considerations When Developing Employee Assistance Services

At a minimum, three questions should be answered before a criminal justice agency decides to extend employee assistance program services to its personnel. The first asks what conditions or sources of stress affect the criminal justice practitioner? Second, how does a criminal justice agency take steps to reduce stress created by its own policies or practices? Finally, what will encourage the targeted practitioners to make use of the services?

There are a number of suggested management strategies for creating a healthy work environment designed to lead to a reduction in organizational stress. For example, Ayers (1990) suggested the following strategies be taken to help achieve this goal:

1. *An examination of the workplace.* In this part of the strategy, Ayers suggested that the organization examine itself, identifying internal stressors and developing plans for needed change. This would include a variety of techniques for obtaining anonymous

information from agency personnel as well as suggestions as to how improvements can be made.

2. ***Believing in the mission.*** This strategy ensures that the department has clear direction that is well understood by all members of the department.

3. ***Living the organization values.*** In this strategy, management must change its approach from autocratic to one which emphasizes democratic principles and input from all of its personnel. This input helps to establish values upon which the organization will carry forth its mission.

4. ***Encouraging upward communication.*** This strategy requires a change from the rigid, military-like atmosphere found in many criminal justice agencies today. Effective communication must be two-way with open communication being allowed to flow from the bottom up and ideas being championed at any level within the organization.

5. ***Pushing autonomy down.*** This strategy implies that educated practitioners should be given more responsibility and discretionary power in performing their tasks. Decision-making will be forced to the lowest level of the organization.

6. ***Ensuring fairness.*** This strategy promotes fairness in all matters to include discipline, performance evaluations, and promotions.

7. ***Caring about people.*** This strategy ensures that all supervisory personnel must care about those employees that work for them. Emphasis here is on the critical role that first line supervisors play in reducing stress by assuming the role of facilitators and coaches (p. 25).

Several similar strategies for reducing organizational stress for correctional personnel were suggested by Woodruff (1993). These steps are to be taken by department managers once organizational stressors have been identified by personnel working within the agency:

1. ***Development of a mission statement, goals and objectives, and values for the organization.*** Policies and procedures should then be consistent with the mission statement and values of the organization.

2. ***Develop consistent written policies.*** For policies to be effective they must be done in writing and consistently applied by management and supervisory personnel.

3. ***Foster participation in decision-making at all levels.*** Personnel work-

ing within the agency should be afforded the opportunity to participate in the development of policies and procedures that effect their work.

4. *Consistent policies, instructions and directives from top management to all levels.* This should serve to reduce role conflict and inconsistent instructions given to subordinates.

5. *Officer education and training prior to and on the job.* All personnel must be adequately trained in order to deal with the stressful situation which they will encounter on the job.

6. *Provide thorough management training programs.* Top level managers should be given training in the consistent application of policies and procedures. Additional training should be provided in all aspects of management and interpersonal communication.

7. *Ongoing training and education in stress awareness and management for all employees.* All individuals in the organization should be made aware of the devastating effects of stress and provided with strategies to help prevent or control their own stress.

8. *Fair and effective selection and performance evaluation procedures.* Promotions and performance evaluations should be conducted in a consistent, objective manner for all individuals.

9. *A comprehensive employee wellness program.* Training should be provided for all personnel in order to develop good health practices including information regarding proper exercise and nutrition (p. 74).

Stratton (1985) suggested that if an Employee Assistance Program is developed within an agency, certain services are essential. Examples include counseling following a critical incident, e.g., if an employee is involved in a shooting incident or if an employee experiences the death of a family member. These services should be made available to agency personnel 24 hours a day. Other programs such as those that deal with substance abuse, financial problems, retirement planning and family concerns can also be of benefit. Stratton (1985) further noted that before establishing a full-scale EAP administrators should review and establish policies regarding the following issues:

1. *Confidentiality and credibility.* The most successful programs are ones in which the persons providing assistance are seen as highly professional and that information provided to them will not be used by the administration against them.

2. *Voluntary versus involuntary.* While it is true that employees may be ordered to attend counseling, the most effective programs are those in which individuals themselves seek out counseling.
3. *Status of the EAP and its staff.* Individuals providing the service must be viewed as ethical and professional.
4. *Location and accessibility of the EAP.* Generally the services should be provided at a location separate from the headquarters of the agency. Again, 24 hour services should be available for critical assistance.
5. *Additional programs.* Programs should be offered on a routine basis for purposes of health screening. Spouse orientation programs are also encouraged for those professionals working in the criminal justice field (p. 31).

Some authorities have suggested that many criminal justice practitioners may be hesitant to share personal or work-related problems with a mental health professional for a variety of reasons (Depue, 1979; Klein, 1989). Reasons include but are not limited to: if information is shared with a mental health professional, how will it be used by administrators; lack of faith in the mental health field, denial—criminal justice practitioners don't have problems, etc. In recognition of these issues some agencies in the 1980s established peer counseling programs wherein fellow employees are trained and offer support and advice.

Klein (1989) described the various aspects of the peer counseling program established in California that was eventually certified by the Commission on Peace Officers Standards and Training:

Training Peer Counselors

1. The three-day course is team-taught by clinical psychologists and police officers.
2. Principles taught include establishing rapport, active listening and taking action.
3. Peer counselors are also trained to recognize serious problems (i.e., delusions, suicidal tendencies) that require referral to a mental health professional (p. 2).

Areas in which the peer counselors have been used successfully include the following:

1. Stress
2. Posttraumatic stress

3. Relationship problems
4. Chemical dependency. (p. 3)

Conclusion

In summary, the occupational world of the criminal justice professional is both emotionally and psychologically demanding. Sources of stress for practitioners include internal and external factors. Therefore, it would seem appropriate for criminal justice executives and assistance service providers to consider the development of comprehensive strategies to assist employees that include, at a minimum, the following components: (a) stress awareness and management training; (b) crisis intervention and postcritical incident services; (c) family counseling; and (d) substance abuse awareness. The International Association of Chiefs of Police has long recognized that police officers needed access to a variety of mental health services. In 1994, this group published a model policy for police agencies to meet these needs. This model policy includes both "peer counseling" and "mental health professional" components in recognition of the different level of services that might be needed for practitioners (IACP, 1995).

As noted earlier, there is substantial literature that indicates a major source of stress for many criminal justice employees related to management and supervisory policies and practices. Therefore, steps must be taken to develop organizational goals and values that recognize the needs of individuals and that seek to maximize their professional potential. Creative problem-solving should take place within criminal justice agencies in order to facilitate and not hinder the efforts of criminal justice professionals. The programs and strategies suggested in this chapter are intended to promote thoughtful dialogue among those persons responsible for reducing stress in the criminal justice work environment thereby enhancing employee productivity.

REFERENCES

Aldag, R., & Brief, A. (1978). Supervisory Style and Police Stress, *Journal of Police Science and Administration,* 6: 362–367.

Ayres, R.N. (1990). *Preventing Law Enforcement Stress: The Organization's Role.* Washington, DC: Bureau of Justice Assistance, US Department of Justice.

Brodsky, C. (1982). Work Stress in Correctional Institutions, *The Journal of Prison and Jail Health,* 2: 74–102.

Bureau of Justice Statistics (1995). *Sourcebook of Criminal Justice Statistics — 1994.* Washington, DC: US Department of Justice.

Champion, D.J. (1990). *Probation and Parole in the United States.* Columbus, OH: Merrill.

Cheek, F., & Miller, M. (1983). The Experience of Stress for Correction Officers: A Double-Bind Theory of Correctional Stress, *Journal of Criminal Justice,* 11: 105–120.

Dahl, J.J. (1981). Occupational Stress in Corrections in B.H. Olson & A. Dargis (eds.), *American Correctional Association Proceedings,* 207–222.

Decker, R.M., Jr. (1991). An Analysis of Telecommunicators Stress in Law Enforcement. Unpublished master's thesis, University of South Florida, Tampa, FL.

Depue, R.L. (1979). Turning Inward: The Police Officer Counselor, *FBI Law Enforcement Bulletin,* 48(2): 8–12, Washington, DC: US Department of Justice.

Eisenberg, T. (1975). Job Stress in the Police Officer: Identifying Stress Reduction Techniques in W.H. Kroes and J.J. Hurrell (eds.), *Proceedings of Symposium,* pp. 26–34. Cincinnati: National Institute for Occupational Safety and Health (HEW Publication #76-187).

Flannery, R.B., Jr. (1986). Major Life Events and Daily Hassles in Predicting Health Status: Preliminary Inquiry, *Journal of Clinical Psychology,* 42: 458–487.

Ganster, D.C., & Schaubroeck, J. (1991). Work Stress and Employee Health, *Journal of Management,* 17: 235–271.

Graupmann, P. (1983). Permanent Shifts as Opposed to Rotating Shifts: An Evaluation of Sick Time and Use Among Police Officers, *Journal of Police Science and Administration,* 11: 233–236.

Holgate, A., & Clegg, I. (1991). The Path to Probation Officer Burnout: New Dogs, Old Tricks, *Journal of Criminal Justice,* 19: 325–327.

Horowitz, S.M., & Baker, W., Jr. (1987, Oct.) The Relationship Between Lifestyle, Distress, and Absenteeism in Male Law Enforcement Officers, *Fitness and Business,* pp. 55–61.

Klein, R. (1989). Police Peer Counseling: Officer Helping Officers, *FBI Law Enforcement Bulletin,* 58(10): 1–4, Washington, DC: US Department of Justice.

Kroes, W.H. (1985). *Societies Victims — The Police: An Analysis of Job Stress in Policing* (2nd ed.). Springfield, IL: Charles C Thomas.

Kroes, W.H., Margolis, B.L., & Hurrell, J.J., Jr. (1974). Job Stress in Policemen, *Journal of Police Science and Administration,* 2: 145–155.

Lindquist, C.A., & Whitehead, J.T. (1986). Burnout, Job Stress, and Job Satisfaction Among Southern Correctional Officers: Perceptions and Causal Factors, *Journal of Offender Counseling, Services, and Rehabilitation,* 10(4): 5–25.

Lombardo, L.X. (1981). Occupational Stress in Corrections Officers: Sources, Coping Strategies, and Implications, *Corrections at the Crossroads: Designing Policy,* 129–149.

McCafferty, R.L., McCafferty, E., & McCafferty, M.A. (1992). Stress and Suicide in Police Officers: Paradigm of Occupational Stress, *Southern Medical Journal,* 85: 233.

Milofsky, C., Ostrov, E., & Martin, M. (19•••). A Stress Management Strategy for US Customs Workers, *E.A.P. Digest,* 14(6): 46–48.

Mitchell, J.T. (1988). The History, Status, and Future of Critical Incident Stress Debriefings, *Journal of Emergency Medical Services,* 13: 47–52.

Mitchell, J.T. & Bray, G.P. (1990). *Emergency Services Stress: Guidelines for Preserving the Health and Careers of Emergency Services Personnel.* Englewood Cliffs, NJ: Prentice-Hall.

Pendleton, M., Stotland, E., Spiers, P., & Kirsch, E. (1989). Stress and Strain Among Police, Firefighters, and Government Workers: A Comparative Analysis, *Criminal Justice and Behavior,* 16: 196–210.

Reaves, B. & Smith, •••. (1995). *Law Enforcement Management and Administration Statistics, 1993: Data from Individual State and Local Agencies with 100 or More Officers.* Washington, DC: US Department of Justice.

Reese, J.T. (1987). *The History of Police Psychological Services.* Washington, DC: US Department of Justice.

Reiser, M. (1974). Some Organizational Stress on Policemen, *Journal of Police Science and Administration,* 2: 156–159.

Reiser, M. (1975). Stress, Distress, and Adaptation in Police Work in W.H. Kroes & J. Hurrel, (eds.) *Job Stress and the Police Officer: Identifying Stress Reduction Techniques.* Proceedings of the Symposium, Cincinnati, OH, May 8–9, 1975, Washington, DC: US Government Printing Office.

Roberg, R.R., Hayhurst, D.L., & Allen, H.A. (1988). Job Burnout in Law Enforcement Dispatchers: A Comparative Analysis, *Journal of Criminal Justice,* 16: 385–393.

Roberts, M. (1975). Job Stress in Law Enforcement: A Treatment and Prevention Program in Kroes, W.H. & Hurrel, J. (eds.) *Job Stress and the Police Officer: Identifying Stress Reduction Techniques.* Proceedings of the Symposium, Cincinnati, OH, May 8–9, 1975, Washington, DC: US Government Printing Office.

Sewell, J. (1981). Police Stress, *FBI Law Enforcement Bulletin,* 50(4): pp. 7–11.

Sewell, J. (1983). The Development of a Critical Life Events Skill for Law Enforcement, *Journal of Police Science and Administration,* 11: 109–116.

Sewell, J.D. (1993). Traumatic Stress of Multiple Murder Investigations, *Journal of Traumatic Stress,* 6: 103–118.

Siegel, B. (1986). *Love, Medicine, and Miracles.* New York: Harper and Row.

Sigler, R. (1988). Role Conflict for Adult Probation and Parole Officers: Fact or Myth, *Journal of Criminal Justice,* 16: 121–129.

Sigler, R., & McGraw, B. (1984). Adult Probation and Parole Officers: Influence of Their Weapons, Rural Perceptions, and Role Conflict, *Criminal Justice Review,* 9: 28–32.

Simmons, C. (1996). The Effects of Job Satisfaction and Stress on Probation Officers' Inclination to Quit. Unpublished master's thesis, University of South Florida, Tampa, FL.

Spielberger, C., Westberry, L., Grier, K., & Greenfield, G. (1981). *The Police Stress Survey: Sources of Stress in Law Enforcement,* Monograph Series 3, No. 6, Tampa: University of South Florida, Human Resources Institute.

Stratton, J.G. (1978). Police Stress: An Overview, *Police Chief,* 45(4): 58–62.

Stratton, J.G. (1985). Employee Assistance Programs: A Profitable Approach for Employers and Organizations, *Police Chief,* 52(12): 31–33.

Smith, J. (1982). Rekindling the Flame, *Federal Probation,* 46(2): 63–66.

The International Association of Chiefs of Police (1995). Model Policy for Providing Mental Health Services.

Whitehead, J., & Lindquist, C.A. (1985). Job Stress and Burnout Among Probation/ Parole Officers: Perceptions of Causal Factors, *International Journal of Offender Therapy and Comparative Criminology,* 29: 109–119.

Whitehead, J.T., & Lindquist, C.A. (1986). Correctional Officer Burnout: A Path Model, *Journal of Research in Crime and Delinquency,* 23(1); 23–42.

Whisler, P.M. (1994). A Study of Stress Perception by Selected State Probation Officers. Unpublished master's thesis, University of South Florida, Tampa, FL.

Woodruff, L. (1993). Occupational Stress for Correctional Personnel—What the Research Indicates (Part 2), *American Jails,* 8(5): 71–76.

PART VIII
FUTURE DIRECTIONS

Dickman and Challenger, in their 1988 "Future Perspectives" writing (Chapter 35), forecasted that stress, physical wellness, and mental and emotional wellness would be the foci of employee assistance programs in the future. Emener and Hutchison, in their Comment/Update, (a) offer that the major theme of Dickman and Challenger's futuristic perspectives "remain true for the 1990s", and (b) highlight 1990s nuances in the work environment, employees and employee assistance programs throughout the United States that also will impact employee assistance programs of the future.

Chapter 33

EMPLOYEE ASSISTANCE PROGRAMS: FUTURE PERSPECTIVES

FRED DICKMAN AND B. ROBERT CHALLENGER

The current trend in the broad field of health care is moving more and more in the direction of addressing the whole person (Hollman, 1981)—a "systems" approach to mental, emotional and physical wellness. Looking at a person as having many parts, functioning as a unit, it is not difficult to see how a problem in one area can have a significant bearing on one's functioning in other areas. An employee assistance program (EAP) sensitive to employee needs will do everything possible to adopt and promote this approach.

Awareness of this holistic concept by the EAP needs to be kept in front of the employees and their families. They need to be reminded continuously of the EAP's existence and philosophy. When an employee can see that the EAP is open to "any problem," that the employee or a member of the employee's family does not have to be in crises, employees will more readily avail themselves of the program's services.

Some of the general components of this holistic approach address:

Stress

Although change seems to be a common denominator for events perceived as stressful, literally anything may be termed stressful if a person is highly vulnerable and lacking a supportive environment. There is extensive research supportive of the relationship between stress and physical and psychological disorders (McGaffey, 1978).

An informed EAP which embraces the concept of "wellness" will include education on stress, its signs and symptoms, and prevention methods and alternate coping strategies.

This chapter is reprinted from *Employee Assistance Programs; A Basic Text* (1988) with permission of the author, the book's editors (Dickman, Emener, & Hutchison, Jr.) and the publisher (Charles C Thomas, Publisher).

411

This can be accomplished by raising employee awareness through lectures, films, seminars and workshops, and newsletters. Periodic monitoring of blood pressures and heart rates, availability of exercise equipment and exercise classes, nutritional and dietary information, and relaxation and meditation techniques all serve to prevent and reduce stress and promote physical wellness.

Physical Wellness

This is not discrete from stress, as noted, however, a few areas may be specifically addressed more appropriately under physical aspects of wellness. EAPs can make available to their employees general information on common prescription drugs and over-the-counter drugs, stressing interactions—especially with alcohol consumption and other drug use.

Seminars, information, and counseling should be available through a progressive EAP to assist employees with stopping smoking and overcoming eating disorders.

Education on the disease concept of alcoholism, the progression of addiction, and early signs of alcoholism and drug abuse is a most effective intervention tool. Alcoholism's effect on the family members and friends of an alcoholic person should not be overlooked.

Mental and Emotional Wellness

Education leads to new awareness, and awareness leads to opportunities for change. A supportive EAP offers programs which promote mental and emotional wellness. These may include:

1. **Communication Skills Training.** Help workers with effective methods for interpersonal communications on and off the job.
2. **Assertiveness Training.** Assist employees in getting what they want, pleasantly and effectively.
3. **Parenting.** Helping parents become more effective and cope with difficult and potentially stressful problems involved in raising children.
4. **Retirement Preparation.** The current economic state is dictating a trend to more early retirements. Most workers can expect to live at least 20 years after retiring, and planning ahead can help this to be a productive, comfortable life stage.

5. **Sexuality and Changing Sex Roles.** Women make up over 40 percent of the national labor force (Solomon, 1983). A component designed to affect stereotypic attitudes and assumptions about women will increase EAPs' penetration. Research literature shows that supervisors with equalitarian attitudes toward women identified and referred more women to EAPs (Reichman, 1983).

6. **Loss and Death.** Support groups offering opportunities for sharing, and programs outlining coping strategies will help employees through difficult periods brought on by death of a loved one, divorce, and major geographical relocations.

7. **Victim Assistance.** EAPs can help immeasurably with personal, emotional and financial wounds resulting from being criminally victimized. Often, these needs have not been attended to by the criminal justice system (Teems & Masi, 1983).

8. **Day Care.** Provisions for caring for young children of working parents would maximize the potential work force available to an employer.

9. **AIDS.** The disease of AIDS is already entering the ever increasing list of problems that fit under the umbrellas of Employee Assistance Programs. Some counselors have the task and responsibility of assisting AIDS victims in developing coping mechanisms and initiated self-help and support groups. In addition, many work organizations are providing educational materials and workshops for their employees. Hopefully, the research and tests of our medical colleagues will eventually remove this fatal disease from our concerns.

10. **Gatekeeping and Brokering of Health Care Costs.** The ever rising costs of health care insurance premiums and treatment has led EAP providers into the total management of mental health, alcoholism and drug abuse benefits. The importance of short term counseling and alternative treatment modalities is presently in the forefront in the containment of these rising costs. The successful EAP providers will need to be even more resourceful in the establishment of cost effective strategies and relationships with the therapeutic and medical community.

11. **Academic Curricula.** The provision of services industry is the fastest growing branch of our present economy. The EAP portion

of that industry is enjoying success in that growth and has resulted in a growing demand upon institutions of higher education to begin to incorporate in their curricula courses aimed at specifically preparing future and present EAP personnel for the growing demand of professionals. The demand will continue for all EAP practitioners to participate in the academic arena to remain abreast and current in the expansion of the EAP field.

12. **Increased Professionalism.** As stated by Masi and Montgomery (1987) EAPs will increasingly demand licensure and other certification as the counseling role is added to that of assessment and referral. Companies who use EAPs as gatekeeper to health care costs containment will have to insure counseling with appropriate quality control.

13. **Various Legal Concerns.** Industry is facing a serious drug problem (Masi & Montgomery, 1987). One way to identify the abuser is through urine analysis. As seen in Chapter 31 this process raises serious problems; constitutional not the least of them. EAPs will be called upon to enter this debate if for no other reason than if they don't we will return to a dismissal policy rather than one of identification, intervention, and remediation.

14. **Displaced Worker Crisis.** Increasing automation and technology may create a new category of employee: the displaced worker. EAPs may (and probably should) be invaluable aids in needed retraining efforts. Testing, referral for retraining and placement can be necessary efforts in the total productivity of the nation.

Although most companies have yet to realize the benefits of a fully functioning EAP, in companies where data on program cost effectiveness is kept, the least return is $3 back for each one dollar spent. One company reported a $17 return on one dollar of EAP funding (Fetterolf, 1983).

Returns like this, coupled with knowledge of costs to industry incurred via on-the-job accidents, absenteeism, health and medical insurance costs, and lost production, the trend is becoming clear that business and industry cannot afford NOT to have some form of an employee assistance program.

There are alternatives for smaller businesses to have an EAP, which are covered elsewhere in this text. Smaller companies can form EAP consortiums, i.e., splitting the cost of a full-time EAP coordinator between two (or more) companies (McClellan, 1982; Quayle, 1983). Another alternative is contracting with local EAP professionals in the area. The more employees are touched by an employee assistance effort, the more effective and worthwhile the effort is—both in terms of human service and bottom-line cost savings.

The trends discussed above have both decided advantages and, to these authors, an obvious danger. Some of the advantages and signs of growth are:

1. Industry and human services will be even more involved in a partnership in the future than previously. This means more people will have the opportunity for early intervention. More human service professionals will learn to relate and be effective in the workplace.
2. These trends mean that industry may be looking seriously at the notion that it not only hired people with problems, or potential problems, but it creates problems (McGaffey, 1978). Studies on industrial stress and its alleviation may teach us how some of this stress may be avoided or, at least, lessened at work.
3. As both government and industry decentralize, we as a society may take more responsibility for prevention and remediation of the kinds of human problems now involved with EAPs.

A Danger

Yet, as advantageous as these trends are, a clear danger exists. Simply put, it is that alcoholism may be lost in the shuffle as the occupational alcoholism program gives way to employee assistance programs which, in turn, is supplanted by the employee enhancement program. There is already evidence to this effect.

Some time ago, the authors surveyed local companies in the Tampa Bay area as to their interest in learning about alcoholism in the workplace. Many were adamant that there was no alcoholism in their companies. Later, some of these same companies contracted with "new" EAP professionals who stressed employee enhancement, "playing down" alcoholism. Apparently stress in the workplace is more acceptable than alcoholism. Recently, the authors asked some of the "new" EAP professionals about penetration rates in general and alcoholism in particular. Penetration rates were reported high, but alcoholism identification and rehabilitation rates were around 5 percent. This is a frightening comparison with the 40 percent–60 percent rates of the occupational alcoholism programs of the 1940s through the 1960s and of the employee assistance programs of the 1970s. There is evidence that the trained interviewer does not find what he or she doesn't know about (Dahlhauser et al., 1983). If the new professionals contracting with industry do not know about alcoholism, they are not apt to see much of it—alcoholic people have been successfully deceiving these professionals for years.

This book ends, as the authors believe it should, where, in a way, it began. Alcoholism and its treatment conceived EAP strategy. Industry, in turn, was recognized as the best intervener for alcoholism treatment. This relationship may be lost unless industrial managers and employee enhancement program professionals maintain a high commitment to alcoholism rehabilitation, which clearly remains the major health problem in the community and in the workplace.

REFERENCES

Dahlhauser, H.F., Dickman, F., Emener, W.G., & Yegidis-Lewis, B. (1982). Alcohol and drug abuse awareness: Implications for intake interviewing. Manuscript submitted for publications.

Fetterolf, C.F. Acceptance remarks upon presentation of Ross Von Wiegand Award at the 12th Annual Meeting of ALMACA. *The Almacan,* 1983 (Oct), *13*(10), 1, 6–7.

Hollman, R.W. Beyond contemporary employee assistance programs. *Personnel Administrator,* 1981 (Sept.).

Masi, D., & Montgomery, P. (1987). Future directions for EAPs. *The Almacan, 17*(3), 20–21.

McGaffey, T.N. New horizons in organizational stress prevention approaches. *Personnel Administrator,* 1978 (Nov.), 26–32.

McClellan, K. An overview of occupational alcoholism issues for the 80's. *Journal of Drug Education, 12*(1), 1982.

Quayle, D. (1983). American productivity: The devastating effect of alcoholism and drug abuse. *American Psychologist, 38*(4), 454–458.

Reichman, W. Affecting attitudes and assumptions about women and alcohol problems. *Alcohol Health & Research World.* Spring, 1983, *7*(3), 6–10.

Solomon, S.D. Women in the workplace: An overview of NIAAA's occupational demonstration project. *Alcohol Health & Research World,* 1983 (Spring), *7*(3), 3–5.

Teems, L., & Masi, D. Victims of crime as EAP clients. *The Almacan,* 1983 (Oct.), *13*(10), 20–21.

Chapter 34

FUTURE PERSPECTIVES—1997

WILLIAM G. EMENER AND WILLIAM S. HUTCHISON, JR.

By and large, the major theme of this book's 1988 futuristic perspectives chapter remains true for the 1990s. If companies continue to move ubiquitously toward a wellness model, alcohol rehabilitation indeed may be lost in the shuffle. (And that certainly would be a shame—there are thousands of good employees who could provide excellent work for companies if the companies' Employee Assistance Programs [EAPs] would genuinely embrace and operationalize an EAP model that would include a viable alcohol rehabilitation program component.) There is, nonetheless, an additional futuristic perspective for EAPs pertinent to what has been, and is, going on in the United States.

Over the first half of the 1990s, the United States has witnessed a suppressed economy. Wage and salary compression, shrinking employment opportunities, "downsizing" and "rightsizing" reconfigurations within business and industry, and rising costs of living, collectively have contributed to a rather severe compression of American economy. One major result of these economic conditions has been a change in "payors"—buyers, purchasers and consumers, in general, have become more cautious and more demanding. This, in turn, has led to increasingly more competitive business practices which have led to dramatic changes in modern business and industry. For example: (1) there have been many cost-cutting and cost-saving initiatives (e.g., businesses are wanting their employees to assume more responsibilities for their own health care costs); and reductions in personnel costs (e.g., employees are being expected to "do more for less"). To assure cost savings with increased worker productivity, coupled with enhanced computer capabilities, businesses and industries are engaging in hyper-vigilant monitoring, in general, and more centralized monitoring (e.g., micro-management) from the top down. As one worker recently said, "No matter what I say or do, I constantly feel that big brother in the front office is watching every move

I make." These changes in the basic infrastructure of most large businesses and industries have had, in turn, many understandable outcome effects on the modern work environment, employees and employee assistance programs (EAPs):

Work Environment:

- worker behavior is being highly monitored
- job tasks are being tightly controlled
- there are more rigid rules for individual behavior (e.g., political correctness)
- there is increased pressure on workers for "doing more"

Employees:

- workers are feeling more suspicious and fearful of losing their jobs
- the "survival mode" has meaningfully lowered employees' job satisfaction
- there is increased job frustration (and lowered levels of worker autonomy)
- workers have increased feelings of paranoia

EAPs

- EAP will be attending to an increased amount of "work-related" problems and difficulties (along with the typical "personal" kinds of problems and difficulties)
- EAPs will feel pressured to do more (for less) as a result of the managed care model of human service delivery, companies cost-cutting efforts, and increased competitiveness with the overall health care industry
- EAP professionals will increasingly feel "in the middle" (e.g., the company will want more specific outcomes for the benefit of the company and the EAP professional will feel more compelled to do what's best for the individual employee)

Overall, these scenarios do not necessarily paint the most exciting and inviting picture for the future of EAPs. The decade ahead will most certainly be extremely challenging!

Concluding Comment

For companies (1) to continue to be profitable and therefore viable in the highly competitive business world of the nineties, *AND* (2) to continue to provide efficient and effective EAPs for their employees, indeed constitutes an extremely demanding set of challenges. Likewise, for EAP professionals (1) to continue to provide efficient and effective EAP services to their clients, *AND* (2) to continue to be professional and ethical in the process, also constitutes an extremely demanding set of challenges. Hopefully, companies, unions and EAP professionals will continue to work together cooperatively and successfully in aiding and assisting troubled employees (in spite of the respective challenges facing them).

APPENDIX I
SELECTED ADDITIONAL RESOURCES

OVEREATERS ANONYMOUS WORLD SERVICE OFFICE
2190 190th Street
Torrance, CA 90504
(213) 320-7941

**SEX INFORMATION AND EDUCATION COUNCIL
OF THE UNITED STATES**
80 Fifth Avenue
New York, NY 10011

SOCIETY FOR SEX THERAPY AND RESEARCH
Sandra R. Leiblum, Ph.D.
Department of Psychiatry
UMD—Robert Wood Johnson Medical School
675 Hoes Lane
Piscataway, NJ 08854

THE SOCIETY FOR THE SCIENTIFIC STUDY OF SEX
Deborah Weinstein, M.S.W., Executive Director
P.O. Box 29795
Philadelphia, PA 19117

APPENDIX II
SELECTED SUPPLEMENTAL BIBLIOGRAPHY

Abramson, E. M., & Snow, C. J. (1982) Alcoholism and kleptomania: looking at the legal inconsistencies. *Employee Relations Law Journal, 7*(4), 619–642.

Adams, J. M. (1982) The problem employee. *New England Business, 4*(7), 62–63, 65.

Akabas, H. (1978) Fieldwork in industrial settings: Opportunities, rewards, and dilemmas. *Journal of Education for Social Work, 14*(3), 13–19.

Albers, R. H. (1982) The theological and psychological dynamics of transformation in the recovery from the disease of alcoholism. (School of Theology). *Dissertation Abstracts International, 43*(4-A), 1198.

Alderman, M. H., & Schoenbaum, E. E. (1975) Detection and treatment of hypertension at the worksite. *New England Journal of Medicine, 293*(2), 65–68.

Allen, H. A., Peterson, J. S., & Keating, G. (1982) Attitudes of counselors toward the alcoholic. *Rehabilitation Counseling Bulletin, 25*(3), 162–164.

Anonymous (1979) Alcoholism programs in the workplace. *Employee Benefit Plan Review, 34*(6), 30, 107.

Anonymous (1980) More companies working with alcoholism. *New England Business, 2*(7), 21–22.

Anonymous (1981) Alcohol abuse and the law. *Harvard Law Review, 94*(7), 1600–1712.

Anonymous (1981) Chemical dependency studies in Minnesota. *Employee Benefit Plan Review, 36*(2), 44, 46.

Anonymous (1981) Detecting drinkers often is not easy for the employer. *Business Insurance, 15*(46), 56–57.

Anonymous (1981) Upgraded medical program extends its reach. *Occupational Hazards, 43*(4), 117–120.

Anonymous (1982) Handling alcohol and drug problems. *Small Business Report, 7*(12), 20–22.

Anonymous (1982) Illinois Bell program helps troubled employees. *Employee Benefit Plan Review, 36*(7), 26–28.

Anonymous (1982) Stress on the job. *Credit Union Magazine, 48*(5), 14–18.

Anonymous (1982) Variety of approaches in employee assistance. *Employee Benefit Plan Review, 37*(1), 28, 30.

Anonymous (1982) What to do about an alcoholic employee. *Effective Manager, 5*(9), 3–4.

Anonymous (1983) Assistance programs help employers reduce alcohol-related wrecks. *Business Insurance, 17*(19), 35–36.

Anonymous (1983) How two companies curb drug abuse. *Occupational Hazards, 45*(4), 93–96.

Anonymous (1983) The narrowing right to fire: How chemical companies are coping. *Chemical Week, 132*(25), 46–50.

Anonymous (1983) EAP potential to save money is unknown. *Business Insurance, 17*(35), 14.

Appelbaum, S. H. (1982) A human resources counseling model: The alcoholic employee. *Personnel Administrator, 27*(8), 35–44.

Appelbaum, S. H. (1982) Rescuing time from the bottle. *Canadian Banker & ICB Review, 89*(6), 22–26.

Bakalinsky, R. (1980) People vs. profits: Social work in industry. *Social Work, 25*(6), 471–475.

Bannon, S. (1975) Alcoholism—a union-management issue. *Labour Gazette* (Canada), *75*(7), 419–423.

Barnett, W. A. (1983) Improving attendance: A formula for success. *Worklife, 3*(2), 7–8.

Barrett, C., & Bickerton, R. (1971) The problem of the sick worker. *Transportation Distribution Management, 11*(9), 47.

Bass, M. (1972) Organizational life in the 70's and beyond. *Personnel Psychology, 25*(1), 19–30.

Belohav, J. A., & Popp, P. O. (1983) Employee substance abuse: Epidemic of the eighties. *Business Horizons, 26*(4), 29–34.

Blacker, F., & Brown, C. A. (1978) Organizational psychology: Good intentions. *Human Relations, 31,* 333–351.

Blomquist, D. C. et al. (1979) Social work in business and industry. *Social Casework, 60,* 457–472.

Bond, T. R. (1981) Drinking: Many employers don't really know the on-the-job indications of alcoholism. *Business Insurance, 15*(46), 37–38.

Boroson, W. (1976) How your career can affect your drinking. *Money, 5*(1), 47–78, 50.

Bower, C. D. (1975) Alcoholism—industry's $9 billion headache. *Personnel Administrator, 20*(1), 32–35.

Brennan, T. P. (1983) Commitment to counseling: Effects of motivational interviewing and contractual agreements on help-seeking attitudes and behavior (University of Nebraska). *Dissertation Abstracts International, 43,* 7-B, 2313–2414.

Brooks, P. R. (1975) Industry-agency program for employee counseling. *Social Casework, 56*(7), 404–410.

Brown, T. E. (1971) Career counseling for ministers. *Journal of Pastoral Care, 25*(1), 33–40.

Burum, P. K. (1968) Counselor involvement and employment stability (Colorado State University). *Dissertation Abstracts, 28,* 11-A, 4442–4443.

Busch, E. J. (1981) Developing an employee assistance program. *Personnel Journal, 60*(9), 708–711.

Cairo, P. C. (1983) Counseling in industry: A selected review of the literature. *Personnel Psychology, 36*(1), 1–18.

Camisa, K. P. (1980) Alcohol abuse. *Business Insurance, 14*(5), 19, 21.

Carr, J. L. & Hellan, R. T. (1980) Improving corporate performance through employee-assistance programs. *Business Horizons, 23*(2), 57–60.

Cohen, I. J. (1981) The anonymous alcoholic. *Inc., 3*(10), 154.

Cook, D. D. (1981) Companies put social workers on the payroll. *Industry Week, 21*(6), 72–79.

Costello, R. M. (1978) Alcoholic mortality: A 12-year follow-up. *American Journal of Drug and Alcohol Abuse, 5,* 199–210.

Dawson, E. R. (1982) Helping employees cope: It takes more than a big heart. *Data Management, 20*(6), 16–18.

Day, C. R. (1983) Pushing pills out of the office. *Modern Office Procedures, 28*(5), 70–71, 74, 76.

Denenberg, T. S. (1980) The arbitration of alcohol and drug abuse cases. *Arbitration Journal, 35*(4), 16–121.

Desilets, R. (1968) Alcoholism and actual pastoral approaches. *Toxicomanies, 1*(1), 51–60.

Dittmer, R. W. (1975) Corporate social responsibility: An overview. *Crisis,* 82, 215–218.

Drummond, T. (1982) The alcoholic and the church: A pastoral response. *International Journal of Offender Therapy & Comparative Criminology, 26*(3), 275–280.

DuBrin, A. J. *The practice of managerial psychology concepts and methods for manager and organization development.* Rochester Institute of Technology, College of Business.

Dugan, R. D. (1979) Affirmative action for alcoholics and addicts—*Employee Relations Law Journal, 5*(2), 235–244.

Ettinger, R. G. (1982) Evaluating a community mental health center's implementation of an employee assistance program (California School of Professional Psychology). *Dissertation Abstracts International, 43,* 1–, 230.

Fappiano, E. R. (1984) The alcoholic priest and Alcoholics Anonymous: A study of stigma and the management of spoiled identity. (New School for Social Research). *Dissertation Abstracts International, 45*(4-A), 1211.

Featherston, H. J., & Bednarek, R. J. (1981) A positive demonstration of concern for employees. *Personnel Administrator, 26*(9), 43–44, 47.

Fitzgerald, M. C. (1982) Correlates of alcoholism among Roman Catholic nuns: Psychological and attitudinal variables. (United States International U.). *Dissertation Abstracts International, 43*(1-B) 246.

Fleming, C. W. (1979) Does social work have a future in industry? *Social Work, 24*(3), 183–185.

Foegen, J. H. (1981) Work-generated pressure: Mental health time bomb. *Management World, 10*(7), 39–40.

Foegen, J. H. (1982) Big motherism. *Business & Society Review,* 41, 73–74.

Follimann, J. F., Jr. (1975) Alcoholism and disability income protection. *CLU Journal, 29*(3), 59–62.

Ford, C., & McLaughlin, F. S. (1981) EAP's: A descriptive survey of ASPA members. *The Personnel Administrator,* 26, 29–35.

Ford, R. C., & McLaughlin, F. S. (1981) Employee Assistance Programs: A descriptive survey of ASPA members. *Personnel Administrator, 26*(9), 29–35.

Fullan, M. (1970) Industrial technology and worker integration in the organization. *American Sociological Review, 35,* 1028–39.

Garcia, K. M. (1982) A psychological and demographic investigation of the rehabilitation counseling process (University of Southern California). *Dissertation Abstracts International, 43,* 3-B, 851–852.

Gardell, B. (1976) Technology, alienation, and mental health: Summary of a social psychological study of technology and the worker. *Acta Sociologica, 19*(1), 83–93.

Garner, E. A. (1983) One way to cut disability costs. *National Underwriter (LifeHealth), 87*(36), 15, 31.

Gavaghan, P. F. (1977) The liquor industry's perspective on prevention of alcohol abuse. *Journal of Alcohol & Drug Education, 23*(1), 63–69.

Ghiselli, E. E. (1974) Some perspectives for industrial psychology. *American Psychologist, 29,* 80–87.

Gibson, W. D. (1978) They're bringing problem drinkers out of the closet. *Chemical Week, 123*(20), 85–91.

Glamser, F. D., & DeJong, G. F. (1979) Efficacy of preretirement preparation programs for industrial workers. *Journal of Gerontology, 30,* 595–600.

Glasser, M. A., & Duggan, T. (1969) Prepaid psychiatric care experience with UAW members. *American Journal of Psychiatry, 126*(5), 675–681.

Gomberg, E. S. (1977) Women, work, and alcohol: A disturbing trend. *Supervisory Management, 22*(12), 16–20.

Gomez-Mejia, L. R., & Blakin, D. B. (1980) Classifying work-related and personal problems of troubled employees. *Personnel Administrator, 25*(11), 27–32.

Googins, B. (1979) EAP's. *Social Work, 20*(6), 464–467.

Greenbaum, M. L. (1982) The "disciplinatrator," the "arbichiatrist," and the "social psychotrator"—an inquiry into how arbitrators deal with a grievant's personal problems and the extent to which they affect the award. *Arbitration Journal, 37*(4), 51–64.

Gregoire, K. C. (1979) An evaluation of several aspects of a consortium employee assistance program (University of Nebraska). *Dissertation Abstracts International, 39* 7 B, 3567.

Grosswirth, M. (1983) Stoned at the office. *Datamation, 29*(2), 30–36.

Gulick, M. A. (1966) Alcoholism and business management. *Annals of the New York Academy of Sciences, 133*(3), 877–879.

Habbe, S. (1973) Controlling the alcohol problem—not by management alone. *Conference Board Record, 10*(4), 31–33.

Hall, D. (1983) Helping employees treat problems of drugs, alcohol. *New England Business, 5*(11), 52–53.

Hallowell, R. E. (1975) Curbing employee alcoholism via the hospital/medical benefit plan. *Newspaper Controller, 29*(1), 2.

Hawkins, B. L. (1983) Dealing with drugs and alcohol: A supervisor's challenge. *Industrial Management, 25*(1), 1–6.

Hayes, L. S., & O'Connor, M. R. (1982) Emotional components of supervision: An EAP workshop. *Social Casework, 63*(7), 408–414.

Hellan, R. T. (1980) Employee assistance programs. *Management World, 9*(10), 18–20.

Hellan, R. T., & Campbell, W. J. (1981) Contracting for EAP services—a guide to making the right choice. *Personnel Administrator, 26*(9), 49–51.

Heyman, M. M. (1971) Employer-sponsored programs for problem drinkers. *Social Casework, 52*(9), 547–552.

Heyman, M. M. (1976) Referral to alcoholism programs in industry: Coercion, confrontation and choice. *Journal of Studies on Alcohol, 37*(7), 900–907.

Heyman, M. M. (1978) *Alcoholism programs in industry—the patient's view.* New Brunswick, NJ: Rutgers U. Press, Center of Alcohol Studies.

Hobson, G. W. Utilizing the systems approach to develop, implement, and evaluate an Employee Assistance Program (Union for Experimenting College & Universities). *Dissertation Abstracts International, 43,* 6-B, 2029.

Hoffer, W. (1983) Consider employee assistance programs. *Security Management, 27*(5), 57–58.

Hoffer, W. (1983) How to help a troubled employee. *Association Management, 35*(3), 69–73.

Hollman, R. W. (1979) Managing troubled employees: Meeting the challenge. *Journal of Contemporary Business, 8*(4), 43–57.

Hollman, R. W. (1981) Beyond contemporary employee assistance programs. *Personnel Administrator, 26*(9), 37–41.

Hollman, R. W. (1983) Employee assistance and employee fitness programs: A growing trend in U.S. business. *Montana Business Quarterly, 21*(21), 12–15.

Hunter, H. R., & Katz, A. H. (1970) Insurance for mental health care. *Community Mental Health Journal, 6*(6), 464–469.

Iutovich, J. M. (1983) The employee assistance program as a mechanism of control over problem-drinking employees (Kent State University). *Dissertation Abstracts International, 43,* 7-A, 2465–2466.

Jackson, V. E. (1979) Alcoholism and the white-collar employee. *Modern Office Procedures, 24*(9), 54–58.

Jensen, A. F. (1968) The process of treatment affiliation among problem drinkers in industry (Washington State University). *Dissertation Abstracts International, 28,* 8-A, 3272–3273.

Jeremy, F. H. (1978) The validation of an instrument to measure hourly worker acceptance of counseling in industry (Western Michigan University). *Dissertation Abstracts International, 39,* 5-A, 2756.

Jernberg, W. R. (1979) Killing with kindness—a fatal approach to alcoholism. *Journal of Applied Management, 4*(5), 28–29, 31.

Jervey, G. (1983) Is the advertising world a mecca for "demon rum"?/Y & R meets the "situation" head on. *Advertising Age, 54*(6).

Johnson, V. E. (1980) *I'll Quit Tomorrow* (Rev. ed.). San Francisco: Harper & Row.

Kaden, S. (1977) Compassion or coverup—the alcoholic employee. *Personnel Journal, 56*(7), 356–358.

Kaplan, J. (1980) Wellness epidemic sweeps companies. *Business Insurance, 14*(35), 1, 31.

Karp, R. E. (1976) Corporate social-responsibility. *Training & Development Journal, 30*(11), 10–15.

Karp, R. E. (1979) More help for emotionally troubled employees. *Business Week* (Industrial Edition), March 12, 97–102.

Kaunitz, P. E. (1974) On the other hand. *Medical World News, 15*(39), 124.

Kay, M. (1982) New slant in human rights: Protection for alcoholics. *Canadian Business, 56*(5), 123–124.

Kenyon, W. H. (1974) The alcoholic at work. *Personnel Management* (UK), *6*(7), 33–36.

Kiechel, W. III (1982) Looking out for the executive alcoholic. *Fortune, 105*(1), 117–118.

Kinney, J., & Leaton, G. (1983) *Loosening the grip* (2nd ed.). St. Louis: C. V. Mosby.

Kirsch, B. A., & Lengermann, J. J. (1972) Empirical test of Robert Blauner's ideas on alienation in work as applied to different type jobs in a white-collar setting. *Sociology and Social Research, 56,* 180–194.

Kur, C. E., & Pedler, M. (1982) Innovative twists in management development. *Training & Development Journal, 36*(6), 88–96.

Kurtz, N. R., & Googins, B. (1979) Managing the alcoholic employee: towards a model for supervisory intervention. *Industrial Management, 21*(3), 15–21.

LaVan, H., Mathys, N., & Drehmer, D. (1983) A look at the counseling practices of major U.S. corporations. *Personnel Administrator, 28*(6), 76–81, 142–146.

Lavino, J. J., Jr. (1978) Personal assistance programs. *Personnel Administrator, 23*(11), 35–36, 42–43.

Lawrence, D. B., & Steinbrecher, D. D. (1979) Occupational alcoholism programs— wave of the future. *Personnel, 56*(4), 43–45.

Lawrence, M. (1982) Don't let the holiday blues get employees down. *Personnel Journal, 61*(12), 898–901.

Lepkin, M. (1975) Program of industrial consultation by a community mental health center. *Community Mental Health Journal, 11,* 74–81.

LeRoux, M. (1982) Employee assistance programs well worth their cost, employers say. *Business Insurance, 16*(39), 3, 16, 20.

Lewis, K. A. (1981) Employee assistance programs: The state of the art of mental health services in government and industry (Northwestern University). *Dissertation Abstracts International, 42,* 6 A, 2504.

Liebowitz, B. (1982) Employee assistance programs as an employee benefit and as risk management. *Employee Benefits Journal, 7*(1), 14–16.

Lynch, P. F. (1973) Q & A on alcoholism. *Supervisory Management, 18*(11), 8–15.

Lynn, G., & Lunn, J. B. (1983) Managing organization caused stress: The challenge for employers and employees. *Management, 35*(2), 20–23.

Maher, T. M. (1980) Control Data presents "wellness" programs. *National Underwriter (LifeHealth), 849*(51), 1, 10.

Mandell, W., & Arneson, S. (1979) Executive success and drinking. *Executive, 5*(2), 14–15.

Mann, K. W. (1972) The mission of the church in a drugs culture. *Journal of Religion & Health, 11*(4), 329–348.

Margolick, D. (1980) The lonely world of night work. *Fortune, 102*(12), 108–114.

Marmo, M. (1982) Arbitrators view alcoholic employees: Discipline or rehabilitation? *Arbitration Journal, 37*(1), 17–27.

Marsh, R. M., & Mannari, H. (1971) Lifetime commitment in Japan: Roles, norms, and values. *American Journal of Sociology, 76,* 795–812.

McClellan, K. (1982) An overview of occupational alcoholism issues for the 80's. *Journal of Drug Education, 12*(1), 1–27.

McCroskey, J. (1982) Work and families: What is the employer's responsibility? *Personnel Journal, 61*(1), 30–38.

McDonald, J. H., & Sparks, P. D. (1974) Employee assistance program for alcoholism and drug abuse: An industry approach. *Industrial Gerontology, 1*(4), 25–27.

McGaffey, T. N. (1978) New horizons in organizational stress prevention approaches. *Personnel Administrator, 23*(11), 26–32.

McKinnon, B. (1979) Sick or just workshy: Who's playing truant? *Chief Executive Monthly,* Nov., 29–30.

Megalli, B. (1978) Alcoholism and drug abuse: A labour-management breakthrough. *Labour Gazette* (Canada), *78* (10), 444–452.

Merrigan, D. M. (1983) Pastoral gatekeeper participation in community alcohol abuse prevention. (Boston U. School of Education). *Dissertation Abstracts International, 44*(6-A), 1700.

Milbourn, G., Jr. (1981) Alcohol and drugs: Poor remedies for stress. *Supervisory Management, 26*(3), 35–42.

Mills, E. (1972) Family counseling in an industrial job-support program. *Social Casework, 53*(10), 587–592.

Morantz, A. (1982) Helping employees cope with personal problems. *Worklife, 3*(1), 10–12.

Morgan-Janty, C. J. (1983) A process evaluation of Employee Assistance Programs in Wisconsin (University of Wisconsin-Madison). *Dissertation Abstracts International, 43* 10-A, 3220–3221.

Nagira, T., Ohta, T., & Aoyama, H. (1979) Low-back pain among electric power supply workers and their attitude toward its prevention and the treatment. *Journal of Human Ergology, 8*(2), 125–133.

Noll, R. L., & Oberwise, R. A. (1982) U. S. production: An effective [sic] approach to worker motivation. *Training & Development Journal, 36*(1), 57–60.

Norris, E. (1981) Alcohol: Companies are learning it pays to help workers beat the bottle. *Business Insurance, 15*(46), 1, 53–54.

O'Brien, D. (1978) Alcoholism referral programs—economic and humane additions to employee benefit packages. *Employee Benefit Plan Review, 33*(2), 67–68.

Osawa, M. N. (1980) Development of social services in industry: Why and how? *Social Work, 25*(6), 464–470.

Otte, F. H. (1982) Creating successful career development programs. *Training & Development Journal, 36*(2), 30–37.

Ozaki, R. S. (1970) Japanese views on industrial organization. *Asian Survey, 10,* 872–889.

Parker, P. H. (1973) Washington state employee alcoholism program. *Public Personnel Management, 2*(3), 212–215.

Pati, G. C., & Adkins, J. I. (1983) The employer's role in alcoholism assistance. *Personnel Journal, 62*(7), 568–572.

Patterson, L. E., Hayes, R. W., & McIntire, P. R. (1974) Careers in operation: Industry as a laboratory for counselor development. *Counselor Education & Supervision, 14*(1), 64–70.

Perham, J. (1982) Battling employee alcoholism. *Dun's Business Month, 119*(6), 48–53.

Perkins, G. (1978) Alcoholism in the workplace. *Management World, 7*(2), 7–8, 10.

Phillips, D. A., & Older, H. J. (1981) Alcoholic employees beget troubled supervisors. *Supervisory Management, 26*(9), 2–9.

Phillips, D. A., Allen, P., & Long, R. J. (1983) Helping alcoholics and other troubled staff. *ABA Banking Journal, 75*(9), 61–71.

Pike, T. P. (1980) Alcoholism in the executive suite—robbing their employers blind. *Vital Speeches, 46*(6), 166–169.

Provost, G. J., Smolensky, W. R., Stephens, R. C., & Freedman, Y. F. (1979) Alcohol or drug use on the job: A study of arbitration cases. *Employee Relations Law Journal, 5*(2), 245–257.

Provost, G. J., Stephens, R. C., Freedman, Y. F. et al. (1978–79) Alcohol in the workplace: A review of recent arbitration cases. *Employee Relations Law Journal, 4*(3), 400–414.

Purcell, T. V. et al. (1974) What are the social responsibilities for psychologists in industry? A symposium. *Personnel Psychology, 27*(3), 435–453.

Ralston, A. (1975) Life-insurance company employee alcoholism management programs. *CLU Journal, 29*(2), 45–55.

Ray, J. S. (1982) Having problems with worker performance? Try an EAP. *Administrative Management, 43*(5), 47–49.

Reardon, R. W. (1975) Tackling the problem of "troubled" employees. *New Englander, 22*(8), 50–52.

Reed, D. J. (1983) One approach to employee assistance. *Personnel Journal, 6*(8), 648–652.

Rendero, T. (1981) Highlights from AMA's Human Resources Conference: Employee assistance programs. *Personnel, 58*(4), 55–57.

Rivers, P. C. et al. (1974) Effect of an alcoholism workshop on attitudes, job satisfaction, and job performance of secretaries. *Quarterly Journal for the Study of Alcoholism, 35*(4A), 1382–1388.

Roberts, K. M. (1977) Good alcoholism plan can cut losses by 15 percent annually—expert. *Business Insurance, 11*(10), 34.

Robichaud, C., Strickler, D., Bigelow, G., & Liebson, I. (1979) Disulfiram maintenance employee alcoholism treatment: A three-phase evaluation. *Behavior Research & Therapy, 17*(6), 618–621.

Rohan, T. M. (1982) Pushers on the payroll: A nightmare for management. *Industry Week, 212*(3), 52–57.

Roman, P. M. (1980) Medicalization and social control in the workplace: Prospects for the 1980s. *Journal of Applied Behavioral Science, 16*(3), 407–422.

Roman, P. M. (1982) Barriers to the use of constructive confrontation with employed alcoholics. *Journal of Drug Issues, 12*(4), 369–382.

Ross, E. A. (1982) Working with industry: A challenge to psychiatry. *Psychiatric Hospital, 13*(3), 909–101.

Rostain, H., Allan, P., Rosenberg, S. (1980) New York City's approach to problem-employee counseling. *Personnel Journal, 59*(4), 305–309, 321.

Rouse, K. A. (1968) Industry can help its problem drinkers. *Personnel Journal, 47*(10), 705–708.

Rozen, L. (1980) Alcoholism—few agencies offer official help. *Advertising Age, 5*(46), 100–101.

Ryan, B. (1981) A new approach to employee alcoholism. *New England Business, 3*(10), 32, 35–36.

Ryan, D. (1978) Alcohol programs in industry. *Work & People* (Australia), *4*(3), 8–14.

Sadler, M., & Hurst, J. F. (1972) Company/union programs for alcoholics. *Harvard Business Review, 50*(4), 22–40.

Sadler, M., & Hurst, J. F. (1972) Confessions of an alcoholic executive. *Dun's Review, 99*(6), 73–79.

Sager, L. B. (1978) Our ten million problem drinkers: What's being done about it. *CLU Journal, 32*(4), 38–46.

Sager, L. B. (1979) The corporation and the alcoholic. *Across the Board, 16*(6), 79–82.

Schachhuber, D. (1977) Local unions in the fight against alcoholism. *Labour Gazette* (Canada), *77*(11), 505–510.

Schaeffer, D. (1979) Alcoholism: Challenge for today's supervisor. *Supervision, 41*(9), 11–13.

Scherr, M. L., & Tainter, P. M. (1982) Health promotion in the workplace: The Sheppard experience. *Psychiatric Hospital, 13*(3), 92–94.

Schneider, P. V. (1979) Preventive maintenance for employees. *Modern Office Procedures, 24*(4), 50–53.

Schneider, P. V. (1979) There is a better way to help troubled employees. *Office, 89*(5), 46, 50, 146.

Schoonmaker, A. N. (1969) *Anxiety and the executive.* New York, NY: American Management Association.

Schramm, C., & DeFillippi, R. J. (1975) Characteristics of successful alcoholism treatment programs for American workers. *British Journal of Addiction, 70*(3), 271–275.

Schreier, J. W. (1983) A survey of drug abuse in organizations. *Personnel Journal, 62*(6), 478–484.

Schuh, A. J., & Hakel, M. D. (1972) The counselor in organizations: A look to the future. *Personnel Journal, 51*(5), 354–359.

Seidler, J. E. (1968) A follow-up study of the employment status and occupational adjustment in three groups of closed rehabilitation cases (University of Oregon). *Dissertation Abstracts, 29,* 1-A, 127.

Shepard, J. M., & Panko, T. R. (1974) Alienation: A discrepancy approach. *Sociological Quarterly, 15,* 253–263.

Sheridan, M. (1977) Contrary to common belief: Business and alcoholism. *New Englander, 24*(8), 54–59.

Sheridan, P. J. (1981) Drug abuse demands action from industry. *Occupational Hazards,* *43*(3), 62–65.

Sinclair, S. (1972) Alcoholism is industry's business. *Canadian Business, 45*(11), 11–12.

Skidmore, R. A., & Skidmore, C. J. (1975) Marriage and family counseling in industry. *Journal of Marriage & Family Counseling, 1*(2), 135–144.

Skidmore, R. A., Balsam, D., & Jones, O. F. (1974) Social work practice in industry. *Social Work,* 280–286.

Smejda, H. (1977) Alcoholism control outlined at BPAI. *Employee Benefit Plan Review, 32*(2), 78–79.

Smejda, H. (1977) How one hospital sells its expertise to industry. *Hospital Financial Management, 31*(10), 8–10, 12.

Smith, R. R. (1974) Social responsibility: A term we can do without. *Business and Society Review, 9,* 51–55.

Smith, T. L. (1981) Coaching the troubled employee. *Supervisory Management, 26*(12), 33–36.

Somers, G. G. (1975–1976) The alcoholic who works at it. *Journal of American Insurance, 51*(4), 1–4.

Somers, G. G. (1976) The alcoholic employee. *Employee Relations Law Journal, 2*(1), 58–65.

Sonnenstuhl, W. J. (1982) A comment on medicalization in the workplace. *Journal of Applied Behavioral Science, 18*(1), 123–125.

Sonnenstuhl, W. J., & O'Donnell, J. E. (1980) EAPs: The why's and how's of planning them. *Personnel Administrator, 25*(11), 35–38.

Sonnenstuhl, W. J., & Roman, P. M. (1982) A comment on medicalization in the workplace/further support for medicalization in the workplace. *Journal of Applied Behavioral Science, 18*(1), 123–127.

Sorensen, A. A. (1973) Need for power among alcoholic and nonalcoholic clergy. *Journal for the Scientific Study of Religion, 12*(1), 101–108.

Stone, J. L., & Crowthers, V. (1972) Innovations in program and funding of mental health services for blue-collar families. *American Journal of Psychiatry, 128*(11), 1375–1380.

Stringer-Moore, D. M. (1981) Impact of dual career couples on employers: Problems and solutions. *Public Personnel Management, 10*(4), 393–401.

Susman, G. I. (1970) Impact of automation on work group autonomy and task specialization. *Human Relations, 23,* 567–577.

Taber, T. D. et al. (1979) Developing a community-based program for reducing the social impact of a plant closing. *Journal of Applied Behavioral Science, 15*(2), 133–155.

Talbott, G. D. (1986) Alcoholism and other drug addictions: A primary disease entity. *Journal of the Medical Association of Georgia,* 490–494.

Talbott, G. D. (1984) An historical review of Georgia's impaired physicians program. *Journal of the Medical Association of Georgia,* 745–748.

Talbott, G. D. (1982) The impaired physician and intervention: A key to recovery. *The Journal of the Florida Medical Association, 69,* 793–797.

Talbott, G. D. (1987) The impaired physician: The role of the spouse in recovery. *Journal of the Medical Association of Georgia,* 190–192.

Talbott, G. D. (1980) Impaired physicians: The dilemma of identification. *Alcohol and Drug Problems, 68*(6), 56–64.

Talbott, G. D. (1984) Relapse & Recovery. *Journal of the Medical Association of Georgia,* 12–14.

Talbott, G. D. (1984) Relapse and Recovery: Special issues for chemically dependent physicians. *Journal of the Medical Association of Georgia, 73,* 763–769.

Talbott, G. D. (1982) The role of the medical student in the treatment of impaired physicians. *Journal of the Medical Association of Georgia, 71,* 275–277.

Talbott, G. D. (1984) Substance abuse and the professional provider: the need for new attitudes about addiction. *Alabama Journal of Medical Sciences, 21*(2), 150–155.

Tavernier, G. (1979) Corporate aid for the alcoholic. *International Management* (UK), *34*(7), 16–20.

Tavernier, G. (1979) How medical executive society developed guidelines on alcoholism. *Association Management, 31*(6), 69–70.

Tersine, R. J., & Hazeldine, J. (1982) Alcoholism: A productivity hangover. *Business Horizons, 25*(6), 68–72.

Trice, H. M., & Belasco, J. A. (1968) Supervisory training about alcoholics and other problem employees: A controlled evaluation. *Quarterly Journal of Studies on Alcohol, 29*(2-A), 382–398.

Trice, H. M., & Beyer, J. M. (1984) Work-related outcomes of the constructive-confrontation strategy in a job-based alcoholism program. *Journal of Studies on Alcohol, 45*(5), 393–404.

Tuthill, M. (1982) Joining the war on drug abuse. *Nation's Business, 70*(6), 64–65.

Twining, J. E. (1980) Alienation as a social process. *Sociological Quarterly, 21,* 417–428.

Uraneck, W. (1981) Providing assistance to state employees. *Public Productivity Review, 5*(1), 80–82.

VonWiegand, R. A. (1972) Alcoholism in industry (U.S.A.). *British Journal of Addiction, 67*(3), 181–187.

Wagner, W. G. (1982) Assisting employees with personal problems. *Personnel Administrator, 27*(11), 59–64.

Walker, J. J. (1978) Supervising the alcoholic. *Supervisory Management, 23*(11), 26–32.

Wallace, J. B. (1981) Impact of employee personal problem counseling on personnel costs in manufacturing industries (United States International University). *Dissertation Abstracts* International, *41,* 7 B, 2813.

Watterson, B. F. (1966) Action on alcoholism. *Annals of the New York Academy of Sciences, 133*(3), 880–882.

Wayman, M. (1980) The corporation as social worker: One response to smart machines that put people out of work. *Canadian Business, 58*(7), 171–172.

Weiner, A., & Sommer. (1973) *Mental health care in the world of work.* New York, NY: Association Press.

Weiss, W. H. (1977) You can't ignore the alcoholic. *Supervision, 39*(4), 6–8.

Weissman, A. (1976) A social service strategy in industry: *Social Work, 20*(5), 401–403.

Weissman, A. (1976) Industrial social services: Linkage technology. *Social Casework, 57,* 50–54.

Wells, P. A., & Amano, M. (1980) Alcoholism drug abuse in the workforce. *Management World, 9*(10), 14–16.

Whitehead, R. (1974) Business' multibillion-dollar hangover. *Nation's Business, 62*(5), 66.

Whitehead, R. (1974) The incredible cost of booze. *Industry Week, 182*(10), 28–32.

Wilkinson, H. L. (1974) Employee addiction—whose problem. *Personnel Administrator, 19*(4), 30–31.

Willatt, N. (1983) Industry's hangover cure. *Management Today,* July, 72–75, 105.

Wilmuth, L. R., Weaver, L., & Donlan, S. (1975) Utilization of medical services by transferred employees: Differential effect of life change on health. *Archives of General Psychiatry, 32*(1), 85–88.

Witte, R., & Cannon, M. (1979) Employee assistance programs: Getting top management's support. *Personnel Administrator, 24*(6), 23–26, 44.

Wolfe, M. N., Werther, W. B., & Bohlander, G. W. (1979) Employee benefits in Arizona: An update. *Arizona Business, 26*(9), 8–14.

Wolff, W. M. (1968) Personality patterns of private clients. *Journal of Consulting and Clinical Psychology, 32*(5), Pt. 1, 621.

Wulf, G. W. (1973) The alcoholic employee. *Personnel Journal, 52*(8), 702–704.

Yasser, R., & Sommer, J. (1974) One union's social service programs. *Social Welfare Forum, 101,* 112–120.

Young, E. (1972) Individuality in a Factory. *American Behavioral Science, 16,* 65–74.

Zemke, R. (1983) Should supervisors be counselors? *Training, 20*(3), 44–53.

Zink, M. M. (1978) Alcoholism—the disease that drains hospital resources away. *Hospital Financial Management, 32*(8), 32–37.

Zink, M. M. (1978) Business drinking: Is it getting out of hand? *Association Management, 30*(6), 57–60.

Zink, M. M. (1978) Congress to aid rehabilitation of occupational alcoholism. *Office, 87*(4), 58, 61.

INDEX